D0752163

Configuring Microsoft Outlook 2003

Configuring Microsoft Outlook 2003

Sue Mosher

with

Robert Sparnaaij
Charlie Pulfer
David Hooker

ELSEVIER
DIGITAL
PRESS

Amsterdam • Boston • Heidelberg • London • New York • Oxford
Paris • San Diego • San Francisco • Singapore • Sydney • Tokyo

Elsevier Digital Press
30 Corporate Drive, Suite 400, Burlington, MA 01803, USA
Linacre House, Jordan Hill, Oxford OX2 8DP, UK

 Recognizing the importance of preserving what has been written, Elsevier prints its books on acid-free paper whenever possible.

Library of Congress Cataloging-in-Publication Data

Application submitted.

British Library Cataloguing-in-Publication Data

A catalogue record for this book is available from the British Library.

ISBN-13: 978-1-55558-326-2

ISBN-10: 1-55558-326-1

For information on all Elsevier Digital Press publications visit our Web site at www.books.elsevier.com

Printed in the United States of America
05 06 07 08 09 10 10 9 8 7 6 5 4 3 2 1

Contents

Introduction

Welcome to Microsoft Office Outlook 2003, the fifth version of Microsoft's premier e-mail and collaboration client! If you're reading this, you're probably anticipating a rollout of Microsoft Outlook 2003 or Office 2003 in your organization, or you have already installed Office or Outlook 2003 and want to know how to deploy and manage certain settings.

This book is designed to help you configure Outlook 2003 to take advantage of its many features, including new, more efficient connectivity methods for Microsoft Exchange accounts. It is not, however, a soup-to-nuts guide to deploying Outlook. The Microsoft Office 2003 Resource Kit, available online at http://office.microsoft.com/en-us/FX011417911033.aspx, contains several books' worth of essential information on how to deploy Office and Outlook in almost every imaginable scenario. It also contains essential free tools, such as the Custom Installation Wizard and Custom Maintenance Wizard, which we'll refer to frequently.

Is this book for you?

We've written this book as a reference for network administrators and help desks in organizations of all sizes that either need to manage Outlook configurations centrally or want to understand the options available for configuring and troubleshooting Outlook features. (Truly curious power users might also find it very interesting, though!)

With the exception of Chapter 5, "Exchange Account Configuration," and Chapter 7, "Managing the Outlook Security Settings Folder," both of which apply only to organizations using Microsoft Exchange as their mail server, the information in this book is applicable to almost any kind of Outlook environment using any kind of mail server.

What you need to know

This book assumes that you already know what techniques are available in your organization to configure end-user settings. These may include Group Policy Objects (GPOs) in Active Directory (AD), which we'll cover in Chapter 2, but also Microsoft System Management Server or a login script utility or an AD/GPO management tool. We are not going to get into the operation of those tools, beyond a brief introduction to GPOs, but will concentrate instead on the Outlook options that you'll want to configure. We'll leave it up to you to adapt the configuration details to your specific tool.

It probably seems obvious, but you will also need to know what operating system(s) you are supporting for Outlook 2003 users and what types of mail server(s) they connect to.

This book also assumes that you have a working knowledge of Outlook 2003 configuration from the user's perspective. If you haven't already, be sure to explore the Tools | Options, Tools | E-mail Accounts, and Tools | Send/Receive Settings | Define Send/Receive Groups dialogs.

As we go along, we'll explain some of the new features in Outlook 2003, such as Cached Exchange mode and support for Windows Rights Management, to help you understand how they might be useful in your organization.

What tools you need

You should download and install the free tools in the Office 2003 Resource Kit, since we will be referring to them—especially the Custom Installation Wizard and Custom Maintenance Wizard—often.

We also recommend that you obtain either Microsoft Virtual PC or a similar tool called VMWare (http://www.vmware.com). Both of these utilities allow you to run "virtual machines" for testing without interfering with the normal programs on your desktop. You can, for example, test how application of a Custom Maintenance Wizard .cmw file will actually affect an end user. Both allow you to roll back the machine to a previous state, so you can do your testing on a clean system, then roll it back to the clean state when you're done, to be ready for the next round of testing.

Two other invaluable testing tools are available from http://www.sysinternals.com. Regmon monitors your system for changes in the Windows registry, while Filemon monitors changes to files on your system. You'll find several other great tools at that site, but Filemon and Regmon are probably the two you'll use the most.

For digging deeply into the Outlook data stores, three tools are available—Mdbvu32.exe, which is included on the Microsoft Exchange installation CD; MFCMAPI, which is discussed in Microsoft Knowledge Base article 291794; and Outlook Spy, which can be purchased from http://www.dimastr.com/outlookspy. We walk through some of the basics of these slightly arcane tools in Chapter 1.

How this book is organized

Here's a sneak preview of what the book covers.

- *Chapter 1: Outlook Data and Settings Locations*—Gives an overview of Outlook data locations, including file and mailbox information stores, and settings locations, including the Windows registry, files in the user's Windows profile folders, and the information store. Also provides an overview of using Mdbvu32.exe, MFCMAPI, and Outlook Spy to explore and modify Outlook settings.

- *Chapter 2: Outlook Configuration Techniques*—Provides walk-throughs for the main Outlook configuration tools—Office Profile Wizard, Custom Installation Wizard, Custom Maintenance Wizard, and GPOs.

- *Chapter 3: Configuring Outlook Mail Profiles*—Discusses how to use the Custom Installation Wizard and Custom Maintenance Wizard to create .prf files used to deploy Outlook mail profiles. Also includes an overview of the .prf file format and some simple practical examples of .prf customization.

- *Chapter 4: Advanced .prf File Usage*—Covers more complex topics related to the .prf files used to create and manage Outlook profiles, including scripts to substitute individual user values and add users' existing Personal Folders .pst files to a new profile, plus a procedure for discovering obscure Exchange settings.

- *Chapter 5: Exchange Account Configuration*—Covers considerations that affect which connectivity method is appropriate for connecting to Microsoft Exchange Server mailboxes, plus details on configuring the new Cached Exchange mode and remote procedure call (RPC) over HTTP methods. Also covers some miscellaneous Exchange issues such as connecting to a new server.

- *Chapter 6: Locking Down Outlook*—Takes a multilayered approach to Outlook security, covering digital signatures and encryption, blocking profile changes, restricting .pst file usage, and managing the Junk E-mail feature and other Outlook security features.

- *Chapter 7: Managing the Outlook Security Settings Folder*—For Exchange environments, covers how to create and maintain a public folder to control attachment blocking and the security features encountered by programs that automate Outlook.

- *Chapter 8: Special Configuration Scenarios*—Discusses Terminal Server deployments, multilanguage installations, upgrades from previous Outlook versions, moving data and settings to a new machine, and applying hotfixes and service packs.

- *Chapter 9: Configuring Other Outlook Options*—Covers configuration changes that are not available in the Office Resource Kit tools or GPOs, including setting custom stationery and signatures, folder permissions, and calendar color labels.

- *Appendix A: Outlook 2003 Policy Settings*—Covers settings available in the administrative template for Outlook.

- *Appendix B: Additional Outlook Registry Settings*—Covers settings from service packs and hotfixes and selected other settings of interest that are not in the administrative template.

- *Appendix C: Disabling Menu and Toolbar Commands and Shortcut Keys*—Covers command ID numbers for use with the Group Policy setting that allows administrators to disable menu and toolbar commands.

- *Appendix D: Other Resources*—Lists other articles and tools to assist with Outlook configuration.

Ready to get started? Let's look first at where Outlook stores its data and settings.

Acknowledgments

The idea for this book dates back several years, when I first heard that Microsoft was working on a white paper to document the format of the .prf files that Outlook can process to create or modify Outlook mail profiles. The author of that white paper, Dan Costenaro, is one of four people who inspired me to write about as many of Outlook's settings as possible. Another is Theron Shreve, publisher at Digital Press, who after the success of my two earlier books for DP, encouraged me to find yet another Outlook topic that I could write passionately about. After reading hundreds of questions from administrators desperate to know how to add an Exchange mailbox to a profile or to block stationery use, it wasn't hard to decide to write about Outlook deployment and configuration issues. But it took some long talks and guidance from my friend and fellow author, Valda Hilley, to get the focus right and to boil down the information into what I hope you will find to be a very practical guide that overlaps only slightly with the information available from the Office Resource Kit. The final member of my inspiring "gang of four" is Jessie Louise McClennan, a fellow Outlook MVP who relentlessly pursues the ideal that every size organization, regardless of whether their mail goes through an Exchange cluster or a simple POP3 server, ought to get the same level of functionality and support from Outlook. JL, I'm sorry your schedule didn't allow you to contribute to this book, but I hope you see your influence throughout it.

My greatest thanks go to the writing and editing team, the largest that I've ever had the pleasure of leading. Robert, Charlie, and David all did deep research into their focus areas and endured a major overhaul of the book's outline. Jeremy Moskowitz, as developmental editor in the early stages, helped define what kinds of questions we should be answering for network administrators. My fellow Most Valuable Professionals (an annual recognition from Microsoft) Diane Poremsky and Vince Averello provided their usual excellent observations as tech editors. I'd especially like to thank Diane for the information on Outlook's MRU lists published at her http://www.slipstick.com Web site.

I was constantly amazed at the thoughtful comments produced by the careful reading of various chapters by many knowledgeable people at Microsoft, particularly Ellen Adams, Randy Byrne, Dan Costenaro, Sloan Crayton, Aaron Hartwell, and Greg Mansius. Ronna Pinkerton, who has been on the Outlook team since the very beginning, provided insight into the top Outlook configuration issues reported to Microsoft Product Support Services. Brandon Hoff and Mike Sampson, the leads responsible for Microsoft's liaison with Outlook MVPs, are both amazing guys and helped me find answers to many questions. KC Lemson provided ideas through her ever-entertaining blog. Others from Microsoft who assisted include Stephen Griffin (developer of the MFCMAPI tool), Bill Jacob, and Mike Jorden.

Fellow Outlook and Exchange MVPs Patricia Cardoza, David Kane, Thomas Lee, Steve Moede, Paul Robichaux, Ben Schorr, Dmitry Streblechenko (developer of the Outlook Spy tool), and Henrik Walther provided ideas and answered questions. I also am grateful to Joseph Neubauer for his article in the *Exchange & Outlook Administrator* newsletter on how to help new users take to Outlook 2003 faster and for his subsequent correspondance on the subject. Bronson Olaso at Imanami, David Sapery at MBH Settlement Group, Mark Smith at Associated Press Broadcast Services, and Kevin Sullivan and Eric Voskuil at AutoProf also reviewed some material. In addition, I'd like to thank the hundreds of administrators and users who posted questions in various community forums or talked with me about Outlook configuration issues at Tech*Ed, especially Madeline McLaughlin at Continental Reporting Service, Paul Raven of the International Monetary Fund, and Ron Thompson at Nortel Networks.

Thank you to the production team at Multiscience Press for their steady professionalism in the magic of turning computer files into a book.

Despite the efforts of all the authors, editors, and reviewers, I'm sure we didn't get everything right. I'll take the blame for any mistakes and will post updates at http://www.turtleflock.com/olconfig/.

Saving the best for last, I couldn't have finished this book without the encouragement of my family, Robert and Annie, who endured with great patience all my complaints about the book that "wouldn't write itself." Robert, who has been working on his Ph.D. the entire time I've been working on this book, gets a special accolade for putting up with my molehills, which look pretty puny in the face of the mountain that he's climbing (and will soon reach the summit!).

Finally, I thank God for the opportunity to share this knowledge and to help people connect with each other.

Sue Mosher
May 2005

Outlook Data and Settings Locations

The goal of this book is to help network administrators and help desks configure, manage, and support users of Microsoft Office Outlook 2003. One of the issues that makes any version of Outlook difficult to manage, compared with other Office applications, is that it stores data and settings in many different locations. Most Outlook settings are stored in the Windows registry or in the user's Windows profile folders. However, some settings are stored in the user's default information store, which normally will be either an Exchange mailbox or a Personal Folders .pst file. In this chapter, you'll learn the following:

- Where Outlook stores its data and settings

- How to use three tools that can help you explore Outlook's inner workings

- What impact Windows roaming profiles may have on an Outlook installation

1.1 Understanding Outlook accounts and data storage

One of Outlook's claims to fame is that it can operate as a "universal inbox," making connections to many different types of e-mail servers while presenting all the information in a unified interface. Outlook 2003 ships with support for these mail accounts:

- Microsoft Exchange Server

- POP3

- IMAP4

- HTTP (Hotmail or Microsoft Network only)

Note: While all Hotmail accounts were supported when Outlook 2003 was released, today only paid Hotmail accounts can be viewed in Outlook. Free Hotmail accounts are accessible only through a Web browser.

Outlook users can also connect to Windows SharePoint Services (WSS) contacts and events lists. Furthermore, Microsoft provides downloadable components to provide enhanced connectivity to Microsoft Network (MSN) accounts and to connect to mail accounts on Lotus Notes or Domino servers. Third-party components are also available to connect to different types of mail, calendar, and other collaboration servers or even directly to databases (see Appendix D).

Note: Since Outlook 2003 runs on Windows 2000 or Windows XP, Outlook users can also add the fax components from those versions of Windows to their Outlook configuration. Users who connect to Microsoft Small Business Server can use its fax component.

Outlook stores information about accounts in mail profiles, which you'll learn more about later in this chapter. In Chapter 3, you will see how to deploy mail profile settings with the tools in the Office 2003 Resource Kit.

1.1.1   Data-storage locations

The choice of mail accounts determines what kind of information store (or stores) Outlook will use to hold the data. Accounts that connect to Microsoft Exchange mailboxes can either display information from the server directly—with no data cached locally—or maintain a local copy of the mailbox and selected public folders in an offline folders .ost file. (You will learn much more about Exchange offline folders files in Chapter 5) IMAP4 and HTTP accounts synchronize the data for each account between the server and a Personal Folders .pst file that is tightly integrated with the account. POP3 accounts do not have a specific store associated with each account but instead download mail into the user's default information store, which will usually be a Personal Folders .pst file. WSS connections use one-way replication to copy data from the server to a .pst file used just for SharePoint connections. Note that this means the data in the SharePoint Folders .pst file is read-only: the user can read but not change any of the items copied from SharePoint contacts or events lists. Users may also have other Personal Folders .pst files, for example those that contain archival data, which are not associated with a particular account.

One of Outlook 2003's important new features is support for Unicode-format .pst and .ost files. These not only make it possible for Outlook to handle non-English-language character sets much better, but they can also grow much larger than legacy .pst and .ost files, which are limited to slightly under 2 GB in size. The default size for Unicode .pst and .ost files is 20 GB, but this can be changed with a Group Policy or user-preference setting in the Windows registry, as you'll see in Chapter 6. The upper limit is well beyond the storage capacity of today's desktop machines—33 terabytes.

Users can manually create Personal Folders .pst files in any file folder. However, all the .pst and .ost files that Outlook creates automatically will be in the %USERPROFILE%\Local Settings\Application Data\Microsoft\ Outlook folder, using default file names.

Note: %USERPROFILE% is an environment variable, information that Windows stores during the current Windows session and that applications can reuse in various contexts. The %USERPROFILE% environment variable refers to the path to the user's Windows user-profile folders on the local machine, usually C:\Documents and Settings\%USERNAME%, where %USERNAME% is another environment variable, the name that the user employs to log onto Windows. Thus, someone who logs onto a machine with the Windows username flaviusj will have a user profile in the C:\Documents and Settings\flaviusj folder.

Exchange. The first offline folders .ost file for an Exchange account will be named Outlook.ost. (If the Exchange account is not using offline folders, no information store file will exist on the local machine.) Subsequent files for other profiles will be named Outlook0.ost, Outlook1.ost, and so on.

IMAP4/HTTP. Outlook constructs the file name for the .pst file associated with an IMAP4, Hotmail, or MSN account from the profile name, the account name, and an eight-digit number, which is incremented each time a new .pst file is created for one of these types of accounts. The default name for an IMAP4 account is the mail-server name. Therefore, if the first IMAP4 account in a profile named Outlook Settings is for an IMAP4 mail server named mail.mydomain.com, the .pst file for that account will be named Outlook Settingsmail.mydomain.com-00000001.pst. If the user adds an MSN account to the same profile using the MSN component that ships with Outlook, the .pst file for the MSN account will be named Outlook SettingsmailMSN-00000002.pst.

Note: Storage files for the MSN Connector that can be downloaded from Microsoft use a different file type and naming convention. Outlook constructs the file name from the user's MSN address. A user with the address myaccount@msn.com will have a file named myaccount.ost. If the user creates a second profile with this account, its file name will be myaccount0.ost. (Don't confuse the MSN .ost files with Exchange offline folders .ost files. They may use the same file extension, but they are not interchangeable.) A user who has worked with the older version of the connector may also have files named Outlook.msnpst, Outlook0.msnpst, Outlook1.msnpst, and so on.

SharePoint. The first SharePoint cache .pst file for a user is named SharePoint Folders.pst. The second is SharePoint Folders(2).pst, and so on.

Default .pst File. If Outlook does not contain an Exchange account, an MSN Connector account, or a third-party account that can be designated as the default information store, Outlook will automatically create a Personal Folders .pst file for use as the default store. The first such file will be named Outlook.pst. The second will be Outlook1.pst, and so on. Also, if the user enables the AutoArchive feature, Outlook automatically creates a .pst file named Archive.pst for use with this feature.

Like the account settings, Outlook stores settings for its information stores in a set of Windows registry values called a mail profile, described later in the chapter. Users can check what data stores are currently in use by choosing File | Data File Management from the main Outlook menu to display the Outlook Data Files dialog, shown in Figure 1.1.

Note that the Outlook Data Files dialog will not include information about any Exchange account that may be present in the profile. In this example, a Personal Folders .pst file is designated as the default store, as shown by the "Mail delivery location" designation in the Comment column.

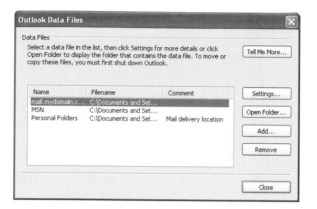

Figure 1.1
Outlook data file settings.

1.1.2   Understanding the default information store

Let's get back to the issue of the default information store, raised in connection with POP3 accounts above. Every Outlook profile has a default delivery location. This is usually either the Exchange mailbox (with the information store being the server itself or an .ost file) or a Personal Folders .pst file. However, the enhanced MSN Connector can also act as a default delivery location, as can some third-party mail components.

The importance of the default delivery location is that it contains the user's main Inbox, Calendar, Contacts, Journal, and Tasks folders. Contacts created from addresses in incoming e-mail messages save to the Contacts folder in the default information store. When the user accepts a meeting request, Outlook creates an appointment in the Calendar folder in the default information store.

A common problem in Exchange environments occurs when the user switches the default store from the Exchange mailbox to a .pst file. In an Exchange organization, users check each other's availability for meetings with what's called a free/busy lookup, which examines information in a special Exchange folder that contains data gleaned from the Calendar folder in the user's Exchange mailbox. If all accepted meeting requests go into a .pst file's Calendar folder because the .pst file is the default store instead of the Exchange mailbox, no free/busy information will be available to other Exchange users about those appointments. Therefore, in an Exchange environment, the best practice is to maintain the Exchange mailbox as the default store. Chapter 6 explains how to prevent users from changing that configuration by blocking changes to their mail profiles.

Note: The reason most frequently given for the use of a Personal Folders .pst file as the default store in a profile that connects to an Exchange mailbox is that the mailbox size is limited, so users are forced to download mail from the mailbox into a .pst file. As the old proverb says, this is penny wise and pound foolish. The potential costs of losing data because a .pst file hasn't been backed up or of not being able to use Outlook's free/busy lookup to facilitate scheduling are usually far greater than the cost of providing adequate hardware and archiving software to maintain a reasonable mailbox size. In addition, organizations under various financial and other regulations may find themselves faced with legal problems if they do not maintain an adequate central record of mail sent and received. You can't maintain such a record if the data is scattered throughout the organization in individual .pst files.

1.2   Outlook settings in the Windows registry

Like all Windows programs, Outlook stores the bulk of its settings in the user portion of the Windows registry. As users make changes to the way Outlook operates by selecting options in the Tools | Options dialog, Outlook updates the corresponding registry entries. Often, administrators will "lock down" certain settings by enforcing them with Group Policy Objects (GPOs). You'll learn more about GPOs in the next chapter.

In addition, as mentioned above, Outlook also stores its mail account settings in a separate section of the Windows registry. Most of these settings are undocumented, but many can be discovered through trial and error, as you'll learn in Chapter 4.

In this section, we'll review the different registry locations that hold Outlook settings so that you'll know where to look. Throughout the remainder of the book, we'll highlight the most important registry settings for Outlook 2003 and then provide a more comprehensive listing in Appendix A.

1.2.1   Mail profiles

A mail profile is a collection of configuration information for address books, item storage, and message delivery for a particular Outlook session. Outlook stores mail-profile account and data-file information in the HKEY_CURRENT_USER\Software\Microsoft\Windows   NT\Current-Version\Windows Messaging Subsystem\Profiles registry key. (You will learn more about mail profiles in Chapter 3.) Figure 1.2 shows the Rege-dit.exe program displaying the settings for a user with two profiles, one named Outlook and one named Outlook Settings. As you can see, each profile has its own registry key. The Outlook Settings profile contains only an Exchange mailbox and the Outlook Address Book, which exposes the content of Outlook contacts folders as address lists that the user can use for address lookup and selection.

Since Outlook 2003 includes extensive support for Unicode, most of the registry values are not easily read REG_SZ string values but REG_BINARY ones. This makes it difficult to see at a glance what aspect of Outlook configuration any particular registry entry might be related to. However, if you double-click a registry value to display it, you'll find that many of the entries do contain readable information. For example, the 001f3006 entry shown in Figure 1.2 indicates that the settings in its subkey are related to the Outlook Address Book.

In most cases, you will not alter the registry settings for an Outlook profile directly but will instead use the mechanisms described in Chapters 3 and 4 to update the profile using a .prf file. Most of the settings that you need to change can be managed with two .prf file creation tools: the

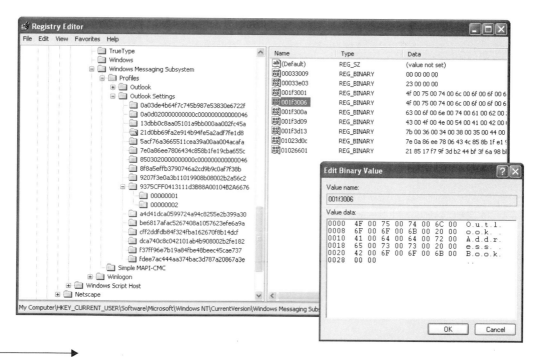

Figure 1.2   *Registry entries for an Outlook mail profile.*

Custom Installation Wizard (CIW) and Custom Maintenance Wizard (CMW). Chapter 4 shows how to discover registry settings that the CIW and CMW don't expose and change them with a .prf file.

Here's an example of where it might be useful to modify a profile registry value directly: When you deploy Outlook 2003 and set up a profile with an Exchange account, the default configuration is to use Cached Exchange mode, which you'll learn more about in Chapter 5. Cached Exchange mode creates a local cache of the user's entire mailbox, a process that could put quite a load on your network if everyone did it at once. Therefore, one approach is to deploy Outlook 2003 in Classic Online mode, then turn on Cached Exchange mode gradually, one group of users at a time. You can use the following registry value to enable or disable Cached Exchange mode:

```
Key: HKEY_CURRENT_USER\Software\Microsoft\Windows NT\
CurrentVersion\Windows Messaging Subsystem\Profiles\
<ProfileName>\13dbb0c8aa05101a9bb000aa002fc45a
Value name: 00036601
Value type: REG_BINARY
Values: 94 01 00 00 (enabled), 14 00 00 00 (disabled)
```

1.2.2   Policy settings

When administrators use GPOs to enforce certain settings, those settings are stored in a special area of the registry, in the HKEY_CURRENT_USER\Software\Policies key. Besides Group Policy tools, any other tool with appropriate administrator access can add or modify the registry values in this key and its subkeys. However, users normally have just read-only permissions. Therefore, options set in the Policies subkeys are mandatory and cannot be changed by the user. In many cases, Outlook hides or disables the user interface that the user would use to change the setting in the absence of a policy.

Figure 1.3 shows a policy setting to force Outlook to display all mail messages in plain-text format, a feature that you'll learn more about in Chapter 6.

A few Outlook and Office policy settings will also be present under the HKEY_LOCAL_MACHINE\Software\Policies\Microsoft key, thus affecting all users who log onto that machine.

1.2.3   User preference settings

Notice that the ReadAsPlain registry value shown in Figure 1.3 resides in the HKEY_CURRENT_USER\Software\Policies\Microsoft\Office\11.0\

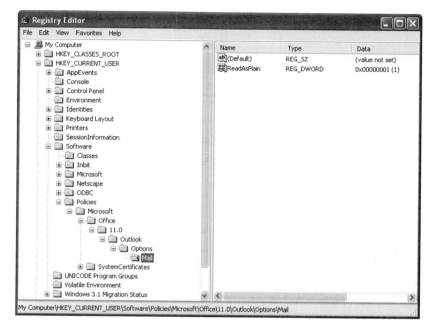

Figure 1.3
Policy to force all mail to display in plain text format.

Outlook\Options\Mail key. If the same ReadAsPlain setting were in place on the user's machine not as a policy setting but as a user preference—in other words, as a setting that the user is allowed to change—it would appear in the HKEY_CURRENT_USER\Software\Microsoft\Office\11.0\ Outlook\Options\Mail key. The difference between the two is that policy settings for Outlook reside under the HKEY_CURRENT_USER\Software\Policies\Microsoft key, while user preference settings are under the HKEY_CURRENT_USER\Software\Microsoft key.

Figure 1.4 illustrates the user preference settings hierarchy in the registry for Outlook. Notice that there is both an Office\11.0\Outlook subkey and an Office\Outlook subkey. Furthermore, the Office\11.0\Common and Office\11.0\Word keys also contain a few settings related to Outlook.

Note: Often, in order to apply a particular setting, you may need to create not just the registry value, but also one or more registry keys or subkeys, because that value and its parent hierarchy don't exist in the registry yet. Tools like the CIW, CMW, and the Group Policy Editor take care of that for you. If you want to test a registry value by adding it by hand, however, you should be aware that you may need to add more than just the value itself.

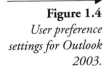

Figure 1.4
*User preference
settings for Outlook
2003.*

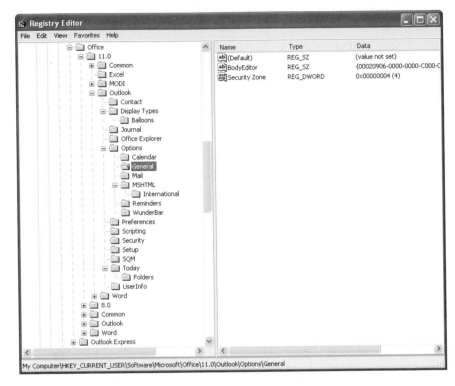

Machine-specific preference settings can be found under the HKEY_
LOCAL_MACHINE\Software\Microsoft key. Under this key's subkeys
you will find other settings that affect all of the machine's users but are not
being enforced as policy settings.

1.2.4   Client extension and Exchange Provider settings

Outlook supports an architecture for tightly integrated add-ins called
Exchange client extensions that predates the more common COM add-in
architecture, which works only in Outlook 2000 and later versions.
Because this architecture originated with the original Exchange mail client
that shipped with Windows 95 and Microsoft Exchange Server 4.0, these
extensions' registry settings are not in the same location as the other Outlook settings. Instead, they are in HKEY_LOCAL_MACHINE\Software\
Microsoft\Exchange\Client\Extensions key, shown in Figure 1.5.

Actually, though, Outlook rarely reads this extension information from
the registry. Instead, it stores the extension settings in a file named
Extend.dat (see Table 1.2). Outlook builds the Extend.dat file if the registry
contains the following value:

Key: `HKEY_LOCAL_MACHINE\Software\Microsoft\Exchange\`
`Client\Extensions`
Value name: `Outlook Setup Extension`
Value type: `REG_SZ`
Value: `4.0;Outxxx.dll;7;000000000000000;0000000000;OutXXX`

Problems with extension settings can arise when a machine is used by multiple users or in Terminal Server configurations. If you install an Exchange client extension for one user, Outlook updates Extend.dat, but that file is specific to each user. When the next user logs on with his or her own Windows profile, the Outlook Setup Extension value is not present in the registry, and the user has not done anything to invoke the extension, so Outlook does not update the second user's Extend.dat file. Deleting Extend.dat so that Outlook can regenerate it from the information in the Exchange\Client\Extensions key is a common troubleshooting operation.

The Client\Extensions registry entries and others under HKEY_ LOCAL_MACHINE\Software\Microsoft\Exchange generally are managed by Outlook and do not have any impact for Group Policy or user-preference settings.

Note: Earlier versions of Outlook used the Rpc_Binding_Order registry value in the HKEY_LOCAL_MACHINE\Software\Microsoft\Exchange key to set the order in which Outlook will try to use different protocols to connect with an Exchange Server. Outlook 2003, however, only uses TCP/ IP, so this entry is no longer relevant, although it will still be present in machines upgraded from a previous version of Outlook.

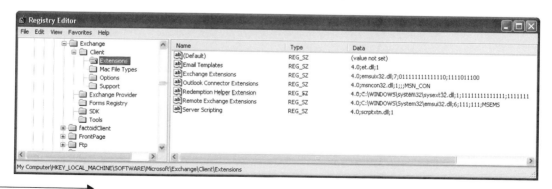

Figure 1.5 *Settings for Exchange client extensions.*

Table 1.1   *Selected Registry Values in HKEY_CURRENT_USER\Software\Microsoft\Exchange*

Value	Type	Description
LogonDomain	REG_SZ	Last used domain when credentials are required to log onto Exchange mailbox
UserName	REG_SZ	Last used user name when credentials are required to log onto Exchange mailbox
Client\Options\PickLogonProfile	REG_SZ	1 = prompt user for mail profile when Outlook starts 0 = do not prompt

Outlook maintains some other information in the user-specific key HKEY_CURRENT_USER\Software\Microsoft\Exchange. For example, the key HKEY_CURRENT_USER\Software\Microsoft\Exchange\Exchange Provider contains a number of values related to the Offline Address Book download for an Exchange account.

Table 1.1 shows three registry values that may be useful in troubleshooting or user configuration.

1.3   Outlook files in the user's Windows profile folders

In addition to the settings in the Windows registry, Outlook also maintains a number of files in subfolders under the user's Windows profile. The default location for this folder is C:\Documents and Settings\%USERNAME%, where %USERNAME% is the environment variable representing the user's Windows logon name. We will refer to this folder as %USERPROFILE%, which is the environment variable that provides the full path to the user's Windows profile folder. Under this folder you will find two folders that contain Outlook settings and data files:

- \Application Data\Microsoft\Outlook
- \Local Settings\Application Data\Microsoft\Outlook

A few other important settings files, such as those for Outlook signatures, are stored in other folders under %USERPROFILE%.

Some files contain user-specific settings, while others contain data. Table 1.2 lists the kinds of settings and data files you can expect to see in the folders under %USERPROFILE%.

Table 1.2   *Outlook Data and Settings Files*

Location	File Name	Description	Mail-Profile Specific
Application Data\Microsoft\ Office	*.acl	AutoCorrect entries	
	*.pip	Personalized menu information for Office applications	
Application Data\Microsoft\ Outlook	*.nk2	Nicknames used for name autocompletion	X
	*.srs	Send/receive settings	X
	*.xml	Navigation pane settings	X
	Offitems.log	Information about Office documents awaiting processing by the Outlook Journal	
	Outcmd.dat	Toolbar customizations	
	Outitems.log	Information about Outlook items awaiting processing by the Outlook Journal	
	Outlprnt	Print format customizations	
	VbaProject.otm	Outlook VBA code project	
Application Data\Microsoft\ Proof	*.dic	Custom spelling dictionaries	
Application Data\Microsoft\ Signatures	*.htm, *.rtf, *.txt	Outlook signature files	
	*.vcf	vCard files saved for use with Outlook signatures	
Application Data\Microsoft\ Stationery	*.htm	User-created stationery files	
Application Data\Microsoft\ Templates	*.oft	Outlook form templates	
	Normal.dot	Default template for Word documents, including WordMail messages	
\Local Settings\Application Data\Microsoft\Forms	Frmcache.dat	Outlook forms cache master file	

Table 1.2   *Outlook Data and Settings Files (continued)*

Location	File Name	Description	Mail-Profile Specific
\Local Settings\Application Data\Microsoft\Forms\IPM*	*.tmp	Cached copies of Outlook forms	
\Local Settings\Application Data\Microsoft\Outlook	*.oab	Exchange Offline Address Book files	
	*.ost	Exchange offline folders files and MSN Connector files	X
	*.pab	Personal Address Book files	
	*.pst	Personal Folders files	IMAP-, MSN-, and SharePoint-related files are profile specific
	Extend.dat	Exchange client extension add-in information	

Note: Microsoft Knowledge Base article 841273, "Administering the Offline Address Book in Outlook 2003," describes how to place the Offline Address Book in a different location by changing a registry value under the user's mail profile.

Since these files reside in the user's Windows profile folders, they are all user specific, but some are also specific to a particular Outlook mail profile. For example, a profile named Outlook Settings would have these files associated with it:

- Outlook Settings.nk2: address autocomplete cache

- Outlook Settings.srs: send/receive settings

- Outlook Settings.xml: navigation pane customizations

1.4   Outlook settings in the information store

As mentioned at the beginning of this chapter, one of the major challenges related to managing Outlook is determining how much of the user's configuration is stored in the default information store itself. Just to make matters

Table 1.3   *Configuration Information in the Default Store*

Type of Information	Global	Folder Specific
Junk mail filter lists	X	
Rules Wizard rules	X	
Custom views	X	X
Custom forms	X	X
Group schedules		X
Calendar color label customizations		X

more confusing, some of this configuration information is folder specific, some affects the whole store, and some can be both! Table 1.3 lists the different kinds of configuration information kept in the store.

For example, you can have both custom views that affect all mail folders and custom views that are specific to a particular mail folder.

Caution: When users who have a Personal Folders .pst file as the default store move to a new machine, they risk losing all this customization information, unless care is taken to copy the old .pst file to the new machine (not export, then import) and to make that file the default for the mail profile on the new machine.

With the exception of the junk filter lists, none of these configuration settings in the store can be deployed using the tools that you'll see in Chapter 2. You can use scripts to publish custom forms and, to a limited extent, create color labels, views, and rules, but you cannot distribute a group schedule. We'll return to the issue in Chapter 9. Also, in Chapter 6, you'll learn how to deploy an initial set of safe senders, safe recipients, and blocked senders for users' junk mail filter.

Even though you generally cannot manage the configuration settings in the information store, three tools are available that allow you to explore the store and view not just what folders and items are present but also see hidden folders and hidden items that help control how Outlook operates. This information can be invaluable both for troubleshooting and for understanding how Outlook data and settings are organized. The three tools are the Information Store Viewer and MFCMAPI, both available for free from

Microsoft, and Outlook Spy, a commercial tool with greater capabilities. While we'll do a quick tour of all three, explaining all of their features would take another entire book, so we encourage you to explore them further on your own.

1.4.1   Using the Information Store Viewer

You can download the Information Store Viewer, also known as Mdbvu32.exe, from the Exchange Server downloads page at http://www.microsoft.com/exchange/downloads/2003/default.mspx. Even though it's listed as an Exchange tool, the viewer works just as well on Outlook configurations that don't include Exchange. It also works fine if you can't or don't want to start Outlook.

When you run the download file, you'll be prompted for a location to install the files. Choose C:\Program Files, and the self-extracting archive will automatically create a subfolder named MDBVU32 and put the Information Store Viewer files there. To run the Information Store Viewer, run C:\Program Files\Mdbvu32\Mdbvu32.exe. Documentation on this tool can be found in the C:\Program Files\Mdbvu32\Information Store Viewer.doc file and includes step-by-step instructions for common tasks, such as deleting a message, emptying a folder, viewing a specific message property, and deleting corrupted rules from a mailbox.

As an example, consider the user's calendar color-code customizations. Perhaps you've noticed that if the user edits the color labels to change the text for the first (pink) label from Important to Critical, that change affects only that one calendar folder. Other calendar folders will still show pink as Important. With this clue that calendar color-code customizations are folder specific, you can use the Information Store Viewer to discover exactly

Figure 1.6
Logging on with the Information Store Viewer.

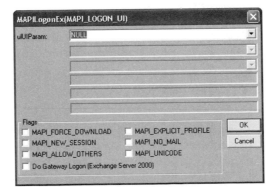

Figure 1.7
*Use the viewer to
open a message
store.*

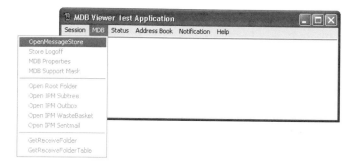

how Outlook stores that information. Start the viewer by running Mdbvu32.exe, and then follow these steps.

1.   After the viewer displays two small windows, it will prompt you for login information using the window in Figure 1.6. If Outlook is already running and you want to work with the accounts in the current mail profile, just click OK. If you want to work with a different mail profile, under Flags, check the box for MAPI_NEW_SESSION, then click OK.

Note: One of the advantages that the Information Store Viewer has over Outlook Spy is that the viewer allows you to log onto other mail profiles without restarting Outlook.

2.   In the MDB Viewer Test Application window (Figure 1.7), choose MDB | OpenMessageStore.

3.   In the Select Message Store to Open window (Figure 1.8), choose the information store you want to work with. If you're working

Figure 1.8
*Select the
information store
you want to view.*

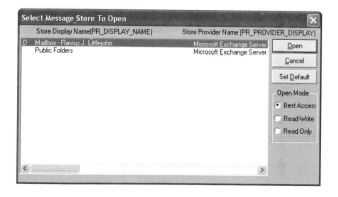

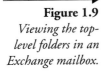

Figure 1.9
*Viewing the top-
level folders in an
Exchange mailbox.*

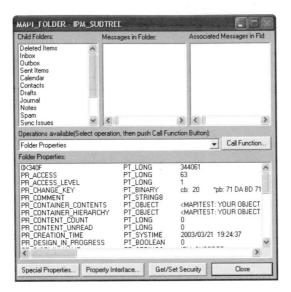

with a mail profile that contains the Exchange service, you'll see at least two stores—the mailbox and the Public Folders hierarchy. For this example, choose the mailbox.

4. Once you open the message store, you'll see the MDB Viewer Test Application window (Figure 1.7) again. This time, choose MDB | Open IPM Subtree. This will display the MAPI_FOLDER window shown in Figure 1.9. It looks complicated, doesn't it! For now, just concentrate on the Child Folders list at upper left. This should look very familiar, because it's the list of folders in the Exchange mailbox. Now you know where you are: Opening IPM_SUBTREE shows you the folders in the Exchange mailbox.

5. Since you suspect that the color label information is in the Calendar folder, double-click the Calendar folder in the Child Folders box in the MAPI_FOLDER window. The window's display will switch to the Calendar folder (Figure 1.10).

    Notice that not only is there an entry under Child Folders for a subfolder of the Calendar folder, but you also see, under Messages in Folder, the list of appointments and events. Then, on the right side of the window, under Associated Messages in Fld, you see three entries. These are called hidden messages because they are stored in the folder the same way as other items but are hid-

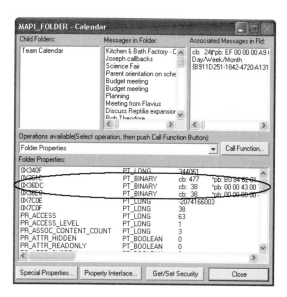

Figure 1.10
Viewing the contents of the Calendar folder.

den from the user. We'll come back to them when we look at this folder with Outlook Spy, for they're also very interesting.

All the properties with names that begin with PR_ are relatively well-documented Messaging Application Programming Interface (MAPI) properties that are common to many different kinds of Outlook objects. Since we're looking for a property that is specific to calendar folders, we should immediately suspect that it's one of the properties at the top that doesn't have a PR_ name. The PT_LONG properties don't seem relevant since they're just numbers.

The properties that look potentially interesting are those in PT_BINARY format, but as it turns out, they don't necessarily store numbers. Outlook 2003 has extensive support for Unicode, a method of encoding text that can handle not just languages like English and Western European languages that use the Roman alphabet, but also languages like Russian or Greek, which have their own alphabets, and even languages like Chinese or Japanese or Korean or languages that work right-to-left like Hebrew and Arabic. Unicode can use any number of bytes per character, but in this instance—as with all Western languages—it uses two bytes of data, each a hexadecimal value, to store a single character. The letter "C" (as in "Critical"—remember how our user changed the calendar label test?) is expressed in Unicode as 00 43. The second and third pairs of digits in the property highlighted in Figure 1.10, 0x36DC, are also 00 43. That's your clue that this property is the one that contains the user's calendar color label customization. The full value of that property is 00 00 43 00 72 00 69 00 74 00 69 00 63 00 61 00 6C, followed by twenty-one more pairs of zeroes. A hexadecimal to ASCII text translator would tell you that the nonzero values, when translated, spell out "Critical."

As you'll see in the next two sections, MFCMAPI and Outlook Spy make it much easier to interpret binary properties because they display both the hex values, as the Information Store Viewer does, and the equivalent text values.

6.   To finish using the Information Store Viewer, click Close on each MAPI_FOLDER window until you return to the MDB Viewer Text Application window (Figure 1.6). Choose Session | Exit, and click OK when you see the two prompts to log out of the store and quit.

The Information Store Viewer is a very powerful tool. You can safely use it to view properties and hidden items, but you can easily create problems if you start deleting or changing properties or hidden messages without knowing their purpose. Be sure to read the documentation before you do anything more with it than view the Outlook hierarchy.

1.4.2   Using MFCMAPI

The free MFCMAPI tool is described in Microsoft Knowledge Base article 291794, "SAMPLE: MFCMAPI Demonstrates MAPI Client Code." It was originally built as a demonstration sample for Exchange MAPI programmers; source code is available.

When you run the download file, you'll be prompted for a location to install the files. Choose C:\Program Files, and the installer will automatically create a subfolder named MFCMapi_Bin and put the MFCMAPI files there. To run MFCMAPI, run C:\Program Files\MFCMapi_Bin\MFCMapi.exe. To make it easy to compare MFCMAPI's operation with that of the Information Viewer, let's walk through the process of looking at the calendar color-code labels.

1.   When MFCMAPI starts, it will display a screen with some basic instructions and an extensive list of keyboard shortcuts. Click OK to dismiss that screen. Then, at the main MFCMAPI window,

choose Session | Logon and Display Store Table, and choose the Outlook profile you want to use.

Tip: If you install MFCMAPI on a machine that does not have Outlook installed, such as the Exchange server, the login prompt will allow you to create a mail profile.

---

2.   As you can see in Figure 1.11, MFCMAPI lists information stores in much the same way as the Information Store Viewer; compare the figure with Figure 1.8. Right-clicking on any store, however, brings up a number of options not available in the Information Store Viewer, such as dumping the contents of the store to a text file and applying a content restriction (in other words, a filter).

3.   For this example, double-click the mailbox store to open it. Click the + sign next to each folder to expand them all into the view shown in Figure 1.12. Compared with the Information Store Viewer display shown in Figure 1.9, MFCMAPI makes it much easier to see the entire folder hierarchy. As in the viewer's window, you can right-click any folder on the left to see a menu of addi-

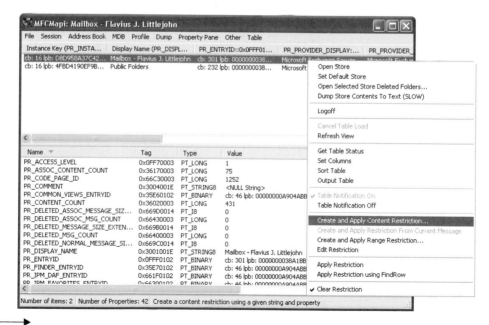

Figure 1.11   *Available information stores in MFCMAPI.*

Figure 1.12
Folders in an
Exchange mailbox,
viewed in
MFCMAPI.

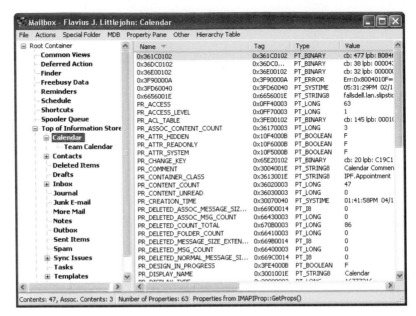

tional options. For example, to see any custom views associated with the Calendar folder, you would right-click the Calendar folder and choose Open Associated Contents Table.

4.   In Figure 1.12, the Calendar folder is selected, so the pane on the right displays the properties of the Calendar folder. The second property from the top, 0x36DC0102, is the one we've identified as holding the folder's customized calendar color labels.

5.   To see more information about that property, double-click it to display the window shown in Figure 1.13. You'll be able to see that this property contains the text C.r.i.t.i.c.a.l, with periods displayed as placeholders for 00 values.

When you have finished using MFCMAPI, close all of its windows. Alternatively, if you want to work with another profile, you can choose Session | Logoff at the main window (Figure 1.11).

1.4.3   Using Outlook Spy

Now that you've seen what the Information Store Viewer and MFCMAPI look like, let's examine the same information using Outlook Spy. You can download a trial version from http://www.dimastr.com/outspy.

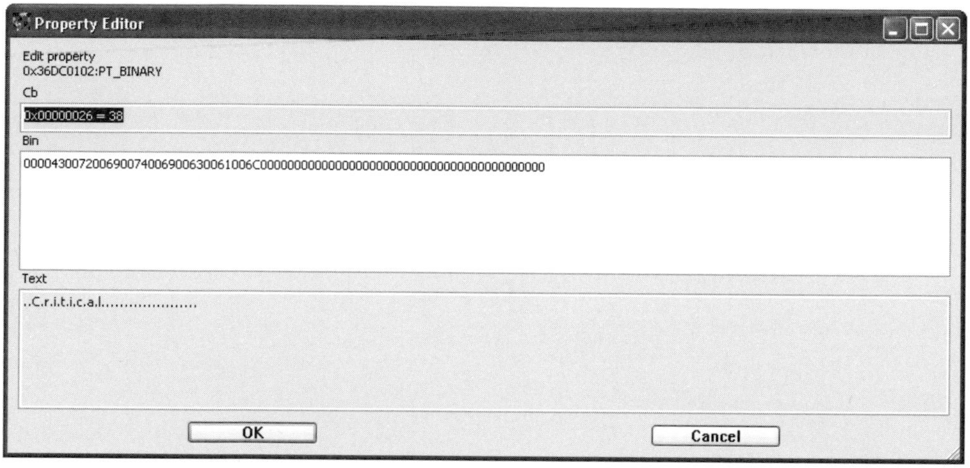

Figure 1.13   *Viewing a property in MFCMAPI.*

Where the Information Store Viewer and MFCMAPI were designed at least in part to help Exchange administrators with troubleshooting, Outlook Spy was designed to help Outlook developers explore Outlook data and hidden settings. The differences show. Where the viewer and MFC-MAPI are stand-alone tools, Outlook Spy integrates directly into Outlook with its own toolbar, shown in Figure 1.14. Where the viewer and MFC-MAPI show only the MAPI interface, Outlook Spy allows you to explore with not just MAPI but two other interfaces—the Outlook object model, commonly used by Outlook developers, and Collaboration Data Objects (CDO), another programming interface that lies midway in features and complexity between the Outlook object model and MAPI. Outlook Spy also has its own built-in script editor that you can use to write and run simple scripts to perform operations with the Outlook or CDO object models.

Remember how many steps it took with the viewer to locate the property that holds the information about the Calendar folder's color codes? Here's how easy it is to do with Outlook Spy:

1.   Switch to the Calendar folder in Outlook.

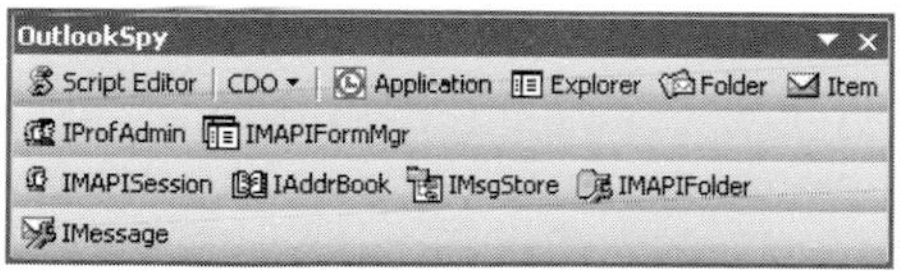

Figure 1.14
The toolbar for Outlook Spy.

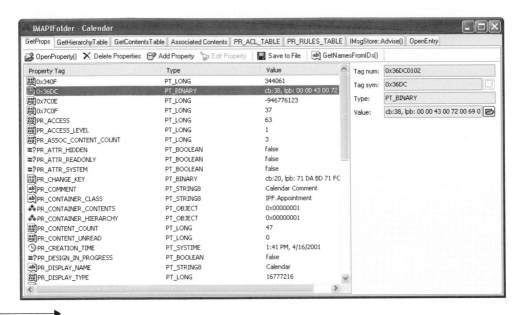

Figure 1.15   *Calendar folder contents shown in Outlook Spy.*

2.   Click the IMAPIFolder button on the Outlook Spy toolbar to
display the IMAPIFolder window shown in Figure 1.15. Compare this display with the viewer display from Figure 1.10 and the
MFCMAPI display from Figure 1.12.

3.   Select the 0x36DC property; then, on the right side of the
IMAPIFolder window, click the button next to the Value box to
display the property value shown in Figure 1.16. This must be the
right property for the calendar color labels, because there on the
right side is the word "C r i t i c a l," showing the modification
the user made, changing the label for "Important" to "Critical."

When you finish working with Outlook Spy, just close all of its windows. You don't need to log off.

As you can imagine, a lot of trial and error is involved in figuring out
which property does what. This property, in particular, 0x36DC, uses a
binary structure that hasn't been documented. However, as you will see in
Chapter 9, it is possible—with a bit of experimentation—to determine the
structure of the property and develop a script that allows you to deploy custom calendar color labels to a folder.

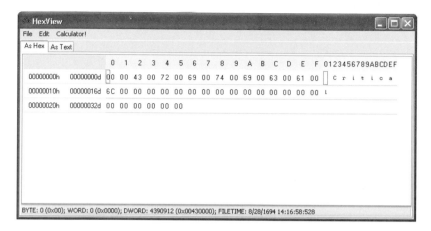

Figure 1.16
Viewing the property value for calendar color labels.

To finish our quick tour of Outlook Spy, let's return to those three hidden messages that you saw in Figure 1.10. To view them in Outlook Spy, in the IMAPIFolder window (Figure 1.15), switch to the Associated Contents tab. Figure 1.17 shows the first item, which turns out to be a custom form named AppointmentRequest published to the Calendar folder. Every item, visible or hidden, has a PR_MESSAGE_CLASS MAPI property (also

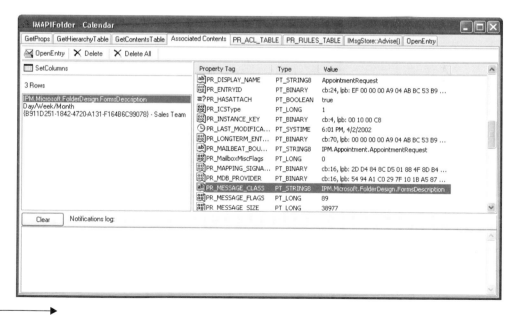

Figure 1.17   *Viewing a published custom form with Outlook Spy.*

known as the Message Class field in an Outlook custom view or the MessageClass property in the Outlook object model) that tells you what kind of item it is. In this example, the class is IPM.Microsoft.FolderDesign.FormsDescription, so you're looking at a custom Outlook form definition for a form with the display name AppointmentRequest.

The second item, shown in Figure 1.18, has a value for the PR_MESSAGE_CLASS property of IPM.Microsoft.FolderDesign.NamedView, which tells us that it is an Outlook folder view definition. Day/Week/Month is the name of one of Outlook's built-in global views that apply to all calendar folders. When a view definition at the folder level has the same name as a global view, the folder-level view definition holds folder-specific modifications of the Day/Week/Month view that the user has made in the course of working with that folder. Outlook caches these folder-specific changes, automatically creating a new view definition at the folder level to hold them.

If you delete that folder-level view definition using MFCMAPI, Outlook Spy, or the Information Store Viewer, the next time the user looks at the Calendar folder with the Day/Week/Month view, it will display the calendar using the settings for the global Day/Week/Month view.

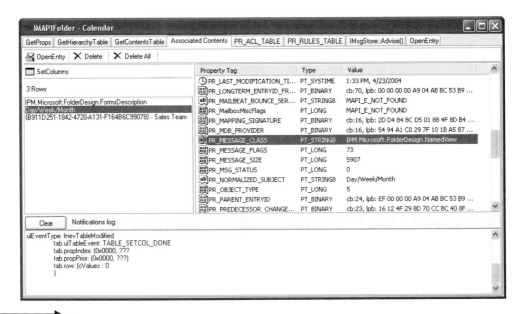

Figure 1.18   *A custom view definition, as seen in Outlook Spy.*

Tip: When you start Outlook with the `/cleanviews` command-line switch, it deletes all custom views that the user has explicitly created and deletes all folder-level view customizations, such as that shown in Figure 1.18. If the user is having a problem with only one view, this is rather a sledgehammer-like solution. Instead, you can first try deleting just the one view that seems to be causing problems, using the Information Store Viewer, MFCMAPI, or Outlook Spy.

The third hidden item in the Calendar folder, shown in Figure 1.19, can be identified as a group schedule item because it is a hidden item with a PR_MESSAGE_CLASS property value of IPM.Appointment. In this case, it's a group schedule item named Sales Team. The group schedule feature in Outlook allows users to view the free/busy availability for a number of people and save that list of people as a group schedule. The free/busy information is shown in a screen similar to the Scheduling page on a normal appointment form. In fact a group schedule item uses the normal appointment form, IPM.Appointment, but only displays the page with the availability information.

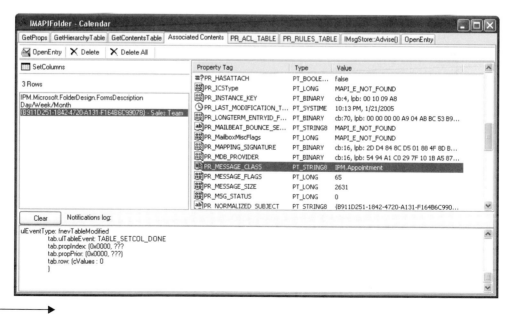

Figure 1.19   *A group schedule as seen in Outlook Spy.*

Seeing that the group schedule item is a hidden message in the Calendar folder helps explain why each group schedule item is specific to a particular calendar folder and can't be saved or copied to another folder or distributed for global use.

1.4.4 Global settings in the information store

In our explorations with the Information Store Viewer and Outlook Spy, we've looked mainly at some folder-specific settings. As you saw in Table 1.2, Outlook also maintains certain global settings for junk mail filter lists, rules, custom views, and custom forms. You can also access these with the Information Store Viewer, MFCMAPI, and Outlook Spy.

This time, let's start with Outlook Spy, and click the IMsgStore toolbar button. In the IMsgStore window (Figure 1.20), click the Open Root Container button, then switch to the GetHierarchyTable tab shown in Figure 1.21.

Tip: Notice the PR_OOF_STATE property highlighted in Figure 1.20. This property tells you whether out-of-office responses are turned on for this Exchange mailbox.

Figure 1.20
Information store properties of an Exchange mailbox, viewed with Outlook Spy.

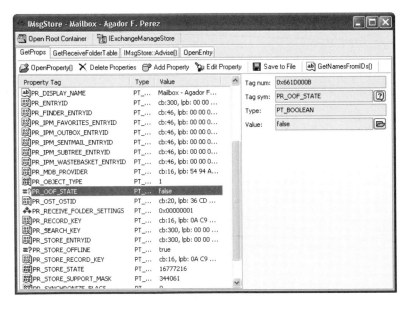

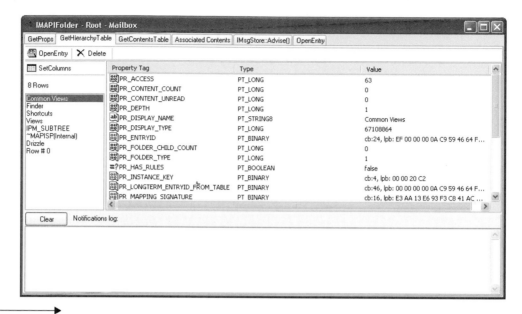

Figure 1.21   *Root-level folders in the default information store, seen with Outlook Spy.*

Each row in the GetHierarchyTable list corresponds to a different set of Outlook data or settings. Depending on whether the information store is an Exchange mailbox or a Personal Folders .pst file and what versions of Outlook have been used with this particular store, you may see different rows from those listed in Figure 1.21. Table 1.4 explains the contents of the folders you are likely to see. Note that in a few cases, the name of the folder may differ, depending on whether you are working with an Exchange mailbox or a Personal Folder .pst file.

To use the Information Store Viewer to access the folders listed in Table 1.4, follow these steps:

1.   Start the viewer by running C:\Program Files\Mdbvu32\Mdbvu32.exe.

2.   If Outlook is already running and you want to work with the accounts in the current mail profile, just click OK in the dialog shown in Figure 1.6. If you want to work with a different mail profile, under Flags, check the box for MAPI_NEW_SESSION, then click OK.

3.   In the MDB Viewer Test Application window (Figure 1.7), choose MDB | OpenMessageStore.

4.   In the Select Message Store to Open window (Figure 1.8), choose the information store you want to work with. If you're working with a mail profile that contains the Exchange service, you'll see at least two stores—the mailbox and the Public Folders hierarchy. For this example, choose the mailbox or, in a non-Exchange profile, the default Personal Folders .pst file.

5.   In the MDB Viewer Test Application window (Figure 1.7), choose MDB | Open Root Folder. You should see the window shown in Figure 1.22. Compare it with Outlook Spy's view of the store root in Figure 1.21 and MFCMAPI's view from Figure 1.12.

To view the contents of any of the folders shown in Figure 1.22, double-click the folder, and it will open in a new MAPI_FOLDER window.

Table 1.4   *Folders in the Root of a Mailbox or Personal Folders .pst File Information Store*

Name	Description
Common Views (or IPM_COMMON_VIEWS)	Search folder definitions Custom forms published to the Personal Forms library Custom view definitions
Deferred Action	Client-side rule actions waiting for the user to start Outlook
Finder (or Search Root)	Named search folders Temporary search folders cached from Advanced Find searches
Freebusy Data	Local free/busy information for the current user (the same information is stored in a public folder on the Exchange server but in a different format)
Shortcuts	Information about folders in Public Folder\Favorites
Views (or IPM_VIEWS)	Custom view definitions
IPM_SUBTREE (or Top of Information Store)	Folder hierarchy that's visible to the user (e.g., Inbox, Contacts, etc.)
~MAPISP(Internal)	Used by Exchange
Drizzle	Used by Exchange
Row # 0	Any folder that does not have a property suitable for a display name appears with this name, Row # 1, and so on.
Subscriptions	Subscriptions to WSS lists
Reminders (.pst store)	Information on all Outlook items that fire reminders.

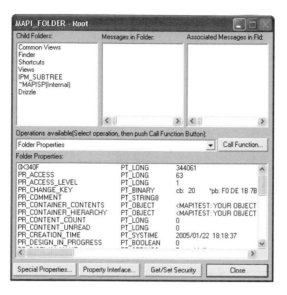

1.4.5   Hidden-message setting items

As you work with the folders in the information store root and with the hidden settings stored in various Outlook folders, you will run across many different kinds of items. You've already seen examples of custom form and view definitions in the earlier section on Outlook Spy. Table 1.5 lists the most common hidden-message setting items, along with the MessageClass property value that distinguishes them.

Note: The rules that users create are stored in the Inbox folder, not in one of the folders at the information store root.

For the most part, the individual properties of these items are undocumented and should not be tampered with.

1.5   Understanding Windows' roaming profiles and folder redirection

As you learned earlier in this chapter, many Outlook settings, including mail-account information stored in an Outlook profile, reside in the user portion of the Windows registry and the user's Windows profile folders on

Table 1.5   *Hidden-Message Setting Items*

MessageClass	Description
IPM.Microsoft.FolderDesign.FormsDescription	Custom form definition
IPM.Microsoft.FolderDesign.NamedView	Custom view definition
IPM.Microsoft.WunderBar.SFInfo	Search folder definition
IPM.Microsoft.WunderBar.Persistence	Used by the navigation pane
IPM.Microsoft.SniffData	Used by Exchange
IPM.Microsoft.ScheduleData.FreeBusy	Free/busy information
IPM.ExtendedRule.Message	Outlook 2003 junk mail settings
IPM.MessageManager	Used by Rules Wizard rules
IPM.RuleOrganizer	Used by Rules Wizard rules
IPM.Rule.Message	Individual rule settings
IPC.MS.Outlook.AgingProperties	Folder archive settings

the client computer. A common strategy in enterprise installations of past versions of Outlook where Exchange is the mail server has been to implement *roaming profiles*, in which the user's registry entries and user's profile folders are stored on the server and downloaded to each client machine where the user logs on. Changes are usually copied up to the server when the user logs off. (Alternatively, Windows XP supports a Group Policy setting that prevents changes from being saved to the server-based profile.) Roaming profiles thus make it possible for a user to have Outlook and other applications work and feel the same, regardless of which machine the user logs on to.

Roaming profiles are effective, though, in fewer situations with Outlook 2003. Remember that the default setting for Outlook 2003 with Exchange is to use Cached Exchange mode, which creates a local cache of the entire mailbox on the local hard drive. You won't want the user to have to wait for this to happen every time he or she logs onto a new machine.

Still, roaming profiles can be a good solution for organizations using Microsoft Exchange Server where people share computers at different times of the day or on different days of the week and all client machines have the same configuration. In those situations, the user's mail profile should be configured to use Classic Online mode, rather than Cached Exchange mode. You'll learn more about Classic Online mode in Chapter 5.

To emphasize the point, roaming profiles are not a good solution in any of these configurations:

- The user is connected to the Exchange server with either Cached Exchange mode or Classic Offline mode, both of which create an offline folders .ost file on the local machine

- The user has only POP3 accounts, and all data is stored in a Personal Folders .pst file.

- The user has only IMAP4 accounts, which cache data locally in Personal Folders .pst files, one per account.

- Users are viewing WSS event and contact lists in Outlook, which caches the WSS data in local .pst files.

- The client computers are running different versions of Outlook.

- The client computers have different Outlook add-ins installed.

What about the situation where the user has POP3 accounts and a Personal Folders .pst file? Why can't the .pst file be stored either on a network drive or in the user's application-data folders and copied down to the local machine at login? In the latter case, the .pst file can be very large, up to about 2 GB for .pst files created with earlier versions of Outlook and 20 GB for files created with Outlook 2003. Copying files of that size to the local machine every time the user logs in could burden the network and frustrate the user. As for network storage of a .pst file, Microsoft supports storing .pst files only on a local drive, not on a network drive. Accessing a .pst file over a local area network (LAN) or wide area network (WAN) connection requires a great deal of overhead: according to Microsoft, write operations can take four times as long as read operations. In addition, if a problem occurs with the network connection, the .pst file may be damaged. Therefore, .pst files should not be stored within the application-data folders for a user's roaming profile; nor should the roaming-profile user use a .pst file stored in his or her home directory on the network server.

Tip: Alternatives to roaming profiles include allowing users to access their Exchange accounts with Outlook Web Access or using Terminal Services.

1.5.1   Settings that roam with a Windows profile

Just in case you do have a scenario where roaming profiles would be appropriate, you'll want to understand just what settings will roam. As you learned earlier in this chapter, most Outlook settings are stored in the Windows registry or in the user's application folders, which are located at %USERPROFILE%\Application Data. Table 1.6 lists the data and settings associated with Outlook that roam by default because they are in one of these two locations. Unless otherwise specified, the Location column lists a subfolder under %USERPROFILE%\Application Data\Microsoft.

Remember that signatures are indirectly specific to a mail profile, not just the user profile. The user can associate each account in Outlook 2003 with a signature for composing new messages and one for replies and forwards. The signature information for each account is stored with the user's Outlook mail profile in the registry.

Table 1.6   Outlook Settings that Roam with a Windows Profile

Data/Setting	Location	Outlook Profile Specific
Outlook mail profiles	Windows registry	
Most user-specific Outlook settings	Windows registry	
View customizations	Outlook information store	
Published custom forms	Outlook information store	
Rules Wizard rules	Outlook information store	
Toolbar customizations	Outlook\Outcmd.dat	
Print-format customizations	Outlook\Outlprnt	
Outlook VBA project	Outlook\Vbaproject.otm	
Address autocomplete cache	Outlook*.nk2	X
Send/receive settings	Outlook*.srs	X
Navigation pane customizations	Outlook*.xml	X
Dictionary file	Proof\Custom.dic	
Signatures	Signatures*.htm, *, rtf, *.txt, *.vcf	See text
Custom stationery	Stationery*.htm	
Custom form template files	My Documents\Templates*.oft	

Note: View customizations, custom forms, and Rules Wizard rules technically are not part of the roaming-profile information. However, because they are maintained in the default information store and the store setting is part of the mail profile, which does roam, a user covered by roaming profiles will see the same views, forms, and rules, no matter what machine is in use.

The %USERPROFILE%\Local Settings folder and subfolders do not roam by default. Table 1.7 lists the types of files contained in the %USER-PROFILE%\Local Settings\Application Data\Microsoft\Outlook folder.

Even though %USERPROFILE%\Local Settings\Application Data\ Microsoft\Outlook is the default location for a .pst or .ost file, the user can actually create such a file anywhere in the file system, including the My Documents folder. If you are using roaming profiles, you may want to restrict the user's ability to create .pst files. Chapter 6 covers this issue.

Note: It is not possible to specify a location for IMAP4 account .pst files. Those are always created in the %USERPROFILE%\Local Settings\Application Data\Microsoft\Outlook folder. This means that if a roaming-profile user has an IMAP4 account in the Outlook mail profile, Outlook will create a new .pst file on each machine that the user logs on to and will download the IMAP4 data into that .pst file to create a new local cache.

Table 1.7   *Outlook Data and Settings That Do Not Roam with a Windows Profile*

File or Extension	Description
Extend.dat	Information on installed Exchange client extensions
Frmcache.dat and related folders	Custom forms cache
.oab	Exchange Offline Address Book files
.ost	Exchange Offline folders and MSN Connector data files
.pab	Personal Address Book files
.pst	Personal Folders files, including archive .pst files and proxy .pst files that cache IMAP, WSS, and Hotmail folders

Another potential problem with roaming profiles is that the user's registry may contain settings in the HKEY_CURRENT_USER\Software\Microsoft\Office\Outlook\Addins or in the HKEY_LOCAL_MACHINE\Software\Microsoft\Office\Outlook\Addins registry keys, which cause Outlook to try to load COM add-ins, regardless of whether the add-ins are actually installed on the machine where the user is working. In that case, the user may get a warning message that a component is not available.

1.5.2 Using folder redirection

Windows 2000 and Windows XP have an additional feature, called folder redirection, that allows an administrator to point certain special folders, such as Application Data, to a network drive. The user works with the data on the server as if it were local. Folder redirection is often used with roaming profiles, but it can also be used independently.

Folder redirection without roaming profiles offers little advantage to Outlook users since some of the key settings and files are specific to particular Outlook profiles or accounts. For example, a profile named Outlook Settings will have a send/receive settings file named Outlook Settings.srs. This file will be useless, however, without the matching Outlook Settings profile that's stored in the registry.

1.6 Summary

In this chapter, you've taken the grand tour of Outlook's data and settings, from the Windows registry to an Exchange mailbox to a Personal Folders .pst file to various files that store separate settings. You should now have a better idea of why Outlook can be a challenge to manage and why troubleshooting Outlook can involve both checking registry entries and drilling down into the information store.

You've seen how three tools, the Information Store Viewer, MFCMAPI, and Outlook Spy, can help you understand Outlook's data and settings better, diagnose problems, and in some cases, even fix problems. Be very cautious in using these tools, though. Because they offer a powerful interface for deleting items and folders and changing properties, careless use could result in lost data or a damaged mailbox or .pst file.

Finally, we've touched on the topics of roaming Windows profiles and folder redirection and explained why they are useful in only a few Outlook 2003 scenarios. If you do encounter a situation where roaming profiles are appropriate, such as Exchange users who work at different machines on different days, you should have a good understanding of which Outlook settings roam and which don't and should plan to configure the mail profile only for Exchange in Classic Online mode.

With the knowledge of Outlook's settings that you've gained in this chapter, we'll look in the next chapter at the key configuration techniques you'll use to deploy these settings, both as part of an Outlook installation and after Outlook has already been installed. Subsequent chapters will go into detail on the effects of specific settings and what the best settings might be for a particular scenario. In Chapter 9, we'll touch on some tips and tricks for configuring Outlook options that require a bit more than the conventional settings. Appendix A provides a comprehensive list of the Group Policy and user-preference settings you can set with the tools that Microsoft provides.

2

Outlook Configuration Techniques

As you saw in Chapter 1, Outlook stores its settings in many different locations—the Windows registry, discrete files, and items and properties in the data stores themselves. To manage these settings, Microsoft provides a collection of free tools in the Office Resource Kit (ORK), plus the powerful Group Policy feature for mandating settings with Active Directory. In this chapter, you'll learn the following:

- How to use the Office Profile Wizard (OPW), Custom Installation Wizard (CIW), and Custom Maintenance Wizard (CMW) to control how Outlook is configured

- How to use Group Policy Objects (GPOs) to enforce Outlook settings

- What tools to use to review settings before you deploy them with the ORK tools or GPOs

2.1   Tools in the Office Resource Kit

The ORK is a collection of articles and tools to assist you in deploying and managing Office installations, including installations of Outlook 2003 as a stand-alone program. The Office 2003 Resource Kit is available online at http://office.microsoft.com/en-us/FX011511471033.aspx. You can download the ORK tools from http://www.microsoft.com/office/ork-archive/2003ddl.htm. Table 2.1 lists those most important to Outlook.

The main Office 2003 Editions Resource Kit (Ork.exe) contains three major configuration tools and three corresponding viewers to show you the settings files that each of those tools can create, all listed in Table 2.2. After you download and run the Ork.exe file to install the tools, you will see them on the All Programs menu under Microsoft Office | Microsoft Office

Table 2.1   *Key ORK Tool Downloads*

Tool	Download File
Office 2003 Editions Resource Kit	Ork.exe
Office 2003 Policy Template Files and Deployment Planning Tools	Office-2003-SP1-ADMs-OPAs-and-Explain-Text.exe [This is the version for Service Pack 1 (SP1)]. Later service packs may release new versions.)
Office 2003 SP1	Office2003SP1-kb842532-fullfile-enu.exe
Office 2003 Setup.exe (Enhanced Version)	EntSetup.exe
Whitepaper: Configuring Outlook Profiles by Using a PRF File	PRFWhtepaper.exe

Tools | Microsoft Office 2003 Resource Kit. You can also locate them in the folders under Program Files\ORKTOOLS\ORK11\TOOLS.

Note: The ORK also contains other tools, such as the HTML Help Workshop and Removal Wizard, which this book does not cover. We will, however, cover the Outlook Administrator Pack in Chapter 7.

Notice that both the CMW and OPW have two purposes. You use the same program both to create a configuration settings file (.cmw or .ops, respectively) and to process such a file and apply those settings.

2.2   Using the Office Profile Wizard

The OPW, Proflwiz.exe, shown in Figure 2.1, allows you to capture settings from an existing Office installation into an .ops file. You can deploy the settings from an .ops file when Office is installed by importing it into the CIW. You can also apply an .ops file later, by running the Proflwiz.exe application again. (You cannot import an .ops file into the CMW.) You can use the OPW to deploy settings even if you do not install Office from an administrative installation point.

The OPW can capture any registry settings, but it can capture files only from those folders located under the user's Windows profile folder, the path which Windows stores as the %USERPROFILE% environment variable. This will usually be C:\Documents and Settings\%USERNAME%, where

Table 2.2 *Configuration Tools and Viewers in the ORK (Ork.exe)*

Tool	File Name	Description
Office Profile Wizard	Proflwiz.exe	Creates or processes an .ops file that contains information on files and registry settings to be added, modified, or removed from an Office installation. The .ops file is created from the settings in an existing Office installation.
Custom Installation Wizard	Custwiz.exe	Creates a transform .mst file that contains information on Office features, files, registry settings, and setup properties to be used during an Office installation. It can also be used to create stand-alone .prf files to configure Outlook mail profiles.
Custom Maintenance Wizard	Maintwiz.exe	Creates or processes a .cmw file that contains information on Office features, files, registry settings, and setup properties. It can also be used to create stand-alone .prf files to configure Outlook mail profiles.
OPS File Viewer	Opsview.exe	Extracts settings from an .ops file created with the OPW and displays them in a text file
MST File Viewer	Mstview.exe	Extracts settings from an .mst file created with the CIW and displays them in a text file
CMW File Viewer	Cmwview.exe	Extracts settings from a .cmw file created with the CMW and displays them in a text file
Outlook Administrator Pack	Admpack.exe	Contains components for managing the Outlook Security Settings folder.

Figure 2.1
The OPW.

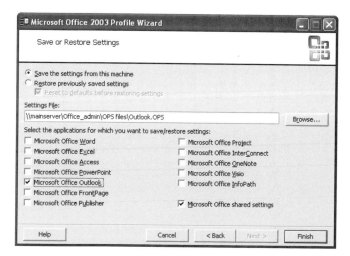

Figure 2.2
Command-line switches for Proflwiz.exe.

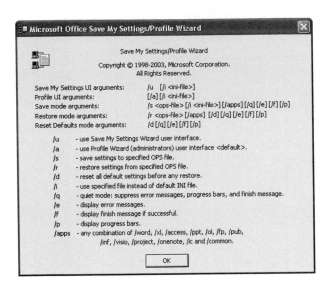

%USERNAME% is the environment variable representing the user's Windows login name.

Figure 2.2 summarizes the command-line switches available for Proflwiz.exe. Any option that you can set in the user interface for the OPW can also be set with a command-line switch. In addition, as you will see in the next section, you can start the OPW with a customized .ini file to tell the OPW exactly which settings to save.

Later, in Section 2.2.4, you'll see how the same program, Proflwiz.exe, functions not just as the OPW but also as the Save My Settings Wizard, which enables users to save and restore Office settings.

2.2.1   Customizing the Office Profile Wizard

By default, the OPW determines what to capture by looking at an .ini file, Opw11adm.ini, which is included in the Program Files\ORKTOOLS\ORK11\TOOLS\Profile Wizard folder. You can edit that file or create your own custom .ini file to capture a different set of settings. If you customize Opw11adm.ini, be sure to make a backup copy of that file first.

Note: The name of the OPW tool is a source of some confusion because an .ops file, by default, does not contain any information about Outlook mail profiles.

To start the OPW with a custom .ini file, use this command line:

```
"C:\Program Files\ORKTOOLS\ORK11\TOOLS\Profile Wizard\
Proflwiz.exe" /s filename.ops /i mycustomfile.ini
```

where Filename.ops is the file you want to create and Mycustomfile.ini is your custom .ini file.

To create a new custom .ini file, make a copy of the Opw11adm.ini file, then open the copy in Notepad or any other text editor for editing. The file includes a number of sections, all documented with comments in the file itself (the lines that begin with #). The [Header] section specifies the product and version. It is followed by 7 sections to back up or remove folders and files and 12 to back up or remove registry values.

[IncludeFolderTrees] section

The [IncludeFolderTrees] section determines what folders the OPW will copy files from. All files in all subfolders of the designated folders are included, except for those file types listed in the [ExcludeFiles] section. Table 2.3 lists the folder tokens that the OPW supports. All of these folders are located under the user's Windows profile folder, the path which Windows stores as the %USERPROFILE% environment variable, except <UserProfile>, which points to the %USERPROFILE% folder itself.

If you compare the information in the .ini file with Table 1.2, you'll see that these lines in the .ini file are crucial to the OPW's default settings for backing up certain key Outlook settings files:

```
<AppData>\Microsoft\Office                      # common
<AppData>\Microsoft\Outlook                     # ol
<AppData>\Microsoft\<SubFolder_Proof>           # common all
<AppData>\Microsoft\<SubFolder_Signatures>      # ol
<AppData>\Microsoft\<SubFolder_Stationery>      # ol
```

The comment at the end of each line—for example, # ol—indicates which application the line is associated with; for example:

- ol: Outlook

- common: Office shared settings

- all: all Office applications

Looking back at Figure 2.1, note that you can select which applications to back up to a given .ops file. If the Microsoft Office Outlook box is checked, then all settings marked with # ol will be included.

—————▶

Table 2.3   *Folder Tokens for the [IncludeFolderTrees] Section*

Folder Token	Location	Description
`<AppData>`	Application Data	Application-specific settings files, including many for Outlook
`<Desktop>`	Desktop	Windows desktop shortcuts and other files
`<Favorites>`	Favorites	Internet Explorer Favorites shortcuts
`<NetHood>`	NetHood	My Network Places shortcuts
`<Personal>`	My Documents	Storage for user-created files
`<PrintHood>`	PrintHood	Shortcuts to printer objects
`<ProgramsMenu>`	Start Menu\Programs	Shortcuts on the Windows Start | All Programs menu
`<RecentFiles>`	My Recent Documents	Shortcuts to recently used files
`<SendTo>`	SendTo	Shortcuts to programs that appear on the Send To submenu on the context menu that the user sees after right-clicking a file in Windows Explorer
`<StartMenu>`	Start Menu	Shortcuts on the Windows Start menu
`<StartupMenu>`	Start Menu\Programs\Startup	Shortcuts to programs that launch when Windows starts
`<UserProfile>`		The %USERPROFILE% folder itself

Note: Not all settings marked with # `ol` will be useful. Some refer to folders, files, and registry values that were used in previous versions of Outlook but are not used in Outlook 2003.

The `<SubFolder_*>` tokens, such as `<SubFolder_Signatures>`, use the folder names found in the corresponding registry values in HKEY_CURRENT_USER\Software\Microsoft\Office\11.0\Common\General. For example, if the Signatures value points to a folder named My Signatures, then the OPW will use this path:

```
%USERPROFILE%\Application Data\Microsoft\My Signatures
```

[IncludeIndividualFolders]

In this section, list individual folders to be included in the backup. Each line must begin with one of the folder tokens in Table 2.3, and you must list each subfolder separately. Wildcards are not supported.

[IncludeIndividualFiles]

In this section, list individual files to be included in the backup, one per line. Each entry must begin with one of the folder tokens in Table 2.3. Wildcards are not supported.

[ExcludeFiles]

In this section, list individual files and file types that you do not want to back up. Both * and ? wildcards are supported in the file name but not in the path. By default, [ExcludeFiles] includes a number of Outlook 2003 settings files, shown in Table 2.4.

[FolderTreesToRemoveToResetToDefaults]

In this section, list folders that you want to delete completely before applying other settings with the OPW. Use the same syntax as in the [Include-FolderTrees] section. All files and subfolders will be deleted.

Table 2.4   *Outlook Settings Files Excluded in [ExcludeFiles]*

File	Description
*.ost	Offline folders files
*.pab	Personal Address Book files
*.pst	Personal Folders files
*.rwz	Rules Wizard backup files
*.nk2	Autocomplete cache files
Extend.dat	Exchange client-extension add-in information
OutlPrnt	Print-format customizations

Note: This section and the other RemoveToResetToDefaults sections will be ignored when the .ops file is used to restore settings, unless the Reset to Defaults before Restoring Settings box is checked (see Figure 2.1) or Proflwiz.exe is started with the /d command-line switch. These sections are always ignored when the .ops file is imported into the CIW.

For example, Listing 2.1 shows an .ini file that, when invoked by the OPW, generates an .ops file that can clear the Outlook customs forms cache, including not just the Frmcache.dat file itself but all subfolders in the Forms folder.

Note: Since the [Header] section is the same for all OPW .ini files, we will not include it in subsequent .ini file listings.

You do not need to include the # ol marker in the sections dealing with folders, files, and registry entries to remove.

[IndividualFilesToRemoveToResetToDefaults]

In this section, list individual files that you want to remove before applying settings in the .ops file. Wildcards are allowed in file names but not folder paths. Each entry must begin with one of the folder tokens in Table 2.3.

The Opw11adm.ini file contains these entries, which will remove Outlook-related settings files:

```
<AppData>\Microsoft\Office\*.*
<AppData>\Microsoft\<SubFolder_Proof>\*.*
<AppData>\Microsoft\<SubFolder_Signatures>\*.*
<AppData>\Microsoft\<SubFolder_Stationery>\*.*
<AppData>\Microsoft\<SubFolder_Templates>\*.*
```

Listing 2.1   *OPW .ini File to Remove the Outlook Custom Forms Cache*

```
[Header]
Version  = 11.0
Product  = Microsoft Office 11.0

[FolderTreesToRemoveToResetToDefaults]
<UserProfile>\Local Settings\Application Data\Microsoft\FORMS
```

[ExcludeFilesToRemoveToResetToDefaults]

In this section, list files that should not be removed, regardless of what folder they reside in. The * and ? wildcards are supported. The Opw11adm.ini file contains these entries that will preserve some key Outlook settings and data files:

- *.PST
- *.DIC
- *.OST

[SubstituteEnvironmentVariables]

This section contains environment variables, such as %USERPROFILE% for expansion in registry values that use the data type REG_EXPAND_SZ.

[IncludeRegistryTrees]

This section includes registry keys to be included in the backup, along with all their subkeys. Wildcards are not supported. Use HKCU as the token for the HKEY_CURRENT_USER registry hive, which contains all of the user settings.

The following keys included in the Opw11adm.ini file are most related to Outlook:

```
HKCU\Software\Microsoft\Office\11.0\Common          # common
HKCU\Software\Microsoft\Office\11.0\Outlook         # ol
HKCU\Software\Microsoft\Office\Outlook              # ol
```

If you are creating an .ops file for use on multiple machines, you should comment out the third line above, the one that backs up HKEY_CURRENT_USER\Software\Microsoft\Office\Outlook, by placing the # character in front of it. This key contains an Addins subkey with settings for all of the COM add-ins that are installed for the current user. (Other COM add-ins may be installed in the HKEY_LOCAL_MACHINE hive.) It is preferable to let such add-ins manage their own settings rather than to try to distribute them through an .ops file and the OPW. If you know that a particular add-in is installed on all machines, you may include it by specifying the path to that add-in; for example:

```
HKCU\Software\Microsoft\Office\Outlook\LookoutAddIn.Connect
#ol
```

[IncludeIndividualRegistryKeys]

This section includes individual registry keys to be backed up, but not with their subkeys. Wildcards are not supported. The following entry in the Opw11adm.ini file is most related to Outlook:

```
HKCU\Software\Microsoft\Exchange\Client\Options
```

[IncludeIndividualRegistryValues]

This section list individual registry values to include in the backup. Wildcards are not supported. To include the default value for a key, end the entry with a backslash.

[ExcludeRegistryTrees]

This section includes registry keys to be excluded from the backup, along with their subkeys. Wildcards are not allowed.

[ExcludeIndividualRegistryKeys]

This section includes individual registry keys to exclude from the backup. Wildcards are not supported.

[ExcludeIndividualRegistryValues]

This section includes individual registry values to exclude from the backup. Wildcards are not supported. To exclude the default value for a key, end the entry with a backslash.

The following entries in the Opw11adm.ini file are most related to Outlook:

```
HKCU\Software\Microsoft\Office\11.0\Outlook\Setup\First-Run
HKCU\Software\Microsoft\Office\11.0\Outlook\UserData
HKCU\Software\Microsoft\Office\11.0\Outlook\Journal\Item
Log File
HKCU\Software\Microsoft\Office\11.0\Outlook\Journal\Outlook
Item Log File
```

[RegistryTreesToRemoveToResetToDefaults]

This section includes registry keys to remove, along with their subkeys, prior to writing values from the .ops file. Wildcards are not supported. The following keys in the Opw11adm.ini file are most related to Outlook:

```
HKCU\Software\Microsoft\Office\11.0
HKCU\Software\Microsoft\Office\Outlook
HKCU\Software\Microsoft\Shared Tools\Proofing Tools
```

The last four sections are similar to their corresponding sections for files and are ignored when the resulting .ops file is imported into the CIW.

- [IndividualRegistryValuesToRemoveToResetToDefaults]

- [RegistryTreesToExcludeToResetToDefaults]

- [RegistryKeysToExcludeToResetToDefaults]

- [RegistryValuesToExcludeToResetToDefaults]

2.2.2 Creating an .ops file

How and when you run the OPW to create an .ops file depends in large part on what you want to accomplish.

Note: You should close all Office programs before running the OPW, even if you're not backing up the settings from all of those programs. While the OPW will offer the opportunity to ignore a running program, it will not be able to finish if it cannot back up open files. Even if the OPW does finish, the resulting .ops file may have unexpected results.

If you want to create an .ops file that contains certain default settings for Outlook and other Office programs, you must first install Office 2003 and configure the settings you want users to have. Then, run Proflwiz.exe either from a command prompt or from the Start menu. Give the name of the .ops settings you want to create, deselect the Office programs you don't want to back up, and then click Finish.

If you want to use a custom .ini file, you will need to run Proflwiz.exe from a command prompt or Windows shortcut and use the /i command-line switch. Table 2.5 lists additional command-line switches that you can use to save settings with Proflwiz.exe. Any of the options that you can invoke in the OPW dialog (Figure 2.1) can also be set with a switch.

For example, this statement starts the OPW with the default Opw11adm.ini file and captures only Outlook and common settings to a file named OLonly.ops:

```
Proflwiz.exe /s OLonly.ops /ol /common
```

After you create an .ini file using the settings in Listing 2.1 and save that .ini file as Resetformcache.ini, you can use it to create an .ops file with this command:

```
Proflwiz.exe /s Resetformcache.ops /i Resetformcache.ini
```

Table 2.5   *Proflwiz.exe Switches to Save Settings*

Switch	Action
/s *<.ops settings file name>*	Save settings to the specified .ops file, which is required if you use the /s switch
/u	Start the wizard with the Opw11usr.ini file and the simplified Save My Settings Wizard interface for end users
/i *<.ini file>*	Use the settings in the specified .ini file to save settings
/q	Suppress error messages, progress bars, and finish message
/p	Display progress bars; suppress error messages
/e	Display error messages; suppress progress bars
/f	Display finish message if successful
/ol	Back up Outlook files and settings
/common	Back up Office common files and settings
/word	Back up Word files and settings
/xl	Back up Excel files and settings
/access	Back up Access files and settings
/ppt	Back up PowerPoint files and settings
/fp	Back up FrontPage files and settings
/pub	Back up Publisher files and settings
/inf	Back up InfoPath files and settings
/visio	Back up Visio files and settings
/project	Back up Project files and settings
/onenote	Back up OneNote files and settings
/ic	Back up files and settings for InterConnect, an electronic business-card program that Microsoft has been testing in Japan

2.2.3   Viewing an .ops file

The .ops file itself is in a binary format and is not designed to be edited. You can, however, view the settings that the .ops file contains using the OPS File Viewer program, Opsview.exe, which installs in the Program Files\ORKTOOLS\ORK11\TOOLS\VIEWERS folder. When you launch

Figure 2.3 *Viewing the settings in an .ops file.*

it either from that folder or from the Start menu, the OPS File Viewer will ask you to select an .ops file, then extract its settings to a text file with the .out file extension and open that file in Notepad. Figure 2.3 shows the settings contained in the OLonly.ops file, created with the command in the previous section, extracted with the viewer.

Tip: If you plan to organize all your .ini and .ops files in a single folder, perhaps with your Office administrative installation point, add a shortcut to Opsview.exe to that folder. You can then drag any .ops file onto the OPS File Viewer shortcut to quickly see the contents of that .ops file.

The size of the .ops file will depend on just what settings and files you've captured; it can be as large as several megabytes. You should carefully review the contents of each .ops file using the viewer, especially one that you plan to use to deploy settings with the CIW. If you need to add or subtract settings, make the necessary changes in the .ini file and then rerun the OPW to create a new .ops file. Repeat the process until you have an .ops file that captures just the settings you need.

2.2.4   Applying an .ops file

Once you have an .ops file that contains settings you want to deploy to the client, you can apply those in settings three different ways:

- Import the .ops file into the CIW and thus deploy it with the transform .mst file that the CIW creates.

- Run the OPW interactively.

- Run the OPW with a command line, specifying the .ops file to process.

Import into the CIW. You'll see the screen for loading an .ops file into the CIW later in Section 2.3.4. Once you load the file, the settings in the .ops file will be deployed in the transform .mst file that the CIW creates.

Run the OPW interactively. To run the OPW interactively on an Office client, look for the Save My Settings Wizard program in the Start | All Programs menu. You'll find it under Microsoft Office | Microsoft Office Tools | Microsoft Office 2003 Save My Settings Wizard. That's right! The Save My Settings Wizard that is part of the default Office or Outlook installation is the same application as the OPW, Proflwiz.exe. The shortcut on the client loads Proflwiz.exe with the Opw11usr.ini file and a simplified user interface. The default location for both Proflwiz.exe and Opw11usr.ini on the client is the C:\Program Files\Microsoft Office\OFFICE11 folder.

Note: Starting Proflwiz.exe with the /u command-line switch is the equivalent of running the Save My Settings Wizard shortcut from the Start menu.

When Proflwiz.exe is started as the Save My Settings Wizard, the user can only choose between saving and restoring settings, then select the destination or source file.

Tip: If you want to control what settings and files the Save My Settings Wizard backs up for the user, modify the Opw11usr.ini and deploy the modified file with the CIW, CMW, or any other tool you use to deploy files to the client. One of the key differences between Opw11adm.ini and Opw11usr.ini, as far as Outlook goes, is that the user version of the .ini file backs up Outlook profile information from the HKCU\Software\Microsoft\Windows NT\CurrentVersion\Windows Messaging Subsystem key. You should use the techniques described in the next chapter to deploy and manage profile settings with a .prf file rather than with the OPW.

Table 2.6   *Proflwiz.exe Switches to Apply Settings*

Switch	Action
/r *<.ops settings file name>*	Apply settings from the specified .ops file, which is required if you use the /r switch
/u	Start the wizard with the Opw11usr.ini file and the simplified Save My Settings Wizard interface for end users
/d	Reset settings to their defaults before applying the .ops file settings
/q	Suppress error messages and progress bars
/p	Display progress bars; suppress error messages
/e	Display error messages; suppress progress bars
/f	Display finish message if successful

Run the OPW with a command line. If you want to apply settings from a specific .ops file, you can use a command line like this, which uses the /r switch to restore settings from an .ops file stored on a network drive:

```
"C:\Program Files\Microsoft Office\OFFICE11\
Proflwiz.exe" /r "\\servername\office_admin\OPS\my
custom.ops" /q
```

The /q switch makes this a "quiet" installation; the user will see no prompts.

Table 2.6 lists additional command-line switches that you can use to apply settings with Proflwiz.exe, for example, in a login script.

2.2.5   Some practical Office Profile Wizard applications

The most common use of the OPW is to create the initial default user-preference settings for an Office deployment, but you may find it useful in other situations as well, especially if you need to deploy new settings or correct an Outlook problem.

As you saw in Section 2.2.1, you can use custom .ini files to create .ops files that perform incremental Outlook cleanup tasks, such as clearing out the custom forms cache folder. If you include such .ops files with your Office deployment or make them available on a network drive, your help desk can refer users to them to help clear up Outlook problems, either providing a shortcut that runs Proflwiz.exe from a command line or walking the user through the process of using the Save My Settings Wizard.

Tip: The default location used by the Save My Settings Wizard when it first runs is the user's My Documents folder; therefore, you may want to place any "maintenance" .ops files in a subfolder of My Documents so that the user doesn't have to navigate far to find them.

Let's look at three more practical applications before we leave the OPW behind. First, on the machine where you installed the ORK, in the C:\Program Files\ORKTOOLS\TOOLS\Profile Wizard\ folder, you'll find a file named Reseto11.ini. Starting Proflwiz.exe with the `/i` switch to invoke this .ini file will create an .ops file that resets almost all Office settings by removing existing files and registry keys and values. You will also find a Reseto11.ops file already built for you in the \Program Files\Microsoft Office\Office11 folder.

Second, you saw how to use the OPW to clear out old forms cache entries. You can do the same thing with unwanted registry values, for example those that hold key "most recently used" (MRU) lists for the Find a Contact box on the Standard toolbar and the Location drop-down list on the appointment form. Listing 2.2 shows the [IndividualRegistryValuesToRemoveToResetToDefaults] section of an .ini file that contains settings to remove a number of MRU lists that users often want to reset.

The three HKCU\Software\Microsoft\Windows NT\CurrentVersion\Windows Messaging Subsystem\Profiles entries require an explicit mail profile name. For example, if the profile is named Outlook Settings, the entry to clear the Other User's Folder history list would be

```
# File | Open | Other User's Folder history list
HKCU\Software\Microsoft\Windows NT\CurrentVersion\Windows
Messaging Subsystem\Profiles\Outlook Settings\
0a0d020000000000c000000000000046\101f0390
```

As you will see in Chapter 3, if you use a .prf file to deploy the default Outlook mail profile for each user, you can control what the name of that default profile will be.

For our final example, we'll use the OPW to distribute Visual Basic for Applications macros. Unlike Word and Excel macros, which exist as part of a document and thus can easily be distributed to other people for their use, Outlook Visual Basic for Applications (VBA) is intended largely for each user's personal use. Yet, there are plenty of situations where you might want to share some code with users to help them work more

---

→

Listing 2.2   *Listing 2.2 OPW .ini File to Reset Various MRU Lists*

```
[IndividualRegistryValuesToRemoveToResetToDefaults]
# History list from the Find a Contact box on the Standard toolbar
HKCU\Software\Microsoft\Office\11.0\Outlook\Contact\QuickFindMRU\QuickFindMRU

# History list from the Location drop-down list on the appointment form
HKCU\Software\Microsoft\Office\11.0\Outlook\Preferences\LocationMRU

# Look in history list from the Find pane
HKCU\Software\Microsoft\Office\11.0\Outlook\Contact\StripSearchMRU\StripSearchMRU

# Search for the Words history list from the Advanced Find dialog
HKCU\Software\Microsoft\Office\11.0\Outlook\Office Finder\MRU 1

# Categories history list from the Advanced Find dialog
HKCU\Software\Microsoft\Office\11.0\Outlook\Office Finder\MRU 3

# File | Open | Other User's Folder history list
HKCU\Software\Microsoft\Windows NT\CurrentVersion\Windows Messaging Subsystem\
Profiles\<profile name>\0a0d020000000000c000000000000046\101f0390

# Move to Folder history list
HKCU\Software\Microsoft\Windows NT\CurrentVersion\Windows Messaging Subsystem\
Profiles\<profile name>\0a0d020000000000c000000000000046\101f031e

# History list from the Actions | New Mail Using | Stationery command
HKCU\Software\Microsoft\Windows NT\CurrentVersion\Windows Messaging Subsystem\
Profiles\<profile name>\0a0d020000000000c000000000000046\101f035e
```

effectively, but you don't have the programming resources in-house to develop a COM add-in, which is the preferred solution for distributing and maintaining code.

As you learned in Chapter 1, all Outlook VBA code resides in a single file, Vbaproject.otm. If you use these entries in an .ini file for the OPW, you'll get an .ops file that will install the Vbaproject.otm from the source machine in the correct location:

```
[IncludeIndividualFiles]
<AppData>\Microsoft\Outlook\Vbaproject.otm   # ol
```

This procedure is not officially supported. Before deploying the resulting .ops file with the OPW, be sure to make users aware that the Vbaproject.otm file being installed will overwrite their original Vbaproject.otm file. If they have existing code, they should use VBA's File | Export command to export the code modules.

2.3   Using the Custom Installation and Custom Maintenance Wizards

As their names imply, the CIW and the CMW are two tools from the ORK that help install and maintain Office. You can use both with either a full installation of Office or an installation of Outlook as a stand-alone program. The CIW and CMW are very similar, as you can see from Table 2.7, which lists the different screens in these wizards. In this chapter, we'll usually show the CIW version of the screen.

The ORK contains hundreds of pages of detailed information on deploying Office and Outlook in a variety of different scenarios. This book does not attempt to duplicate that information but instead concentrates on configuration issues, such as which registry values to configure to make Outlook as secure as possible and how to modify Outlook mail profiles. Accordingly, when we look at the CIW and CMW shortly, we'll concentrate on the screens that cover those configuration settings. Those marked with * in Table 2.7 are covered in this chapter; those marked with † are covered in Chapter 3.

We assume that you have a basic familiarity with the CIW and CMW. The next section provides a brief review.

2.3.1   Understanding Office setup and maintenance

Both the CIW and CMW require access to the original setup files. (The OPW doesn't.) If you have done enterprise installations of past versions of Microsoft Office, you may have run Setup.exe /a—/a being a command-line switch—to create an administrative installation point, a central copy of Office on a network drive that users connect to and run the Setup.exe program to install Office. Office 2003 supports both this type of administrative installation point and a new type of central installation point created by copying the compressed files from the Office or Outlook 2003 CD to a network folder. If you install Office using a compressed CD image, you have the option of caching the installation files on the local machine, creating a local installation source (LIS). When the LIS is present, users installing hotfixes or service packs, applying updates created with the CMW, or running Help | Detect and Repair will not need to access the original installation media or network folder.

Like other Microsoft programs, Office 2003 uses Windows Installer technology to perform the actual software installation. Windows Installer allows you to apply a *transform .mst file*, along with an application's installation files, to produce a customized Office installation that includes particular features, registry settings, and other options, as shown in Figure 2.4. The

Table 2.7   *Screens in the CIW and CMW*

Title	CIW Screen	CMW Screen
Welcome	1	1
Open the MSI File	2	2
Open the MST/CMW File	3	3
Select the File to Save	4	4
Specify Default Path (CIW only) and Organization Name	5	5
Remove Previous Versions	6	n/a
Set Feature Installation States[*]	7	6
Configure Local Installation Source	8	n/a
Customize Default Application Settings[*]	9	n/a
Change Office User Settings[*]	10	7
Add/Remove Files[*]	11	8
Add/Remove Registry Entries[*]	12	9
Add, Modify, or Remove Shortcuts[*]	13	n/a
Identify Additional Servers	14	10
Specify Security Settings[*]	15	11
Add Installations and Run Programs[*]	16	n/a
Outlook: Customize Default Profile[†]	17	12
Outlook: Specify Exchange Settings[†]	18	13
Outlook: Add Accounts[†]	19	14
Outlook: Remove Accounts and Export Settings[†]	20	15
Outlook: Customize Default Settings[*]	21	16
Outlook: Specify Send/Receive Settings[*]	22	17
Modify Setup Properties	23	n/a

[*] Covered in this chapter.
[†] Covered in Chapter 3.

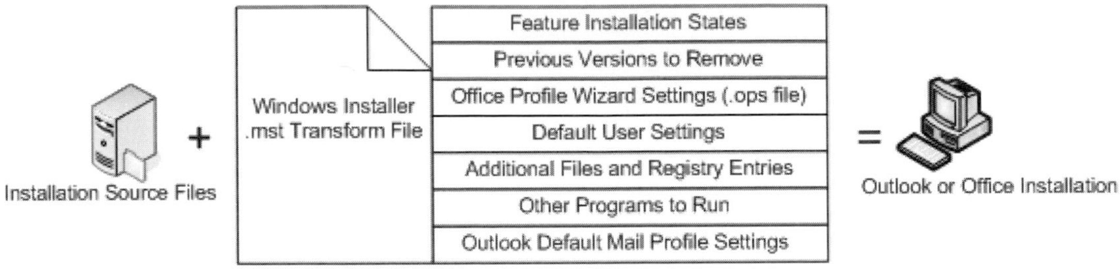

Windows Installer .mst Transform File	Feature Installation States
	Previous Versions to Remove
	Office Profile Wizard Settings (.ops file)
	Default User Settings
	Additional Files and Registry Entries
	Other Programs to Run
	Outlook Default Mail Profile Settings

Installation Source Files   +   = Outlook or Office Installation

Figure 2.4 *Combining a transform .mst file with an Office or Outlook installation source to perform an installation.*

CIW is a tool for creating such transform .mst files with the settings necessary for an Office installation.

A typical Office setup command invokes the .mst file as follows:

```
\\servername\office_admin\setup.exe TRANSFORMS="\\
servername\office_admin\mycustom.mst" /qb-
```

Note: The `/qb-` switch causes the Office 2003 setup program to display only simple progress indicators and error messages and to suppress any modal dialog boxes. A complete list of setup switches is available in Microsoft Knowledge Base article 826530, "Description of Setup Command-Line Switches for Office 2003."

While Setup.exe is the program you use to apply an .mst file created with the CIW, to apply a .cmw file created with the CMW, you use the CMW program itself—Maintwiz.exe. A typical command to apply a .cmw file from a shared network folder looks as follows:

```
\\servername\office_admin\maintwiz.exe "\\servername\
office_admin\CMW files\mycustom.cmw" /qb-
```

Note that if the path to the .cmw file has spaces in it, you must enclose the entire path in quotation makes. This is also true for the path to an .mst file used with Setup.exe.

Tip: To make it easier to deploy settings with .cmw files, you can include the Maintwiz.exe file among the files deployed during Office setup, using the settings on Screen 11 of the CMW, Add/Remove Files. That way, the user can run a local copy of Maintwiz.exe from a known location.

2.3.2   Starting the Custom Installation and Custom Maintenance Wizards

When you run the CIW or CMW, the first few screens cover four steps:

1.   Specify the location of the Windows Installer .msi package that contains the Office or Outlook setup files.

2.   Specify the location of the output file (.mst for the CIW, .cmw for the CMW).

3.   Set the default folder where Office will be installed on the client machine (CIW only) and the organization name.

4.   Set which earlier versions of Office programs to remove (CIW only). Earlier versions of Outlook are always removed since a machine can have only one version of Outlook installed.

The next sections cover the subsequent screens, where you actually select the configuration options.

2.3.3   Selecting Outlook and Office features

Screen 7 in the CIW (screen 6 in the CMW) is the first of several screens where you can select exactly which Office applications you want to install and which features you want to include. As you can see in Figure 2.5, the features are organized in a hierarchy. In some cases, the parent feature is just a container for the child features. In others, the parent is a feature itself, and any change in its feature installation state will cause a similar change in its children's state. You should plan to check the state of all child features rather than rely on the feature state of the parent.

Tip: If you want screen 7 to open with all of the application-feature state trees expanded, run Custwiz.exe with the /x command-line switch.

If you are installing the stand-alone Outlook 2003 that comes with Exchange 2003, you will not see the other Office applications on this screen, only Microsoft Office Outlook, Office Shared Features, and Office Tools.

For each feature, you will have up to seven choices of installation state (eight in the CMW), which are listed in Table 2.8.

If you are using a compressed CD-image installation point and allow setup to create an LIS, you will not be able to choose "Run from Network"

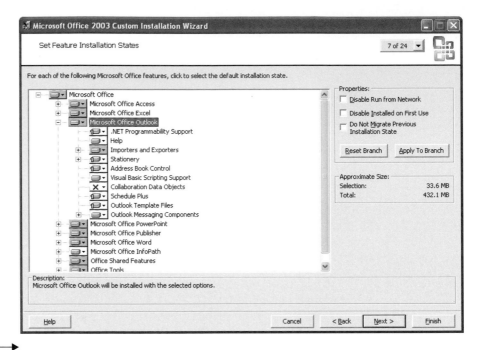

Figure 2.5   *Choose which Office 2003 applications and features to install.*

or "Run all from Network" as a feature since the files are contained in compressed .cab files, and it is not possible to run Office from a compressed file. If you want to prevent the user from changing the feature state during an interactive setup, right-click the feature and choose Hide. Similarly, you can use Unhide to make a hidden feature visible to the user during interactive setup.

The controls in the CIW shown on the right side of Figure 2.5 under Properties can help you apply broad settings to a single feature or an entire branch when you plan to allow users to select which features to install. (These controls are not available in the CMW.) Checking the first two check boxes—Disable Run from Network and Disable Installed on First Use—makes those installation options, both of which depend on having a network connection, unavailable for the selected feature. If you check the third box, Do Not Migrate Previous Installation State, the setup process will apply the installation state set in the transform .mst file that the CIW generates, if necessary removing features that the user might have added during a previous installation of Office. To apply any of those three settings to an entire branch in the feature hierarchy, select the top level of the branch, then click Apply to Branch. To reset a branch to the default installation settings, select the top level of the branch and click Reset Branch.

Table 2.8   *Feature Installation States*

Installation State	Description
Leave Unchanged	This leaves the feature in its original installation state (CMW only).
Run from My Computer	This copies all files and registry entries necessary for the feature to the user's computer so that the feature can be run locally.
Run All from My Computer	This applies the "Run from My Computer" installation state to the selected feature and all its child features.
Run from Network	The feature is available to the user. The necessary components are not copied to the local machine but instead are run from the administrative installation point. Not available for all features.
Run All from Network	This applies the "Run from Network" installation state to the selected feature and all its child features.
Installed on First Use	The components for the feature will be installed from the administrative installation point or LIS the first time the user invokes the feature. Not available for all features.
Not Available	Do not install the feature.
Not Available, Hidden, Locked	Do not install the feature, and do not display it to the user as an available feature during setup.

To help you configure Outlook to meet your organization's needs, Table 2.9 indicates which features are installed by default and which only on first use. For example, if you know that users often import data from Excel, you will probably want to set the ODBC feature under Importers and Exporters/Import from Other Formats to "Run from My Computer" instead of accepting the default state of "Installed on First Use." Similarly, if you know that certain commonly used in-house applications or Outlook utilities require Collaboration Data Objects (CDO), you will want to change the feature state for CDO from "Not Available" to "Run from My Computer."

In addition to the Outlook features shown in Table 2.9, you should also review the Office Shared Features and Office Tools, even if you are installing only Outlook 2003 and not the full Office 2003 package. Table 2.10 lists those features most relevant to Outlook and their default installation state.

As an example, power users who build Outlook custom forms or write VBA code will probably want to change the feature state for Digital Certificate for VBA Projects, Visual Basic Help, and Web Debugging from

Table 2.9 *Outlook Features*

Feature	Description	Default Installation State
.NET Programmability Support	Primary interop assemblies required by Outlook-related applications built on the .NET Framework. Required if you use any .NET add-ins in Outlook.	Installed on First Use
Help	Local Outlook Help files	Run from My Computer
Importers and Exporters Import from Other Formats ■ PAB	Components for importing data from a Personal Address Book .pab file.	Run from My Computer
Importers and Exporters Import from Other Formats ■ Act 3.0 ■ Text (DOS) ■ Text (Windows) ■ ODBC ■ Lotus Organizer ■ Schedule Plus ■ Schedule Plus Interchange	Components for importing data into Outlook from: ■ ACT! 3.0, 4.x, and 2000 ■ Comma-separated and tab-separated values in text files created in DOS or Windows ■ Microsoft Excel or Access ■ Lotus Organizer 4.1 and 5.0 ■ Microsoft Schedule Plus	Installed on First Use
Stationery	Basic files Extended files	Installed on First Use
Address Book Control	ActiveX control that displays the Outlook Address Book, used by Windows SharePoint Services Web pages, among others.	Installed on First Use
Visual Basic Scripting Support	VBScript support for custom Outlook forms; forms cannot run code without this component.	Run from My Computer
CDO	Programming library used by Outlook-related applications to provide certain functionality that Outlook's own programming interface does not support.	Not Available
Schedule Plus	Microsoft Schedule Plus application, for backward compatibility.	Installed on First Use
Outlook Template Files	Mail.oft file installed in Program Files\Microsoft Office\Templates.	Installed on First Use
Outlook Messaging Components Outlook MAPI Service Providers ■ Outlook Address Book	Components to display Outlook contacts in the address book.	Run from My Computer

Table 2.9 *Outlook Features (continued)*

Feature	Description	Default Installation State
Outlook Messaging Components Outlook MAPI Service Providers ■ Microsoft Exchange Server	Components to connect to a Microsoft Exchange mailbox.	Run from My Computer
Outlook Messaging Components Outlook MAPI Service Providers ■ Microsoft LDAP Directory	Components to display a Lightweight Directory Access Protocol (LDAP) directory in the address book.	Run from My Computer
Outlook Messaging Components Outlook MAPI Service Providers ■ Personal Folders	Components to store data in Personal Folders .pst files. If not installed, users will be unable to archive, use POP3, IMAP4, or Hotmail accounts, or link to a Windows SharePoint Services list.	Run from My Computer

Table 2.10 *Office Shared Features and Office Tools*

Office Shared Features	Description	Default Installation State
Alternative User Input Speech Handwriting	Provides support for voice recognition and handwriting input	Speech—Installed on First Use Handwriting—Disabled
Digital Certificate for VBA Projects	Installs the Selfcert.exe tool for generating a certificate to sign the user's own VBA project so that VBA security can be set to high	Installed on First Use
Microsoft Handwriting Component	Provides support for drawing and writing in Office applications	Installed on First Use
International Support Universal Font	Provides fonts to allow display of most languages, if the computer system supports them	Not Available
Office Assistant	Provides on-screen characters to provide tips and other help	Installed on First Use
Proofing Tools English French Spanish	Provides spelling and grammar checkers, hyphenation support, thesaurus, translation tools, and optical character recognition	English—Run from My Computer French and Spanish—Installed on First Use
VBA	Consists of the built-in VBA programming environment	Run from My Computer

Table 2.10 *Office Shared Features and Office Tools (continued)*

Office Shared Features	Description	Default Installation State
VBA Visual Basic Help	Provides Help topics for VBA	Installed on First Use
HTML Source Editing Web Scripting Web Debugging	Provides Microsoft Script Editor, which acts as the debugging environment for VBScript behind custom Outlook forms	Installed on First Use
Language Settings Tool	Provides support for setting language options in Office programs	Installed on First Use
Windows SharePoint Services Support	Provides components that help integrate Office with the SharePoint collaboration platform	Run from My Computer
Save My Settings Wizard	Installs Proflwiz.exe to provide support for backing up most Outlook and other Office settings to a file	Run from My Computer
Smart Tag Plug-ins	Provide Smart Tags to recognize dates, names, addresses, and stock ticker symbols in Excel and Word, including e-mail messages using Word-Mail as the editor	Run from My Computer

"Installed on First Use" to "Run from My Computer" since they know they'll need those components. Alternatively, if you wanted to disable VBA support completely, change the feature state for VBA under Office Shared Features from "Run from My Computer" to "Not Available."

Note: CIW screen 8 allows you to change the settings for the LIS, the cache of Office installation files that the setup process copies to the local machine when you install Office from a compressed CD image. If you are installing Office or Outlook from a compressed CD image, you need to use screen 8 to accept the license agreement and enter the volume license product key. Otherwise, each user will need to accept the license and enter the key when setup runs. If you are installing Outlook or Office from an administrative installation point rather than a compressed CD image, the options on screen 8 do not apply, even though you can configure them as part of the CIW.

2.3.4   **Configuring Outlook and Office default settings**

As you learned in Chapter 1, most Office and Outlook settings are stored in the Windows registry. When you install Office 2003 over a previous version, the default behavior is to migrate any settings that the user may have from a previous installation of Office to the corresponding registry entries for Office 2003. In many cases, however, you will want to set default values for certain options, particularly when you are installing Office or Outlook for the first time on new computers. Screens 9, 10, 12, 15, 21, and 22 in the CIW (in the CMW, 7, 9, 11, 16, and 17) allow you to configure various Office and Outlook properties, using the different methods listed in Table 2.11. Note that using any of these methods only sets default values for the options, most of which the user can change to his or her own preferences using the Tools | Options dialog or other commands in Outlook. To enforce particular settings so that users cannot override them, you need to use GPOs, as described later in Section 2.4.

Before looking at each of these screens, let's consider the issue of precedence. If you configure the same setting differently in more than one place, which setting does the installation process actually apply? In general, options set later in the CIW or CMW process take precedence over those set earlier. In other words, an option set with a registry entry on CIW screen 12 will override any value for that option set with an .ops file on screen 9 or with the Office User Settings hierarchy on screen 10. However,

Table 2.11   *Methods for Setting Default Options*

CIW Location	CMW Location	Description
Screen 9	n/a	Import settings from a profile .ops file created with the OPW. Allow or disable migration of existing user settings.
Screen 10	7	Select options from a hierarchy, similar to that used for administering settings with GPOs.
Screen 12	9	Add or remove entries from the Windows registry.
Screen 15	11	Set the security level for add-ins, VBA macros, and ActiveX.
Screen 21	16	Control the default e-mail format and editor for Outlook. Specify whether the Outlook Personal Address Book should migrate.
Screen 22	17	Configure send/receive group settings (Exchange only).

if on screen 9, you choose to migrate the user's existing Office settings, those settings are applied after all of the other settings in the transform, so their values take precedence over any new settings.

Note: Using the CIW, it is also possible to apply settings collected with the OPW after Office or Outlook setup has completed by adding a command on screen 16, Add Installations and Run Programs. In that case, the settings in an .ops file are applied after the settings in the transform .mst file and will override any user settings that were migrated from a previous version.

As you learned earlier in this chapter, you can capture the settings for most Office application options by running the OPW to create an .ops file. Typically, you will perform a clean installation of Office or Outlook 2003, configure the desired settings, and then run the OPW. On screen 9 of the CIW (Figure 2.6), you import the .ops file.

You also have a choice on CIW screen 9 of migrating the user's settings from a previous Office installation. This migration takes place after all of

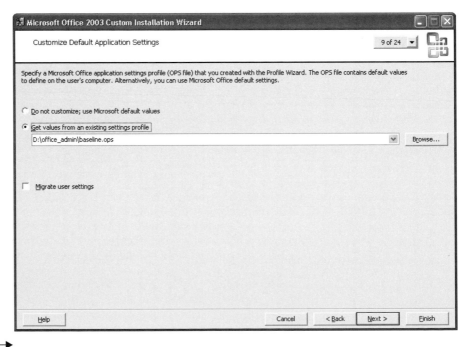

Figure 2.6   *Adding an OPW .ops file to the CIW.*

the settings in the CIW's transform .mst file have been applied during the setup process.

Screen 10 in the CIW (Figure 2.7) and the corresponding screen 7 in the CMW, Change Office User Settings, allow you to configure the most important registry settings for Office programs one by one rather than in a batch as the .ops file does. (Many of these settings can also be set with GPOs. Those relevant to Outlook are listed, along with their corresponding registry values, in Appendix A.)

When you switch to either screen, you'll see a brief onscreen message that says, "Reading settings . . ." Both programs read the available settings from files with the extension .opa. These .opa settings files are located in the Program Files\ORKTOOLS\ORK11\TOOLS\SHARED subfolder on the machine where the ORK tools are installed.

If you are deploying or configuring Office 2003 with Service Pack 1 (SP1) applied, you should replace the original .opa files with the files that

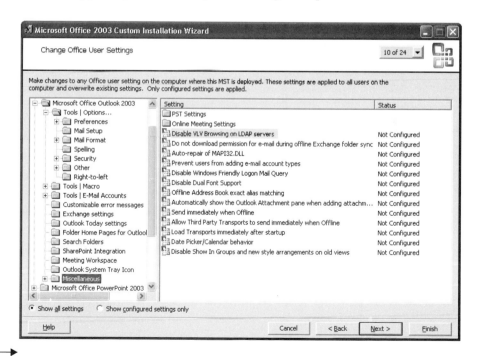

Figure 2.7   *Setting specific user settings.*

have been updated for SP1, which introduces some new registry settings. Microsoft provides a file, Office-2003-SP1-ADMs-OPAs-and-Explain-Text.exe, that contains the updated .opa files, updated administrative template .adm files for use with the Group Policy Editor, and two Excel worksheets. One worksheet lists all user-interface options in Office, along with the corresponding Group Policy or CIW/CMW settings. The other worksheet lists all Office-related Group Policy and CIW/CMW settings, including those that are not exposed in the user interface. Information on how to obtain this update and how to install it is available at http://office.microsoft.com/en-us/assistance/HA011513711033.aspx. Expect to see similar updates for subsequent service packs.

Another important thing to keep in mind is that some settings that affect Outlook may be found under other applications or under the settings for Office itself. As you can see in Figure 2.8, some key settings for the Offline Address Book (OAB) appear not under the Microsoft Office Outlook 2003 branch but under Microsoft Office 2003 (machine)/Exchange Settings.

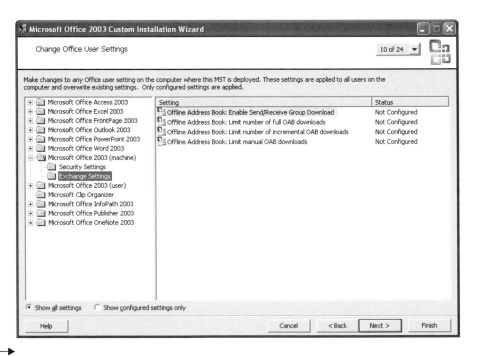

Figure 2.8   *Office user settings available in the CIW.*

Figure 2.9
*Setting a
WordMail option.*

These particular settings are applied on a per-machine basis, installing in the HKEY_LOCAL_MACHINE hive.

To configure any option, double-click the setting in the window on the right, choose Apply Changes, and select the desired value for the setting. For example, to filter HTML and thus reduce the size of HTML messages composed when Word is the e-mail editor (a configuration known as Word-Mail), expand the Microsoft Office Word 2003 branch to drill down to Tools | Options/General/E-mail Options, then double-click Filter HTML before Sending. In the Properties dialog for that setting (Figure 2.9), select Apply Changes, then check the check box for the setting. To set the other options related to WordMail that appear under E-mail Options, click Next Setting.

Note: You will see a few more Outlook configuration options later in this chapter in Section 2.3.8.

We're going to skip screen 11 (Add/Remove Files) in the CIW, which is screen 8 in the CMW, and come back to it in Section 2.3.5 so that we can complete the discussion of configuring program options by looking next at screen 12 (Add/Remove Registry Entries) in the CIW (screen 9 in the CMW).

Tip: Remember that you can use the screen selector drop-down list at the top right corner of the CIW to switch back and forth between pages. If you decide later in the wizard that you need to change a setting, you don't need to click Back a dozen times. Instead, just select the screen you want directly from the drop-down list.

The Add/Remove Registry Entries screen (Figure 2.10) allows you to add or remove entries from the Windows registry. These can be settings for Outlook or Office or even Windows settings that you want to change as part of your Office installation. You might even choose to do all of your settings configuration on this screen and skip the previous two screens completely. Or you might do most of the configuration on those screens and on the Add/Remove Registry Entries screen, configure only those changes that the earlier screens don't support. Personal preference and the number of options you want to set will both probably play a role in your decision.

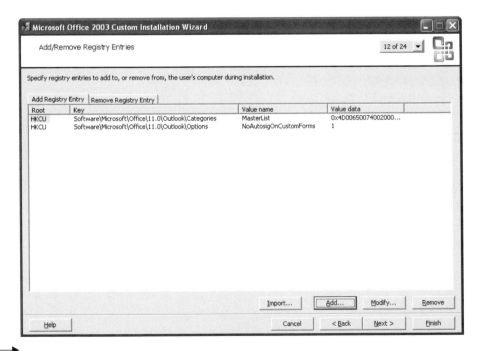

Figure 2.10   *Configure registry values for Outlook or other programs.*

Chief among the registry changes you'll want to make on this screen are those related to Office service packs and Outlook hotfixes that you may be deploying as part of your installation. You will probably want to deploy any new installation with Office Service Pack 1, and as later service packs are issued, you'll probably want to update your base installation to include them as well. Hotfixes are interim patches that Microsoft issues between service packs to address significant security and other issues. Most are specific to just one application and are not available as public downloads; you can get them quickly with a call to Microsoft support, though. Many service packs and hotfixes introduce new registry settings to fix problems or configure new features. While a service pack may include a new .opa file, a hotfix won't. Also, the .opa file for a service pack may not expose all of the new registry options available.

For example, Office 2003 SP1 added a feature that many Outlook users and administrators have long asked for—putting the user's automatic signature on messages created with custom forms. However, this meant that forms that implemented their own workarounds to insert the signature would wind up with two signatures. Therefore, Microsoft provided a new NoAutosigOnCustomForms registry entry, described in Microsoft Knowledge Base article 840393, to suppress automatic signatures on custom forms, in other words, to retain the behavior of previous versions. To set this registry value on CIW screen 12 or CMW screen 9, click Add, then accept the default Root of HKEY_CURRENT_USER and change the data type to REG_DWORD. For the key, enter Software\Microsoft\Office\11.0\Outlook\Options. For the value, enter NoAutosigOnCustomForms, and for the value data, enter 1. The results should look like Figure 2.11. Click OK to add that registry entry.

Figure 2.11
Configuring a Windows registry entry.

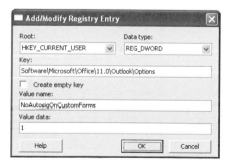

Warning: The dialog shown in Figure 2.11 only validates that the data entered under Value data is appropriate for the chosen data type. For example, a REG_DWORD value can have only decimal or hexadecimal data. It does not validate whether the data itself is appropriate for that registry value. All registry modifications should be thoroughly tested before you distribute them to large numbers of users.

Note that this screen also provides the ability to import a .reg file. You can create a .reg file by exporting a branch from the Registry Editor (Regedit.exe) or by generating one manually in Notepad or any other text editor. An important application for Outlook 2003 would be to provide a starting list of categories for the master category list. This list, held in the registry in a binary value, displays whenever the user clicks the Categories button on an Outlook item, but it's specific to each user. Outlook has no dedicated configuration option to set the master category list, but you can incorporate it on this screen by performing the following these steps:

1. On any Outlook item, click Categories, and edit the master category list to reflect the categories that you want users to see as their default list.

2. Start the Registry Editor by running Regedit.exe.

3. Navigate to the HKEY_CURRENT_USER\Software\Microsoft\ Office\11.0\Outlook\Categories key.

4. Right-click the Categories key, choose Export, choose the location where you want to save the .reg file, give it a name, and then click Save.

5. On screen 12 of the CIW (screen 9 in the CMW), click Import, select the .reg file you exported in step 4, and then click Open.

This procedure imports the binary, Unicode master category list into the CIW for addition to the transform .mst file.

Note: You can also configure the master category list by setting it before you run the OPW, then including the resulting .ops file in the transform.

The final option on this screen is to remove registry entries. Switch to the Remove Registry Entry tab and click Add to specify the root, key, and value name of any registry entry that you might want to remove.

2.3.5   Configuring files

Let's back up one screen to look at screen 11 in the CIW (Figure 2.12), or screen 8 in the CMW, where you enter the location of files that you want to add to the installation or specify files that you want to remove when Office or Outlook is installed.

To add a file, click Add, and specify the location. The file does not need to be located on a network drive that the user can access when setup occurs because the CIW adds the file itself to the transform .mst file. The CMW adds the file to its .cmw output file. For example, as noted in Section 2.3.1, you may want to deploy the CMW application Maintwiz.exe so that users can run it locally. Figure 2.11 shows how the CIW lists this file after it has been added.

To remove a file from the user's machine, switch to the Remove Files tab, then click Add. In the File Path dialog (Figure 2.13), choose the location, then type in the name of the file. In most cases, you will be removing a file found under <ProgramFiles\Microsoft Office>, the parent folder where Office program files are installed, or <ApplicationData>\Microsoft\Outlook,

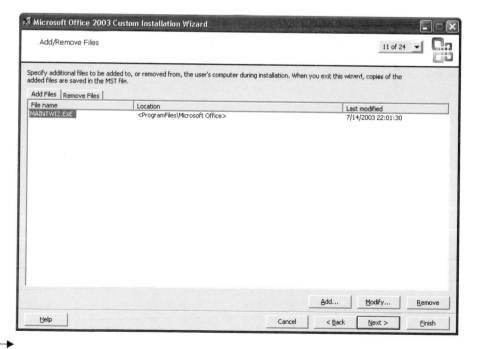

Figure 2.12   *Adding files to be installed.*

Figure 2.13
Designating the path to a file to be removed as part of the installation process.

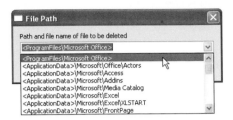

the default location for user's Outlook data and configuration files, but you can also choose from several other system paths. In addition, you can also enter the exact path to a known file.

For example, you might want to reset users' toolbar customizations so that they start fresh with the default toolbars when they start using the new version of Outlook. To accomplish that, you can use this screen to remove the <ApplicationData>\Microsoft\Outlook\Outcmd.dat file, which holds the user's customized toolbar settings.

Note: Table 1.2 lists the location of Outlook user settings files, such as Outcmd.dat.

2.3.6 Configuring shortcuts

Screen 13 in the CIW allows you to add and configure shortcuts to Office programs on the Start menu and the Windows desktop in order to control how the user launches Outlook and other Office applications and tools. There is no equivalent screen in the CMW. You can also add shortcuts to any files or applications on the user's machine or to Web pages and place them in locations such as Internet Explorer's Links toolbar or the Quick Launch bar in Windows XP.

As Figure 2.14 shows, the default for shortcuts to basic applications like Outlook and Word is to place them in the Programs menu under a submenu named Microsoft Office. That submenu, in turn, has its own submenu, Microsoft Office Tools, which contains shortcuts to Office utilities such as the Save My Settings Wizard.

The default list of shortcuts will include the applications and tools that you selected on screen 7 (Set Feature Installation States). Use the Add, Modify, and Remove buttons at the bottom of screen 13 to configure the

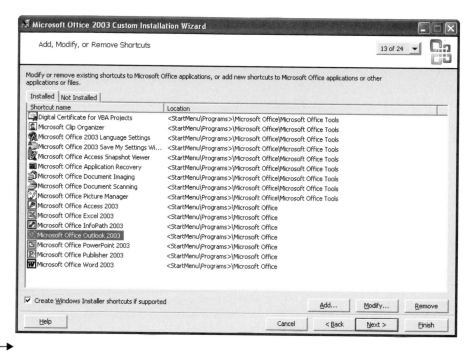

Figure 2.14 *Configuring shortcuts.*

shortcuts. When you add a shortcut, the Target list on the Add/Modify Shortcut Entry dialog (Figure 2.15) will include not just the Office applications but any other files that you added on screen 11 (Add/Remove Files).

Figure 2.15
Configuring an application shortcut.

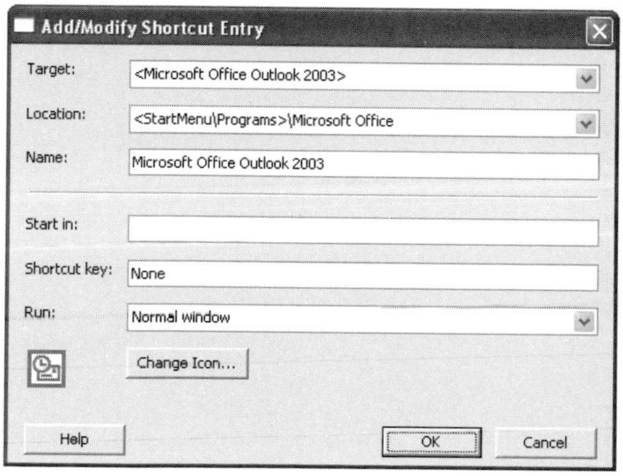

For example, you might prefer to have Outlook appear in the main Start menu, not under the Programs menu. To make that change, follow these steps:

1.   On screen 13, select Microsoft Office Outlook 2003.

2.   Click Modify.

3.   On the Add/Modify Shortcut Entry dialog, change the location from <StartMenu\Programs>\Microsoft Office to <StartMenu\Programs>.

4.   Click OK to save the shortcut.

You can also add command-line switches to a shortcut. The extensive, full list of switches for Outlook 2003 is available in the Help topic "Command-line switches."

For example, even though the reading pane in Outlook is safe, as you'll see in Chapter 6, some administrators may prefer to disable it. There is no registry entry to do this. Instead, you can add or modify an Outlook shortcut and append the /nopreview switch to the target. Figure 2.16 shows that switch added to an Outlook shortcut for the Quick Launch bar. Notice the space before the switch.

If you add a command-line parameter that contains a space, such as the name of a document or template file, enclose the parameter in quotation marks. For example, you could add a desktop shortcut to a custom Outlook message form with the message class IPM.Note.Vacation Request by placing this text in the Target property:

```
<Microsoft Office Outlook 2003> /c "IPM.Note.Vacation
Request"
```

Figure 2.16
Adding a Quick Launch shortcut that disables the reading pane.

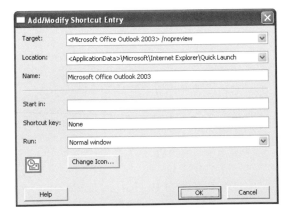

When you add a shortcut to the Outlook application on the Windows desktop using this technique, it will not have the properties of the desktop shortcut in earlier versions, where right-clicking the Outlook shortcut brought up the option to configure mail accounts and Outlook profiles.

Note: We will skip CIW screen 14 and CMW screen 10, which are not directly related to Outlook configuration. If you are using an administrative installation point rather than a compressed CD image, especially in a large organization, you may want to set up more than one administrative image. These screens provide a place to enter the location of those other images.

2.3.7 Configuring add-in and macro security settings

Outlook 2003 includes many security features that it shares with other Office applications and some specific to Outlook, which you'll read about in Chapter 6. Screen 15 in the CIW (screen 11 in the CMW) lists options for COM add-ins and VBA macros.

Warning: As explained earlier in the Section 2.3.4, a user can override these security settings. For that reason, it is more common to apply security settings with GPOs than with a transform created with the CIW or a .cmw file created with the CMW.

If you make no changes on this screen, leaving all options set to <do not configure>, Outlook will operate with this default behavior:

- All COM add-ins will run.

- If you are upgrading from a previous version of Outlook, the user's VBA security setting will not change.

- If you are installing Outlook on the machine for the first time, VBA will be set with a macro security of High, which means that no Outlook VBA code will run unless the VBA project has been digitally signed with a valid, trusted certificate. (Remember, one of the Office components you can install is the Selfcert.exe utility for creating a digital certificate to sign VBA projects.)

- If an Office application needs to use an ActiveX control that might be unsafe, the user receives a prompt. If the user authorizes the control to run, it is initialized with the capability to store and retrieve data.

Note: Remember that you can disable VBA completely by setting its feature installation state to Not Available on CIW screen 7 or CMW screen 6.

To tighten the default security as much as possible, use the options shown in Figure 2.17.

Under this configuration, Outlook will operate with the following more restrictive behavior:

- The only COM add-ins that will run are those signed with certificates added to the list of trusted publishers. You can select certificates to be installed with Outlook using the Add button on screen 15.

- Outlook VBA will be set with a macro security of High, which means that no Outlook VBA code will run unless the VBA project has been digitally signed with a valid, trusted certificate.

- If an Office application needs to use an ActiveX control that might be unsafe, the user receives a prompt. If the user authorizes the control to run, it is initialized without the capability to store and retrieve data.

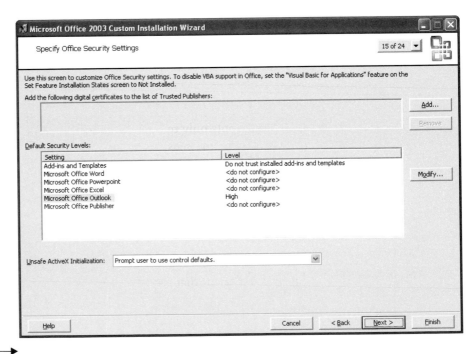

Figure 2.17   *Most secure default settings for Outlook 2003.*

Table 2.12   *Security for Add-ins and Templates*

Setting	Description
Do not configure the security level	Do not change the user's setting. Office applications being installed by this transform use the default setting "Trust all installed add-ins and templates."
Trust all installed add-ins and templates	Allow all add-ins and templates to run, even those without digital signatures.
Do not trust installed add-ins and templates	Only run add-ins and templates that have been signed with a valid, trusted digital signature.

Note: Office 2003 uses the same trusted publishers list, that is, sources for which the user has digital certificates installed, as Internet Explorer.

An add-in that is "trusted" in the sense of having a certificate from a trusted publisher is not necessarily trusted to the point that it can run Outlook automation code without triggering security prompts. You will learn about the concept of code trusting for the object model security guard in Chapters 6 and 7.

Let's look at these add-in security settings in more detail.

Under Default Security Levels, add-ins and templates support the three options shown in Table 2.12.

These options apply only to Outlook COM add-ins. Even though Outlook has templates in the sense of Outlook form template (.oft) files, no code runs on these and other unpublished forms, unless the Exchange administrator overrides this default setting using the Outlook Security Settings folder, as described in Chapter 7.

Under each application, you will see the four VBA security options, as shown in Figure 2.18.

As listed earlier in Table 2.9, Office includes a Digital Certificate for VBA Projects component that allows users to generate a digital certificate to sign their VBA projects so that they will run when macro security is set to high.

Figure 2.18
VBA security levels.

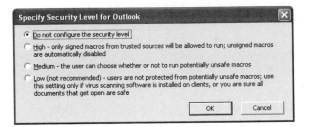

Note: The reference to documents under the Low setting is misleading since Outlook is not a document-centric application. These security settings apply only to the VBA project in Outlook, VBAProject.otm. They do not affect code behind custom Outlook forms; nor are they related to the object model guard security prompts discussed in Chapters 6 and 7.

The final option on this screen of the wizard is for Unsafe ActiveX Installation, which offers the four options shown in Table 2.13.

On installations where Unsafe ActiveX Installation has not been previously configured, choosing <do not configure> causes Outlook to use the default behavior, which is "Prompt to use persisted data."

Table 2.13   *Security Settings for ActiveX Controls*

Setting	Description
<Do not configure>	Do not change the user's setting.
Prompt user to use control defaults	If an application invokes an ActiveX control that might be unsafe, the user sees a prompt and can choose whether to trust the source. If the user trusts the control, then it initializes with its default settings rather than with any data that might have been previously stored with the control.
Prompt user to use persisted data	If an application invokes an ActiveX control that might be unsafe, the user sees a prompt and can choose whether to trust the source. If the user trusts the control, then it initializes with any data that might have been stored with the control.
Do not prompt	This is the least secure setting. ActiveX controls run without the user receiving a prompt and use any persisted data.

Note: We will skip the next few screens. Screen 16 of the CIW provides a place to include additional programs that you want to run after Office or Outlook setup has completed. In general, these will be programs that do not use a Windows Installer package. (For Windows Installer packages, you can chain the package installation using settings in the Setup.ini file for the main Office or Outlook installation.) For example, you might have a setup program for a MAPI provider that allows Outlook to connect to a non-Exchange enterprise mail server.

Screens 17 to 20 in the CIW and screens 12 to 15 in the CMW help you configure Outlook mail profiles. We'll return to them in Chapter 3.

2.3.8 Managing additional Outlook settings

On screen 21 in the CIW (Figure 2.19) or screen 16 in the CMW, the options are all related to Outlook and set corresponding entries in the Windows registry.

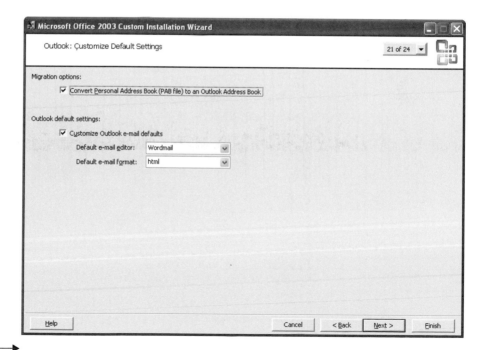

Figure 2.19 *Setting message defaults and the Personal Address Book Migration option.*

If you check the Convert Personal Address Book (PAB file) . . . box, the CMW will add three registry values into the .cmw file:

Key: HKEY_CURRENT_USER\Software\Microsoft\Office\11.0\
Outlook\Setup
Value name: ImportPAB
Value type: REG_SZ (string)
Value: yes

Value name: First-Run
Value type: REG_DWORD
Value: 0

Value name: FirstRun
Value type: REG_DWORD
Value: 0

When these three values are present, the next time Outlook starts, it will import data from the .pab file in the user's mail profile (if there is one) to the user's default Contacts folder.

The other two options control the e-mail message defaults. Choose WordMail as the editor only if you are also installing Word 2003. Outlook

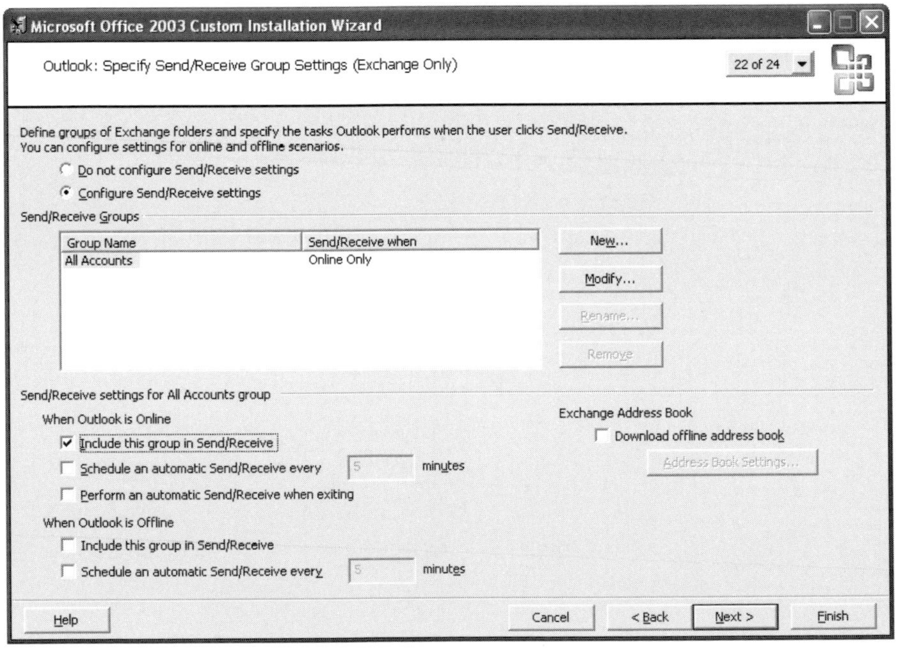

Figure 2.20   *Managing settings for send/receive groups for an Exchange account.*

2003 cannot use an earlier version of Word as its editor. The default e-mail format is HTML, with rich text and plain text as the other available choices.

For mail profiles containing an Exchange account, you can use screen 22 in the CIW (screen 17 in the CMW) to manage the send/receive group settings, as shown in Figure 2.20. You'll see some practical applications of these settings in Chapter 5.

Note: If you plan to deploy send/receive group settings, you may need to apply the post-SP1 hotfix detailed in Microsoft Knowledge Base article 885243, "Description of the Outlook 2003 Post-Service Pack 1 Hotfix Package: September 13, 2004."

This concludes our walk-through of the settings available in the CIW and CMW. We will return to these tools in Chapter 3 to walk through the process of building Outlook mail profiles.

2.3.9 Viewing .mst and .cmw files

Just as you can view .ops files created with the OPW using the OPS File Viewer, you can also use the MST File Viewer and CMW File Viewer to examine the .mst and .cmw files created by the CIW and CMW, respectively. These viewers are available in the Program Files\ORKTOOLS\ORK11\TOOLS\VIEWERS folder and on the Start menu.

When you launch the MST File Viewer, you will see the prompt in Figure 2.21, asking you not only for the .mst file location but also the location of the .msi file for the product that you want to use the .mst file to install.

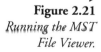

Figure 2.21
Running the MST File Viewer.

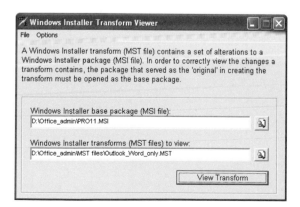

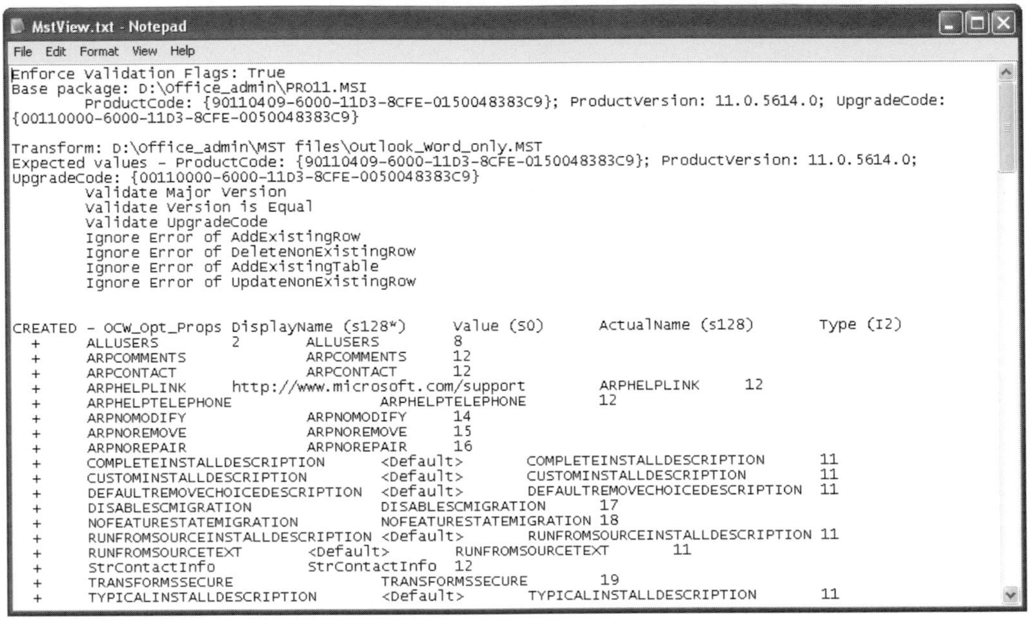

```
Enforce Validation Flags: True
Base package: D:\office_admin\PRO11.MSI
        ProductCode: {90110409-6000-11D3-8CFE-0150048383C9}; ProductVersion: 11.0.5614.0; UpgradeCode:
{00110000-6000-11D3-8CFE-0050048383C9}

Transform: D:\office_admin\MST files\Outlook_Word_only.MST
Expected values - ProductCode: {90110409-6000-11D3-8CFE-0150048383C9}; ProductVersion: 11.0.5614.0;
UpgradeCode: {00110000-6000-11D3-8CFE-0050048383C9}
        Validate Major Version
        Validate Version is Equal
        Validate UpgradeCode
        Ignore Error of AddExistingRow
        Ignore Error of DeleteNonExistingRow
        Ignore Error of AddExistingTable
        Ignore Error of UpdateNonExistingRow


CREATED - OCW_Opt_Props DisplayName (s128*)     Value (S0)      ActualName (s128)       Type (I2)
  +     ALLUSERS        2       ALLUSERS        8
  +     ARPCOMMENTS             ARPCOMMENTS     12
  +     ARPCONTACT              ARPCONTACT      12
  +     ARPHELPLINK     http://www.microsoft.com/support        ARPHELPLINK     12
  +     ARPHELPTELEPHONE                ARPHELPTELEPHONE        12
  +     ARPNOMODIFY             ARPNOMODIFY     14
  +     ARPNOREMOVE             ARPNOREMOVE     15
  +     ARPNOREPAIR             ARPNOREPAIR     16
  +     COMPLETEINSTALLDESCRIPTION      <Default>       COMPLETEINSTALLDESCRIPTION      11
  +     CUSTOMINSTALLDESCRIPTION        <Default>       CUSTOMINSTALLDESCRIPTION        11
  +     DEFAULTREMOVECHOICEDESCRIPTION  <Default>       DEFAULTREMOVECHOICEDESCRIPTION  11
  +     DISABLESCMIGRATION              DISABLESCMIGRATION      17
  +     NOFEATURESTATEMIGRATION         NOFEATURESTATEMIGRATION 18
  +     RUNFROMSOURCEINSTALLDESCRIPTION <Default>       RUNFROMSOURCEINSTALLDESCRIPTION 11
  +     RUNFROMSOURCETEXT       <Default>       RUNFROMSOURCETEXT       11
  +     StrContactInfo          StrContactInfo  12
  +     TRANSFORMSSECURE                TRANSFORMSSECURE        19
  +     TYPICALINSTALLDESCRIPTION       <Default>       TYPICALINSTALLDESCRIPTION       11
```

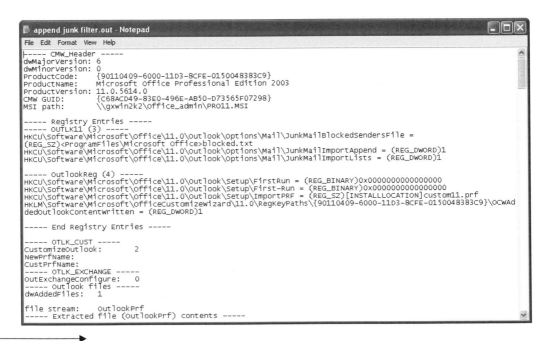

Figure 2.22 *Viewing the contents of an .mst file.*

```
----- CMW_Header -----
dwMajorVersion: 6
dwMinorVersion: 0
ProductCode:    {90110409-6000-11D3-8CFE-0150048383C9}
ProductName:    Microsoft Office Professional Edition 2003
ProductVersion: 11.0.5614.0
CMW GUID:       {C68ACD49-83E0-496E-AB50-D73565F07298}
MSI path:       \\gxwin2k2\office_admin\PRO11.MSI

----- Registry Entries -----
----- OUTLK11 (3) -----
HKCU\Software\Microsoft\Office\11.0\Outlook\Options\Mail\JunkMailBlockedSendersFile =
(REG_SZ)<ProgramFiles\Microsoft Office>blocked.txt
HKCU\Software\Microsoft\Office\11.0\Outlook\Options\Mail\JunkMailImportAppend = (REG_DWORD)1
HKCU\Software\Microsoft\Office\11.0\Outlook\Options\Mail\JunkMailImportLists = (REG_DWORD)1

----- OutlookReg (4) -----
HKCU\Software\Microsoft\Office\11.0\Outlook\Setup\FirstRun = (REG_BINARY)0x0000000000000000
HKCU\Software\Microsoft\Office\11.0\Outlook\Setup\First-Run = (REG_BINARY)0x0000000000000000
HKCU\Software\Microsoft\Office\11.0\Outlook\Setup\ImportPRF = (REG_SZ)[INSTALLLOCATION]custom11.prf
HKLM\Software\Microsoft\OfficeCustomizeWizard\11.0\RegKeyPaths\{90110409-6000-11D3-8CFE-0150048383C9}\OCWAd
dedOutlookContentWritten = (REG_DWORD)1

----- End Registry Entries -----

----- OTLK_CUST -----
CustomizeOutlook:       2
NewPrfName:
CustPrfName:
----- OTLK_EXCHANGE -----
OutExchangeConfigure:   0
----- Outlook files -----
dwAddedFiles:   1

file stream:    OutlookPrf
----- Extracted file (OutlookPrf) contents -----
```

Figure 2.23 *Viewing the contents of a .cmw file.*

The CMW File Viewer just prompts you for the location of the .cmw file. Figures 2.22 and 2.23 display examples of the extracted contents of an .mst file and a .cmw file as the viewers display them in Notepad.

2.4 Using Group Policy to configure Microsoft Outlook

Microsoft Group Policy is a powerful technology for centralized management of Outlook desktops. For administrators managing large deployments of Outlook, which may comprise hundreds or thousands of desktops, Group Policy is supported by effective tools to allow configuration of the Outlook desktops from a central location. Group Policy used in this way can significantly reduce the cost of configuration and ongoing management of the Outlook desktop. The basic concept behind Group Policy is that administrators configure policies once, then the policy is applied continuously to the users. These policies, such as setting up the basic Outlook Junk Mail configuration, cannot be changed by the user.

In later chapters, we will see examples of how Group Policy can be used to configure the basic Outlook user interface, Outlook security, junk mail settings, and other Outlook features.

Originally introduced in Windows 2000, Group Policy is dependant on Active Directory to distribute and apply defined policies to the correct groups of users. The Group Policy settings that you create to manage Outlook can be linked with selected Active Directory service system containers such as sites, domains, and organizational units (OUs). You can apply policy (settings) to specific users or computers in those Active Directory containers. Applying different policy to different containers or different security groups will allow you to customize Outlook in different ways for different user groups if you wish.

Group Policy can be used to perform a number of administrative tasks, such as configuring settings for registry-based policies, implementing common corporatewide security, centralizing software deployment, deploying scripts to the desktop, redirecting folders, and configuring many Microsoft software applications, such as Microsoft Office and Microsoft Internet Explorer. This section focuses particularly on the use of Group Policy for the configuration of Microsoft Outlook 2003. Here is what we will cover in this section:

- Getting started with Group Policy for Outlook

- Describing the Group Policy Management Console

- Using Group Policy Modeling (GP Modeling) and Group Policy Results (GP Results) to build and test better GPOs

- Using Office 2003 and Outlook 2003 Administrative Templates

- Building a custom administrative template .adm file

Note: Third-party tools are also available to use the power of the Group Policy technology to manage just about any Windows configuration setting. See Appendix D for information on these.

2.4.1　Getting started with Group Policy for Outlook

It is not our intention in this section to cover all of the basics of Microsoft Group Policy in detail. Microsoft and a number of third parties have already published a variety of resources including books, whitepapers, and simulations on Group Policy. For references to some of this material see Appendix D. Our goal in this section is to give a quick overview of the steps for getting Group Policy functioning, followed by a discussion of how some of the features of Group Policy can be used to configure Microsoft Outlook.

As mentioned earlier, Group Policy relies on Active Directory for implementation and enforcement of the policies defined by GPOs. As a result, it is not possible to use Group Policy in a non–Active Directory environment. Deployment of Windows 2000 Server or Windows Server 2003 with Active Directory is a prerequisite for using Group Policy. It is highly recommended that you familiarize yourself with Active Directory concepts before implementing Group Policy. In addition to the server prerequisites, desktops to which you want to apply Group Policy must be running the Windows 2000 operating system or Windows XP. These, of course, are the operating systems required for Outlook 2003 as well.

GPOs are objects that contain defined policy settings. Usually, an organization will have many GPOs, one for each cluster of policy settings related to a particular application feature. For example, in an Outlook environment, you may want to have one GPO to configure the basic look and feel of Outlook for your users, another to manage the Outlook security settings, another to manage junk mail settings, and so forth. Although it is possible to put all of these policies into one GPO, doing so is not recommended as this makes it harder to apply specific policy settings for certain groups of users. With only one GPO that contains all settings, your only choice would be to deploy all of the settings or none of the settings to a particular group of users or computers. Often you will want to apply certain policy settings to certain users and different policy settings to others. Also, having only one GPO for all policies can be difficult to manage and troubleshoot as you are trying to enforce so many settings at the same time. Thus, you should focus on creating GPOs that contain only the minimum settings needed.

Previously, GPOs could only be defined and managed using the Active Directory Users and Computers tool. With the release of Windows Server 2003, Microsoft released a new tool dedicated to defining and managing GPOs called the Group Policy Management Console (GPMC). Once Active Directory has been deployed in your environment, your next step is to install GPMC. GPMC will be covered in more detail in the next section.

Figure 2.24 shows the editor that is used to create GPOs, called the Group Policy Object Editor, which can be invoked from within GPMC. This editor is the same tool that's used with Active Directory Users and Computers if you don't have GPMC. GPO settings are divided into two broad categories, computer-configuration settings and user-configuration settings. A single GPO can contain both computer or user settings or only one or the other. Typically, though, you will probably have GPOs for managing computer settings and separate GPOs for managing user settings.

Settings will be applied based on what computer the user is working at, as well as the user's membership in a particular OU or more security groups. (Generally, you will want to manage GPOs with security groups, not assign them to individual users.) In some cases, the same setting will be available as both a computer-configuration setting and a user-configuration setting. In this case, the computer-configuration setting will take precedence over the user-configuration setting.

Note: A feature called loopback allows you to manage how policy settings are applied when a user logs on to a computer and the computer's policy settings need to take precedence over the user's policy settings. This is generally needed when several GPOs may conflict, some being applied to computer OUs and some being applied to user OUs. To manage this feature, navigate in the Group Policy Editor to Computer Configuration/Administrative Templates/System/Group Policy and enable the "User Group Policy loopback processing mode" policy. If you want only the computer's user policies to apply, as you probably would on classroom machines, choose the Replace mode. If you want the computer's user policies to override the corresponding user policies for the logged on user, choose the Merge mode.

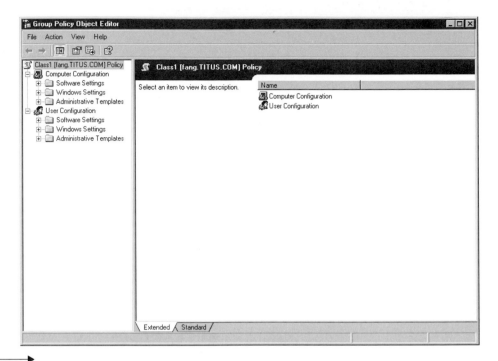

Figure 2.24   *Group Policy Object Editor with computer- and user-configuration settings.*

In order to define a specific policy, you will define the appropriate settings within a GPO. For instance let's create a GPO called Outlook Forms Policy. This policy will be used to disable your users' ability to define custom Outlook forms. You can accomplish this by enabling the "Disable command bar buttons and menu items" setting and selecting the Tools | Forms | Design option, as shown in Figure 2.25.

Note: The policy settings listed under Microsoft Office Outlook 2003 in Figure 2.23 come from an administrative template .adm file. You'll see how to add administrative templates to the editor later in Section 2.4.5.

Once you have finished defining all of the settings for your GPO, you simply close the GPO window. Since disabling menu items is a user-configuration setting, your next step is to apply the GPO to a domain or OU that contains the users you wish to have covered by this GPO. This is a simple matter of linking the GPO to the appropriate Active Directory container using GPMC. Figure 2.26 illustrates the linking of the Outlook policy GPO to the HQ OU.

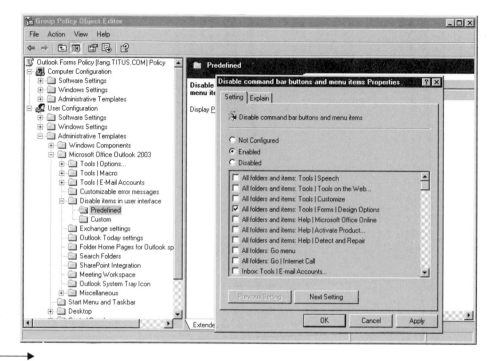

Figure 2.25   *Defining settings in the Group Policy Object Editor.*

If the group of users to which you want to apply the GPO is in a particular security group rather than an OU, you can use security-group filtering to apply the policy. In this situation, you link the GPO to the domain or OU that contains all of the users in the security group, then you apply a security-group filter.

To apply a security-group filter, perform the following steps:

1.   In GPMC, click on the GPO you want to filter.

2.   In the right-hand pane of GPMC, you will see the Security Filtering area.

3.   Click Add, and add the security group(s) to which you wish to apply the policy.

2.4.2   The Group Policy Management Console

As noted earlier, in conjunction with the release of Windows Server 2003, Microsoft released a new tool for managing GPOs. The new tool, GPMC, is free to any licensed user of Windows Server 2003 and can be obtained from the Microsoft download site.

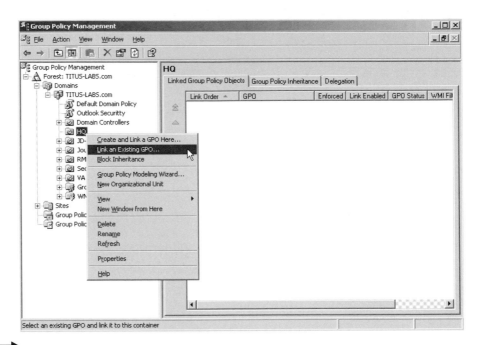

Figure 2.26   *Linking a GPO to an AD OU.*

GPMC can be used to manage either a Windows 2000 or a Windows Server 2003 network. The tool can be installed directly on Windows Server 2003, or it can be installed on Windows XP. If you wish to install it on Windows XP, you must have Windows XP SP1, and you must have the Microsoft .NET Framework 1.0 installed. If you are managing a Windows 2000 Server network, your domain controllers must be running Windows 2000 Server SP2 or greater.

Tip: If you are managing Group Policy settings for Windows XP SP2, you should install the hotfix described in Microsoft Knowledge Base article 842933, "'The Following Entry in the [strings] Section Is Too Long and Has Been Truncated' Error Message When You Try to Modify or to View GPOs in Windows Server 2003, Windows XP Professional, or Windows 2000."

For each domain, GPMC will manage GPOs by default using the domain controller that holds the Operations Master token for the primary domain-controller emulator. Make sure that all of the administrators working on common GPOs are pointed at the same domain controller. This will avoid replication conflicts caused by different administrators working on the same GPO at the same time on different domain controllers.

GPMC provides a single solution for managing all Group Policy–related tasks. GPMC lets administrators manage Group Policy for multiple domains and sites within one or more forests in a simplified user interface with drag-and-drop support. Besides creating and editing new GPOs, GPMC provides backup, restore, import, copy, and reporting of GPOs. These operations are also scriptable, which lets administrators customize and automate management of GPOs.

2.4.3   Using Group Policy Modeling and Group Policy Results to build better GPOs

GP Modeling and GP Results are two tools available within GPMC that help administrators build more effective policies. Because large enterprises can often have dozens of GPOs managing different aspects of their Active Directory network, it is sometimes difficult to determine the effect of multiple GPOs being applied to the same user or computer. GP Modeling and GP Results are tools that enable administrators to view the effect of multiple policies or settings on a single user or computer. The main difference between the two tools is that GP Modeling provides a simulation of applying GPOs to a user or computer, whereas GP Results shows the exact effective policy currently being applied to a user or computer.

Microsoft allows Group Policy settings to be applied in a very granular fashion to a specific set of users or computers using various procedures. For example, it is possible to block the application of certain domain policy settings to particular OUs or sites by using block inheritance (generally, all GPOs applied to a domain will be inherited by all OUs or sites in the domain). As previously mentioned, it is also possible to filter the application of Group Policy to particular users within an OU. This feature is called security filtering and is accomplished by using Active Directory security groups to filter which users will receive the GPO. The disadvantage of using such procedures is that it can be very hard for administrators to determine what set of GPOs is actually being applied to certain users. This is why GP Modeling and GP Results are so useful. They allow administrators to determine quickly what GPOs and settings are being applied to a specific user or computer. This makes it much easier for administrators to test GPOs before they are placed into a production environment.

The GP Modeling tool allows administrators to simulate the deployment of a Group Policy that would be applied to users and computers. GP Modeling requires a Windows Server 2003 domain controller because the simulation is done by a service that is only available with Windows Server 2003.

Before the availability of GPMC, similar functionality was available through the Resulting Set of Policy (RSoP) MMC snap-in. The Group Policy Modeling Wizard is a newer version of the RSoP MMC snap-in. The Group Policy Modeling Wizard has new functionality including HTML reporting of RSoP data; as a result, it is the recommended tool to use.

Using the GP Modeling tool is easy. It's a wizard that steps you through what you want to model. To start the wizard, right click on GP Modeling in GPMC and select the Group Policy Modeling Wizard. The most important step is specifying the user or computer that you want to model, as shown in Figure 2.27.

When you finish the wizard it creates a report, as shown in Figure 2.28. The report contains the following:

- *Summary:* This contains an HTML report of the summary information, including the list of GPOs being applied or denied to the specific user or computer, security group membership, and Windows Management Instrumentation (WMI) filters. WMI filters are GPO filters that can be applied based on the attributes of a target computer. Please see the Microsoft white papers listed in Appendix D for more information on WMI filters.

Figure 2.27
Group Policy Modeling Wizard user and computer selection.

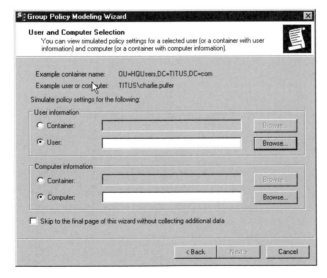

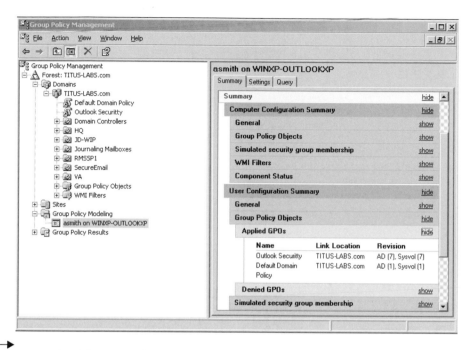

Figure 2.28   *Results of the GP Modeling tool.*

- *Settings:* This contains an HTML report of the simulated policy settings that would be applied in this simulation.

- *Query:* This lists the parameters used to generate the query.

Looking at the report, an administrator will quickly be able to see what GPOs are being applied or denied to a particular user or computer and, on the Settings tab (Figure 2.29), the summary of the resulting GPO settings being applied. Make sure the settings you want to have applied are really being applied!

The GP Results tool is similar to the GP Modeling tool, but GP Results is not a simulation. GP Results is the actual resultant set of policies obtained directly from the client. This involves getting results for an actual user on an actual computer. The user must have previously logged on to this computer in order to obtain the results. In addition, the client must be running Windows XP or Windows Server 2003. GP Results cannot be obtained from a Windows 2000 machine. If you want to test a Windows 2000 machine, you will need to use GP Modeling.

The GP Results tool is also a wizard that will step you through what is required. To start this wizard, right-click on GP Results in GPMC, and select the Group Policy Results Wizard. The wizard will prompt you for the

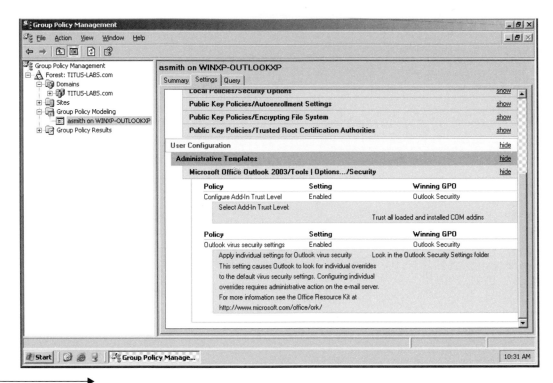

Figure 2.29   *GPO Settings applied to a specific user.*

computer for which the report will be generated, the particular user for which the report will be generated, and whether you want to show user results, computer results, or both.

Like the GP Modeling Wizard, when finished the GP Results Wizard creates a report. The GP Results report contains the same information in the Summary and Settings sections as is contained in the GP Modeling report. Only the Events section is different.

- *Summary:* This contains an HTML report that contains information on the user or computer, the Group Policies applied or denied, security-group memberships, and WMI filters.

- *Settings:* This contains an HTML report that shows user settings and/ or computer settings applied.

- *Events:* This tab shows all policy-related events from the target computer. These events are useful for troubleshooting Group Policy issues. For example, if the summary report indicates that a particular Group Policy component failed to process, look here for errors and warnings in the event log.

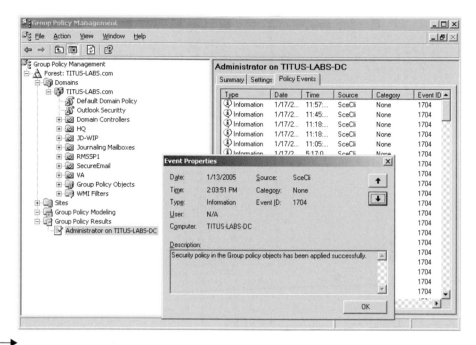

Figure 2.30   *Event properties as displayed by the GP Results tool.*

Figure 2.30 shows an example events log.

2.4.4   The Office 2003 and Outlook 2003 administrative templates

Administrative templates facilitate centralized configuration and control of registry settings used by applications. These administrative templates (.adm files) are basically text files that are stored on the computer used to configure Group Policy. These .adm files can be imported into the Group Policy Object Editor's Administrative Templates nodes, where they can be used to configure Group Policy.

An .adm file defines how registry-related Group Policy settings are displayed under the Administrative Templates nodes in the Group Policy user interface. In addition, the .adm file specifies the registry locations where changes should be made if an administrator makes a particular selection. These registry locations are not shown in the Group Policy user interface because an administrator generally doesn't need to know the specific registry details. In addition, .adm files contain all of the choices for a particular registry setting that can be enabled, disabled, or set to a specific value; specify any options or restrictions that are associated with the selection; and can specify a default value to use if a selection is activated.

Administrative templates can be used to configure certain operating system settings and to configure application settings. Microsoft makes templates available for most of the Microsoft Office applications. You can download the latest Office 2003 SP1 templates from the Microsoft download site. Look for the file called Office-2003-SP1-ADMs-OPAs-and-Explain-Text.exe. This contains administrative templates for basic Office 2003 settings, Outlook 2003, Word 2003, Excel 2003, PowerPoint 2003, Publisher 2003, Access 2003, Front Page 2003, and a few others. To manage Outlook 2003, you need to import the Office11.adm and Outlk11.adm files onto the computer you are using for GPMC. The Office11.adm template is needed because it contains some settings that relate to management of Outlook such as the Restricted Permissions settings that manage Rights Management Services permissions for Outlook users.

Follow this process to make the templates available:

1.   Save the Office11.adm and Outlk11.adm files to the \windows\ inf directory on the machine you will be using to create the Group Policy.

2.   In GPMC, create a new GPO.

3.   Edit the GPO.

4.   Under User Configuration, right click on Administrative Templates, and click Add/Remove Templates.

5.   In the Add/Remove Templates dialog, click Add, and select the Outlk11.adm and Office11.adm files you have previously saved.

6.   This should add the templates to the list of choices. Click Close.

7.   Under User Configuration, expand the administrative templates tree; you should see the Microsoft Office 2003 and the Microsoft Office Outlook 2003 folders.

Please note that if you want to apply the new SP1 .adm files for Office and Outlook 2003 SP1 (or the .adm files for subsequent service packs), you will first need to remove the Office and Outlook 2003 .adm files that were shipped with the original versions from the Administrative Templates section.

Figure 2.31 shows the Office and Outlook templates after they have been made available in the Group Policy Object Editor.

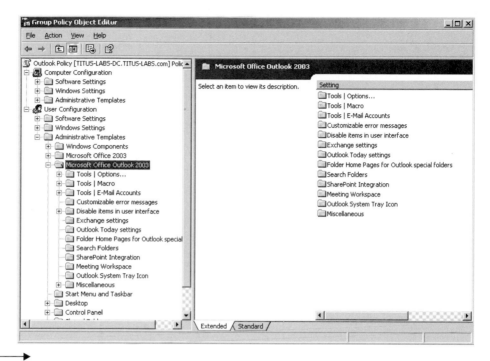

Figure 2.31 *Microsoft Office 2003 and Office Outlook 2003 administrative templates.*

The general groups of settings available to control and customize Outlook 2003 are in subnodes of the Microsoft Office Outlook 2003 administrative template as seen in Figure 2.31, which shows that a large number of settings can be used to manage the Outlook user interface, e-mail accounts, Exchange settings, mail format, security, and much else. For a complete listing of the Outlook settings available, see Appendix A.

2.4.5 How to create a new administrative template

In some cases, the Outlook 2003 administrative template may not contain a setting for a registry entry that Outlook supports. This may be because it is a fairly new feature, and Microsoft has not yet added that setting to the administrative template. Or, it may be a hotfix item that has not yet been slipstreamed into the main product. In these cases, it is possible for you to create a new administrative template that will complement the existing Outlook administrative template. Once the new administrative template you've created is added to the GPO, you can manage the settings via Group Policy.

Administrative templates are basically text files that follow a certain syntax. Let's look at Microsoft's Outlook 2003 template. Administrative templates can be viewed and edited using the Windows Notepad application. The Outlook 2003 template starts as follows:

```
CLASS USER

CATEGORY "Microsoft Office Outlook 2003"
CATEGORY "Tools | Options..."
CATEGORY "Preferences"
CATEGORY "E-mail options"
POLICY "Message handling"
```

The CLASS property describes whether the settings will appear under the computer-configuration settings (COMPUTER) of the Group Policy Object Editor or under the user-configuration settings (USER). In the case of Outlook, almost all of the settings are user-configuration settings. The CATEGORY is the name displayed in the Group Policy as a node in either the computer-configuration or the user-configuration settings. These nodes can be nested, as in the above example where "E-mail options" is nested under "Preferences," which is nested under "Tools | Options," as shown in Figure 2.32. The name of the policy setting is identified with the POLICY property.

Once the policy has been identified, you need to list the actual registry key that will be modified, then the possible values that can be placed into this registry setting. Again, let's look at the example in the Outlook 2003 template shown in Figure 2.32. This policy is used to define centrally what will happen after a user moves or deletes an open mail item.

```
KEYNAME "Software\Policies\Microsoft\Office\11.0\Outlook\
Preferences"
    PART "After moving or deleting an open item:"
DROPDOWNLIST
        VALUENAME AfterMove
    ITEMLIST
        NAME "Open the next item" VALUE NUMERIC 0
        NAME "Return to the Inbox" VALUE NUMERIC 1
        NAME "Open the previous item" VALUE NUMERIC 2 DEFAULT
```

The KEYNAME property identifies the exact registry key location that will be modified when this policy is modified. Because this Outlook policy is listed in the administrative template under CLASS USER, the user-configuration section, the registry keys modified will be in the HKEY_CURRENT_USER key.

The PART property identifies text that appears in the user interface when the policy is opened by an administrator in the Group Policy Editor, as in

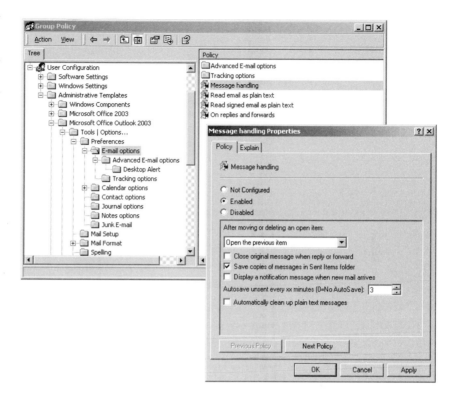

Figure 2.32
Viewing the policy-setting hierarchy that corresponds to the administrative template.

Figure 2.8, and what control will be used to display it, in this case, a drop-down list.

The VALUENAME property identifies the name of the string value, binary value, DWORD, or other registry value that will be modified under the registry key named in the KEYNAME property.

Since this example uses a drop-down list, this policy setting includes an ITEMLIST property that sets the choices available in the drop-down list— "Open the next item," "Return to the Inbox," or "Open the previous item." The choice will be represented in the registry as a numeric value of 0, 1, or 2.

Now let's look at an example of a registry entry not included in the Outlook 2003 administrative template that you may want to control via Group Policy. As mentioned earlier, we will create a new .adm file to manage this registry entry.

When you use Microsoft Office Outlook 2003 in Cached Exchange mode, Outlook 2003 verifies and resolves the names of e-mail recipients with the OAB stored on the user's machine. The process of matching names against actual addresses is called *automatic name resolution* (ANR); however, because the OAB may not contain the same information as the full online global address list (GAL), Outlook looks in fewer fields in the OAB to try to find a matching name. You may have users who need to resolve names against the GAL at all times. To support such scenarios, Microsoft provides a registry value, ANR Include Online GAL, that allows you to force Outlook 2003 always to use the online GAL to resolve ambiguous names or e-mail aliases.

Note: See Chapter 5 for a complete list of the fields used for name resolution against the OAB, compared with those used for name resolution against the GAL.

You can force the use of the GAL by creating the following registry value, which can be managed with GPOs:

```
Key: HKEY_CURRENT_USER\Software\Policies\Microsoft\
Office\11.0\Outlook\Cached Mode
Value name: ANR Include Online GAL
Value type: REG_DWORD
Value: 0 (default) or 1
```

If the value is set to 0, Outlook 2003 uses the OAB to resolve ambiguous names or e-mail aliases when you create an e-mail message.

If the value is set to 1, Outlook 2003 uses the global address book to resolve ambiguous names or e-mail aliases when you create an e-mail message, instead of using the OAB.

Let's add this registry setting to a new administrative template called Additional Outlook 2003 Settings, placing it under the user-configuration settings. Since you may want to add other policy settings later, we'll begin building a logical organizational structure for these extra Outlook settings by creating a node for Exchange settings and, under that, a node for settings specific to Cached Exchange mode.

In order to create the new .adm file, open Notepad, enter the text shown in Listing 2.3, and then save the file, giving it a file name with the .adm extension.

Note that each section—PART, POLICY, and CATEGORY—requires a matching END statement. Also, the KEYNAME and VALUENAME must be the exact registry key and value that Outlook supports and the available values (1 for VALUEON and 0 for VALUEOFF in this example) must be supported for that registry value. But the CATEGORY, POLICY, and PART text can be what-

Listing 2.3 *Administrative Template to Manage the ANR Include Online GAL Registry Value*

```
CLASS USER

CATEGORY "Additional Outlook 2003 Settings"
CATEGORY "Exchange Settings"
CATEGORY "Cached Exchange Mode"
POLICY "Address Book Used for Name Resolution"
KEYNAME "Software\Policies\Microsoft\Office\11.0\Outlook\Cached
Mode"
        PART "Use Global Address List for Name Resolution" CHECKBOX
            VALUENAME "ANR Include Online GAL"
            VALUEON NUMERIC 1
            VALUEOFF NUMERIC 0
        END PART
        END POLICY
END CATEGORY
END CATEGORY
END CATEGORY
```

ever you want them to be. Use terms that will make it easy for the administrator to understand the purpose of the policy settings.

Once you've saved the .adm file just created, add it to a new or existing GPO. As described earlier, in the Group Policy Editor, right-click the Administrative Templates node, choose Add/Remove Templates, click Add, and select the .adm file you just created. When you expand the nodes of the newly added administrative template, you should see the organizational structure shown in Figure 2.33, matching the three CATEGORY properties in Listing 2.3.

The text for the POLICY property appears in the Policy pane on the right side of the Group Policy Editor, while the text for the PART property appears in the Properties dialog for the policy setting.

This example uses CHECKBOX as the type for the PART property. If you examine the Outlk11.adm file or any other administrative template, you'll see several other part types to provide user interfaces appropriate for other types of registry entries. These include the following:

- DROPDOWNLIST

- NUMERIC (uses a spin control)

- EDITTEXT

- LISTBOX

You can manage any registry setting with an .adm file, not just those in the HKCU\Software\Policies key. However, any POLICY under CLASS

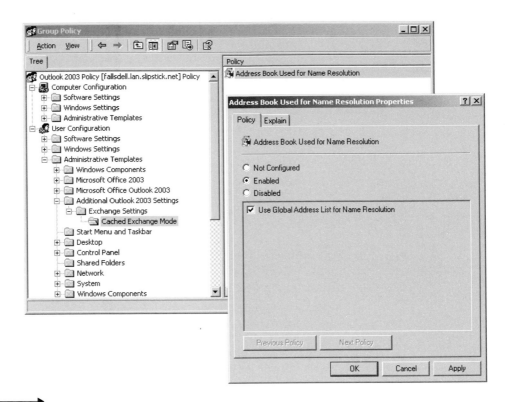

Figure 2.33   *New .adm template added to Administrative Templates.*

USER that does not refer to a registry value under the HKCU\Software\Policies key is a user-preference setting, not a policy setting, and the user will be able to override it. You can configure the Group Policy Editor to show only actual policy settings by right-clicking any node in the Administrative Templates hierarchy and choosing Show Polices Only from the context menu.

Also, if you configure user preferences with a GPO, you will need to set a computer-configuration policy to force these settings to be applied even if the GPO has not changed. In the Group Policy Editor, navigate to Computer Configuration/Administrative Templates/System/Group Policy and enable the "Security policy processing" policy setting. Within that setting, check the box for "Process even if the GPOs have not changed." This will ensure that the user preferences are reapplied periodically, overwriting any change the user may have made.

In the examples in this section, we've just scratched the surface to help you see how you can create your own administrative template file to help manage more Outlook settings with GPOs. Appendix D includes information on where to find the complete reference to the syntax for administrative template files in the Windows Platform SDK documentation.

2.5   Choosing the configuration method

In this chapter, you've learned about four different ways to configure Outlook settings, both those that exist in the Windows registry and certain settings stored as files. By now, you're probably wondering which method to use when. The answer to that question will depend mainly on these factors:

- Whether you want to enforce settings or set defaults that the user can override

- Whether you need to apply settings when you deploy Outlook or modify the settings some time after the initial deployment

- Just how much configuration you need to do

- Whether the user has access to the initial setup files (e.g., pro11.msi for an Office 2003 Professional installation)

Table 2.14 reviews common scenarios and suggests what procedure(s) to use.

Remember that you can apply a .cmw file only if the user has access to the setup files. If the user might not have access to the setup files, you can—with a little effort to develop a custom .ini file—generate an .ops file that

Table 2.14   *Procedures for Setting Outlook Options*

If you want to . . .	Then do this:
Customize an existing copy of Office or Outlook and then deploy those settings to users	Use the OPW to generate an .ops file and deploy it either as part of a custom installation transform .mst file or with the OPW/Save My Settings Wizard
Deploy settings files, such as signature files or a custom dictionary	Enter the file location in the CIW or CMW and deploy the resulting .mst or .cmw file
	-or-
	Use the OPW to generate an .ops file from a custom .ini file and deploy it with the OPW/Save My Settings Wizard
Enforce certain user registry settings	Create GPOs and select settings in the Group Policy Editor

Table 2.14   *Procedures for Setting Outlook Options (continued)*

If you want to . . .	Then do this:
Apply new registry values added by a hotfix	Use the CMW to generate a .cmw file that you deploy with MaintWiz.exe
	-or-
	Create a custom .adm file and add it to the Group Policy Editor
	-or-
	Add setting to the Windows registry, and create a custom .ini file to capture the setting in an .ops file that you deploy with the OPW/Save My Settings Wizard
Add or remove an Outlook feature after installation	Use the CMW to generate a .cmw file that you deploy with MaintWiz.exe

will allow you to deploy any registry setting using the OPW/Save My Settings Wizard.

In addition to these methods, of course, you may also have tools such as a login script utility, Microsoft Systems Management Server, and other aids to deployment that help you deploy policy settings, user-preference settings, and files associated with Outlook settings.

2.6   Summary

The tools in the ORK—particularly the OPW, CIW, CMW, and their associated viewers—provide a powerful toolbox for deploying and maintaining feature states, setting options in the Windows registry, and deploying Outlook settings files. To enforce settings in an Active Directory environment, you use GPOs to set options exposed by the administrative templates included in the ORK.

In the next chapter, you'll see how to use the CIW and CMW to create Outlook mail-profile settings that you can deploy either as part of .mst or .cmw files or as stand-alone .prf files.

3

Configuring Outlook Mail Profiles

Especially in large organizations, ensuring that each user's copy of Outlook connects to the correct mail account is a critical deployment issue. No administrator wants to touch every desktop to configure the mail account and the other settings that make up the Outlook mail profile. In Chapter 2, you saw how you can use the Custom Installation Wizard (CIW) to deploy settings along with a new installation of Outlook and use the Custom Maintenance Wizard (CMW) to deploy settings to existing installations. The CIW and CMW also allow you to build a text file with a .prf extension containing mail-profile settings either for separate processing by Outlook or for deployment as part of either the CIW's transform .mst file or the CMW's .cmw file.

In this chapter, you will learn how to build these .prf files and the basics of how they work. Topics include the following:

- How to create a .prf file with either the CIW or CMW

- The way Outlook processes .prf files

- The basic structure of a .prf file

- How to import an existing .prf into the CIW or CMW for deployment with an .mst or .cmw file

- How to use a .prf file to update an existing profile, as well as to create a new mail profile

The examples in this chapter deal with both Exchange and Internet mail accounts. We will get into the settings for Exchange accounts in more depth in Chapters 4 and 5.

3.1   Understanding mail profiles

As you learned in Chapter 1, a mail profile is a collection of configuration information for address books, item storage, and message delivery for a particular Outlook session. Mail profiles are specific to each Windows user and are stored in the Windows registry, in the HKEY_CURRENT_USER\Software\ Microsoft\Windows NT\CurrentVersion\Windows Messaging Subsystem\ Profiles key. Every active Outlook user has at least one mail profile. However, the profile does not have to contain any mail accounts. It can contain only a Personal Folders .pst file.

Some examples of the address books, item storage, and message delivery mechanisms that you can find in a mail profile include the following:

- Lightweight Directory Access Protocol (LDAP) address books that contain SMTP addresses with other directory information, available through Exchange or over the Internet.

- Personal Folders .pst files that contain Outlook items and are particularly important for holding mail accessed from IMAP or POP3 accounts.

- IMAP4, POP3, and SMTP settings for using standard Internet protocols to access mailboxes and send messages.

- Account settings for Microsoft Exchange, the corporate e-mail and collaboration server from Microsoft. Outlook 2003 provides the most feature-rich experience of Exchange 2000 and Exchange 2003.

- Configuration information for accounts on other corporate mail or collaboration servers, such as Oracle CorporateTime, Lotus Notes or Domino, Samsung Contact, or SAP.

Note: An Outlook profile is not the same as a Windows profile, which contains other user-specific application settings as well as the Outlook mail-profile settings. It is also not the same as the profile of Office settings built by the Office Profile Wizard for use with the CIW. An Outlook mail profile is limited to configuring messaging, address book, and information store components such as those described above.

Sometimes an Outlook profile is referred to as a MAPI profile since the underlying programming mechanism for creating and configuring Outlook profiles is Messaging Application Programming Interface (MAPI). Indeed, the use of MAPI profiles is not limited to Outlook but is available to other applications.

Some users will have more than one than mail profile. For example, since each profile cannot contain accounts from two Exchange organizations, a consultant might have one profile for the Exchange server in her company and a second profile to access an Exchange account provided by one of her clients to facilitate her work with that company. Or, a user working from home might keep his personal mail accounts in one profile and use a separate profile for his work mail account.

Tip: Even though you cannot have two Exchange accounts from different organizations, there are ways to bring at least the mail messages from an account at another company into a profile that already has an Exchange account. One is to use POP3 or IMAP4, assuming the Exchange administrator has enabled those protocols. Another is to connect to the mailbox as an HTTP mail account, using the URL for Outlook Web Access, the browser-based interface for Exchange. You'll see how in Section 3.4.4.

3.2 Understanding .prf files

Administrators are often puzzled to learn that they cannot use a simple Group Policy setting to add an account to an Outlook mail profile. (That said, Appendix D lists some third-party tools that can add mail-profile deployment features to Active Directory.) Instead, Microsoft uses .prf files—either explicitly or implicitly—for mail-profile creation and updating.

Versions of Outlook prior to Outlook 2002 required the use of a separate tool (Newprof.exe or Modprof.exe) to apply profile settings from a .prf file. Starting with Outlook 2002, users could create or modify an Outlook mail profile simply by running a .prf file, without the need for those extra tools (which, in fact, won't work at all with Outlook 2003). In addition to running .prf files directly, you can use the CIW or CMW from the Office Resource Kit to deploy a .prf file in such a way that Outlook imports it automatically. You'll learn about all those methods later in Section 3.3.2.

Note: It is also possible to develop custom applications that perform mail-profile configuration functions using the Extended MAPI programming interface. Documentation on Extended MAPI can be found in the Microsoft Platform Software Development Kit (SDK). We do not cover Extended MAPI programming in this book.

What aspects of a mail profile can you configure with .prf files? In theory, you can use .prf files to deploy or configure almost any component of an Outlook mail profile. In practice, it's not so simple because all of the possible settings are not documented. Any application that includes a MAPI information store, address book provider, or mail transport can add its own arbitrary settings to the mail profile. In essence, the MAPI community—both Microsoft and the developers of other MAPI components that work with Outlook—collectively owns the documentation for MAPI profiles. What Microsoft provides in the .prf file mechanism is a flexible, open framework for configuring any setting that a MAPI component might need, without the need to document that setting in advance.

Outlook's support for .prf files provides several advantages when it comes to deploying and updating mail profiles:

- The ability to process .prf files is built into Outlook. You don't need any extra software-deployment tool running on the client to give Outlook instructions for handling a .prf file. In other words, when an end user double-clicks on a file with the extension .prf, Outlook simply imports the settings with some limited user interaction.

- Since .prf files are plain text files, they can be edited by hand or, for more complex deployment scenarios, customized with scripts. For example, a large organization may need to deploy profiles to computers where Microsoft Outlook is already installed. The .prf files can be easily customized to allow for different user names, different Exchange servers, and a variety of settings.

- Customization of a .prf file can support properties that the CIW and the CMW do not allow you to set. In Chapter 4, you will see how to customize a .prf file to add settings, such as the location of the default archive .pst file, that are not supported by the CIW or CMW.

3.3   Using the resource kit tools to build .prf files

Even if you plan to customize a .prf file by hand, you should always start with a .prf file built with the CIW or the CMW. As you will see later in Section 3.4, the .prf file has a complex structure. Entries in different sections need to match, and some sections—the mapping sections that come last in a typical .prf file—are not usually edited at all. Let the CIW or CMW do the heavy lifting of creating a basic .prf file that you can then modify to suit particular needs.

Tip: You can build and export .prf files from the CIW or CMW even if you are not using either of those tools to deploy or maintain your Outlook of Office installations. If you are planning only to export a .prf file and not to build an .mst or .cmw file, it does not matter which of these two tools you use to build the .prf file.

Table 3.1 is a road map to the four screens in the CIW and CMW that control Outlook mail-profile settings.

As you saw in Chapter 2, both the CIW and CMW have two additional screens related to Outlook (21 and 22 and 16 and 17, respectively), but these do not have any impact on mail-profile .prf files.

As Table 3.1 shows, you can use a .prf file to remove a Lotus cc:Mail or Microsoft Mail account (CIW screen 20 or CMW screen 15). However, you cannot remove an existing POP3 or IMAP4 mail account, as you might want to do if your organization is migrating from those types of Internet accounts to Exchange. In that scenario, you may want to create a completely new profile and use the ExMerge tool to merge data from .pst files into the users' mailboxes. (Microsoft Knowledge Base article 174197, "XADM: Microsoft Exchange Merge Program (Exmerge.exe) information," provides a good introduction to this tool. Alternatively, if you want to leave the option of how to handle old .pst data up to the users, you could create a new profile with only the Exchange account and Outlook Address Book

Table 3.1   *Mail-Profile Screens in the CIW and CMW*

Screen	Screen Numbers		Description
	CIW	CMW	
Customize Default Profile	17	12	Choose whether to modify an existing mail profile, create a new profile, or apply an existing .prf file
Specify Exchange Settings	18	13	Configure an Exchange account, including Cached Exchange mode and other settings
Add Accounts	19	14	Add Internet mail accounts, Personal Folders .pst files, and address books
Remove Accounts and Export Settings	20	15	Remove Lotus cc:Mail and Microsoft Mail accounts and export profile settings to a .prf file

and instruct users how to import or copy their old Outlook data from a Personal Folders .pst file into the Exchange mailbox.

Warning: If you plan to use the CMW to deploy your updated .prf file, which is Microsoft's recommended way to deploy a new or modified profile, take care to start with a new .cmw file each time and to change no other settings besides those for the mail profile. Otherwise, you run the risk of accidentally modifying other Office components or settings. For example, an optional component such as Collaborative Data Objects could be unintentionally removed by the CIW even though it might be needed by other applications besides Outlook. A good practice is to use the CMW File Viewer discussed in the previous chapter to check the operations that the .cmw file will perform.

The next section will walk us through the creation of a mail profile that contains an Exchange account and an IMAP4 account, using the CMW. If you already have a .prf file and want to implement it, feel free to skip ahead to Section 3.3.2.

3.3.1 Example: Configuring a profile for Exchange and IMAP4

IMAP4 is an Internet mail standard that offers some advantages over the older POP3 standard, chief among them being that it stores all mail on the server until the user (or the user's mail application) deletes it. IMAP4 is offered by many Internet service providers and also is supported by many low-cost mail servers, even some that don't require a dedicated machine. These factors may make IMAP4 attractive to small organizations that don't need the additional collaboration features provided by Microsoft Exchange Server.

You can also use IMAP4 to connect to an Exchange server, assuming the server has that protocol enabled. This makes it possible, for example, for a consultant to connect to an in-house Exchange server and also to an Exchange account at a client's site, all in one profile.

Every Outlook mail profile needs the Outlook Address Book so that users can use their Outlook Contacts folders as address lists for name resolution and address lookup. Therefore, a mail profile to support both an Exchange account and an IMAP4 account needs three components:

- Exchange account (which will also act as the default information store)

- IMAP4 mail account

- Outlook Address Book

If you are building a profile in which an IMAP4 account is the only e-mail account, you will encounter IMAP4's chief disadvantage: you will need a separate Personal Folders .pst file to act as the default information store for the profile. This means that the user will have an Inbox in the Personal Folders folder hierarchy that contains no information and a separate Inbox in the IMAP4 account hierarchy that contains the incoming messages for that account. (For more information on the default information store, turn back to Chapter 1.) There are, however, third-party IMAP4 applications that integrate with Outlook, such as InsightConnector from http://www.bynari.net, that do allow the IMAP4 data store to be the default information store. But with the components that ship with Outlook, a mail profile to support an IMAP4 account by itself would need the following three components:

- IMAP4 mail account

- Personal Folders .pst file for the default information store

- Outlook Address Book

Let's walk through the steps involved in using the CMW to configure a profile for Exchange and IMAP4 and to deploy it either as a .prf file or as a .cmw file. (The steps to include a default profile as part of the initial Outlook deployment would be essentially the same, only you'd perform them in the CIW.)

1. Start the CMW and select the .msi file to open.

2. On screen 3, select "Create a new CMW file."

3. On screen 4, specify the name and path of the CMW file. Since we are going to use the CMW only to create an Exchange and IMAP profile, you might use Exchange-IMAP Profile.cmw as the file name.

4. Skip to screen 12, Outlook: Customize Default Profile. Select New Profile to create a new default profile, and give the profile a name. In this case, we've used Default Outlook Profile as the name (see Figure 3.1). (Note that the profile name and the .prf

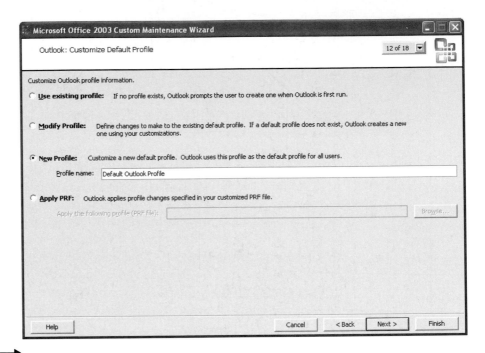

Figure 3.1   *Creating a new default profile with the CMW.*

file name are not related in any way. They can be different or the same.)

Note: We'll cover the Apply PRF option shown in Figure 3.1 later in Section 3.4.1.

5.   In screen 13 (Figure 3.2), select "Configure an Exchange Server connection" and provide the user name and Exchange server name. Use the %USERNAME% environment variable if everyone who will be using this profile has an Exchange mailbox associated with his or her Windows login. The = prefix will force Outlook to resolve the name using the exact Windows username. This is a big help in organizations with hundreds or thousands of users, some of whom may have similar aliases (billg and billga, for example). Otherwise, if Outlook cannot resolve the name, the user will see a dialog at startup asking which is the correct account. Figure 3.2 also shows the default settings that the CMW applies when you choose to use Cached Exchange mode, a new

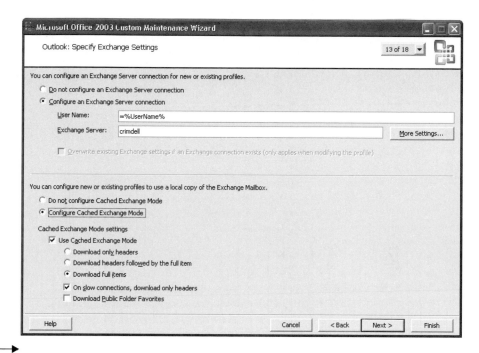

Figure 3.2   *Configuring an Exchange account.*

connectivity method in Outlook 2003 that you'll learn more about in Chapter 5.

Note: The environment variables %USERNAME% and %USERPRO-FILE% are the ones most commonly used in .prf files, although others should also work fine. (Be sure to test first.) As you will see in Chapter 4, it also is possible to use other environment variables by writing a script to pre-process the .prf file to substitute actual values for environment variables before Outlook processes it.

---

6. To set the location of the offline folders .ost file and Offline Address Book .oab files used by Cached Exchange mode, click the More Settings button shown in Figure 3.2. At the top of the dialog shown in Figure 3.3, you can change the location of the .ost file and .oab files.

7. Figure 3.3 also shows the default settings that Outlook uses when you select *Connect to Exchange Mailbox using HTTP* and enter the URL to the server. This connectivity method is called remote

Figure 3.3
*Configuring
additional
Exchange account
settings.*

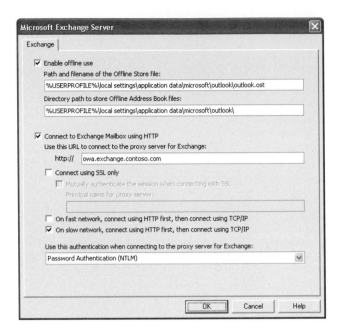

procedure call (RPC) over HTTP and provides a better way to connect to Exchange over the Internet compared with earlier versions of Outlook. You can use RPC over HTTP either with or without Cached Exchange mode, although in most cases you'll want to use them together. You'll learn more about RPC over HTTP in Chapter 5.

8.   On screen 14 (Figure 3.4), select "Customize additional Outlook profile and account information."

9.   To add an IMAP4 account, click Add, and in the Add Account dialog (Figure 3.5), select IMAP, and click Next.

10. In the IMAP Settings dialog (Figure 3.6), give the account a name, which the user will see in the Outlook folder list, and provide the information necessary to log onto the account. Note that you can use the environment variable %USERNAME% for both the user name and the user portion of the e-mail address. When it processes the .prf file, Outlook will replace that variable with the user's Windows login name. This might not be appropriate for all scenarios, of course. You might need to use a script like those shown in Chapter 4 to add the individual account information to each user's .prf file.

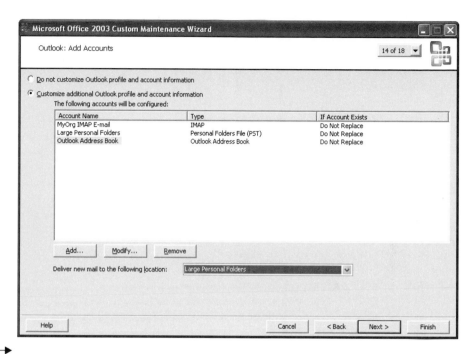

Figure 3.4 *Accounts added to a default profile.*

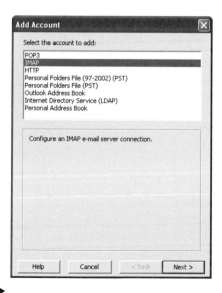

Figure 3.5 *Adding an Internet account, address book, or Personal Folders .pst file to a mail profile.*

Figure 3.6
Configuring an IMAP account.

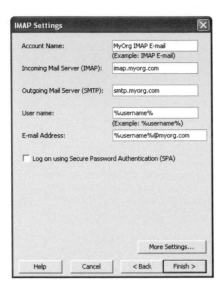

Figure 3.6 shows a More Settings button, which displays a dialog similar to what the user would see when configuring an IMAP account manually. Most of the settings are so user or machine specific that they cannot be set with a simple .prf file. However, on the Advanced tab (Figure 3.7), you can configure the server ports and timeouts and, if the IMAP server requires it, add a root folder path, such as ~/Mail.

Figure 3.7
Configuring advanced IMAP account settings.

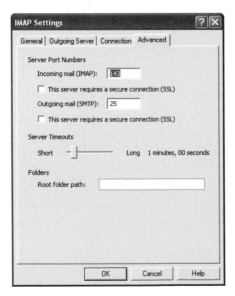

The IMAP account configuration dialogs do not provide any way to enter the user's IMAP account password. The first time the user starts Outlook with this profile, the password prompt dialog will appear, and the user will have the opportunity to specify that Outlook should remember the password.

Note: User-password information for POP3 and LDAP accounts also cannot be deployed with a .prf file. The user will need to specify the password the first time that Outlook starts with one of those accounts.

When you have completed configuring the IMAP account settings, click Finish on the IMAP Settings dialog (Figure 3.6) to return to CMW screen 14 (Figure 3.4).

11.   If you want to add a Personal Folders .pst file to this profile, click Add again to add another account. This time in the Add Account dialog, choose Personal Folders File (PST) to create a Unicode .pst file. (Chapter 1 has information on the two different types of .pst files that Outlook 2003 supports.) As you can see in Figure 3.8, the CMW suggests a file location built from the %USER-PROFILE% environment variable, which points to the user's Windows profile folders on the local system. You can either accept this location or choose a different one that the user will have access to on the local machine. (Remember that Microsoft does not support locating .pst files on network drives.) The store name—Large Personal Folders is the default name for a new Unicode .pst file—will be the display name for the root folder that the user sees for this store in the Outlook folder list.

If you have an Exchange account in the profile, you do not also need a .pst file in the profile. Technically, you do not even need to add a .pst file to a profile that has only an IMAP account. If the user starts Outlook, and there is no .pst file or other default information store already defined, Outlook automatically will create a Unicode Personal Folders .pst file in the same location as shown in Figure 3.8 and make it the default information store. Creating a .pst file as part of the mail profile gives you the opportunity, though, to specify a different location, to specify a particular store name, or to use a different encryption option besides the default (compressible). The encryption options are discussed in Chapter 6.

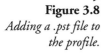

Figure 3.8

Adding a .pst file to the profile.

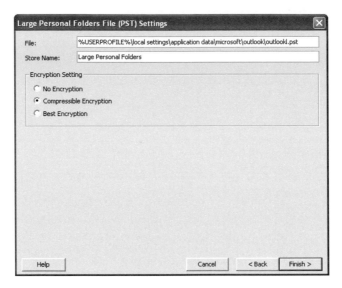

Note: A bug in the CIW and CMW adds the wrong EncryptionType setting to the .prf file, causing Outlook to disregard the preference for a Unicode .pst file and instead to create an Outlook 97 to 2002–compatible Personal Folders .pst file. Perhaps this bug will be fixed by the time you read this. If not, you can still get a Unicode .pst file through two different methods. As just described, you can simply omit adding a Personal Folders .pst file to the profile and let Outlook configure a .pst file if it needs one for the profile. Alternatively, you can edit the .prf file manually to change the EncryptionType setting value to 0x50000000, as shown in Listing 3.1 and Section 3.4.3.

We'll go ahead and add a .pst file to this profile, even though it isn't really needed, so that we'll have an opportunity to see how a .pst file is represented in the resulting .prf file. When you have completed the .pst file settings, click Finish on the Large Personal Folders File (PST) Settings dialog (Figure 3.8) to return to CMW screen 14 (Figure 3.4).

12.   Click Add once more; however, this time, in the Add Account dialog, choose Outlook Address Book. Click Next, then Finish. The Outlook Address Book has no settings that you can configure with a .prf file.

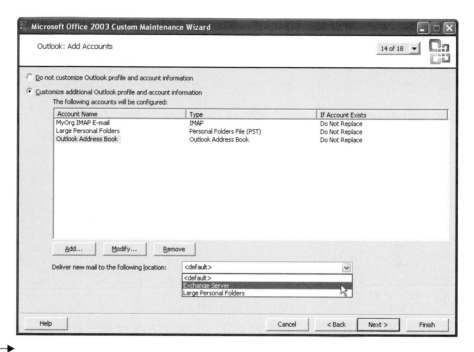

Figure 3.9   *Designating the default information store for a profile.*

13.   The last task on screen 14, setting the default information store, is optional in profile-building scenarios where you have only one information store. However, in this instance, we've added both an Exchange account and a Personal Folders .pst file, so we should indicate which is the default store. From Figure 3.4 "Deliver new mail to the following location" drop-down list, choose Exchange Server, as shown in Figure 3.9.

Note: Note that the name of the drop-down list on screen 14, "Deliver new mail to the following location," is somewhat misleading. It sets the mail delivery location only for Exchange and POP3 accounts but not for IMAP4 accounts. New mail arriving to an IMAP account will be delivered to that account's Inbox folder, not to the Inbox folder in the default store.

Since we are making only mail-profile changes with the CMW this time, you're almost done. Switch to screen 15 (Figure 3.10).

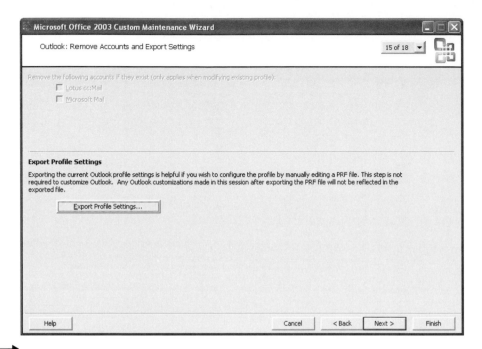

Figure 3.10   *Finishing a mail profile.*

Note: The options at the top of screen 15 to remove Lotus cc:Mail and Microsoft Mail are disabled in this example because we are creating a new default profile. If we were modifying an existing profile, those options would be available.

To export the mail-profile settings to a .prf file that you can modify or reuse later, click Export Profile Settings, choose a file location, and click Save.

To incorporate the .prf file into a .cmw file that you can deploy with the CMW, click Finish on screen 15.

Listing 3.1 shows the first five major sections of the .prf file created by following the steps above and modifying the EncryptionType for the Large Personal Folders service to the correct value for a Unicode .pst file, which is 0x50000000.

Note: The remaining sections not shown in Listing 3.1 are called mapping sections and are explained later in Section 3.4.5.

Later in Section 3.4, we'll review the different sections of the .prf file in some detail.

Listing 3.1   *A .prf File to Configure a New Default Profile with Exchange and IMAP Accounts*

```
;Automatically generated PRF file from the Microsoft Office
Customization and Installation Wizard

; ***************************************************************
; Section 1 - Profile Defaults
; ***************************************************************

[General]
Custom=1
ProfileName=Default Outlook Settings
DefaultProfile=Yes
OverwriteProfile=Yes
ModifyDefaultProfileIfPresent=FALSE
DefaultStore=Service1

; ***************************************************************
; Section 2 - Services in Profile
; ***************************************************************

[Service List]
ServiceX=Microsoft Outlook Client
ServiceEGS=Exchange Global Section
Service1=Microsoft Exchange Server
ServiceEGS=Exchange Global Section
Service2=Unicode Personal Folders
Service3=Outlook Address Book

; ***************************************************************
; Section 3 - List of Internet Accounts
; ***************************************************************

[Internet Account List]
Account1=IMAP_I_Mail
```

Listing 3.1   *A .prf File to Configure a New Default Profile with Exchange*
                    and IMAP Accounts (continued)

```
;***************************************************************
; Section 4 - Default Values for Each Service
;***************************************************************

[ServiceX]
CachedExchangeMode=0x00000002
CachedExchangeSlowDetect=TRUE

[ServiceEGS]
CachedExchangeConfigFlags=0x00000100
MailboxName==%UserName%
HomeServer=crimdell

[Service1]
OverwriteExistingService=No
UniqueService=Yes
MailboxName==%UserName%
HomeServer=crimdell
AccountName=Microsoft Exchange Server

[Service2]
UniqueService=No
Name=Large Personal Folders
PathToPersonalFolders=%USERPROFILE%\local settings\application
data\microsoft\outlook\outlookl.pst
EncryptionType=0x50000000

[Service3]

;[ServiceX]
;FormDirectoryPage=
;-- The URL of Exchange Web Services Form Directory page used to
create Web forms.
;WebServicesLocation=
;-- The URL of Exchange Web Services page used to display unknown
forms.
;ComposeWithWebServices=
;-- Set to TRUE to use Exchange Web Services to compose forms.
;PromptWhenUsingWebServices=
;-- Set to TRUE to use Exchange Web Services to display unknown
forms.
;OpenWithWebServices=
;-- Set to TRUE to prompt user before opening unknown forms when
using Exchange Web Services.
```

Listing 3.1 *A .prf File to Configure a New Default Profile with Exchange and IMAP Accounts (continued)*

```
;******************************************************************
; Section 5 - Values for Each Internet Account
;******************************************************************

[Account1]
UniqueService=No
AccountName=MyOrg IMAP E-mail
IMAPServer=mail.myorg.com
SMTPServer=smtp.myorg.com
IMAPUserName==%USERNAME%
EmailAddress=%USERNAME%@myorg.com
IMAPUseSPA=0
DisplayName=
ReplyEMailAddress=
SMTPUseAuth=1
SMTPAuthMethod=0
ConnectionType=0
RootFolder=
ConnectionOID=MyConnection
IMAPPort=143
IMAPUseSSL=0
ServerTimeOut=60
SMTPPort=25
SMTPUseSSL=0
```

3.3.2 Deploying a .prf file

The steps in the previous section created both a .prf file and a .cmw file. You can use either file to deploy the profile settings. As described in Chapter 2, to modify settings using a .cmw file and the CMW (Maintwiz.exe), the user must have access to the Office or Outlook setup files.

You can use any of the six methods shown in Table 3.2 to deploy the profile settings contained in the .prf or .cmw file. Note that it is not possible to import profile settings without running Outlook because Outlook itself is the application that processes the information in the .prf file. If, however, you want to process the profile settings silently, you can use any of the last three methods in the table. Both wait until the next time Outlook starts before processing the .prf file.

Table 3.2   *Methods for Deploying .prf File Settings*

Method	Description	Prompts User?	Applies .prf to All Users
Run the .prf file directly	Starts Outlook with the `/promptimportprf` switch, prompts the user, and if the user says yes, processes the .prf file	Yes	No
Start Outlook with the `/promptimportprf` switch and the path to the .prf file	Starts Outlook, prompts the user, and if the user says yes, processes the .prf file	Yes	No
Start Outlook with the `/importprf` switch and the path to the .prf file	Starts Outlook without prompting the user and processes the .prf file	No	No
Use the ImportPRF registry value	Creates or modifies the default profile the next time Outlook starts	No	No
Run a .cmw file with Maintwiz.exe	Creates or modifies the default profile the next time Outlook starts	No	Yes
Install Outlook or Office with the .mst file created by the CIW	Creates or modifies the default profile the next time Outlook starts	No	Yes

Note: One method that is not available, at least not without making a prior change to Outlook's file-attachment security settings, is sending users a .prf file via e-mail and asking them to run that file. Outlook blocks access to .prf file attachments by default. Chapters 6 and 7 explain how to manage the attachment-block settings with GPOs, user-preference registry entries, or a special folder on an Exchange Server.

A detailed description of each method listed in Table 3.2 follows.

■ *Method 1—Run the .prf file.* Place the .prf file in a network folder or distribute it to users' machines as part of their logon script, then run the .prf file. Files with the .prf extension are associated with Outlook. Running a .prf file launches Outlook with the `/promptimportprf` command-line switch, which prompts the user with the dialog shown in Figure 3.11.

If the user clicks Yes, Outlook will process the .prf file, then start. If the .prf file creates a new default profile and if Outlook was previously

Figure 3.11
User is prompted to import .prf settings.

set not to prompt the user to select a profile, Outlook will start with the new default profile. Otherwise, Outlook will operate as it normally does, either prompting the user or using the previous default profile.

- *Method 2—Start Outlook with the* /promptimportprf *switch.* A Windows shortcut or command to use this method would look as follows:

```
"C:\Program Files\Microsoft Office\OFFICE11\OUTLOOK.EXE"
/promptimportprf "C:\Program Files\Microsoft Office\IMAP
Profile.prf"
```

This method works exactly the same as method 1.

Tip: For best results with methods 1 through 4, place the .prf file on the user's local machine. If you place it in a network folder and the .prf file is not available, Outlook will not be able to apply the settings. Keeping a copy of the .prf file locally will also make it easy for a technician to help the user repair or replace the default mail profile.

- *Method 3—Start Outlook with the* /importprf switch. A Windows shortcut or command to use this method would look as follows:

```
"C:\Program Files\Microsoft Office\OFFICE11\OUTLOOK.EXE"
/importprf "C:\Program Files\Microsoft Office\IMAP
Profile.prf"
```

This method works exactly the same as method 1, only the user is not prompted.

- *Method 4—Use the ImportPRF registry value.* You can use this method to deploy mail-profile settings silently the next time Outlook starts. In other words, the user does not need to start Outlook just to process the .prf file. Follow these steps:

  1. Copy the .prf file to the client computer using a login script or other mechanism, or place it in a network folder that will be accessible to the user.

2.   In the registry key HKEY_CURRENT_USER\Software\ Microsoft\Office\11.0\Outlook\Setup\, delete the registry key values FirstRun and First-Run or set the value of each to 0.

3.   In the same key, HKEY_CURRENT_USER\Software\ Microsoft\Office\11.0\Outlook\Setup\, add a REG_SZ string value named ImportPRF.

4.   Set the value of ImportPRF to the path of the .prf file that you deployed in step 1.

You can use the Add/Remove Registry Entries screens in the CIW or CMW, or any other registry management tool you choose, to deploy these registry changes. The next time Outlook starts, it will process the .prf file—without prompting the user—then remove the ImportPRF value.

- *Method 5—Run the .cmw file.* This method is effectively the same as method 4, except that running the .cmw file actually handles the task of writing the .prf file to the local machine. As described in Chapter 2, to run the .cmw file, you use the CMW, Maintwiz.exe. If you have deployed the Maintwiz.exe file to the local Office folder on the user's machine and placed a file named Update.cmw File on a network drive, the command will look as follows:

```
"C:\Program Files\Microsoft Office\Office\Maintwiz.exe"
"\\my server\my share\update.cmw"
```

You can execute this command from a logon script. Using the information in the .cmw file, the CMW will write a .prf file with the name Custom##.prf, where ## represents some number, to the Microsoft Office folder on the user's local drive (usually C:\Program Files\Microsoft Office). The next time Outlook starts, because you have executed Maintwiz.exe, Outlook will invoke a special instruction to set the necessary registry values (ImportPRF, FirstRun, and First-Run) in the HKEY_CURRENT_USER\Software\Microsoft\ Office\11.0\Outlook\Setup\ key, then process the .prf file, as in method 4.

You only need to run Maintwiz.exe's Update.cmw once per machine. Outlook will process the .prf file for each user who logs in to that machine.

Tip: After Outlook processes the .prf file, it will remove the ImportPRF value from the HKEY_CURRENT_USER\Software\Microsoft\Office\ 11.0\Outlook\Setup\ key. However, when you deploy a .prf file using method 5, the Custom##.prf file remains in place in the C:\Program Files\ Microsoft Office folder after Outlook starts and processes the .prf. This means that you can use that .prf file later if you need to reapply the same settings for any user on that machine.

- *Method 6—Deploy the .mst file.* If you used the CIW to create or import .prf file settings, those settings will be deployed when you install Outlook or Office with the resulting .mst file. As with method 5, the ImportPRF key will be created and the .prf file written to the user's local drive to be processed the next time Outlook starts. This process will take place for each user who logs in.

3.3.3   Practical considerations

Now that you know how to deploy new and modified profiles, you might be interested in some practical considerations that commonly arise when working the Outlook mail profiles. Let's start with controlling the default profile.

As you've seen, a .prf file can create a new default profile or modify the existing default profile. Two registry entries hold the name of the default profile and control whether the user sees a prompt to select a profile when Outlook starts:

```
Key: HKEY_CURRENT_USER\Software\Microsoft\Windows NT\
CurrentVersion\Windows Messaging Subsystem\Profiles
```
Value name: `DefaultProfile`
Value type: `REG_SZ`
Value: Name of the default profile

```
Key: HKEY_CURRENT_USER\Software\Microsoft\Exchange\
Client\Options
```
Value name: `PickLogonProfile`
Value type: `REG_DWORD`
Value: `0` to log on with the default profile, `1` to present the Choose Profile dialog

If you are deploying a new default profile, for example, you might want to make it a little more difficult for the user to revert to his or her old profile. To do this, you can set PickLogonProfile to 0, thereby preventing the user from seeing the Choose Profile dialog.

When you are migrating from Internet mail accounts to Microsoft Exchange as the mail server, you must decide whether to try to modify the user's old default profile or create a new default profile. In most cases, you will probably want to create a new default profile that holds the Exchange account so that the user immediately stops using the Internet mail account. If you have used consistent naming for the default .pst file in the old profile, then you can add that .pst file to the new profile so that users can easily access their old information. Otherwise, you may want to provide instructions to users on how to use the File | Import and Export command or the File | Open | Outlook Data File command to access their old Outlook data. Use Import and Export if you want to import the data from the .pst file into the Exchange mailbox. Use Open | Outlook Data File if you want to access the data in its original .pst file rather than import to the mailbox.

Note: Chapter 4 includes a script to look for Personal Folders .pst files in the default location and add them to the .prf file to create a new Exchange profile.

As noted in the walk-through for creating profile settings with the CMW, you should always include the Outlook Address Book in a profile. Otherwise, users will not see any of their contacts folders when they display the address book to select recipients. In Section 3.4.2, you'll see how to use a .prf file to modify a profile to add the Outlook Address Book if it is not already present. While it is not possible to change the address display order from First Last to Last, First with a .prf file, it can be done with a script, as you'll see in Chapter 9.

3.4   **The structure of a .prf file**

Now that you have seen a simple example of a .prf file, it is time to begin looking at the overall structure. Knowing the structure of a .prf file allows you to determine, for example, whether an existing profile is to be overwritten or how to include multiple messaging services—address books, PST files, and so on—in a single profile.

Like the .ini files that you may have used as configuration files for various programs in the past, a .prf file is a plain-text file consisting of several sections. Upper-level sections generally depend on lower-level sections. In general, the closer to the top of the .prf file a section appears, the more likely it is that you will need to understand it and modify it. You are unlikely to need to modify sections near the end.

A .prf file generally consists of seven sections. Some sections include subsections with the details for different accounts and services. You saw these first five sections in Listing 3.1 in order of appearance from top to bottom in the .prf file:

In section 1, the [General] subsection determines how the profile is deployed in relationship to other profiles. This subsection always has the name General.

Note: The section numbers—sections 1 through 5 in Listing 3.1 and sections 6 and 7, which you'll see later when we discuss mapping sections—are arbitrary and do not affect the operation of the .prf file. The semicolon (;) character at the beginning of each line in those section headings means that those lines are actually comments in the .prf file. The section numbers do, however, provide a convenient organizational framework for the .prf file, so we will continue to refer to them throughout this chapter.

In section 2, the [Service List] subsection lists messaging services in the profile, including address books and message-storage services such as Exchange. This subsection always has the name Service List.

In section 3, the [Internet Account List] section lists Internet mail accounts to retrieve and send e-mail, specifically IMAP, POP3, and HTTP accounts. This section always has the name Internet Account List.

Section 4 consists of a service-account section for each messaging service that is included in the profile and listed in the [Service List] section. For example, in Listing 3.1, the [Service List] section includes this line:

```
Service1=Microsoft Exchange Server
```

In section 4, you see a corresponding service-account subsection named [Service1].

Similarly, section 5 consists of an Internet account subsection for each account that is included in the [Internet Account List] section. In Listing 3.1, the [Internet Account List] includes this line:

```
Account1=IMAP_I_Mail
```

In section 5, you see a corresponding subsection named [Account1], which contains the settings for the IMAP account.

If the .prf file has additional messaging services or accounts, you will see additional services and accounts listed under [Service List] and [Internet Account List] and corresponding service and account subsections named [Service2], [Service3], and so on, or [Account2], [Account3], and so on. When you build a .prf file with the CIW or CMW, the tool takes care of assigning the service and account names. If, however, you need to modify a .prf file, you need to be aware that the actual name of the service or account itself does not matter. What is critical is that the name for each service or account subsection must exactly match the name under the [Service List] or [Internet Account List] section that refers to that messaging service. In other words, if the statement in the [Internet Account List] section were

```
FirstIMAPAccount=IMAP_I_Mail
```

then the corresponding subsection in section 5 would be named [FirstIMAP-Account].

3.4.1   Deploying a hand-modified .prf file

In the next few sections, and in Chapter 4, you will see many ways to customize a basic .prf file created with the CIW or CMW by editing it in Notepad or any other text editor. You can deploy such a .prf file using any of the first three methods in Table 3.2, the ones that run a stand-alone .prf file.

You can also import your edited .prf file into the CIW or CMW so that it can be distributed with the .mst file created by the CIW or the .cmw file created by the CMW. Refer back to Figure 3.1 and notice the Apply PRF option at the bottom of screen 12 in the CMW (screen 17 in the CIW). After you select Apply PRF, you can browse and select any existing .prf file and import its settings into the CIW or CMW.

Note: If you import your .prf file, screens 13 to 15 in the CMW and 18 to 20 in the CIW will be disabled. In other words, if you choose to apply an existing .prf file, you cannot use the CMW or CIW to modify the .prf settings imported from that file.

3.4.2 The [General] section

Take a second look at Listing 3.1. The first section that appears in any CIW-generated .prf file, the [General] section, provides the following options for processing a profile:

- Which profile is overwritten or modified, using the ProfileName keyword and the ModifyDefaultProfileIfPresent keyword

- Whether a profile is overwritten or modified, using the OverwriteProfile keyword

- Whether the resulting profile is the default profile for the Outlook user, using the DefaultProfile keyword.

Table 3.3 summarizes the options for the [General] section. For example, to specify that the default profile is always overwritten, regardless of the name of the default profile, set OverwriteProfile to Yes and ModifyDefaultProfileIfPresent to TRUE, as follows:

```
[General]
Custom=1
ProfileName=Default Outlook Profile
DefaultProfile=Yes
OverwriteProfile=Yes
ModifyDefaultProfileIfPresent=TRUE
DefaultStore=Service1
```

Note: The bold type that appears in the above example will not appear in a .prf file itself, which is simply a text file. We will use bold, however, to call your attention to important aspects of .prf files.

The value for the ProfileName can be just about any name that you choose. You cannot, however, use an environment variable, such as

Table 3.3 *Summary of Keywords for the General Section*

Keyword for General Section	Settings and Their Effects
ProfileName	Set to the name of the profile.
ModifyDefaultProfileIfPresent	Set to TRUE to ignore ProfileName and modify the user's default profile if one exists. If one does not exist, the default profile is created.
DefaultProfile	Set to Yes or omit to make the profile created the default profile. If the profile is already the default, setting this keyword to No will make the profile no longer the default.
BackupProfile	Set to Yes to back up the profile being replaced.
OverwriteProfile	Set to Yes to overwrite the profile determined by ProfileName or ModifyDefaultIfPresent. Otherwise, set to Append to modify the selected profile if it exists, or set to No to avoid overwriting an existing profile.
DefaultStore	Set to a section referenced in the [Service List] section to specify where messages are delivered, as in `DefaultStore=Service1`, where Service1 contains the settings for a Personal Folders .pst file.
Custom	Set this to 1 to indicate the .prf file is customized.

%USERNAME%, to customize the profile name to be the name of an individual user. This may seem odd, but it makes sense when you consider that there is no need for a customized profile name when you're tailoring the profile to the logged-in Windows user. You would only need custom profile names when you were supporting multiple Outlook users under the same Windows login. In that case, the %USERNAME% environment variable would not be unique to the Outlook user anyway and, therefore, would not be appropriate to use for the profile name.

Tip: Using a consistent profile name through the organization actually can help with support and troubleshooting. When a user has a problem, a support technician can suggest that the user start Outlook with the default Outlook profile or whatever the universal name of the main profile is in your organization. External programs and scripts that need to start Outlook can also specify the name of this profile as part of their logon statement.

When creating a new profile, Outlook will, by default, make a backup of the existing profile if a profile is being overwritten. For example, if the profile being created is named MyProfile, then this profile will be backed up to a profile named BACKUP of MyProfile, BACKUP2 of MyProfile,

Figure 3.12
Backup profiles from previous .prf imports.

and so on. If you do not want the user to be able to revert to earlier profiles and have PickLogonProfile set to 1, as described earlier in Section 3.3.3, you may want to disable this backup feature by including a `Back-upProfile=No` statement in the [General] section. Otherwise, the user may be confronted with a long list of profile backups such as that shown in Figure 3.12.

The following example adds the `BackupProfile=No` statement to create an entirely new default profile named Default Outlook Profile without backing up the existing default profile:

```
[General]
Custom=1
ProfileName=Default Outlook Profile
DefaultProfile=Yes
OverwriteProfile=Yes
ModifyDefaultProfileIfPresent=FALSE
BackupProfile=No
```

Running a .prf file with these settings will overwrite the default Outlook profile without making a backup. If the user is using some other profile as the default, Outlook also will make Default Outlook Profile the new default profile.

Table 3.4 summarizes the useful combinations of DefaultProfile, OverwriteProfile, and ModifyDefaultProfileIfPresent settings for common profile-deployment scenarios. Where n/a is listed for a particular setting, it means that the value of that setting does not affect the scenario.

Warning: Using `DefaultProfile=No` together with `OverwriteProfile=Yes` produces unexpected and undesirable results. If ProfileName is set to the profile that is the current default, that profile will no longer be the default after the .prf file is processed. Instead, the default will be the profile that comes first in the alphabet. What happens is that `DefaultProfile=No` causes Outlook to remove the default status from the named profile. Since Outlook doesn't know which profile to use as the new default, it just picks the one at the top of the alphabetical list.

Something similar happens if ModifyDefaultProfileIfPresent is set to TRUE: the current default profile is overwritten and is no longer the default. The new default profile is the one first in alphabetical order.

Because of this side effect, you should use `DefaultProfile=No` and `OverwriteProfile=Yes` together only in one scenario—when Profile-Name is set to a profile that you know for certain is not the current default profile and when ModifyDefaultProfileIfPresent is set to FALSE.

If you use the CIW or CMW to make your profile changes, you'll never run into this problem since those tools always create a .prf file with appropriate settings for DefaultProfile and OverwriteProfile.

Table 3.4   *Common Profile Deployment Scenarios*

Scenario	ProfileName	DefaultProfile	OverwriteProfile	ModifyDefault-ProfileIfPresent
Create a new named profile if one doesn't already exist, but don't make it the default	Is present	No	No	FALSE
Create a new named profile if one doesn't already exist, and make it the default	Is present	Yes	No	FALSE
Overwrite the settings for a particular named profile that is not currently the default	Is present	No (see warning above)	Yes	FALSE (see warning above)
Overwrite the settings for a particular named profile, and make it the default	Is present	Yes	Yes	FALSE
Overwrite the settings for the default profile	n/a	Yes	Yes	TRUE
Add or modify services for a particular named profile that is not the default profile	Is present	No	Append	FALSE
Add or modify services for a named profile, and make it the default profile	Is present	Yes	Append	FALSE
Add or modify services for the default profile	n/a	Yes	Append	TRUE

You may have noticed that Table 3.4 does not contain any scenario to overwrite an existing profile and preserve its default status (i.e., whether or not it is the default profile). Outlook 2003 cannot handle that scenario, at least not with a .prf file alone.

Let's look next at an example of where you might use the setting `Overwrite Profile=Append`. As noted earlier in Section 3.3.3, occasionally you may encounter a mail profile that does not contain the Outlook Address Book service and, therefore, does not properly expose the user's Contacts folders as address lists. You can correct that situation by invoking a .prf file with `OverwriteProfile=Append`. Listing 3.2 shows the first four sections of a .prf file intended to update a profile named Default Outlook Profile to add the Outlook Address Book and make that profile the default.

Listing 3.2   *Sample .prf File to Add the Outlook Address Book*

```
; ****************************************************************
; Section 1 - Profile Defaults
; ****************************************************************

[General]
Custom=1
ProfileName=Default Outlook Profile
DefaultProfile=Yes
OverwriteProfile=Append
ModifyDefaultProfileIfPresent=FALSE


; ****************************************************************
; Section 2 - Services in Profile
; ****************************************************************

[Service List]
;ServiceX=Microsoft Outlook Client
Service1=Outlook Address Book


; ****************************************************************
; Section 3 - List of Internet Accounts
; ****************************************************************

[Internet Account List]

; ****************************************************************
; Section 4 - Default Values for Each Service.
; ****************************************************************

[Service1]
```

If, instead, you wanted to make sure the default profile—regardless of its name—contains the Outlook Address Book service, you would use these settings in the [General] section:

```
[General]
Custom=1
DefaultProfile=Yes
OverwriteProfile=Append
ModifyDefaultProfileIfPresent=TRUE
```

If you are modifying a profile that contains the Microsoft Exchange service, setting OverwriteProfile to Append will not result in adding additional Exchange mailboxes to the profile. (In fact, it is not possible to add a secondary mailbox with a .prf file.) For other messaging services that can appear in a profile multiple times, such as POP, IMAP, or LDAP, setting OverwriteProfile to Append will result in the addition of a new account or messaging service.

3.4.3   The [Service List] sections

Section 2, the [Service List] section, lists messaging services, such as address books or message-storage services that are included in a profile. For each service in the [Service List], a corresponding subsection exists in section 4. For example, Listing 3.3 is a partial listing of a .prf file that configures the same Exchange and IMAP services as Listing 3.1, but adds a personal address book.

To create Listing 3.3, two changes have been made to Listing 3.1. The first change is the addition of a line to the [Service List] section:

```
Service4=Personal Address Book
```

The second change is the addition of a new subsection in section 4 named [Service4] that corresponds to Service4 in the new line above. Note also that the right-hand side of the line above corresponds to a [Personal Address Book] mapping section that appears later in the .prf file but is not shown in Listing 3.3 above. (You'll see it shortly in Section 3.4.5.) The new section, shown below, contains settings for an instance of the Personal Address Book (PAB) messaging service:

```
[Service4]
NameOfPAB="Personal Address Book"
Path="%USERPROFILE%\local settings\application data\
microsoft\outlook\mailbox.pab"
ShowNamesBy=1
```

Listing 3.3   *A .prf File with an Added Personal Address Book*

```
;Automatically generated PRF file from the Microsoft Office Customization and
Installation Wizard


; ***************************************************************
; Section 1 - Profile Defaults
; ***************************************************************

[General]
Custom=1
ProfileName=Default Outlook Settings
DefaultProfile=Yes
OverwriteProfile=Yes
ModifyDefaultProfileIfPresent=FALSE
DefaultStore=Service1


; ***************************************************************
; Section 2 - Services in Profile
; ***************************************************************

[Service List]
ServiceX=Microsoft Outlook Client
ServiceEGS=Exchange Global Section
Service1=Microsoft Exchange Server
ServiceEGS=Exchange Global Section
Service2=Unicode Personal Folders
Service3=Outlook Address Book
Service4=Personal Address Book


;****************************************************************
; Section 3 - List of Internet Accounts
;****************************************************************

[Internet Account List]
Account1=IMAP_I_Mail

;****************************************************************
; Section 4 - Default Values for Each Service
;****************************************************************

[ServiceX]
CachedExchangeMode=0x00000002
CachedExchangeSlowDetect=TRUE

[ServiceEGS]
CachedExchangeConfigFlags=0x00000100
MailboxName==%UserName%
HomeServer=crimdell
```

Listing 3.3   *A .prf File with an Added Personal Address Book (continued)*

```
[Service1]
OverwriteExistingService=No
UniqueService=Yes
MailboxName==%UserName%
HomeServer=crimdell
AccountName=Microsoft Exchange Server

[Service2]
UniqueService=No
Name=Large Personal Folders
PathToPersonalFolders=%USERPROFILE%\local settings\application data\microsoft\
outlook\outlookl.pst
EncryptionType=0x50000000

[Service3]

[Service4]
NameOfPAB="Personal Address Book"
Path="%USERPROFILE%\local settings\application data\microsoft\outlook\mailbox.pab"
ShowNamesBy=1


;****************************************************************
; Section 5 - Values for each Internet Account
;****************************************************************

[Account1]
UniqueService=No
AccountName=MyOrg IMAP E-mail
IMAPServer=mail.myorg.com
SMTPServer=smtp.myorg.com
IMAPUserName==%USERNAME%
EmailAddress=%USERNAME%@myorg.com
IMAPUseSPA=0
DisplayName=
ReplyEMailAddress=
SMTPUseAuth=1
SMTPAuthMethod=0
ConnectionType=0
RootFolder=
ConnectionOID=MyConnection
IMAPPort=143
IMAPUseSSL=0
ServerTimeOut=60
SMTPPort=25
SMTPUseSSL=0
```

Note: Outlook 2003 supports the PAB service mainly for backward compatibility with data from earlier versions. New installations of Outlook 2003 generally will not use it. It does, however, provide a good, quick example of how to install an address book service using a .prf file.

You might also want to take note that screen 21 in the CIW and screen 16 in the CMW offer the option to import any .pab file that exists in the user's current mail profile

As noted earlier during the walk-through for creating a profile for an IMAP account, a bug in the CIW and CMW outputs the wrong EncryptionType setting to the .prf file for a Unicode Personal Folders .pst file. By changing one line in the appropriate [Service List] subsection, you can fix that problem before you distribute the .prf file. Follow these steps:

1.   Look in the [Service List] section to locate the name of the service for the Personal Folders .pst file. In Listing 3.3, that will be

      ```
      Service2=Unicode Personal Folders
      ```

2.   Next, look for the corresponding section named [Service2]. In that section replace the statement

      ```
      EncryptionType=0x40000000
      ```

      with the correct setting for EncryptionType:

      ```
      EncryptionType=0x50000000
      ```

3.   Save the .prf file, and deploy it using any of the methods that you saw in Section 3.3.2.

One other thing to notice in all of the .prf listings that you have seen so far is that the service section for the Outlook Address Book has no settings. All of the listings have a line similar to this one under the [Service List] section:

```
Service3=Outlook Address Book
```

However, the corresponding [Service3] section has no settings listed under it because the Outlook Address Book has no settings that can be configured with a .prf file.

Another oddity appears in the [Service List] section. The following statement appears twice:

```
ServiceEGS=Exchange Global Section
```

That is not an error, and you should not remove the second instance of that statement. In some scenarios, [Exchange Global Section] needs to be processed before the [Microsoft Exchange Server] section, while in other scenarios, the processing order needs to be reversed. The solution, therefore, is to include the Exchange Global Section statement both before and after the Microsoft Exchange Server statement.

In a corporate environment where users connect to an IMAP4 mail server and don't have access to an Exchange server, they might use an LDAP address book as the shared corporate address book. The settings in Listing 3.4 add support to a .prf file for using an Active Directory domain controller as an LDAP server.

To adapt this section to your particular LDAP server, you would need to change the ServerName setting and possibly also the UserName setting, which is necessary if your LDAP server requires authentication. The Server-Name setting should be an LDAP server and can be an Active Directory domain controller. For larger directories, you may want to experiment with the value for MaxEntriesReturned. If you make it larger, Outlook may appear to hang while it waits for those entries to return from the LDAP server, especially if the server or network is slow. However, a greater number of returned entries may make users' LDAP searches more useful.

Listing 3.4   *Adding Support for an LDAP Server to a .prf File*

```
[Service List]
;ServiceX=Microsoft Outlook Client
Service1=Unicode Personal Folders
Service2=Outlook Address Book
Service3= LDAP Directory

[Service3]
UniqueService=No
ServerName=LDAPServer
DisplayName=Corporate Active Directory ; should be a name of your
choice
ConnectionPort=389
UseSSL=FALSE
UseSPA=FALSE
DisableVLV=0
UserName=%UserName%
SearchBase=
SearchTimeout=60
MaxEntriesReturned=100
```

Tip: You don't need to edit a .prf file manually to add an LDAP service. The Outlook: Add Accounts screen (screen 19 in the CIW, screen 14 in the CMW) allows you to add an LDAP service and configure all of the settings shown in Listing 3.4

3.4.4   The [Internet Account List] sections

The [Internet Account List] section obeys the same rules as the [Service List] section, except that only IMAP, POP, and HTTP mail accounts are added to this section. Each account listed under [Internet Account List] has its corresponding subsection with specific settings.

For example, Listing 3.5 is similar to Listing 3.1, except that an HTTP account has been added. Microsoft officially supports HTTP connections only to Hotmail and Microsoft Network accounts. However, it is also possible to access an Exchange 2000 or 2003 mailbox as an HTTP account, using the same URL that the user would enter in a browser to connect with Outlook Web Access.

Note: Accessing an Exchange mailbox as an HTTP account using the URL for Outlook Web Access is not the same as the new RPC over HTTP connectivity for Exchange 2003, which we will cover in Chapter 5. In fact, it's not even officially supported by Microsoft. However, using the HTTP method can be very handy if you already have an Exchange mailbox in your Outlook profile or if you're working with a client who allows only OWA access from outside its organization. As with an IMAP connection to an Exchange mailbox, special folders such as Calendar, Contacts, Journal, and Tasks will not have the special Outlook item types in them, but you will be able to send, receive, and view messages and meeting requests without any problem.

The two changes needed to add the HTTP account are shown in bold in Listing 3.5. They are very similar to the changes demonstrated previously for the [Service List] section to add a PAB or LDAP account.

The first change is that a line has been added to the [Internet Account List] section:

```
Account2=INET_HTTP
```

Listing 3.5   *A .prf File for Configuring Two Internet Mail Accounts*

```
; ********************************************************************
; Section 1 - Profile Defaults
; ********************************************************************

[General]
Custom=1
ProfileName=My OWA
DefaultProfile=Yes
OverwriteProfile=Yes
ModifyDefaultProfileIfPresent=FALSE


; ********************************************************************
; Section 2 - Services in Profile
; ********************************************************************

[Service List]
;ServiceX=Microsoft Outlook Client
ServiceEGS=Exchange Global Section
Service1=Unicode Personal Folders
Service2=Outlook Address Book

;********************************************************************
; Section 3 - List of Internet Accounts
;********************************************************************

[Internet Account List]
Account1=IMAP_I_Mail
Account2=INET_HTTP

;********************************************************************
; Section 4 - Default Values for Each Service
;********************************************************************

[ServiceEGS]

[Service1]
UniqueService=No
Name=Large Personal Folders
PathToPersonalFolders=%USERPROFILE%\local settings\application data\microsoft\
outlook\outlookl.pst
EncryptionType=0x50000000

[Service2]
```

Listing 3.5 *A .prf File for Configuring Two Internet Mail Accounts (continued)*

```
;*****************************************************************
; Section 5 - Values for Each Internet Account
;*****************************************************************

[Account1]
UniqueService=No
AccountName=MyOrg IMAP E-mail
IMAPServer=imap.myorg.com
SMTPServer=smtp.myorg.com
IMAPUserName=%USERNAME%
EmailAddress=%USERNAME%@myorg.com
IMAPUseSPA=0
DisplayName=
ReplyEMailAddress=
SMTPUseAuth=1
SMTPAuthMethod=0
ConnectionType=0
RootFolder=
ConnectionOID=MyConnection
IMAPPort=143
IMAPUseSSL=0
ServerTimeOut=60
SMTPPort=25
SMTPUseSSL=0

[Account2]
UniqueService=No
HttpServer=http://www.your_org.com/exchange/%USERNAME%/
UserName=%USERNAME%
Organization=
Reply=
Account=OWA
EmailAddress=%USERNAME%@your_org.com
Connection Type=0
ConnectOID=
```

The second change is that a subsection named [Account2] has been added to section 5, providing settings for the HTTP service.

Tip: To disable the inclusion of a messaging service or Internet mail account in a .prf file, don't delete the service or account. Instead, simply insert a semicolon in front of the appropriate entry from the [Service List] section or the [Internet Account List] section. The service or Internet mail account will then be easy to include in the .prf file, if you change your mind later, by removing the semicolon.

3.4.5   **Mapping sections**

At the end of the .prf file and not shown in Listing 3.1, there are also several mapping sections under the section headings Section 6—Mapping for Profile Properties and Section 7—Mapping for Internet Account Properties; these determine how profile settings are written to the registry. The names of these sections include [Microsoft Exchange Server], [Exchange Global Section], [Personal Folders], [Unicode Personal Folders], [Outlook Address Book], [Microsoft Outlook Client], and [Personal Address Book]. The service-account sections use the information in the mapping sections. You can modify these sections when you need to add settings to a profile that the CIW and CMW do not expose. You will learn more about those in Chapter 4, especially in regard to tracking down obscure Exchange settings. For now, we'll just use the example of the PAB. If you look back at Listing 3.3, you'll see that it added the following line to the [Service List] section:

```
Service4=Personal Address Book
```

with this matching service section:

```
[Service4]
NameOfPAB="Personal Address Book"
Path="%USERPROFILE%\local settings\application data\
microsoft\outlook\mailbox.pab"
ShowNamesBy=1
```

The third section that contributes to the settings for the PAB is the following mapping section:

```
[Personal Address Book]
ServiceName=MSPST AB
NameOfPAB=PT_STRING8,0x001e3001
Path=PT_STRING8,0x001e6600
ShowNamesBy=PT_LONG,0x00036601
```

As you can see, the name of the section, [Personal Address Book], corresponds to the setting for the Service4 keyword in the [Service List] section. Furthermore, the keywords under the [Service4] section each have a matching statement in the [Personal Address Book] section. The cryptic-looking values for the keywords in the [Personal Address Book] section are actually values that tell Outlook where in the Windows registry settings for the mail profile to store the PAB service options.

3.5 Summary

Outlook's ability to process .prf files to create, overwrite, or modify mail profiles provides a powerful tool for deploying mail profile changes in many different environments—from rolling out connections to a new mail server to troubleshooting a missing Outlook Address Book service. Most .prf files start with the settings produced by the CIW or CMW, but once you know how they work, you can begin to customize them with any text editor.

To help you get a feel for the structure of .prf files, we've looked at several different examples:

- Deploying a profile that includes both Exchange and IMAP4 accounts

- Updating an existing profile to add the Outlook Address Book service

- Adding a PAB or LDAP address list

- Manually editing a .prf file to fix a bug related to Unicode Personal Folders .pst files

- Adding an Exchange mailbox to a profile as an HTTP account using the Outlook Web Access URL

In the next chapter, we'll take a closer look at .prf files to delve more deeply into how you can discover and change settings that the CIW and CMW do not expose.

4

Advanced .prf File Usage

The .prf files that you learned how to create in Chapter 3 by using the Custom Installation Wizard (CIW) and the Custom Management Wizard (CMW) cannot handle every possible mail-profile customization chore. In fact, there are many customizations that cannot be propagated with .prf files at all. This chapter shows you additional scenarios where it makes sense to edit a .prf file by hand or where you might need to customize .prf files for multiple users by using a script. The following topics are covered:

- How to use a script to expand environment variables in a .prf file so that you can customize the .prf file for a particular user or department

- How to add connections to the user's existing .pst files using a script

- How to read the mapping sections of a .prf file

- How to use before and after snapshots of the registry to determine which registry value corresponds to a particular account option

- Where to find values in the Windows registry that you can manage with a .prf file, including settings not supported in the CIW or CMW

4.1 Using scripts to modify .prf files

In Chapter 3, you saw how the CIW and CMW can create basic .prf files containing the basic settings for Outlook accounts. Sometimes the task at hand is more than these basic .prf files can handle. For example, you might need to configure a mail account where the user name doesn't match the Windows login user name. Or, as part of a migration from a POP3 or IMAP4 server to Microsoft Exchange, you might want to make all of a user's Personal Folders .pst files available in the new profile that connects to the Exchange mailbox. One solution in situations like these is to write a script to tailor the .prf file to the individual user. We'll look at two examples that use two different techniques.

4.1.1   Expanding environment variables in a .prf file

Given that a .prf file is just a plain-text file, you might be wondering how it can accommodate the multitude of mail account and other service settings that can vary from user to user or even from one computer to another. One way is through environment variables. You've already seen in Chapter 3 that Outlook can process the %USERNAME% environment variable when it appears in a .prf file and replace that variable with the user's Windows login name. This makes it very easy to set up mail accounts using a generic .prf file that all users can apply; of course, this technique works only if the mail-account user name matches the Windows user login name.

Another important environment variable is %USERPROFILE%, which returns the path to the user-specific folders on the client computer. In the service section for the Personal Folders service in Chapter 3, you saw how the %USERPROFILE% environment variable can be used to construct a file path:

```
PathToPersonalFolders=%USERPROFILE%\local settings\
application data\microsoft\outlook\outlook1.pst
```

Outlook provides no guarantee that it will be able to expand any given environment variable. You can depend on it to be able to process %USER-NAME% and in some contexts %USERPROFILE%, which are defined by the operating system based on the user's Windows login and account information. Most other environment variables should also work, so it's worth testing to find out. But if you want to play it totally safe, don't count on Outlook to be able to process all environment variables that might be available from the operating system or that custom scripts or other methods might have added.

On the other hand, environment variables provide a familiar mechanism for setting user-specific information on a machine. Besides the standard environment variables, others can also be defined, for example, with a login script or the Setx utility for Windows 2000 and later versions, available in the Windows resource kits. Administrators frequently use environment variables to pass information from one script to another. A .prf file itself is very much like a script in that it is a plain-text file that contains instructions for an application. One approach that you may want to consider when you need to tailor a .prf file to individual users is to replace the environmental variable placeholders in the .prf file with the actual environmental variable values, then save the .prf file for later use. In this fashion, by the time Outlook processes the .prf file, all it will contain is static text. As an example, we'll construct a sample script to deploy IMAP4 account settings with environment variables.

Note: You could actually use any text in the .prf file as a placeholder, but using environmental variables is both familiar and flexible.

In an organization using Microsoft Exchange as its mail server, the user's Windows login name and Exchange e-mail account alias are very likely to be the same. Therefore, the %USERNAME% environment variable can be used in the .prf file to substitute for the account name, as you saw in Chapter 3. The same might not be true, however, in other mail environments. For example, to set up IMAP accounts, you might need to match up login names with e-mail account names. One way to do this is to use environment variables in the .prf file as placeholders for the account information, then to use another script to expand those environment variables into the actual static values. This process assumes that you are already using a login script or other mechanism to set environment variables on each machine to provide the necessary account information for the individual user. The Outlook profile part of the process includes the following steps:

1. Construct the .prf file using environment variables.

2. Construct a script to replace the environment variables in the .prf file with their actual values.

3. Run the script.

4. Invoke the .prf file using any of the methods discussed in Chapter 3.

A detailed description of steps 1 to 3 follows, along with a sample script.

Note: The sample script is only one way to accomplish this substitution. For example, utilities such as the UNIX-based stream editor (SED) can also be used in place of scripting in order to substitute strings on a file. (SED for Windows as available as part of the Cygwin open-source package from http://www.cygwin.com.)

Step 1: Place environment variables in the .prf file

The first step is to construct a .prf file that contains the account and other settings you want to deploy. You should start with a .prf file generated by the CIW or CMW, entering placeholder text for such settings as the user name and e-mail address.

Listing 4.1 shows the [Account1] service section from a .prf file designed to deploy an IMAP account. Many of the required IMAP settings require customization. Use environment variables as the values for these settings, as shown in bold in Listing 4.1.

Step 2: Implement a generic environment variable substitution script

The next step is to implement a generic method to substitute actual values for the environment variables in the .prf file. For example, the script in Listing 4.2 will take input from the standard input device and send modified output to the console.

Since the script in Listing 4.2 uses the JScript programming language, it will need to be saved with the .js file type. For example, save

Listing 4.1   *Account Settings for an IMAP Account*

```
[Account1]
UniqueService=No
AccountName=%accountname%
IMAPServer=%imapserver%
SMTPServer=%smtpserver%
IMAPUserName=%imapuser%
EmailAddress=%emailaddress%
IMAPUseSPA=0
DisplayName=%USERNAME%
ReplyEMailAddress=
SMTPUseAuth=1
SMTPAuthMethod=0
ConnectionType=0
RootFolder=
ConnectionOID=MyConnection
IMAPPort=143
IMAPUseSSL=0
ServerTimeOut=60
SMTPPort=25
SMTPUseSSL=0
```

Listing 4.2 *Script to Expand Environment Variables in Any File*

```
var stdin = WScript.StdIn;
var stdout = WScript.StdOut;
var WshShell = WScript.CreateObject("WScript.Shell")

var str2
while (!stdin.AtEndOfStream)
{
 var str = stdin.ReadLine();
 str2 = WshShell.ExpandEnvironmentStrings(str)
 stdout.WriteLine(str2)
}
```

the script as SubstEnv.js. To execute the script, at a command prompt or in a script, enter a command similar to the following:

```
cscript /nologo SubstEnv.js < template_file.prf > output_
file.prf
```

where

template_file.prf should be replaced with the name of the master .prf file that contains the environment variables. Ordinarily, the name used will include the full path of the file. This file can be placed on a shared drive or distributed to user computers for deployment.

output_file.prf should be replaced with the name of the .prf file that will be executed to install a profile. In an enterprise deployment on a local area network (LAN), this file can be placed in the user's home folders.

Note: The /nologo switch for the cscript command suppresses the display of Microsoft copyright and product information. Without it, this extra information would be erroneously written to the output .prf file.

Step 3: Implement a command file to execute the script

The final step is to implement a command file that will set the environment variables from step 1 and then execute the script from step 2. (This might also be done with a login script.) Listing 4.3 shows such a command file.

If any of the file names (SubstEnv.js, *template_file.prf, output_file.prf*) contains spaces, enclose it in double quotation marks.

Listing 4.3   *Commands to Set Environment Variables and Create a Custom .prf File*

```
setlocal
set accountname=Abraham Lincoln
set imapserver=server1
set smtpserver=server2
set imapuser=AbeL
set e-mailaddress=AbeL@somedomain.com
set username=Lincoln
set userprofile=
cscript /nologo SubstEnv.js < template_file.prf > output_file.prf
endlocal
```

Listing 4.4 shows the portion of the output_file.prf file altered by running the commands in Listing 4.3. The [Account1] section has been modified to replace environment variables with static values.

Note that the %USERPROFILE% environment variable is removed from the set of environment variables in the command file in Listing 4.3 with the following line:

```
set userprofile=
```

The effect of this command is that the script SubstEnv.js will leave all occurrences of %USERPROFILE% in *template_file.prf* untouched in *output_file.prf*. Consequently, when *output_file.prf* is executed on the client computer, %USERPROFILE% will be substituted with the Windows profile name (not to be confused with the Outlook profile) of the actively logged on user. Other environment variables, such as %USERNAME%, can be treated in a similar fashion, depending on how .prf files are being deployed, if you prefer to use the Windows user name rather than substitute some other name.

Listing 4.4   *A Portion of the Modified .prf File*

```
[Account1]
UniqueService=No
AccountName=Abraham Lincoln
IMAPServer=server1
SMTPServer=server2
IMAPUserName=AbeL
EmailAddress=AbeL@somedomain.com
IMAPUseSPA=0
DisplayName=Lincoln
```

Tip: For Exchange server, Outlook will prompt the user to pick a name from a list if Exchange cannot resolve the name. For example, if both FredS and FredSi are in the Exchange organization and FredS is specified as the user name in the .prf file, Outlook will prompt the user to pick between the two names. To solve this, if you use a script to personalize .prf files with users' details, append the user name with an "at" sign (@) to force Exchange to resolve the name.

4.1.2   Inserting .pst file paths into a .prf file

In our second script example, you'll see how to discover what Personal Folders .pst files the user has been working with during the past 30 days (in the default folder for such files) and how to add them to a .prf file. This might be useful because you cannot remove a POP3 or IMAP4 service from a profile with a .prf file. Thus, in a migration situation from Internet mail accounts to Exchange, you have two choices:

- Add the Exchange service to the existing default mail profile and make the Exchange mailbox the default delivery store. This leaves any POP3 and IMAP4 accounts still active in the profile. The user will have to remove them manually.

- Create a new default mail profile that contains the Exchange service and the Outlook Address Book.

The second technique makes a clean break from the old mail server(s) but can leave users wondering where their old data might be. The script solution in Listing 4.5 supports a workaround: create a new default mail profile for the Exchange mailbox, but add the user's .pst files before Outlook processes the .prf file.

The VBScript code in Listing 4.5 searches the default location for .pst files—%USERPROFILE%\Local Settings\Application Data\Microsoft\Outlook\—to locate any .pst files that have been used in the past 30 days and updates a target .prf file to add the necessary service sections to the [Service List] section. You can place the script in a .vbs file or include it in the user's login script.

The AddPSTsToPRF subroutine is the heart of the script and takes two arguments—the location of the generic .prf file, which you might deploy as

Listing 4.5   *Script to Insert Active .pst File Names into a .prf File*

```
Dim userPath
Call AddPSTsToPRF( _
"C:\Program Files\Microsoft Office\" & _
"Office11\basic new Exchange.prf", _
"installme.prf")

Sub AddPSTsToPRF(prfPath, prfOutputFile)
    Const FORREADING = 1
    Const FORWRITING = 2

    arrPST = FindPSTs()
    For i = 0 To UBound(arrPST)
        strServiceList = strServiceList & vbCrLf & _
                        "ServicePST" & i & _
                        "=Unicode Personal Folders"
        strServices = strServices & vbCrLf & _
                    "[ServicePST" & i & "]" & _
                    vbCrLf & "UniqueService=No" & _
                    vbCrLf & _
                    "PathToPersonalFolders=" & _
                    userPath & arrPST(i) & vbCrLf
    Next

    If Len(strServiceList) > 2 Then
        strServiceList = Mid(strServiceList, 3)
        strServices = Mid(strServices, 3)

        Set fso = _
        CreateObject("Scripting.FileSystemObject")
        Set prfFile = fso.GetFile(prfPath)
        If Not prfFile Is Nothing Then
          Set ts = _
            prfFile.OpenAsTextStream(ForReading)
          prfContents = ts.ReadAll
          prfContents = Replace(prfContents, _
                        "[Service List]", _
                        "[Service List]" & _
                        vbCrLf & strServiceList, _
                        1, 1, vbTextCompare)
          prfContents = Replace(prfContents, _
                        ";[ServiceX]", _
                        strServices & vbCrLf & _
                        ";[ServiceX]", _
                        1, 1, vbTextCompare)
          ts.Close

          Set ts = fso.CreateTextFile(userPath & _
                    prfOutputFile, True)
          ts.Write prfContents
          ts.Close
        End If
    End If
End Sub
```

Listing 4.5   *Script to Insert Active .pst File Names into a .prf File (continued)*

```
Function FindPSTs()
    Get path to default location for PST files
    Set WshShell = CreateObject("WScript.Shell")
    userPath = WshShell.expandenvironmentstrings _
                ("%USERPROFILE%") & _
                "\Local Settings\Application Data" & _
                "\Microsoft\Outlook\"

    Set fso = CreateObject("Scripting.FileSystemObject")
    Set fld = fso.GetFolder(userPath)

    For Each myFile In fld.Files
        If Right(UCase(myFile.Name), 4) = ".PST" Then
            days = DateDiff("d", _
                    myFile.DateLastModified, Date)
            If days < 31 Then
                If Left(myFile.Name, 18) <> _
                  "SharePoint Folders" Then
                    strFileList = strFileList & ";" & _
                                    myFile.Name
                End If
            End If
        End If
    Next
    If strFileList <> "" Then
        strFileList = Mid(strFileList, 2)
        FindPSTs = Split(strFileList, ";")
    End If
End Function
```

part of your Outlook installation, and the name of the customized .prf file that the script will create in the user's %USERPROFILE%\Local Settings\ Application Data\Microsoft\Outlook folder. (You can, of course, modify the script to save it in some other folder.)

The script makes extensive use of the FileSystemObject object from the Microsoft Scripting Runtime Library to evaluate the names and dates of files in the user's Outlook data folder, to read the source .prf file, and to write data to the customized .prf file. Windows 2000 and XP automatically install this library (Scrrun.dll). The script ignores Sharepoint Folders .pst files but includes .pst files associated with IMAP4 accounts. Listing 4.6 shows an example of the changes that the script makes in the [Service List] section and in the service sections. The new lines are shown in bold. They add three .pst files for a user named flaviusj. ServicePST0 is apparently an archive file, ServicePST1 is probably the user's main .pst file, and ServicePST2 is a .pst file associated with an IMAP4 account in the user's previous profile, which was named Outlook.

Listing 4.6   *A Portion of a .prf File Updated by the AddPSTsToPRF Procedure*

```
; **********************************************************
; Section 2 - Services in Profile
; **********************************************************

[Service List]
ServicePST0=Unicode Personal Folders
ServicePST1=Unicode Personal Folders
ServicePST2=Unicode Personal Folders
ServiceX=Microsoft Outlook Client
ServiceEGS=Exchange Global Section
Service1=Microsoft Exchange Server
ServiceEGS=Exchange Global Section
Service2=Outlook Address Book


;**********************************************************
; Section 4 - Default Values for Each Service
;**********************************************************

[ServiceX]
CachedExchangeMode=0x00000002
CachedExchangeSlowDetect=TRUE

[ServiceEGS]
CachedExchangeConfigFlags=0x00000100
MailboxName=%UserName%
HomeServer=crimdell

[Service1]
OverwriteExistingService=No
UniqueService=Yes
MailboxName=%UserName%
HomeServer=myserver
AccountName=Microsoft Exchange Server

[Service2]

[ServicePST0]
UniqueService=No
PathToPersonalFolders=C:\Documents and Settings\flaviusj\Local
Settings\Application Data\Microsoft\Outlook\archive.pst

[ServicePST1]
UniqueService=No
PathToPersonalFolders=C:\Documents and Settings\flaviusj\Local
Settings\Application Data\Microsoft\Outlook\outlook.pst

[ServicePST2]
UniqueService=No
PathToPersonalFolders=C:\Documents and Settings\flaviusj\Local
Settings\Application Data\Microsoft\Outlook\
Outlookapp4.mailblix.com-00000005.pst

;[ServiceX]
```

You can process the customized .prf file using any of the methods discussed in Chapter 3. When the user runs Outlook with the new profile, the folder list will contain not just the new Exchange mailbox but also the user's previous archive and other .pst files.

Note: The script in Listing 4.5 assumes that the source .prf file was built with the CIW or CMW and thus includes the standard [Service List] section and a commented-out ";[ServiceX]" statement that is present in CIW/CMW-generated .prf files. You could also set up the source .prf file with your own placeholder text and adjust the script to replace that placeholder text in order to position the service-list entries and the service sections properly. Another possible modification would be to look in additional locations for .pst files.

An alternative approach would be to read the registry entries for a particular Outlook profile to determine which .pst files are associated with the profile. This, however, might not tell you what other .pst files the user might have used recently, such as archive files. Furthermore, the names of the registry subkeys where that information resides differ with every profile. In Chapter 9, you will see an example of using the Windows Management Instrumentation scripting interface to iterate registry keys in a profile. This technique could be adapted to locate each subkey related to a .pst file, then obtain the path to that file from the 001f6700 registry value under that key.

Note: See Appendix D for information on the third-party ProfMan programming library, which can also handle profile modifications in scripts, assuming the ProfMan.dll library is installed on the client machine.

4.2   Adding settings not supported by the Custom Installation Wizard

Almost all of the examples of .prf files you have seen so far, both in this chapter and in Chapter 3, have used settings built with the CIW or CMW. These tools, however, do not provide support for all possible messaging-service settings. By adding properties to the mapping sections of a .prf file, you can add or configure many other settings.

To deploy a setting that is not supported by the CIW or CMW, you should follow this basic two-step procedure:

1.   Include a line for the setting in the appropriate mapping section in the .prf file.

2.   Implement the setting in the appropriate service section in the same way that other features are implemented, as you saw in Chapter 3.

Typically, the information that you need to add to a .prf file to support a new setting will come from a Microsoft Knowledge Base article, such as article 836755, which shows how to set the default archive file name. However, such information may also be obtained by careful examination of the Windows registry. You'll see how to do that later in Section 4.3.

Before we present a general technique for discovering such settings, let's look at two specific examples—setting the location for the default Personal Folders .pst file used for archiving and changing the TCP/IP ports used in connection with an Exchange account.

4.2.1   Example: Setting the location of the default archive file

As noted above, Microsoft Knowledge Base article 836755, "How to Set the Location of an Archive .pst File in Outlook," explains how to modify a .prf file to set the location of the default archive file. The Microsoft Knowledge Base example shows how to deploy a completely new profile and overwrite the existing profile. In our example, you'll see how to modify an existing profile to add a new Unicode Personal Folders .pst file and make that new .pst file the default archive file.

Using a Unicode .pst file for the archive means that the user can store up to 20 GB of data, by default, in the archive file and can successfully archive multilingual data from an Exchange 2000 or 2003 mailbox or another Unicode .pst file. As you saw in Chapter 3, the CIW and CMW have a bug that causes any unmodified .prf file to create .pst files in the old format, not the new Unicode format. By editing the .prf file manually, you can correct that problem.

Note: The user may set any folder to archive to any specific .pst file, not just the default archive file. The technique illustrated in this example will not override any such folder-specific archive settings.

Start by using the CIW or CMW to create a basic .prf file that you can modify. On screen 12 of the CMW (screen 17 of the CIW), choose Modify Profile. This choice will create a .prf file that modifies the user's default mail profile. On screen 14 of the CMW (screen 19 of the CIW), add a new Personal Folders File (PST) account to create a .pst file in the new Unicode format that Outlook 2003 supports. Give it the file name Archive_l.pst and the store (or display) name Archive Folders, as shown in Figure 4.1.

On screen 15 of the CMW (screen 20 of the CIW), export the profile settings to a file named Add Archive File.prf. Open that file in Notepad (or any other text editor) to make the additional changes described in this section.

The first change will be to the [Microsoft Outlook Client] mapping section. Recall that the CIW and CMW automatically add the mapping sections at the bottom of each .prf file. In this scenario, add the line shown in bold in Listing 4.7.

Note that you are not required to use the specific label ArchiveFileName to set this property. You can replace this label with another label as long as you use the same label in the service section to specify the actual path for the archive file.

Note: Don't be concerned that the information after the equal sign of the new line looks rather cryptic. The format of this line will be covered below.

Figure 4.1

Adding a new Unicode Personal Folders .pst file for use as an archive.

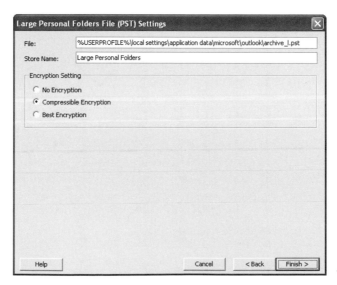

Listing 4.7   *Modified Mapping Section to Include the Archive File Location*

```
[Microsoft Outlook Client]
SectionGUID=0a0d020000000000c000000000000046
FormDirectoryPage=PT_STRING8,0x0270
WebServicesLocation=PT_STRING8,0x0271
ComposeWithWebServices=PT_BOOLEAN,0x0272
PromptWhenUsingWebServices=PT_BOOLEAN,0x0273
OpenWithWebServices=PT_BOOLEAN,0x0274
CachedExchangeMode=PT_LONG,0x041f
CachedExchangeSlowDetect=PT_BOOLEAN,0x0420
ArchiveFileName=PT_UNICODE,0x0324
```

Next, specify the archive file name using the label from the left side of the new line that you added to the [Microsoft Outlook Client] mapping section. For example, in Listing 4.8, in the [Service List] section, the [ServiceX] section maps to the [Microsoft Outlook Client] section from Listing 4.7 by way of the following line:

```
ServiceX=Microsoft Outlook Client
```

Then, the [ServiceX] section includes the actual path value for Archive-FileName:

```
ArchiveFileName=%USERPROFILE%\local settings\application
data\microsoft\outlook\archive_1.pst
```

Tip: If you are working with a .prf created by the CMW or CIW to modify a profile, the [Service List] section may have a semicolon in front of the line for the Microsoft Outlook Client service. Similarly, the heading line for the matching service section for the Microsoft Outlook Client service may have a semicolon in front of it. Be sure that you remove these semicolons. Otherwise, those lines will be treated as comments and not processed by Outlook as part of the .prf file.

Under the [Service1] section, which adds the archive .pst file, the EncryptionType is set to 0x50000000 to correct a known bug in the CMW and CIW. As you read in Chapter 3, when you create a .pst file and specify the new Personal Folders format, not the Outlook 97–2000 format, the EncryptionType in the resulting .prf file is set incorrectly to 0x40000000. If you edit the .prf file to change it to 0x50000000, Outlook will correctly create a Unicode format .pst file.

Listing 4.8   *Specifying the ArchiveFileName Path*

```
; ********************************************************
; Section 1 - Profile Defaults
; ********************************************************

[General]
Custom=1
DefaultProfile=Yes
OverwriteProfile=Append
ModifyDefaultProfileIfPresent=TRUE


; ********************************************************
; Section 2 - Services in Profile
; ********************************************************

[Service List]
Service1=Unicode Personal Folders
ServiceX=Microsoft Outlook Client


;********************************************************
; Section 3 - List of Internet Accounts
;********************************************************

[Internet Account List]

;********************************************************
; Section 4 - Default Values for Each Service
;********************************************************

[ServiceEGS]

[Service1]
UniqueService=No
Name=Archive Folders
PathToPersonalFolders=%USERPROFILE%\local settings\application
data\microsoft\outlook\archive_1.pst
EncryptionType=0x50000000

[ServiceX]
ArchiveFileName=%USERPROFILE%\local settings\application data\
microsoft\outlook\archive_1.pst
```

Warning: If the .pst file that you specify in the `PathToPersonalFolders=` line already exists, Outlook will use the existing file rather than create a new file. Therefore, when you want to create a new .pst file for the user, try to use a file name that the user will be unlikely to have chosen on his or her own. You can use the %USERNAME% environment variable to create a file name such as archive-%USERNAME%.pst.

When you save and deploy the resulting .prf file, Outlook will display the Archive_l.pst file in the folder list. It will appear with the display name set by the Name property, which is Archive Folders in this example. Outlook will also set Archive_l.pst to be the default archive file. If you want to turn on AutoArchive or change that feature's options, you can either deploy user-preference settings with the CIW, the CMW, or a script, or you can use a Group Policy Object (GPO) to enforce certain settings. In the Group Policy Editor, look under User Configuration / Administrative Templates / Microsoft Office Outlook 2003 / Tools | Options / Other / AutoArchive. These settings are in a similar location in the settings hierarchy in the CMW or CIW.

4.2.2   Example: Fixing the TCP/IP ports used with Exchange

Many organizations have implemented firewall restrictions and standards for better network security. Unfortunately, standard remote procedure call (RPC) traffic, since it uses a wide range of TCP/IP ports, is not very firewall friendly. Microsoft Knowledge Base Article 833799, "How to Configure Static Communication Ports in Outlook 2003," shows a way around this. The technique, however, requires configuration changes on the Exchange 2000 or 2003 server and in Outlook profiles. Effectively, both the Exchange server and Outlook have to be configured to use a fixed TCP/IP port for RPC traffic.

To configure Outlook to use specific TCP/IP ports with Exchange, first add additional lines to the [Exchange Global Section] (a mapping section); these lines are shown in bold in Listing 4.9.

Next, configure the [ServiceEGS] section (the "EGS" in ServiceEGS stands for "Exchange Global Section") to use the labels added in Listing 4.9

Listing 4.9   *Adding TCP/IP Port Settings to the Exchange Global Section*

```
[Exchange Global Section]
SectionGUID=13dbb0c8aa05101a9bb000aa002fc45a
MailboxName=PT_STRING8,0x6607
HomeServer=PT_STRING8,0x6608
HTTPExchangePort=PT_I2,0x662d
HTTPReferralPort=PT_I2,0x6631
HTTPDirectoryPort=PT_I2,0x662f
TCPExchangePort=PT_I2,0x662c
TCPReferralPort=PT_I2,0x6630
TCPDirectoryPort=PT_I2,0x662e
```

Listing 4.10 *Setting RPC over HTTP Ports*

```
[ServiceEGS]
HTTPExchangePort=81
HTTPReferralPort=90
```

Listing 4.11 *Setting TCP/IP Ports*

```
[ServiceEGS]
TCPExchangePort=3100
TCPReferralPort=3101
```

to set specific port values. Note that not all of the new labels need be used. For example, Listings 4.10 and 4.11 show two alternative combinations of settings, one to set the ports used by RPC over HTTP clients and the other to set the ports used by normal TCP/IP clients.

Warning: Specific settings for TCP/IP ports for Exchange should be used only with a full understanding of the configuration issues with Exchange and possibly other back-end-side facilities such as firewalls. Microsoft Knowledge Base article 270836, "Exchange 2000 and Exchange 2003 Static Port Mappings," is a good starting point to understand these configuration issues.

4.3 How to find additional settings

In the above examples, you added settings to .prf files to specify the location of the archive file name and TCP/IP ports for connecting to Exchange 2000 or 2003. Each of these examples required adding lines to mapping sections in a .prf file, as shown in Listings 4.7 and 4.9.

It would be great if Microsoft documented all possible settings in .prf files, but this is not always the case. What if you want to set an Outlook option that appears to be related to the mail profile but that is not directly supported or shown clearly in a .prf file? As you will see, if you can find that setting in the Windows registry, then you may be able to add it to a .prf file for testing and possible deployment.

The good news is that many Outlook and Exchange settings can indeed be found in the registry. Settings for Lightweight Directory Access Protocol (LDAP) and Internet accounts generally tend to be well documented and handled by the .prf file, so there's less need to dig into the registry to discover the settings for these types of messaging services. The technique that you're about to learn really comes in handy in configuring complex services like an Exchange account.

4.3.1   Understanding .prf file-mapping sections

The first step in discovering new settings is to understand the format of the mapping sections, which we will look at in detail. With that information, you'll be able to see the connection between Outlook profile settings stored in the Windows registry and the lines in a .prf file that can configure those settings. Once you understand that connection, you can follow the same steps in the other direction, that is, discover a setting in the registry that you want to deploy, then figure out how you might set it with a .prf file.

We're going to look at two mapping sections that you're already familiar with from previous examples—the [Microsoft Outlook Client] section, where you added the ArchiveFileName setting in Listing 4.7, and the [Exchange Global Section] mapping section shown in Listing 4.9

Each line of interest in a mapping section can be broken down into three parts. Take another look at the line that adds the ArchiveFileName setting:

```
ArchiveFileName=PT_UNICODE,0x0324
```

You'll see that it has three parts:

- *Label:* The leftmost part of the line, ArchiveFileName, is a label, a reference point used to set the property for the archive file name in the corresponding service section, such as in Listing 4.8. The label is symbolic only and can therefore just as easily have some other name, such as AutoArchivePath. The important issue is that the same label must be used both in the mapping section that defines the property and in the service section that sets the property value.

- *Data type:* To the right of the equal sign is the PT_UNICODE data type. This indicates that the data for the property corresponding to the ArchiveFileName label is a Unicode text string. If you look back at Listing 4.7, you'll see other data types, such as PT_LONG. Each of these determines what sort of data is associated with the property represented by the label. These data types are documented in Table 4.1.

- *MAPI property tag:* The rightmost element of the line, separated from the data type with a comma, consists of a number in hexadecimal for-

---

Table 4.1	*Data Types for Mappings*

Data Type	How the Data Appears in .prf file
PT_BOOLEAN	Boolean value, either TRUE or FALSE, also represented by 1 or 0, respectively
PT_LONG	A long integer, between –2,147,483,648 and 2,147,483,647, often represented in hexadecimal format
PT_I4	Equivalent to PT_LONG
PT_SHORT	A short integer, between –32,768 and 32,767, possibly represented in hexadecimal format
PT_I2	Equivalent to PT_SHORT
PT_STRING8	A text string, possibly in quotation marks
PT_UNICODE	A date type designation generally used instead of PT_STRING8, particularly for international versions of Outlook

mat. By convention, hexadecimal numbers begin with "0x," followed by the actual numbers in order to distinguish them from decimal numbers. In the next section, you will see how the data type and this hexadecimal number combine to form a registry entry.

4.3.2 Relating mapping sections to the profile registry settings

Once you understand the format of a mapping section's lines, you also need to understand where to look in the Windows registry for profile settings. As you learned in Chapter 1, Outlook stores settings for mail profiles in the HKEY_CURRENT_USER\Software\Microsoft\Windows NT\CurrentVersion\Windows Messaging Subsystem\Profiles key of the registry. For your explorations, you will probably find it convenient to create a test profile. The remainder of this section demonstrates the steps for using such a test profile to discover profile settings that are stored in the registry.

Step 1: Find the profile in the registry

Let's say you have an Outlook mail profile named Demo that contains an Exchange account. Run the Registry Editor (Regedit.exe or Regedt32.exe), and navigate to the Windows Messaging Subsystem key. Expand the Profiles key, and you will see a list of the profiles that are currently installed for the currently logged-on user. Figure 4.2 shows the Demo profile that we are looking for.

Figure 4.2
*The Demo profile
in the registry.*

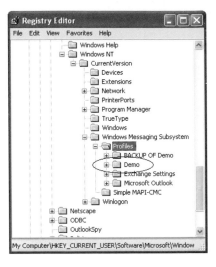

Step 2: Find the key for the messaging service

Listings 4.7 and 4.9 each contain the label SectionGUID. Unlike the other mapping section lines that contain a data type and a MAPI property name, the SectionGUID line has the string to the right of the equal sign that is a unique identifier. This is a number in hexadecimal format used to distinguish some mapping sections, including the [Microsoft Outlook Client] and [Exchange Global Section] sections. This identifier is also the name of the registry key that contains most of the settings for the corresponding mapping section in the .prf file.

Figure 4.3 shows the key that corresponds to the SectionGUID entry in the [Microsoft Outlook Client] mapping section in Listing 4.7. Note that the name of the key is the same as the data for the SectionGUID entry, 0a0d020000000000c000000000000046.

Step 3: Locate the registry value

Click on the 0a0d020000000000c000000000000046 key highlighted in Figure 4.3 to see the individual registry values for that key. The name of each value shown in Figure 4.4 is an eight-digit hexadecimal number. The first four digits of each correspond to the one of the data types (PT_UNICODE, and so on) listed in Table 4.1. Table 4.2 lists which data types correspond to which registry entries. For example, the top value shown in the right-hand pane of the Registry Editor in Figure 4.4 is 0003033d. Since the first four digits are 0003, you can look at Table 4.2 to determine that the corresponding data type is PT_LONG.

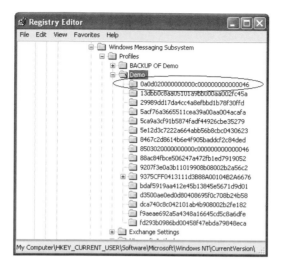

Figure 4.3
Registry key for the [Microsoft Outlook Client] mapping section.

Note: Some of the registry entries for a profile may not correspond to any data type in Table 4.2. These will usually be additional data types, such as binary data, that cannot be configured with .prf files.

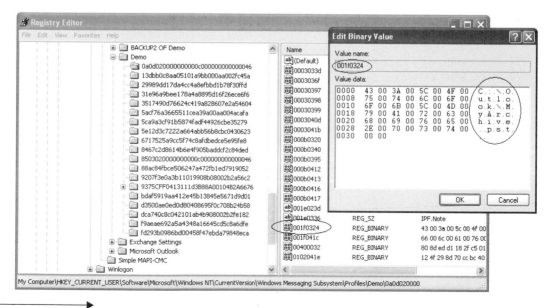

Figure 4.4   *The archive file name setting in the registry.*

Table 4.2 *How Data Types Correspond to Registry Entries*

Data Type	First Four Digits in Registry Value Name
PT_BOOLEAN	000b
PT_LONG or PT_I4	0003
PT_SHORT or PT_I2	0002
PT_STRING8	001e
PT_UNICODE	001f

As a simple example, we can look for the archive file name property that you already know how to set with a .prf file. First, start Outlook with the Demo profile and set the default archive file name from within Outlook using the Tools | Options | Other | AutoArchive dialog. For this example, the default archive file name specified within Outlook is C:\Outlook\MyArchive.pst.

Since the default archive file name is a string, it seems likely that it will be stored as either data type PT_STRING8 or PT_UNICODE. Note that by examining the registry hive in Figure 4.4, you can see that there are two Unicode settings, each having a name beginning with 001f, the prefix listed in Table 4.2 for values that use the Unicode data type. Displaying value 001f0324, as shown in Figure 4.4, clearly shows the default archive file name that we have specified within Outlook, C:\Outlook\MyArchive.pst.

The last four characters of the registry value name—in other words, the part after the data type indicator—make up the MAPI property name that appears in the corresponding line for the property in the mapping section in the .prf file. Therefore, since the registry value's name is 001f0324, the last four characters are 0324, and the line to include in the service section is

```
SomeLabel=PT_UNICODE,0x0324
```

where SomeLabel can be replaced by the label of your choice. In the case of the example in Listings 4.7 and 4.8, we used the label ArchiveFileName.

Look at Figure 4.5 to see how the information in the mapping section of a .prf file corresponds to the registry keys and values that Outlook creates for a mail profile. The value for the SectionGUID label, 0a0d020000000000c000000000000046, under the [Microsoft Outlook Client] mapping section, becomes the registry key for that portion of the profile. The value for the ArchiveFileName label, PT_UNICODE,0x0324,

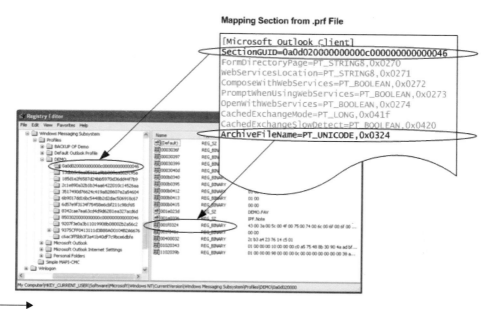

Figure 4.5 *How the .prf mapping section corresponds to profile registry values.*

provides the information needed to create the 001f0324 value under that key.

Note: You might be wondering why Figure 4.5 does not show registry values for any of the [Microsoft Outlook Client] settings besides ArchiveFileName; for example, you may wonder why there is no 001e0270 value corresponding to FormDirectoryPage. Remember that the mapping section only tells Outlook what registry value to use for a particular setting. The corresponding service section determines whether to add a particular setting and what its value will be.

4.3.3 Finding profile settings for Exchange

You can use the same procedures to discover settings for an Exchange Server account. If you look at the [Exchange Global Section] mapping section in a .prf file, you will see that it contains a value for SectionGUID of 13dbb0c8aa05101a9bb000aa002fc45a. This tells you that Exchange account settings will appear in the profile under the registry key 13dbb0c8aa05101a9bb000aa002fc45a. A basic approach to discovering Exchange account settings would be to set the desired account options within Outlook or the Mail applet in Control Panel applet and then examine the registry settings for the profile under that key. (Chapter 5 explains in detail the Exchange account features, such as Cached Exchange mode and RPC over HTTP, that are mentioned below.)

You can get bleary-eyed looking at the Registry Editor to try to see what's changed. Instead, consider using the File | Export command to take before and after snapshots of registry changes, exporting them as .reg files, which are just text files with the .reg extension. Because they are text files, you can compare them with a file-comparison utility to determine what has changed. You may already have such a utility in your system administrator's toolkit, such as the Windiff.exe tool from Microsoft.

Note: Windiff.exe is available as part of the Windows XP SP2 support tools. Microsoft Knowledge Base article 838079, "Windows XP Service Pack 2 Support Tools" provides the download link. Other tools specifically for monitoring registry changes include RegShot from http://the7thlab.mybesthost.com and RegMon from http://www.sysinternals.com.

If you don't already have such a utility, you can use Microsoft Word's document-comparison feature to compare two .reg files. Follow these steps:

1. Start Word, and use the File | Open command to open the first .reg file. If you're prompted for the format, choose Unicode.

2. Choose Tools | Compare and Merge Documents, then select the second .reg file. Check the box for Legal Blackline, then click Compare.

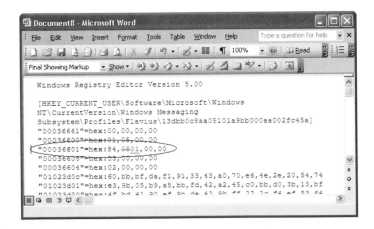

Figure 4.6   *Comparing before and after registry export files with Word.*

Table 4.3   *Cached Exchange Mode Options for Registry Value 00036601*

Cached Exchange Mode	Download Public Folders/ Favorites	Registry Value (hex)
Off	n/a	04 00 00 00
On	Off	84 01 00 00
On	On	84 05 00 00

Word will open a copy of the first .reg file marked to show how it differs from the second .reg file and will display the Reviewing toolbar. You can ignore formatting changes by clicking Show on the Reviewing toolbar and choosing Formatting off. Figure 4.6 shows the result of comparing registry export .reg files before and after turning off the option for downloading Public Folders\Favorites folders in Cached Exchange mode. Possible values for the 00036601 registry value are shown in Table 4.3.

Armed with that information, you can now construct a .prf file that contains the information necessary to turn Cached Exchange mode on or off or to enable or disable downloading Public Folders/Favorites to the cache. Looking at Table 4.2, you determine that the value 00036601 is a PT_LONG long value and add the appropriate new line to the [Exchange Global Section] mapping section, shown in bold in Listing 4.12.

Note: Don't look for a registry value named 00036629 corresponding to the CachedExchangeFlags label in the [Exchange Global Section] mapping section. Outlook imports data from that label but does not create a registry value named 00036629. Instead, it uses the information to set other registry values.

Listing 4.12   *Adding a CachedExchangeMode Label*

```
[Exchange Global Section]
SectionGUID=13dbb0c8aa05101a9bb000aa002fc45a
MailboxName=PT_STRING8,0x6607
HomeServer=PT_STRING8,0x6608
RPCoverHTTPflags=PT_LONG,0x6623
RPCProxyServer=PT_UNICODE,0x6622
RPCProxyPrincipalName=PT_UNICODE,0x6625
RPCProxyAuthScheme=PT_LONG,0x6627
CachedExchangeConfigFlags=PT_LONG,0x6629
CachedExchangeMode=PT_LONG,0x6601
```

Listing 4.13   *Turning on Cached Exchange Mode Public Folders\Favorites Downloads*

```
[General]
Custom=1
DefaultProfile=Yes
OverwriteProfile=Append
ModifyDefaultProfileIfPresent=TRUE

[Service List]
ServiceEGS=Exchange Global Section

[ServiceEGS]
CachedExchangeMode=0x00000584
```

Next, edit the general and service sections of the .prf file to include only the change in the Cached Exchange mode setting. Listing 4.13, for example, shows the appropriate value to enable Cached Exchange mode with Public Folders\Favorites downloads. Note that the order of bytes for the setting's value in the .prf file is the reverse of what you see in the Registry Editor and in Table 4.3—0x00000584 in the .prf file versus 84 05 00 00 in the Registry Editor.

You've now seen how to dissect a .prf file to match its settings with those in the Windows registry and, conversely, how to locate a registry entry known to control a particular account setting and use its location in the registry to create a corresponding property setting in a .prf file. You should do extensive testing, though, before deploying any setting that you have researched in this manner. It's very easy—especially in the case of registry values like 00036601, which control multiple settings—to miss a possible configuration option. For example, in addition to enabling Cached Exchange mode, the 00036601 registry value also controls whether Outlook always prompts for the user name and password and whether Outlook automatically detects the network connection state. The values shown above in Table 4.3 will set Outlook to detect the connection state automatically and not prompt for the user name and password; these are the default settings.

4.3.4   Additional Exchange settings

As you saw in Listing 4.12, the [Exchange Global Section] contains settings for the mailbox name and home server, as well as settings related to RPC over HTTP and Cached Exchange mode, both of which you will learn more about in Chapter 5. Table 4.4 lists the registry values for these set-

Table 4.4   *Profile Settings in Exchange 2000 and Exchange 2003*

Description of Settings	Registry Values
Logon network security	00036119
Connection state and Cached Exchange mode options	00036601
Encryption of data between Outlook and Exchange	00036606
RPC over HTTP options	00036623
RPC proxy server for RPC over HTTP	001f6622
RPC proxy server principal name	001f6625
RPC over HTTP authentication	00036627
Directory for Offline Address Book (OAB) files	001e660e
Sequence number, used by OAB differential downloads	0003667d
Path to offline folders .ost file	001f6610
User full name	001f3001

tings, along with some other known registry values for Exchange accounts. Note that these settings may vary with future releases of Exchange. All are found in the same HKEY_CURRENT_USER\Software\Microsoft\Windows NT\CurrentVersion\Windows Messaging Subsystem\Profiles\<*profile name*>\13dbb0c8aa05101a9bb000aa002fc45a key that you saw in the previous section.

In some cases, a single numeric registry value may encode multiple settings. You've already seen one example, registry value 00036601, which controls two different options for Cached Exchange mode—whether Cached Exchange mode is enabled and whether Public Folders/Favorites are downloaded to the cache, plus additional options related to connection-state detection and user-name and password prompting.

Another example is registry value 00036623, which controls six different RPC over HTTP options. Each of the lowest six digits in a byte is used to represent a different option. It's easiest to see this when you look at the byte in its binary rather than hexadecimal format. For example, turning on RPC over HTTP sets the lowest digit to 1, resulting in the following values:

- Binary   0000 0001
- Hex   0x0001

Table 4.5   *RPC over HTTP Options in Registry Value 00036623*

No.	Option	Binary Value
1	Enable RPC over HTTP	0000 0001
2	Connect using Secure Sockets Layer only	0000 0010
3	Mutually authenticate	0000 0100
4	Use HTTP first on fast networks	0000 1000
5	Don't show Authentication Configuration Warning	0001 0000
6	Use HTTP first on slow networks	0010 0000

If you also turn on the option to connect using HTTP first on a fast network, that sets the sixth bit to 1, with the following result:

- Binary   0010 0001

- Hex   0x0021

Table 4.5 shows the different settings. In each case, a value of 1 enables the option, while 0 disables it.

The fifth option in Table 4.5 suppresses the dialog shown in Figure 4.7.

To find out which value for the 00036623 property represents any combination of options, add the binary values for the desired options from Table 4.5 and convert that number to hexadecimal format. In the example above, to get the value for enabling RPC over HTTP and choosing the option to use HTTP first on slow networks, you add the binary values 0000 0001 and 0010 0000 to get 0010 0001, which converts to a hexadecimal value of 0x0021. This will appear in the 00036623 registry value with the bytes reversed, as 21 00 00 00.

Figure 4.7
You can suppress this dialog with a registry setting deployable with a .prf file.

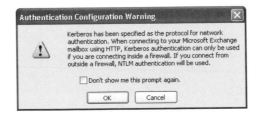

4.4   Limitations to .prf files

All of the examples of advanced .prf file customization in this chapter have dealt with settings represented in the [Microsoft Outlook Client] and [Exchange Global Section] mapping sections. There's a good reason for this: each of these mapping sections contains a SectionGUID property whose value is used to set a consistent registry key for that service. In other words, the registry keys for the Microsoft Outlook Client and Exchange Global Section settings are the same in every mail profile on every Outlook client. These are the exception, rather than the rule, however. Most other accounts and services do not have consistent or unique registry keys. This makes it less likely that you can use the discovery process described in the previous section to find settings you can easily configure by adding a label to the appropriate .prf file mapping section.

This does not mean that these settings cannot be automated, however. Just as Outlook uses Extended MAPI internally to configure profile settings in the Windows registry, an external program can use Extended MAPI to read or set the same options. As Extended MAPI is not a scripting language and requires C++ or Delphi programming skills, we do not cover it in this book. However, in Chapter 9, you will see examples of a third-party library, ProfMan, that does allow you to script such profile-related options as secondary Exchange mailboxes.

4.5   Summary

This chapter has provided you with three valuable techniques that can enhance the value of .prf files for deploying mail profiles in your organization: (1) modifying a .prf file with a script to expand or customize it for the current user, (2) adding to the mapping sections in the .prf file to configure additional properties, and (3) constructing new labels for the mapping section from information found in the Windows registry. While .prf files cannot deploy every profile-related setting, they do cover most of the common settings you are likely to need to configure, especially for Exchange accounts.

The .prf files that Outlook uses to deploy mail-profile settings operate as scripts, providing processing instructions to the Outlook application. Because they are text files, you can write a script to preprocess a .prf file, replacing environment variables or other placeholder text with the required values for an individual user (or all users in a department).

Certain mapping sections in a .prf file can easily be matched up with the corresponding Windows registry values. Once you know how this correspondence works, you can look for other registry values that might be useful to deploy with a .prf file but that are not directly supported by the CIW or CMW. As an example, you've seen how to deploy a new Unicode .pst file and make it the default destination for Outlook's AutoArchive feature.

Exchange Account Configuration

Microsoft Outlook was designed with an architecture that allows it to handle many different types of mail accounts. However, most frequently in enterprise deployments, you'll find it used as the client for Microsoft Exchange Server. In fact, purchasing a client-access license for Microsoft Exchange 2003 or Microsoft Small Business Server (SBS) 2003, which includes Exchange, gives an organization the right to install Outlook 2003 as the client software.

Every version of Outlook has made improvements in its Exchange connectivity, and Outlook 2003 is no exception. One of the goals of this chapter is to sort out the different connectivity options, then help you achieve the optimal configuration for the one you choose. In this chapter you'll learn the following:

- The benefits of two new connectivity methods—Cached Exchange mode and remote procedure call (RPC) over HTTP

- Which connectivity method is best for which type of Exchange user

- How to configure Cached Exchange mode and RPC over HTTP

- Why the Offline Address Book (OAB) might sometimes take longer than users expect to show updated and new addresses

- How to update Exchange accounts to point to a new server

Chapter 3 showed you how to use the tools in the Office Resource Kit (ORK) to create and modify Outlook mail profiles that include an Exchange account. This chapter reviews and builds on those settings.

5.1   Choosing your Exchange connectivity

If Exchange is your organization's mail server, part of your Outlook 2003 deployment planning and ongoing user support will involve making decisions on which method of connecting to Exchange will work best for which users. Outlook 2003 offers more connectivity choices than previous versions. Let's first get a brief overview of the connectivity choices, then explore each one in depth so you can make an informed choice.

- *Connect in Cached Exchange mode.* This is a new feature in Outlook 2003; folders in the user's mailbox and, optionally, in the Public Folders\Favorites hierarchy are cached on the local hard drive. This is the new default Exchange connectivity setting in Outlook 2003. The cache is contained in an offline folders .ost file, but Outlook 2003 improves on the offline folders .ost file used in previous versions of Outlook. The user can disconnect from the network and keep working without having to restart Outlook. When used with Exchange 2000 or 2003, this newer .ost file provides support for Unicode and is set by default to a maximum of 20 GB. Although Microsoft does not recommend exceeding that size, a Unicode .ost file can grow to a maximum of 33 terabytes. Of course, the local file system will probably limit the maximum size to far less than that. (For more information on .ost files, see Chapter 1.)

- *Connect in Classic Online mode.* The data is stored on the server and not cached at all on the client.

- *Connect in Classic Offline mode.* Selected folders are cached locally in an offline folders .ost file. To switch between Classic Online and Classic Offline modes, the user must restart Outlook. By contrast, a Cached Exchange mode user can switch between the online and offline state without restarting Outlook.

- *Use Outlook 2003 in Classic Online mode in a Terminal Services environment.* Working offline is not supported or necessary in this scenario since the Terminal Services server is always online with the Exchange server. No data is stored on the user's local machine.

- *Connect to the Exchange server as a POP3 or IMAP4 client.* This method is typically used in a situation where one user, for example a consultant with mailboxes at different client sites, needs to connect to mailboxes on several different Exchange servers. An Outlook mail profile allows only one connection to an Exchange server but multiple POP3 or IMAP4 accounts.

- *Connect to the Exchange server with Outlook Web Access (OWA).* OWA—that is, an Exchange mailbox accessed through the user's browser—works well for users with light e-mail and collaboration usage who do not need to use Outlook custom forms or add-ins. OWA also does not support Outlook's Journal feature for keeping track of the time you spend on different activities. A good example of where OWA might be an ideal solution is an environment where shift workers check their e-mail at a kiosk shared by everyone in a department. Travelers also find it handy to use OWA to check their Inbox from airport or hotel Internet kiosks. Since OWA is a browser-based connectivity option, we do not cover it in this book.

- *Connect to the Exchange mailbox as an HTTP account.* In this connectivity option, Outlook uses the Web address and credentials for an OWA account but displays the e-mail messages in Outlook, as it would a Hotmail or Microsoft Network account. While Microsoft does not officially support this technique, it does work and, like the POP3/IMAP4 option, can be handy to connect to an Exchange 2000 or 2003 mailbox from an Outlook mail profile that already has an Exchange account.

Note: OWA isn't the only access feature for Exchange users who are out of the office. Exchange 2003 also includes Exchange ActiveSync and Outlook Mobile Access to support mailbox access for mobile devices such as smart phones and PDAs.

In addition to Cached Exchange mode, the other major new connectivity feature in Outlook 2003 is the ability to connect to an Exchange 2003 server over the Internet using RPC over HTTP without the need for a virtual private network (VPN). This method can be used with Cached Exchange mode, Classic Online mode, or Classic Offline mode.

After reviewing the characteristics of these different Exchange connectivity modes, we'll take a look at typical user scenarios to determine what type of connectivity fits different users.

5.1.1   Cached Exchange mode

As the name implies, Cached Exchange mode stores a cached copy of the user's mailbox on the user's machine in an offline folders .ost file. Optionally, it can also cache folders from the shared Public Folders hierarchy on the Exchange server that the user has designated as favorites by adding them into their personal Public Folders\Favorites hierarchy in the folder list in Outlook. In addition, Cached Exchange mode downloads a copy of the enterprise address book (the global address list or GAL). This offline address book (OAB) allows users to send messages to other people in the organization without the need to make a round-trip to the server to look up the address for a name in the GAL. Outlook will still try to go to the server if the user requests details that are not in the OAB.

Cached Exchange mode has a number of advantages over the connectivity scenarios in earlier Outlook versions. Previously, the basic connectivity model was a client-server model that assumed that the user either had a fast and near flawless network connection or could work offline most of the time and live without the features that weren't available when working offline. Most users will see better performance simply because, in this Cached Exchange mode, most interaction with Outlook data takes place on the local machine. For example, if you read the same message three times, Outlook downloads it from the server just once on the initial download into the cache—not three times, once for each time the message is read. In Cached Exchange mode, Outlook downloads and uploads new and updated items and sends outgoing messages automatically in the background while the user is online. Outlook needs a direct connection to the Exchange server only to access other users' mailboxes and Public Folders that are not in the user's Public Folders\Favorites hierarchy, to perform a free/busy lookup, or to get GAL details that are not included in the OAB.

Note: Being online and being connected to the network are two different states. It is possible to be connected to the network and yet working offline, at least where Outlook is concerned. In Cached Exchange mode, the user can switch Outlook to an offline state or, in Classic Offline mode, start Outlook offline. The online or offline state determines whether Outlook will send and receive messages essentially continuously (online) or only on a schedule or when the user manually starts a send/receive session by pressing F9 (offline). A user may choose to work offline in order to have more control, through the Send/Receive settings, over which folders will download headers only and which will download full items—or none at all.

A good way to keep these concepts straight is to distinguish the machine's network state—connected or disconnected—from the Outlook application state—online or offline.

Cached Exchange mode's greatest contribution to user productivity, though, is the ability to switch between working online and offline without restarting Outlook. This makes it possible to unplug from the network, move to a new location, reconnect to the network, and start using Outlook again immediately. This is a benefit even for stationary users: if the office network goes down for a few minutes, Cached Exchange mode users can continue working on whatever they're doing in Outlook without skipping a beat.

Note: The classic demonstration of this feature at conferences is to cut the network cable with a large pair of scissors. It's always an applause getter!

Where Exchange 2003 is the server, another improvement aimed at users with less-than-perfect network connections is that Outlook adjusts the way that it downloads data from the server in Cached Exchange mode, depending on the available bandwidth and network latency. On slow networks or those with delays, Outlook can download message headers first so that the user can begin reviewing new items as Outlook continues to download message bodies and attachments as a background task. When used with Exchange 2003, Outlook 2003 also downloads most recent items first, rather than the oldest items. Reading the current item is always a foreground task and takes priority.

Cached Exchange mode tries to reduce the amount of traffic transmitted with all versions of Exchange with a feature called Smart Change synchronization. When certain common changes are made to messages, Outlook 2003 synchronizes only a minimum set of attributes. For example, when a user flags a message, Outlook 2003 synchronizes only the attributes related to the flag, not the entire message.

Note: This type of smart synchronization depends on Outlook 2003's being the only client. If the user is also using OWA or Outlook Mobile Access against the same mailbox or is using ActiveSync to make changes on a PDA, then synchronizes with Outlook, any changes made through those clients will require Outlook to synchronize the entire item with the server, not just the modified properties.

According to Microsoft, using Outlook 2003 with Exchange 2003 can result in a 50 to 70 percent reduction in network traffic as compared with Outlook 2002 synchronization with an offline folders file. This improvement is due to additional optimization features, including data compression, buffer packing, the ability to resume an interrupted synchronization session without starting over and to skip bad or virus-quarantine items, and a reduction in the total number of requests for information between client and server.

Another consideration related to Cached Exchange mode is that Outlook 2003's built-in junk mail filter works only in Cached Exchange mode. One of the key features of the client-side junk filter is to allow the user to create safe and blocked senders lists. These lists are used not just by Outlook's junk filter but also by Exchange 2003. If your organization has installed the Intelligent Message Filter (IMF), an add-in for Exchange 2003 that Microsoft provides, each incoming message gets a Spam Confidence Level (SCL) score from the IMF that represents the likelihood that the message is spam. If a message's SCL is lower than a threshold set on the IMF server by the administrator, the IMF passes the message through to the mailbox store. When a message's SCL score is below the store threshold and the Junk E-mail feature is enabled, the IMF checks the sender against the user's blocked senders list, which is stored in the user's mailbox. If the sender is on the list, the message is placed in the user's Junk E-mail folder; otherwise, it goes into the Inbox or into a folder determined by a server-based Rules Wizard rule. Conversely, if a message's SCL exceeds the store threshold, the IMF checks the sender against the safe senders list, which is also stored in the mailbox, and against a list of addresses from the user's Contacts folder. If the sender is not on either of those lists, the message goes into the Junk E-mail folder; otherwise, it goes into the Inbox unless a rule moves it to another folder.

If your organization is not using the IMF and the user is not configured for Cached Exchange mode, Exchange 2003 will still check the message against the user's safe and blocked senders lists, plus the Contacts folder addresses. Even a user who is not working in Cached Exchange mode can take advantage of this server-side junk mail filtering by adding frequent correspondents to their Contacts folder and connecting to the mailbox with OWA to build up safe and blocked senders lists with OWA's Junk Mail feature.

5.1.2   Classic Online mode

Users of past versions of Outlook should be familiar with the Classic Online mode, where the Outlook user connects directly with the Exchange server. Outlook maintains no local cache file in this mode. This configuration is still supported and is the method used when Outlook 2003 is configured to run as an application under Terminal Services. As you'll see in Section 5.1.6, this is also a method suitable for roaming users.

Exchange Recovery mode   Exchange administrators know that situations do occur when a mailbox is accidentally deleted, and it may be more convenient to try to restore data from an .ost file than from the full backup of the Exchange information store on the server. Even if the mailbox store can be recovered after a problem occurs, users probably will need to send and receive mail while recovery is under way, and they may also need access to their calendar, tasks, and contacts.

In past versions of Outlook, all too often when a mailbox was replaced, the user attempted to connect to the new mailbox and found that the .ost file was "orphaned" and no longer usable. The Cached Exchange mode connectivity method in Outlook 2003 includes a new feature called Exchange Recovery mode to prevent this situation. This feature works with any version of Exchange but performs especially well with Exchange 2003, when a recovery storage group is used to recover the mailbox store while users work from a temporary "dial-tone" store that lets them send and receive messages. (See Appendix D for more information on this Exchange 2003 feature.)

If Outlook 2003 starts, tries to make a connection to the Exchange server, and discovers that the server is there but the mailbox is missing or that the mailbox has been replaced, it displays the dialog shown in Figure 5.1. The user can either connect directly to the mailbox, in which case the data in the local .ost file cache will not be available, or can choose to work offline with the .ost file data and not be able to send or receive messages. This preserves the data in the .ost file so that the user can, if necessary, export it to a .pst file and import it later into the restored mailbox.

In most Exchange 2003 scenarios, however, exporting and importing will not be necessary. The first time Outlook starts after the administrator restores the original mailbox, Outlook will automatically switch back into normal Cached Exchange mode, giving the user access to both the data in the .ost file again and the connection to the server for sending and receiving messages and synchronizing other data.

Figure 5.1   *Outlook 2003's Exchange Recovery mode prevents the loss of .ost file data when the Exchange mailbox is being recovered.*

Note: In either of the classic modes, the user must exit and restart Outlook to switch between online and offline operation.

5.1.3   Classic Offline mode

In Classic Offline mode, Outlook synchronizes a local cache, held in an offline folders .ost file, with the data on the server. Outlook uses the .ost file, however, only when the user is working offline. This is one of the biggest distinctions between Classic Offline mode and Cached Exchange mode, in which Outlook always reads from the cache first. A further limitation of Classic Offline mode is that its offline folders .ost file can grow no larger than just under 2 GB, while the default maximum size for a new offline folders file for Exchange 2000 or 2003 in Cached Exchange mode is 20 GB, and the maximum can be set to support even larger .ost files.

One potential advantage that Classic Offline mode offers over Cached Exchange mode is the ability to designate which folders in the mailbox and the Public Folders\Favorites hierarchy Outlook will cache locally. In Cached Exchange mode, Outlook automatically downloads the contents of all mailbox folders and (optionally) Public Folders\Favorites while the user is working online. Although it is possible to use a Send/Receive group to control the folders that Outlook caches if the Cached Exchange mode user always works offline after the initial population of the .ost file, this capability is difficult for the average user to discover and is difficult to manage. If the user has very limited space on the hard drive and a need for tight control of what folders are in the local cache, Classic Offline mode may offer an advantage to the Outlook 2003 user.

5.1.4   POP3 and IMAP4

Exchange also supports POP3 and IMAP4 connections, but these offer limited functionality to the user. A POP3 connection can retrieve only messages in the user's Inbox. An IMAP4 account can access any message folder in the user's mailbox or in the Public Folders hierarchy. Users connecting to an Exchange mailbox with POP3 or IMAP4 can still exchange meeting and task requests with other Exchange users and access the GAL through the Lightweight Directory Access Protocol (LDAP) if the administrator makes it available, but users will not have free/busy lookup or access to data in nonmail folders. As usually implemented, POP3 and IMAP4 are less secure mail protocols because passwords are sent as clear text.

Cached Exchange mode offers a better and more secure experience to these users, even in poor-network-connection scenarios. However, POP3 or IMAP4 may be the only supported option if the user needs to connect to more than one Exchange server in a single mail profile.

5.1.5 Outlook Web Access with HTTP

As noted above, we're not going to cover OWA in this book since it is a browser-based application and not technically part of Outlook 2003. It is possible, although not supported, to add an HTTP account to Outlook 2003 and provide the URL credentials and login information for an Exchange 2000 or 2003 mailbox. Outlook can then access the mail (but not contacts or other types of items) from an Exchange account, in a way similar to how an IMAP4 account would work.

5.1.6 Typical user scenarios

Most Exchange users fall into one of four categories, illustrated in Figure 5.2, to distinguish them by their use of one or multiple computers and by whether they're usually in the office or often working from some other location.

- *Stationary*—Always working at the same computer (desktop or laptop) in the office

- *Roaming*—Working at different computers, depending on the day or shift, but always in the office

Figure 5.2
Your organization may include all of these different types of users.

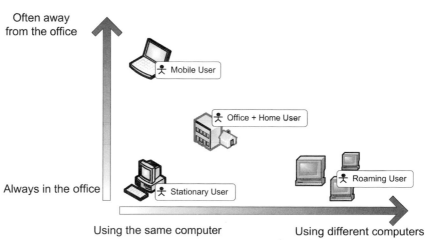

- *Office + Home*—Sometimes working in the office, usually at the same computer, sometimes working from home

- *Mobile*—Working on a portable computer, sometimes in the office, sometimes outside the office

Note that the first two user types always connect to the Exchange server over the office network. The other types of users connect, at least some of the time, from outside the office network. If you have Exchange 2003, you have the option of supporting RPC over HTTP. Otherwise, unless they use OWA, these users will need either direct dialup access to your network or an Internet-based connection via a VPN.

For some of these user scenarios, there is one best Outlook 2003 configuration. For others, there is more than one good solution. We'll briefly review the most appropriate connectivity for each type of user.

The stationary user

The stationary user sits at the same computer every day and can take full advantage of Cached Exchange mode, maintaining a local cache of the Exchange mailbox and favorite Public Folders on the local machine. Unless there is a problem with low disk space, no other connectivity mode does as good a job for this type of user. In a low-disk-space scenario, Classic Online mode would be the best choice if the full feature set of Outlook is needed. (Otherwise, you might consider using OWA.)

The roaming user

The roaming user sits at different computers throughout the week but needs access to the same data at each location. It would be very inefficient, both in network bandwidth and local storage, to maintain an offline folders file for the roaming user on each machine or in the user's home data directory on the network server. Therefore, one good solution for this user is Classic Online mode, with no offline folders file, using a roaming Windows profile to ensure that the user's Outlook profile is available on each machine where the user logs on, along with the other basic application data that you learned about in Chapter 1, such as signatures and the nickname cache file.

Another solution, compatible with fairly low-end desktop computers, would be to access Outlook via Terminal Services. In this case, no data is stored locally. The program runs on the server, and the data remains in the Exchange mailbox and public folder store. Yet another option would be OWA, where the user accesses the mailbox through a browser.

The office + home user

The challenge for the office + home user is to gain access to the same data both from a machine in the office and from one or more machines outside the office that may or may not be under your organization's control. Depending on the backend configuration, this user may have RPC over HTTP available for the external connection or may need to use a direct dialup connection or a VPN. It may not be possible to have a full-time connection from outside the office.

If the office usage is all from one machine, then Exchange Cached mode is the preferred connectivity for that machine.

Otherwise, the in-the-office part of this scenario is similar to that of the roaming user, where Classic Online mode may work best. For the connection from outside the office, Cached Exchange mode will work best as it allows full access to the data even when a full-time connection is not available. (OWA is also a potential solution if full Outlook functionality is not needed.)

The mobile user

The mobile user is more likely to be working in a disconnected state, especially if the user travels a great deal and will definitely want to use Cached Exchange mode in order to have data available in Outlook at any time, in any place, with new data being downloaded at a pace appropriate for the network connection.

5.2   Configuring Cached Exchange mode

Cached Exchange mode is on by default when a user creates a new Outlook mail profile that includes Exchange, except in a Terminal Server environment. Issues related to Cached Exchange mode generally fall into one of three categories:

- Data storage and synchronization

- Address book access and storage

- Application responsiveness in other areas

This section explores those issues and suggests optimal settings and other strategies for dealing with them.

5.2.1   Data storage and synchronization

Each Outlook 2003 user with Cached Exchange mode will be downloading the entire contents of his or her Exchange mailbox and the OAB to the local hard drive upon starting Outlook for the first time. You probably don't want everyone in your organization to do that on the same day! Instead, you can use the Custom Installation Wizard (CIW) or Custom Maintenance Wizard (CMW) from the ORK to create a custom .prf file, as described in Chapter 3, with the Cached Exchange mode option enabled (see Figure 5.3). With this option you can enable Cached Exchange mode for your users in phases by deploying that .prf file to groups of users, rather than everyone at once.

When creating an .mst transform file with the CIW, a .cmw file with the CMW, or a .prf file with either tool, you can control how Cached Exchange mode will operate. By default, Outlook will download full items when connected via a fast connection (faster than 128 Kbps) and headers only when connected via a slow connection (slower than 128 Kbps). If the mailbox is on an Exchange 2003 server, you can modify this default behavior using the

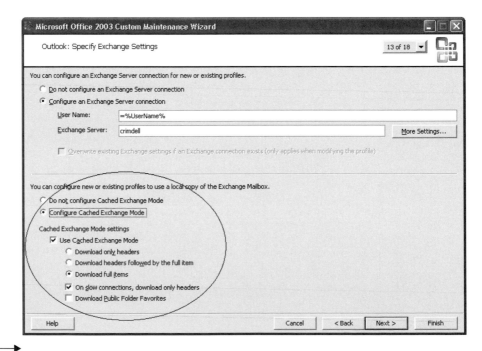

Figure 5.3   *When creating an Outlook profile with the CIW, you can control Cached Exchange mode settings.*

settings in Figure 5.3, for instance, always to download full items (even on slow connections) or to download headers first and then full items.

When users have Public Folders marked as Favorite, you can also choose to have these favorites made available offline with Cached Exchange mode. Keep in mind that this adds extra initial network traffic and that the building of the cache could take a while, especially when the folders are large in size.

Note: In some cases, even though Outlook is on a slow link and should be downloading headers, it seems to download full items. For example, if you have multiple machines connected together on a 10-MB local area network (LAN) sharing a slow Internet connection via Internet Connection Sharing, Outlook will see that the connection to the LAN is 10 MB and not realize that the connection to the Exchange server is really 56 Kbps. You can verify whether or not Outlook realizes that it's on a slow connection by looking in the lower right corner of the status bar. It should report "connected (headers)" while you're on the slow connection. If it reports that you're in "header" mode and is still downloading full items, then one of two things is likely happening.

- A mailbox rule is processing all incoming messages and is requesting a property that's not included in the header.

- An add-in is doing some sort of processing on inbound items via the Outlook object model. Likely culprits include virus scanners, anti-spam products, and synchronization software. In this case, you can disable any COM add-ins that interact with Outlook data; see Section 6.6.1. For testing purposes, you can also start Outlook 2003 with the command-line switch `/safe` or `/safe:3` to prevent any Exchange client extensions from loading.

5.2.2 Cached Exchange Mode optimization

To optimize Cached Exchange mode, Outlook uses a timing method for synchronization. By default Outlook uploads local changes to a message to the server after 15 seconds. If within 15 seconds another local change occurs, this timer is restarted. When multiple changes are made and each change is within the 15-second period, in theory Outlook may hold off synchronization for a long time because the timer gets reset each time. To make sure this doesn't happen, an upload will also occur 60 seconds after the first change if Outlook notices that changes haven't been uploaded yet.

By default, Outlook downloads server changes, for instance when a new message arrives, 30 seconds after Outlook is notified of this change by the Exchange server. If more server-side changes occur within these 30 seconds, they will be downloaded together with the first change.

You can adjust these timings by deploying three registry entries:

Key: `HKEY_CURRENT_USER\Software\Policies\Microsoft\Office\11.0\Outlook\Cached Mode`
Value name: `Upload`
Value type: `REG_DWORD`
Default value: `0000000f` (15 seconds)

Value name: `Download`
Value type: `REG_DWORD`
Default value: `0000001e` (30 seconds)

Value name: `Maximum`
Value type: `REG_DWORD`
Default value: `0000003c` (60 seconds)

Note: These registry values can be added to the group policy editor with the Outlk11.adm administrative template file for Service Pack 1 (SP1).

On a really slow network, it may seem like it takes a long time before the first inbox headers start appearing after Outlook is started. This is because a complex handshake is going on between the client and server when Outlook first starts up and connects with the Exchange server. Over a really slow link, such as a normal mobile phone connection, this could take more than a minute.

On first use of Outlook with Cached Exchange mode enabled, the synchronization of the folders occurs in the following order:

1.   Utility folders (common views, views, and security settings)

2.   Calendar

3.   Contacts

4.   Drafts

5.   Inbox

6.   All other folders (defined by the user)

7.   Sent Items

8.   Deleted Items

9.   Public Folder\Favorites (added by the user)

After this initial synchronization, Outlook will learn and eventually change the priority on the folders so that the folder used most frequently is synchronized first.

5.2.3 Address Book access and storage

In addition to the data in the user's mailbox, Outlook 2003 in Cached Exchange mode also automatically downloads the offline address book (OAB) from the Exchange Server. This address book contains the bulk of the information from the GAL that Outlook users access most often. Users can, for example, use the OAB to look up colleagues' phone numbers or add them as recipients in e-mail messages and meeting requests. The Exchange administrator can configure the OAB for each mailbox store to contain either all of the entries in the GAL or a subset and also control how often the OAB is updated, usually according to a fixed schedule. On the client side, the OAB download options can be configured by the user in the Send/Receive settings or deployed by using the CIW or CMW, as described in Chapter 3. Figure 5.4 shows the available settings for a Send/Receive group.

The default setting is for Outlook to download the OAB automatically approximately every 24 hours. In an Exchange environment where the OAB is updated more frequently on the server, you may want to have Outlook download the OAB more often. (However, Microsoft recommends that this capability be used rarely—primarily when the OAB is relatively small.) You can accomplish this by modifying the Send/Receive group settings either at Outlook deployment using the CIW or after deployment using the CMW. In the settings for the All Accounts Send/Receive group, under the When Outlook is Online heading, check the box for "Schedule an automatic Send/Receive every" and provide the number of minutes in the scheduling interval. Figure 5.5 shows the All Accounts Send/Receive group set to perform a send/receive every two hours. This will download any changes in the OAB made since the last send/receive.

Figure 5.4
The way the OAB updates is controlled by the Send/Receive settings.

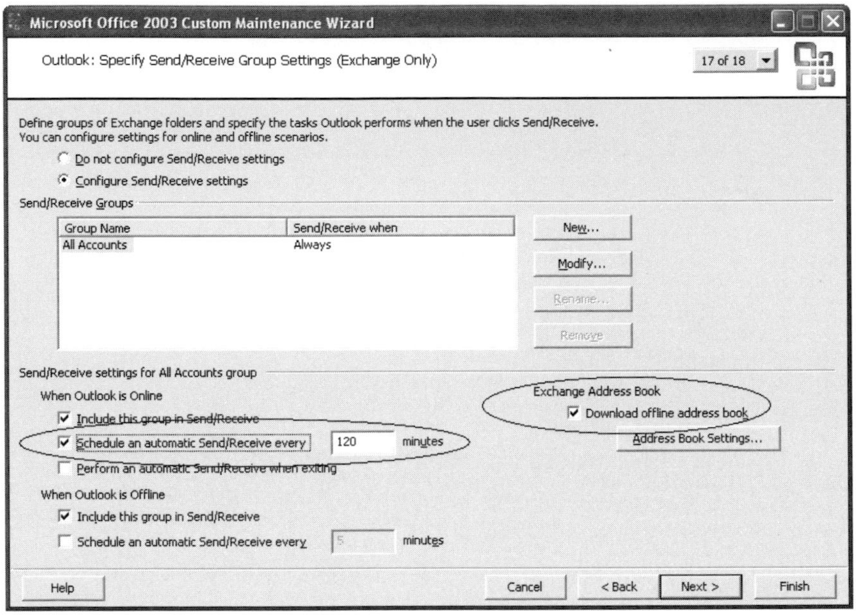

Figure 5.5　*Download the OAB every two hours.*

Normally updates to the OAB are small and do not cause a lot of network traffic. When the update of the OAB is larger than one-eighth of the total size of the OAB, clients will download the full OAB instead of an update. Downloading the OAB in full can cause high network usage.

Note: Microsoft Knowledge Base article 839826, "High network usage occurs while Outlook clients download the offline Address Book from Exchange 2003 at the same time," describes a number of scenarios that can trigger full OAB downloads. When your network experiences high usage because of many full OAB downloads, Exchange 2003 with SP1 installed allows you to protect the network from future overloads by modifying the registry on the Exchange server. Microsoft Knowledge Base article 867623, "Throttling full offline Address Book downloads to limit the effect on a LAN in Exchange Server 2003," describes this setting. You can use the MSExchangeIS Performance Monitor counter "OAB: Full downloads bytes/sec" to determine if the companywide download of the OAB is indeed the cause of a network overload.

Table 5.1   *OAB Files*

File Name	Description
Details.oab	Contains all of the object details (those that were included in generation of the OAB) except for display name. This file is not present in a no-details OAB.
Browse.oab	This is the core file. It contains the object type, display name, and a pointer into the Details.oab for each object.
Rdndex.oab	This is an index for resolving parental and relative distinguished names.
Anrdex.oab	This is an index for resolving ambiguous names.
Pdndex.oab	This file allows expansion of the PDN table during differential downloads of the OAB and holds changes to domain names.
Tmplts.oab	This file contains the dialog box strings and any information that is static in accordance with the OAB. This file does not increase in size if you add additional objects to your directory.

The OAB consists of five or six files that can be found in the %USER-PROFILE%\Local Settings\Application Data\Microsoft\Outlook folder. Table 5.1 lists the OAB files and their purpose. When the OAB is in Unicode format, the name of the file will have a "U" in front of it (e.g., Udetails.oab). The OAB will be in Unicode format only if the user connects to an Exchange 2003 server, and the Cached Exchange mode offline folders .ost file is in Unicode format.

To change the OAB download behavior after the initial download, you need to delete all of the .oab files, then implement this registry value:

```
Key: HKEY_CURRENT_USER\Software\Policies\Microsoft\
Office\11.0\Outlook\Cached Mode
Value name: DownloadOAB
Value type: REG_DWORD
Value:  0 =  Do not download the OAB automatically.
        1 =  Always use the Download Full Items mode (default).
        2 =  When the Cached Exchange download mode is set to
             Header only, perform a differential OAB update.
        3 =  Download the OAB and a differential update
```

After you delete the OAB files and set DownloadOAB to one of the nonzero values, the next automatic or manual synchronization with the server will download new copies of the OAB files.

To provide a manageable download, the OAB does not contain and does not support relationship-related lookups and is missing some properties. When users access the following information, Outlook will attempt to get it from the server if Outlook is connected to the Exchange server:

- Information about managers and direct reports from the Organization tab of the address-entry Properties dialog

- Information about distribution and security-group membership from the Member Of tab of the address-entry Properties dialog

- Custom address book properties

For users who are not connected to the server, the Organization and Member Of tabs will display no information because the pointers that keep track of organizational relationships and group membership are not included in the OAB. When users who are connected to the server switch to one of those tabs, they may experience a slight delay as Outlook makes a call to the server to look up the information.

Tip: Because custom properties require a trip to the server, the Exchange administrator should not modify the address-entry display template to show custom properties on the General tab, which is the tab that appears first when the user displays the details of an entry in the GAL. Any time a custom property is present on a display-template page, Outlook will try to retrieve that property information from the server.

As you saw in Figure 4.4, when setting up the download of the OAB as part of the user's profile, you can choose between Full Details or No Details. The full-details OAB, which is the default, includes digital-certificate information needed to encrypt messages to other GAL users. At first, Outlook will look in the Active Directory for another user's digital certificate. When a connection to the Active Directory cannot be made, Outlook will use the OAB.

When resolving and verifying names and addresses, the OAB checks fewer properties of a contact than the GAL. Table 5.2 lists the properties available from the OAB and those available by default from the online GAL.

If you have a specific need always to use the GAL when resolving names to actual addresses, you can force Outlook to do this by modifying the registry as follows:

```
Key: HKEY_CURRENT_USER\Software\Policies\Microsoft\
Office\11.0\Outlook\Cached Mode
Value name: ANR Include Online GAL
Value type: REG_DWORD
Value: 1 = enabled, 0 = disabled
```

5.2.4 Other Cached Exchange Mode recommendations

Because Cached Exchange mode depends on the local .ost file cache, the performance of that cache is critical to a good user experience. While the new Unicode .ost format defaults to a maximum size of 20 GB, Microsoft cautions that large .ost files of more than 1 GB or more than 5,000 items per folder may show reduced performance. The most certain approach to controlling the .ost size is to limit the Exchange mailbox size with settings on the server and to use the default setting so as not to download users' Public Folders\Favorites hierarchy to their local cache. Downloading Public Folders\Favorites is one of the settings the administrator can control with the settings in the CIW (screen 18) or CMW (screen 13) for configuring Outlook mail profiles, which you saw in Chapter 3.

Table 5.2   *Fields Available for Name Resolution*

Active Directory Property	Description	Available in OAB	Available in Online GAL
displayName	Display name	X	X
mail	SMTP address		X
givenName	First name		X
legacyExchangeDN	Distinguished name for backward compatibility with older Exchange systems		X
mailNickname	Exchange alias name	X	X
physicalDeliveryOfficeName	Office name	X	X
proxyAddresses	All e-mail addresses for the user		X
name	LDAP common name		X
sAMAccountName	Windows NT 4.0 logon name		X
Sn	Surname	X	X

How do you estimate how large an .ost file will result from a given mailbox? The .ost file will generally be larger than the mailbox size. A good starting assumption would be that the .ost file will be 25 percent larger than the mailbox; however, a better approach would be to test with some mailboxes that are typical both in size and content (messages versus files) for your organization.

Each new Outlook 2003 mail profile that uses Exchange will have Cached Exchange mode turned on by default. When the user starts Outlook, a new .ost file will be created, and Outlook will begin populating it with the contents of the mailbox. Since this creates network traffic and potentially uses up a lot of hard drive space, especially if the user is also downloading Public Folders\Favorites, you may want to block the user from creating a new profile. Chapter 6 explains how to do this with the "Prevent users from making changes to Outlook profiles" Group Policy setting.

It is not recommended to use Cached Exchange mode on more than one machine. In other words, if you have roaming users, their Outlook profiles should not be set up for Cached Exchange mode because of the number of changes Cached Mode needs to make when you haven't been on a machine for a long time. As a result, the startup of Outlook will take longer and could cause a lot of network traffic. A situation where it would be appropriate to use Cached Exchange mode on more than one machine is when a user works at both a desktop computer and on a laptop. In that scenario, the user can have the daily performance advantages on the desktop and also be able to travel with the mailbox.

By default, Outlook informs the end user about Exchange connectivity status by displaying pop-up warning messages like the following:

- Network problems are preventing connection to the Microsoft Exchange Server *servername*.

- Outlook is trying to retrieve data from the Microsoft Exchange Server computer.

- Outlook is preparing a local copy of your Exchange mailbox. This one-time process may take several minutes to complete. Some of your data may not be shown until the process is complete.

You can configure the type of warning message being displayed with regards to Exchange connectivity. As Figure 5.6 shows, these settings can be set with the Change Office User Settings screen in the CIW or CMW and control these registry values:

Key: HKEY_CURRENT_USER\ Software\Microsoft\Office\11.0\ Outlook\Display Types\Balloons

CIW/CMW display name: Show Network Warnings
Value name: NetWarn
Value type: REG_DWORD
Value: 1 = Enabled (default), 0 = Disabled

CIW/CMW name: Show Exchange Server Messages
Value name: Exchange
Value type: REG_DWORD
Value: 1 = Enabled (default), 0 = Disabled

CIW/CMW name: Show Network Connectivity Changes
Value name: NetConn
Value type: REG_DWORD
Value: 1 = Enabled (default), 0 = Disabled

The "Time before notifying . . ." options shown in Figure 5.6 can also be controlled with the Group Policy Editor, as well as with the CIW or CMW.

If you are using Windows Rights Management (described in detail in Chapter 6) to protect e-mail messages and attachments, Microsoft recom-

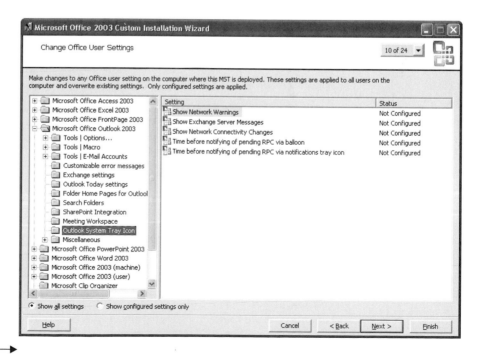

Figure 5.6   *Setting the Exchange connectivity warnings in the CIW.*

mends that you set Outlook 2003 Cached Exchange mode clients so that they automatically retrieve user licenses for Outlook messages, instead of prompting the user each time. This option is available both as a Group Policy setting and in the CIW and CMW. In the Group Policy Editor, navigate to User Configuration/Administrative Templates/Microsoft Office Outlook 2003/Miscellaneous. The setting is named "Do not download permission for e-mail during offline Exchange folder sync" and appears in a similar location on the Change Office User Settings screen (screen 12 in the CIW and screen 7 in the CMW). Microsoft's recommendation is to enable the setting and leave the "Check to disable download of permission" box unchecked. As a Group Policy setting, this controls the following registry value:

```
Key: HKEY_CURRENT_USER\Software\Policies\Microsoft\
Office\11.0\Common\Drm
Value name: DoNotAcquireDRMLicenseOnSync
Value type: REG_DWORD
Value: 1 = Enabled, 0 = Disabled (default)
```

The key for a user-preference option set with the CIW or CMW is as follows:

```
HKEY_CURRENT_USER\Software\Microsoft\Office\11.0\
Common\Drm
```

5.3   Configuring Exchange 2003 RPC over HTTP

Outlook uses remote procedure calls (RPCs) to communicate with the Exchange server. RPC over HTTP is a connectivity method available only between Outlook 2003 and Exchange 2003 that provides a secure way for Outlook to connect to the Exchange server over the Internet without the need for a VPN and without opening potential vulnerabilities in the firewall that protects your organization from electronic intrusions. With previous versions of Outlook, remote users who connected to an Exchange server had to rely on a VPN connection. Since a VPN requires a special configuration and TCP/IP ports to be opened, a VPN connection cannot always be made in a locked-down network. RPC over HTTP allows remote users to make a connection to the Exchange server via HTTP so that wherever they can browse the Internet, they can make an Exchange connection.

More precisely, the technology is often called RPC over HTTPS, because a Secure Sockets Layer (SSL) connection is strongly recommended. In that scenario, Outlook 2003 will not be able to connect unless the server's SSL certificate is valid, and the Outlook client computer has a copy of the certificate in the client's trusted-root certification authority or the certificate is derived from a trusted-root authority such as Verisign or Entrust.

You can use RPC over HTTP to connect to Exchange in Cached Exchange mode, Classic Online mode, or Classic Offline mode. The RPC over HTTP proxy server operates as an Exchange front-end server normally would, supporting pass-through authentication and delivering messages and other data to your back-end Exchange servers. In addition, it can also handle lookups for the Global Address List and pass them along to your Global Catalog (GC) server. (The GC server is a special domain controller in an Active Directory network that contains a copy of all objects in every domain in the forest, that is, in your entire network, but stores only those attributes used in the most common queries.)

Note: If you have only one Exchange Server in your organization, it is possible to configure it to accept RPC over HTTP connections; however, the more common and recommended topology is to use separate front-end and back-end servers. Information on setting up Exchange 2003 to support RPC over HTTP can be found in Appendix D.

You saw the basic configuration for RPC over HTTP connectivity in Chapter 3.

For best results when deploying RPC over HTTP, upgrade client computers to at least Windows XP Service Pack 2 (SP2). SP2 corrects some issues with RPC over HTTP performance or failure. If your organization has not yet deployed SP2, client computers will at least require the Windows hotfix described in Microsoft Knowledge Base article 331320, "Outlook 2003 Performs Slowly or Stops Responding When Connected to Exchange Server 2003 Through HTTP." SP2 is strongly recommended because it provides a much more secure desktop environment.

Tip: To provide security, RPC over HTTP uses SSL. A certificate must be installed on the server that is running the RPC proxy service. This certificate must be validated by a trusted certificate authority. A connection will fail when the connecting client computer doesn't recognize that certificate authority or when the certificate is misconfigured on the server. If you are using an internal-root certificate authority, then each client will need the certificate installed. This is usually done by exporting a .cer file from the certificate authority, then saving it and running it on the client computer.

Note that while the symptoms (i.e., inability to complete the connection) will appear on the client, the issue must be resolved on the server. Lack-of-connectivity symptoms on the client may also occur if there are problems with the front-end/back-end server configuration.

5.3.1   Proxy configuration

RPC over HTTP is designed mainly for users who connect to an Exchange server that is not on the local network. Therefore, you'll generally want it to try to use the Internet (HTTP) first before the LAN (TCP/IP). The default setting, however, is to attempt to connect with TCP/IP first. You can easily change this option when configuring a mail profile by using the CIW or CMW, as described in Chapter 3 and depicted in Figure 5.7. This modifies the RPCoverHTTPflags option in the .prf file.

To display the dialog shown in Figure 5.7, navigate to screen 18 in the CIW or screen 13 in the CMW, Outlook: Specify Exchange Settings, and click the More Settings button.

5.3.2   Deleted-item recovery

Users who are connected to an Exchange server with RPC over HTTP basically have the same functionality as they would on a direct LAN connec-

Figure 5.7
Customizing Exchange proxy settings for RPC over HTTP.

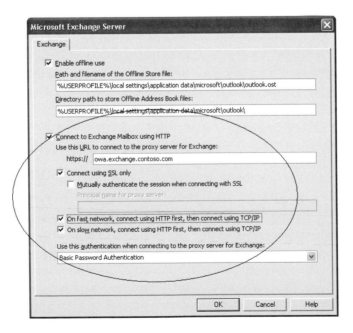

tion, including access to the deleted-item recovery feature, assuming it has been configured on the server. In some cases, however, the Recover Deleted Items option may not be available on Outlook's Tools menu even though it has been enabled on the server. This seems to be especially true when connecting to Microsoft Small Business Server.

You can enable the Recover Deleted Items option by modifying the registry value on the client computer:

```
Key: HKEY_LOCAL_MACHINE\SOFTWARE\Microsoft\Exchange\
Client\Options
Value name: DumpsterAlwaysOn
Value type: REG_DWORD
Value: 1 = Enabled (default), 0 = Disabled
```

This will allow the user to recover Outlook items that the user deletes after the DumpsterAlwaysOn registry value is set to 1. Items deleted earlier cannot be recovered.

5.3.3 Preventing fallback to RPC over TCP/IP

In Figure 5.6, you saw Outlook configured to attempt to connect with RPC over HTTP first, then to fall back to RPC over TCP/IP. If you use this setting to test RPC over HTTP in a corporate environment, Outlook will probably connect fine—even if something is wrong with the RPC over HTTP configuration—because it falls back successfully to RPC over TCP/IP. To test your organization's RPC over HTTP setup, therefore, you may want to disable, at least temporarily, the TCP/IP fallback. You can use this registry value to accomplish that:

```
Key: HKEY_CURRENT_USER\Software\Microsoft\Office\11.0\
Outlook\RPC
Value name: DisableRpcTcpFallback
Value type: REG_DWORD
Value: 0 = Fall back normally from TCP to HTTP or HTTP to TCP (default);
       1 = Disable fall back; if start with HTTP, only use HTTP. If start with
           TCP, only use TCP
```

5.4 Connecting to a new Exchange server

When you move a mailbox within the same Exchange organization or administrative group to a different mail server, Outlook automatically updates the client mail profile to reflect the new mailbox location when Outlook starts for the first time after the move. This automatic referral mechanism does not work when you move a mailbox out of its Exchange organization or administrative group, as you would when migrating from an Exchange 5.5 server to Exchange 2003. For such scenarios, Microsoft provides the Exchange Profile Update tool, also known as ExProfRe. This command-line tool allows you to update a client's mail profile and reset only the parts of the profile that reflect the move of the mailbox. To download the tool and obtain detailed information on how to use it, see Microsoft Knowledge Base article 873214, "How to Use the Exchange Profile Update Tool." This tool, which needs to be run for each user—for example, through a login script—makes a backup of the user's default mail profile and makes these changes to the user's configuration:

- Renames the .xml file that controls the navigation behavior from *<profile name>*.xml to *<profile name>*.exprofre. (This behavior can be suppressed with the `/f` command-line switch.)

- Deletes the .oab files for the OAB and resets Outlook to look for a new set of .oab files on the server. (This behavior can be suppressed with the `/a` command-line switch.)

- Deletes the most recently used list of other mailboxes seen in the File | Open | Other User's Folder dialog.

- Clears the .nk2 nickname cache for the profile if the `/n` command-line switch is specified.

Another thing to take into consideration when you move mailboxes from an Exchange 5.5 server to an Exchange 2000 or 2003 server is that the offline folders .ost file will still be in the old ANSI format that is subject to the 2-GB size limit. As long as the .ost file is in ANSI format, Outlook will also download the ANSI version of the OAB.

To force Outlook to create an .ost file in the new Unicode .ost file format, you can set a user-preference option in the CIW or CMW or use a Group Policy Object (GPO). The Group Policy setting is located under User Configuration/Administrative Templates/Microsoft Office Outlook 2003/Exchange Settings and in a similar location on the Change Office User Settings screen (screen 10 in the CIW and screen 7 in the CMW). For the Exchange Unicode Mode—Ignore OST Format setting, you will see the three choices listed in Table 5.3 and shown in Figure 5.8.

The Group Policy setting sets a value in this key:

```
HKEY_CURRENT_USER\Software\Policies\Microsoft\Office\
11.0\Outlook\EMSP
```

Table 5.3   *Options for Exchange Unicode Mode—Ignore OST Format*

Option	Description	IgnoreOSTFormat Value
OST format determines mode	Outlook leaves the .ost file as it is.	0
Create new OST if format doesn't match mode	If the .ost file doesn't match the server type, Outlook creates and populates a new .ost file to match the server type (Unicode for Exchange 2000/2003, ANSI for earlier versions).	1
Prompt to create new OST if format doesn't match mode	If the .ost file doesn't match the server type, Outlook prompts the user to create a new .ost file to match the server type each time Outlook starts.	2

Figure 5.8
Forcing OST format by using GPOs.

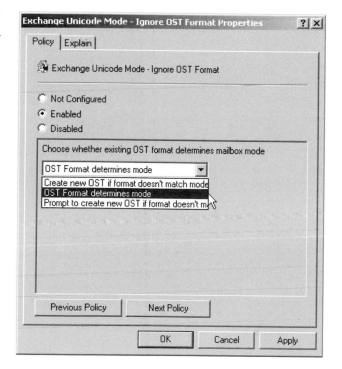

---

while the user-preference setting in the CIW or CMW sets a value in

```
HKEY_CURRENT_USER\Software\Microsoft\Office\11.0\
Outlook\EMSP
Value name: IgnoreOSTFormat
Value type: REG_DWORD
Value key: 0 (default), 1, 2
```

A post-SP1 hotfix is required to make Outlook correctly detect the IgnoreOSTFormat value. (By the time you read this, it may be included in the most recent Office 2003 service pack.) For information on this hotfix, see Microsoft Knowledge Base article 892089, "An Outlook 2003 Group Policy Setting That Forces Outlook Clients to Only Use a Unicode Offline Folder Is Not Applied Correctly."

This hotfix also adds a new registry value to enable Outlook to create an .ost file in the desired format without prompting the user:

```
Key: HKEY_CURRENT_USER\Software\Policies\Microsoft\
Office\11.0\Outlook\EMSP
Value name: SilentOSTFormatChange
Value type: REG_DWORD
Value: 1 (enabled) or 0 (disabled)
```

If you use a GPO to force Outlook to generate a new Unicode .ost file, you may want to filter the GPO so that not all users will change to the new .ost file format at the same time and cause a performance hit on the Exchange server.

5.5   Miscellaneous Exchange issues

In this section, we discuss several settings that can help resolve particular common problems that Outlook 2003 users with Exchange accounts may experience:

- Lack of new-mail notifications

- Locating a Global Catalog server

- Default mail account switching to Exchange

5.5.1   Managing new-mail notifications

New-mail notification packets are transmitted by the Exchange server with Universal Datagram Packets (UDP). When Outlook starts, it automatically chooses a port in the range of 1023 to 65535 to receive UDP packets and tells the server the port and the IP address of the machine where Outlook is running. If, however, this port is blocked—for example, by a firewall—Outlook users will not automatically receive notification of new messages. They may also see Outlook freeze if the Find feature is invoked. The solution to this problem is to specify a fixed port that Outlook will use for UDP.

To specify a fixed port, create this value:

```
Key: HKEY_CURRENT_USER\Software\Microsoft\Office\11.0\
Outlook\RPC
Value name: FixedUDPPort
Value type: REG_DWORD
Value: (Decimal value of the port you want to use, e.g., 10000)
```

Tip: FixedUDPPort can take a value between 1023 and 65535. If the UDP port is in use by another program, Microsoft Outlook 2003 will acquire another port in the ephemeral range (1023 to 5000) to be used in registering for notification events from Exchange. Therefore, you may want to try setting a value for FixedUDPPort greater than 5000.

Also note that Windows XP SP2 turns on its built-in firewall by default. In an enterprise environment where all connectivity is through the local network, it can safely be disabled, assuming the organization has its own firewall. If the organization does not have a firewall or if the user is using a machine that also connects to the Internet directly, you should leave the firewall enabled but make an exception for Outlook.exe to allow communication via the chosen UDP port.

5.5.2   Controlling the Global Catalog server

As you learned earlier in this chapter, the GC server is a special domain controller in an Active Directory network that contains a copy of all objects in your entire network but stores only the most commonly used attributes. Outlook needs to connect to a GC server in order to locate the server containing the user's Exchange mailbox. In some situations, especially where the Outlook client is remote from either the GC or Exchange server, you may want to force Outlook to use either the closest GC server or a specific GC server.

To make Outlook locate and use the closest GC, apply this registry value:

```
Key: HKEY_CURRENT_USER\Software\Microsoft\Exchange\
Exchange Provider
Value name: Closest GC
```

Value type: `REG_DWORD`
Value: `1`

To specify a GC, apply this registry value:

Key: `HKEY_CURRENT_USER\Software\Microsoft\Exchange\`
`Exchange Provider`
Value name: `DS Server`
Value type: `REG_SZ`
Value: Fully qualified domain name of the GC server, for example,
`myserver.mydomain.com`

5.5.3 Managing the default mail account in Small Business Server 2003

If the Exchange server is running on Microsoft SBS 2003, users with non-Exchange accounts in the same profile as the Exchange account may see the default mail account always revert to the Exchange account, regardless of the user's previous choice. A registry entry is available to prevent the SBS login script from changing the transport order:

Key: `HKLM\Software\Microsoft\SmallBusinessServer\`
`ClientSetup`
Value name: `NoTransportOrder`
Value type: `REG_DWORD`
Value: `1`

5.6   Summary

This chapter has discussed Exchange account configuration in Outlook and its improvements compared with previous versions. You have learned about the various ways that a user can connect to an Exchange server and the advantages of various connectivity methods for different types of users.

You have also learned that the way in which Cached Exchange mode is deployed can have a direct impact on your network's performance and the user's interaction with Outlook and should therefore be carefully considered. You can change the way the synchronization occurs and how the OAB is downloaded.

Configuring RPC over HTTP can, in most cases, replace the VPN connection to your corporate network to enable Exchange availability from the Internet. A good RPC over HTTP configuration also can increase the responsiveness of Outlook on a slow network.

The new Unicode format for offline folders .ost files in Cached Exchange mode is also an important change that should be taken into account when mailboxes are being switched from an Exchange 5.5 server to an Exchange 2000 or 2003 server. Updating the mail profile of the Outlook client after a mailbox has been moved to a different Exchange organization or administrative group can be automated by using the Exchange Profile Update tool.

Additional Exchange registry settings are described in Appendix A.

6

Locking Down Outlook

In an era where virus-carrier and spam messages outweigh the volume of legitimate e-mail messages, mail administrators have been supportive of Microsoft's efforts since 2000 to add security features to Outlook. This chapter covers how to use those features to make Microsoft Outlook a safe and secure e-mail client, including the following:

- Using encryption to protect sensitive e-mails

- Applying security to Personal Folders .pst files

- Protecting message content using Windows Rights Management Services (RMS)

- Configuring the Outlook Junk E-mail Filter and filter lists

- Protecting against malicious e-mail Web content

- Blocking dangerous attachments

- Understanding the protections guarding against malicious programs that automate Outlook to harvest addresses or send messages

6.1   Locking down Outlook—the big picture

Deploying a secure platform for your Outlook users involves examining and responding to threats in three separate categories:

- Threats to information in transit and at rest

- Threats to unwanted information dissemination

- Threats to incoming e-mail, including spam

Besides securing the Outlook client, your messaging security plan should also consider security for the Exchange server (or other mail server) and the server's base operating system. For information on Windows Server and Exchange Server security, see the references provided in Appendix D.

6.2 Threats to information in transit and at rest

This section discusses threats to outbound Outlook messages sent to recipients inside or outside the user's organization and to Outlook message stores, primarily the .pst file, which is generally stored on a user's computer. (Items in an Exchange Server mailbox are protected by security measures on the server.)

When a user composes and sends e-mail, especially over the Internet, the message is subject to attack by hackers using network monitors, packet sniffers, and other hacking tools. The messages are also vulnerable to attack on your own corporate network. The Simple Mail Transfer Protocol (SMTP), the standard used to deliver most e-mail messages today, was originally developed to carry small, informal types of messages on a private network. SMTP was never designed to carry critical and sensitive information across public, interconnected networks like the Internet.

SMTP sends information across the Internet in a way that allows anyone to read the messages, thus leaving sensitive e-mail subject to attack. The most common method used to prevent these types of attack is encryption of the information. Encryption can take many forms. At the basic network level, you may be able to use network devices or Exchange Server to encrypt all traffic between two points, such as from one Exchange SMTP server to another. This type of encryption is independent of the mail client and does not affect Outlook configuration, so it will not be covered in depth here. Such network encryption can give you some assurance that the e-mail traffic you send between Exchange Server computers in different offices cannot be read by someone other than the intended recipients. On the other hand, such encryption does not guarantee that an attacker who has taken control of a network device or Exchange Server, thereby gaining access to e-mail before it is encrypted, will not be able to read the message.

6.2.1 Understanding S/MIME

To lessen the vulnerability of information within your e-mail network, you can implement end-to-end encryption starting at the Outlook client using the Secure/Multipurpose Internet Mail Extensions (S/MIME) standard. The S/MIME standard provides two basic security services:

- Message encryption
- Digital signatures

Most organizations deploy S/MIME for its message-encryption capability, which performs an encryption operation on a message when it is sent, making the text of the message unreadable. When the recipient of the message reads it, a decryption operation makes the text readable again.

You can think of digital signatures as the digital version of a legal signature on a paper document. Digital signatures validate the identity of the sender of the message, provide nonrepudiation (i.e., the sender cannot deny having sent the message), and ensure data integrity so that the recipient can be certain that the message body has not been tampered with in transit.

Note: A digital signature does not need to match the From address on a message in order to be valid.

Both message encryption and digital signatures are enabled in S/MIME via a mechanism known as *digital certificates*. These digital certificates are the digital equivalents of IDs you might keep in your wallet, such as a driver's license or a birth certificate. Digital certificates are issued to users as a means to prove their identity.

Outlook allows users to import digital certificates for use with S/MIME messages. These digital certificates are issued by a certificate authority (CA). The CA can be private (run by a company for its own purposes) using a public-key infrastructure (PKI) like the one in Windows Server 2003, or it can be public. Public CAs provide public trust and are generally recognized automatically by browsers or e-mail clients like Outlook, Verisign (http://www.verisign.com) and Thawte (http://www.thawte.com) are examples of public CAs that can sell you certificates that they vouch for.

Despite the logical appeal behind it, S/MIME use is not widespread. Most S/MIME implementations deal only with messages sent within an organization. Messages that go to external addresses are not signed or encrypted because without a central directory, it is very hard to exchange the certificates needed to encrypt mail for others. Still, the availability of public CAs certainly makes it possible to build an S/MIME infrastructure that works for both internal and external messages.

6.2.2   Configuring Outlook for S/MIME

Full support in Outlook for S/MIME and X.509 V3 digital certificates was first introduced with Outlook 2000 Service Release 1 (SR-1); they are fully supported in Outlook 2003. When you install Outlook, you have all of the components you need to support S/MIME. The one additional task you will need to perform in order to configure S/MIME V3 is to get digital certificates for your users. As mentioned above, these certificates can be obtained by implementing your own CA using the Windows Server 2003 PKI or by purchasing them from a public CA.

Tip: This chapter does not discuss in depth managing a PKI and generating certificates for S/MIME. If you are using the Windows Server 2003 PKI and your mail server is Microsoft Exchange, ask your PKI administrator to generate and publish the "Exchange User" and "Exchange Signature Only" certificate templates that are included in the Windows Server 2003 PKI.

A recommended practice is to use two certificates per user for S/MIME, one for encryption and one for digital signatures. The encryption private key should be archived in case the user ever loses his or her key pair. This will ensure that encrypted mail can be recovered. In order to ensure non-repudiation, you don't want to back up the other private key used for digital signatures. Also, because digital signatures generally do not add any content that would need to be saved and recovered, you don't really need to archive the private key for recovery.

If you are using the Windows Server 2003 PKI and the client operating system is Windows XP, the best way to deploy S/MIME to users is to use the certificate autoenrollment feature with a Group Policy Object (GPO). You will find the autoenrollment settings properties in the Group Policy Editor under User Configuration/Windows Settings/Security Settings/Public Key Policies, as shown in Figure 6.1. (Chapter 2 explains how to create and modify GPOs.)

In an Exchange environment, the "Exchange User" and "Exchange Signature Only" certificate templates will also have to be configured for autoenrollment. The groups and users targeted for autoenrollment will have to be added to the security configuration of the templates with Read, Enroll, and Autoenroll permissions. Once the PKI administrator has published the two certificate templates, you can create a GPO that will autoenroll user for these certificates.

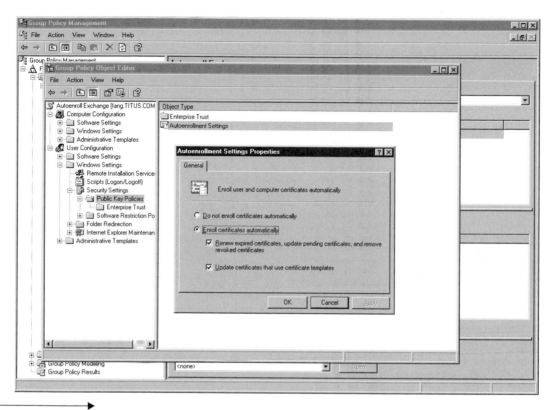

Figure 6.1 *Setting up Group Policy to autoenroll users for certificates.*

After applying the GPO to a group of users (generally via an Active Directory organizational unit), these users will see a pop-up (Figure 6.2) that alerts them to the fact that they have received certificates.

Outlook 2003 will automatically examine the available certificates and use the correct one for digital signatures and for encryption. As a result, once autoenrollment is completed, users are ready to start using S/MIME. They can check their S/MIME in Outlook by choosing Tools | Options,

Figure 6.2
Users are automatically alerted that they have received certificates.

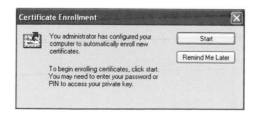

Figure 6.3
Outlook user
S/MIME settings.

then on the Security tab clicking Settings under "Encrypted e-mail." Figure 6.3 shows a screen shot of the resulting dialog.

If you decide to obtain the certificates from a public CA rather than setting up your own CA, you may need to do some additional configuration to make it easy for users to obtain their certificates. Issuers of public certificates such as the Verisign OnSite service will normally ask users to go to a specific Web site to register for their certificates. Outlook users click the Get a Digital ID button on the Security tab in the Tools | Options dialog in Outlook 2003. In order to direct your users to a prearranged Web site, you can configure a GPO to change the URL to which the Get a Digital ID button directs the user. In the Group Policy Editor, go to User Configuration / Administrative Templates / Microsoft Office Outlook 2003 / Tools | Options / Security / Cryptography and select the URL for S/MIME Certificates setting. This setting controls the following registry value:

```
Key: HKEY_CURRENT_USER\Software\Policies\Microsoft\
Office\11.0\Outlook\Security
Value name: EnrollPageURL
Value type: REG_SZ
Value data: URL where the user can obtain an S/MIME certificate
```

Enable this setting, and set its URL parameter to point to the Web page that has been set up by the public CA for our users' enrollment, as shown in Figure 6.4 (The URL can contain %1, %2, and %3, which will be replaced by the user's name, e-mail address, and language respectively.)

The advantage of using a public CA is that Microsoft Outlook automatically trusts certificates issued by most public CAs. This generally means

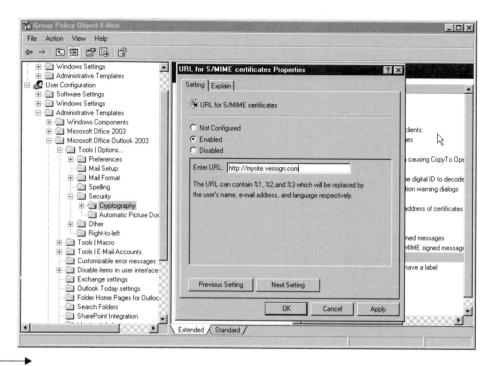

Figure 6.4   *Redirect the Get a Digital ID location.*

better interoperability with people outside of your organization. Public CA certificates used to encrypt and sign messages will be trusted by the Outlook client used by people in other organizations, making S/MIME interoperability easier.

If you choose to use your own Windows Server 2003 CA, your CA will not automatically be trusted by Outlook clients outside your organization. As a result, if you send digitally signed messages to people outside your organization, they will get a message that says that the certificate is unknown or untrusted. The only way around this is for the other organization to publish the root certificate of your CA into all of its users' Trusted Root Certification Authority Store.

Tip: The Trusted Root Certification Authority Store can be viewed in Internet Explorer. Choose Tools | Internet Options, and on the Content tab, click Publishers.

If, however, most of your secure-message traffic will be within your enterprise, you may be better off using the Windows Server 2003 CA. Running your own CA may be less expensive and will also provide higher levels of trust as you will be in complete control of the certificates issued from your own CA.

6.2.3 **Protecting the .pst store**

As described in Chapter 1, a Personal Folders .pst file is a local storage file where users can keep their e-mail and other Outlook data. In some cases, organizational policy may dictate that all corporate information and e-mail must be stored centrally for backup and archiving. If users are storing e-mail locally on their own machine using a Personal Folders .pst file, it will be difficult to manage this information centrally as a corporate asset. In this case, administrators may want to disable the user's ability to create or open a .pst file. While it is not possible to block .pst use by a determined, knowledgable user absolutely, you can largely accomplish this using GPOs.

Using the Microsoft Office Outlook 2003 administrative template in the Group Policy Editor, under the Miscellaneous policy settings, there is a setting called "Prevent users from making changes to Outlook profiles." Enabling this setting will prevent users from changing their profiles through the Tools | E-mail Accounts dialog or the Mail applet in the Control Panel. However, it will not stop users from opening existing .pst files or creating a new one through the Outlook user interface.

This setting also does not prevent the user from modifying the options for an Exchange account. The user will still be able to right-click the root folder of his or her Exchange mailbox, select the Properties dialog, and click Advanced to access all of the options for the Exchange account.

Note: Several other settings related to .pst files can be controlled via GPOs. In the PST Settings options under Miscellaneous (shown in Figure 6.5), you can use the "Large PST: Absolute maximum size setting." Setting a very small maximum size will basically prevent users from storing anything in their .pst files. Unfortunately, these .pst size settings also apply to the offline folders .ost files used to cache Exchange Server data. As a result, administrators will probably not want to use these settings to suppress use of .pst files.

If you want to disable the ability to create a .pst file through the Outlook user interface completely, you can use this registry entry:

```
Key: HKEY_LOCAL_MACHINE\Software\Microsoft\Office\11.0\
Outlook
```

Value name: `DisablePST`
Value type: `REG_DWORD`
Values: `1` (disable .pst use), `0` (allow .pst use)

You can deploy this registry setting with the Custom Maintenance Wizard (CMW), as described in Chapter 2. Note that it affects all users on the machine since it is deployed to the HKEY_LOCAL_MACHINE hive of the Windows registry. Also, the DisablePST setting cannot be deployed as a GPO policy setting unless you apply the hotfix described in Microsoft Knowledge Base article 896515, "A network administrator can add the DisablePST registry value to a registry key so that all the users of a computer cannot create or access Outlook .pst files in Outlook 2003."

When DisablePST is set to 1, users will not be able to create Personal Folders .pst files and will see these additional behaviors:

- If you click Tools, then Options, then the Other tab, the AutoArchive section is hidden. You cannot set AutoArchive options.

- The AutoArchive tab in each folder's properties dialog box is hidden.

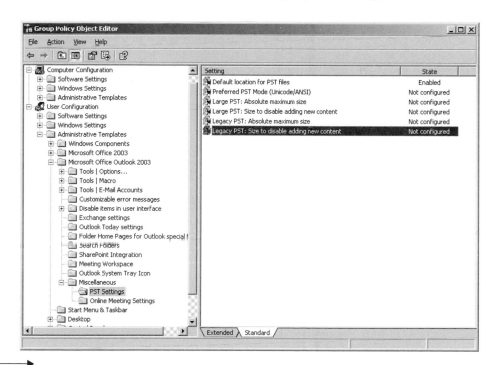

Figure 6.5   *Group Policy settings for managing .pst files.*

- All of the AutoArchive settings that were previously set are no longer enabled. For example, if you previously configured AutoArchive to move messages older than six months from your Sent Items folder to a personal folder's .pst file, this feature no longer functions.

- On the File menu, the Archive command is hidden.

- On the File menu, the Import and Export command no longer imports or exports to a .pst file. If you attempt to export or import from a .pst file, you will see the message ".pst (Personal Storage) usage is disabled on this computer."

- On the File | Data File Management dialog, the Add button no longer offers Personal Folders .pst file as an option.

- On the File | New | Outlook Data File dialog, Personal Folders .pst File is no longer an option.

- Users who try to link a Windows SharePoint Services events or contacts list to Outlook will not be able to do so and will receive a warning message "Outlook can't add the folder because creating a new Personal Folders (.pst) file isn't allowed on this computer." However, Microsoft Knowledge Base article 897658, "You receive an 'An error occurred adding the following Windows SharePoint Services folder to Outlook' error message when you link a Windows SharePoint Services Calendar or Events list to Outlook 2003," describes a hotfix and a new registry value, AlwaysAllowSharePointPST, that make it possible to link to SharePoint lists even when DisablePST=1.

Setting DisablePST to 1 does not, however, disable the ability to open an existing .pst file. You can, however, disable the File | Open | Outlook Data File command with a GPO using the setting "Disable command bar buttons and menu items," as discussed in Appendix C.

Even with DisablePST set to 1 and the File | Open | Outlook Data File command disabled, users who know how to automate Outlook can use a script to run code that uses the Namespace.AddStore method to create or open an existing .pst file. Disabling or not installing Visual Basic for Applications (VBA) does not prevent external scripts from automating Outlook. Therefore, it is not possible to block .pst use entirely.

A .pst file typically resides locally on the user's hard disk. The .pst file could be placed on a central server, but Microsoft does not officially support storing .pst files on network drives and warns that corruption may occur in such configurations. When stored locally, the .pst file should be configured with NTFS security to restrict who can read the file. If the .pst file is not thus protected and also has no password protection, it can be opened by anyone using an Outlook client or even a text editor like Notepad. Opening the .pst file in a text editor would most certainly be messy. If it were unencrypted, the file would appear as message text mixed in with Outlook control information and HTML tags from HTML-format messages.

When you create a new .pst file, Outlook offers a choice of three different types of encryption: No Encryption, Compressible Encryption (the default), and High Encryption. You cannot change the encryption level after the file is created.

Under the No Encryption option, Outlook does not encode your .pst file. A user may be able to read the .pst file with a text-editor program or with a hexadecimal-editor program.

Compressible Encryption will encode the data in your .pst such that other users will not be able to read the message with text or hexadecimal editors. Hackers may be able to defeat this encryption with special tools. This type of encryption still allows compression of the .pst file with compression tools like PKZIP utilities or the built-in compression that's available on some Windows file systems.

High Encryption uses a stronger form of encryption that is more difficult to hack. It's also potentially more time-consuming for Outlook to read and write. The .pst file can be compressed but to a lesser degree than if you were using the Compressible Encryption option.

The default security setting is the Compressible Encryption option. Use this option if disk space is more important than security. If security is more important that disk space, use the High Encryption option.

Administrators can create .pst files for users and preselect the location and level of encryption of .pst files by using the Custom Installation Wizard (CIW). Step 19 in the CIW (or step 14 in the CMW) allows administrators to customize additional Outlook profile and account information. In this step the administrator can select to add a .pst file, then define the location and encryption strength for users, as shown in Figure 6.6. This can be a useful feature when administrators want to be able to configure the type of archive file that Outlook will use. Chapter 3 provides more information on how to deploy this type of mail-profile customization, while Chapter 4 explains how to set the location of the default archive file and how to force a new .pst file to use the new Unicode format that allows files larger than the 2-GB limit in earlier versions.

The .pst file can also be password protected. In this case, even a hacker who had the right tools to crack the encryption would not be able to open

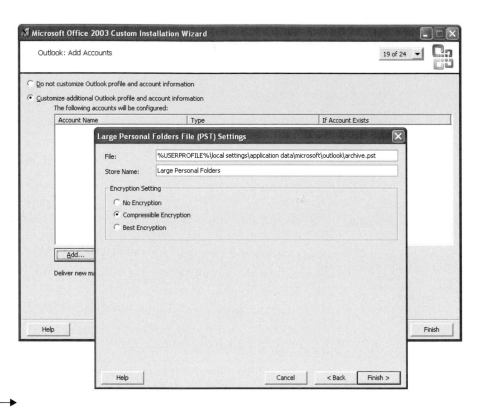

Figure 6.6   *Configuring a .pst file with the CIW.*

Figure 6.7   *Configuring a password for a .pst file.*

the file without knowing the password. Users can define passwords for their
.pst files as shown in Figure 6.7 by using the Personal Folders settings dia-
log, which can be found in Tools | Options, under Mail Setup | Data Files.
Unfortunately, given the availability of .pst password-removal/crack tools
on the Internet, this password protection is not infallible.

6.2.4   Protecting the offline folders .ost file

While there is no way to password protect the offline folders .ost file used
by Outlook in Cached Exchange mode or Classic Offline mode, as you can
for .pst files, it is protected in other ways. The .ost file is both encrypted
and uniquely associated with a particular mailbox. Applications exist, however, to hack an .ost file's security and convert it to an unprotected .pst file.
Therefore, for additional protection, the drive where the .ost file is stored
should be an NTFS volume, and the .ost file should reside in a folder where
only the user has the right to read and write files. In addition, if the
machine is using Windows XP, it should be set up to require a password
when the machine returns from hibernation or standby. The System.adm
administrative template for Windows XP includes a policy setting under
System/Power Management called "Prompt for password on resume from
hibernate/suspend." It sets this registry value:

> Key: `HKEY_CURRENT_USER\Software\Policies\Microsoft\`
> `Windows\System\Power`
> Value name: `PromptPasswordOnResume`
> Value type: `REG_DWORD`
> Values: `1` (require a password), `0` (don't prompt for a password)

6.2.5   Locking down other e-mail accounts

Earlier in Section 6.2.3, you learned how to lock down mail profiles so that
users cannot make changes. If you don't want to go that far, you can still
prevent users from adding specific e-mail account types by using GPOs. In
the Group Policy Editor, under User Configuration/Administrative Tem-
plates/Microsoft Office Outlook 2003/Miscellaneous, the "Prevent users
from adding e-mail account types" setting allows you to specify what type
of e-mail accounts you want to prevent users from adding. Figure 6.8 shows
the choices available via this setting. This setting may be a useful way to
block users from setting up e-mail accounts to check their home or personal
e-mail. These additional e-mail account types could potentially be support
headaches for your organization.

Figure 6.8
*Preventing users
from adding other
e-mail accounts.*

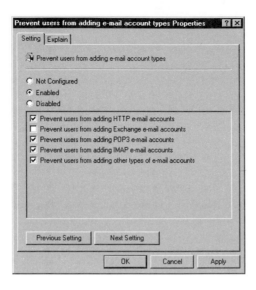

Note, however, that each option corresponds to a separate entry in the registry, and if you enable this Group Policy setting, you set all five registry values. If you prefer not to set some of those values, you may want to use another method besides GPOs to roll out the desired registry value(s), which are found in Table 6.1. All are REG_DWORD values in the HKEY_CURRENT_USER\Software\Policies\Microsoft\Office\11.0\Outlook\ Options key and take a value of 1 to enable the option and 0 to disable it. In other words, setting DisableHTTP to 1 will prevent users from adding Microsoft Network, Hotmail, or Exchange OWA accounts to their Outlook mail profiles.

Table 6.1   *Registry Values to Prevent Users from Adding Different Types of Mail Accounts*

Group Policy Setting	Registry Value
Prevent users from adding HTTP e-mail accounts	DisableHTTP
Prevent users from adding Exchange e-mail accounts	DisableExchange
Prevent users from adding POP3 e-mail accounts	DisablePOP3
Prevent users from adding IMAP e-mail accounts	DisableIMAP
Prevent users from adding other types of e-mail accounts	DisableOtherTypes

6.3   Threats to unwanted information dissemination

Today's information worker creates an abundance of valuable digital information in many different forms. E-mail communications, proprietary product plans, confidential reports, and human-resource reports are just some examples of valuable digital information. Once these documents are created, they are regularly shared through e-mail messages. Organizations today face the challenge of how to protect this valuable digital information against careless mishandling and malicious use. In addition, external factors such as new legislative requirements to protect sensitive data are pushing business to develop methods to protect digital information better.

Historically, security has focused on perimeter-based security methods. Authentication technologies and access control lists (ACLs) are used to restrict access to specific systems or specific data. As previously discussed, organizations may also use encryption to secure e-mail messages in transit and to help positively identity the sender of the information. The problem with these methods is that once recipients have access to digital information, they are free to distribute the information by various means such as e-mail, printing, and copying. After access is granted, no restrictions control what can be done with the data or where it can be sent.

6.3.1   Understanding Windows Rights Management Services

In order to control what can be done with digital information, Microsoft has introduced Windows Rights Management Services (RMS), an add-on product for Windows Server 2003. In addition, Microsoft has built support for RMS into the Microsoft Office 2003 suite, including Microsoft Outlook 2003.

Note: Only the Microsoft Office Professional Enterprise Edition 2003 includes RMS features. The version of Outlook 2003 distributed with Exchange 2003 does not. It's also worth noting that you do not need to be using Exchange as the mail server in order to use RMS; it operates independently of the mail server.

The Microsoft RMS product can persistently protect any binary format of data so that the usage rights remain with the information—even in transport—rather than merely residing on an organization's network. This also enables usage rights to be enforced after the information is accessed by an authorized recipient, both online and offline, inside and outside of the organization.

In order to protect documents and e-mail, RMS encrypts the information, making access conditional on having the appropriate rights. Once the information is encrypted, only trusted entities with the appropriate usage rights can decrypt the information in an RMS-enabled application.

In order to make use of RMS technology, an organization must install RMS Server on Windows Server 2003. Once this is done, the RMS client software can be deployed to users. Then, using RMS-enabled applications such as Microsoft Office 2003, users can implement RMS-enforced usage rights on digital information. Over the long term, Microsoft intends to integrate the RMS client into the Windows operating system so that this component will no longer need to be installed separately. Today, however, the RMS client must be installed as a separate component for Windows XP and supported earlier operating systems (back to Windows 98 Second Edition with the Active Directory Client Extension).

If a user on a machine without the RMS client attempts to create or access a rights-protected document or e-mail message, the dialog in Figure 6.9 will appear and advise the user that the RMS client needs to be installed.

Currently, Windows Rights Management Client 1.0 is available for download from the Microsoft Web site (see Appendix D). It can be installed either before or after the installation of Office 2003 or chained to the Office or Outlook installation. Once the RMS client is installed, the client computer must be activated, and the RMS server must issue an RMS account certificate (RAC) to allow the user to apply RMS rights in Outlook 2003 and Office 2003.

Figure 6.9
Message displayed when user does not have the RMS client installed.

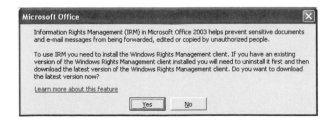

At present, all machines that need to be activated for RMS must connect to the Microsoft Web site (https://activation.drm.microsoft.com) to obtain a unique "lockbox." For activation, machines can connect to the Internet via proxy through the RMS server or can connect directly to the Internet. The lockbox is the location where some sensitive information, such as the computer's private key, is stored. The private key is used in the encryption process for some RMS operations. The need to connect to the Internet for activation may cause problems where machines do not have Internet connection. (Future versions of RMS may not require an Internet connection for activation.)

Once the machine is activated and has a unique lockbox, users must obtain an RAC. These certificates identify trusted users within a corporate RMS system and enable users to access and use protected files and information. Each certificate contains a public and private key that is used to license information intended for that user's consumption. The user-certification process creates an RAC, which associates a user account with a specific computer and enables the user to access and use rights-protected information from that computer.

6.3.2 Creating and using rights-protected content

The easiest way to become activated and receive an RAC is by rights-protecting an Outlook 2003 message or a document created in Microsoft Word, Excel, or PowerPoint 2003. The first time a user publishes rights-protected information or attempts to access rights-protected information on a client computer, the RMS-enabled application sends a request for an account certificate to the Windows RMS root installation identified in the Active Directory. In order for this to complete successfully, an organization must have installed and configured an RMS server that has published its existence to the Active Directory. If an enterprise RMS server has not been installed, the user will be prompted to sign up with the Microsoft Passport RMS trial service, as show in Figure 6.10. This service is intended only as a trial service for users who do not have access to an RMS server within their organization. Microsoft does not guarantee its availability. To maximize trust and security, organizations will want to have their own RMS server. Use of the Microsoft Passport trial service is not recommended for organizations that want to use the security features of RMS.

Once the user has been activated and has obtained an RAC from the organization's RMS server, he or she can begin to use the features of RMS within Outlook 2003. Figure 6.11 shows a message that has been rights

Figure 6.10
Initiating use of the
Microsoft Passport
RMS Service.

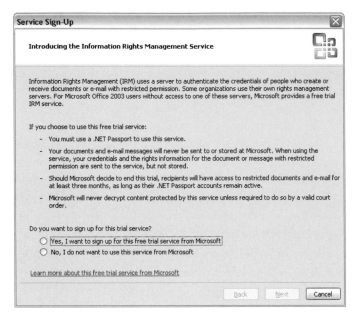

protected using the basic protection in Outlook 2003 available from the
File | Permission menu or the Permission button on the toolbar (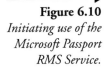). The
recipient can read the message but cannot forward, print, or copy it.

When the recipient replies to an RMS-protected message, Outlook does
not include the body of the original message in the reply. It does automatically apply the same permission restriction on the outgoing message that

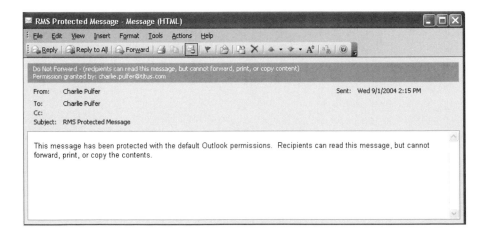

Figure 6.11   *A rights-protected Outlook 2003 message.*

the incoming message had. The user can turn RMS protection off on the reply by choosing File | Permission | Unrestricted Access.

The expiration date that a user sets on an Outlook 2003 message with the View | Options dialog has special meaning for an RMS-protected message. Once that date passes, the recipient will no longer be able to read the message or any attached files.

In order to apply more advanced or more granular rights, organizations can define RMS policy templates, which can then be applied to Outlook messages.

Users who do not have Office or Outlook 2003 can still read RMS-protected content by using the Windows Rights Management Add-on (RMA) for Internet Explorer. The RMA can be downloaded from the Microsoft Web site and provides a way for users of supported Windows operating systems to view, but not to alter, files with restricted permission. In order to use the RMA, clients must first install the RMS client software.

To send an RMS-protected Office document in an e-mail message so that an RMA user can read it, the user needs to create, protect, and save the file first. In Word, for example, choose File | Permission | Do Not Distribute. In the dialog shown in Figure 6.12, under "Additional settings," choose

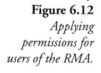

Figure 6.12
Applying
permissions for
users of the RMA.

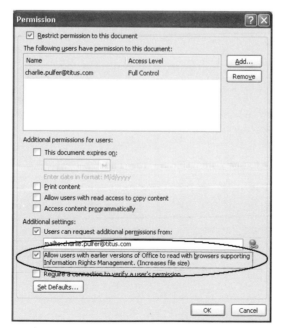

"Allow users with earlier versions of Office to read with browsers supporting Information Rights Management." Save the file and then attach it to the outgoing message. Do not protect the message itself.

Note: There are actually three ways to apply rights-management protection to an Office attachment such as a Word document, but only one of them results in a file that the RMA can read. If you want recipients to be able to read the document with the RMA, you must apply rights-management protection and save the document, then attach it to an existing Outlook message. Do not apply rights-management protection to the Outlook message itself. If you do that, or if you create the message by using the File | Send To | Recipient (as Attachment) command in Word, the resulting document will be readable only by Office 2003 users with the rights-management client, not by recipients who have only the RMA.

Many of the RMS features for Office 2003 can be centrally enabled or disabled using GPOs. Alternatively, if you don't want to lock down these features settings, you can customize the default user preferences using the CIW for a new installation or the CMW for an existing installation. In the Group Policy Editor, go to User Configuration/Administrative Templates/ Microsoft Office 2003/Manage Restricted Permissions to see the available options. These options control registry entries in the HKEY_CURRENT_ USER\Software\Policies\Microsoft\Office\11.0\Common\DRM key. Here are some of the key settings you are most likely to set. Note that they are part of the Office administrative template, not the Outlook template. All except Admintemplatepath, which is a REG_SZ value, are REG_DWORD values with possible values of 1 to enable the setting and 0 to disable it.

- *Disable Information Rights Management user interface.* If this setting is enabled, the rights-management-related options within the user interface of all Office 2003 programs are disabled.

   Value name: `Disable`

- *Disable Microsoft Passport service for content with restricted permission.* If this setting is enabled, users cannot open content created by a Passport-authenticated account. This policy will most likely be used where a corporate RMS server is deployed and the enterprise decides not to trust outside entities (such as Passport IDs).

   Value name: `DisablePassportCertification`

- *Allow users with earlier versions of Office to read with browsers.* If this setting is enabled, rights-management-protected content will automatically be created so that users can read it without Office 2003 programs, using the RMA for Internet Explorer.

  Value name: `IncludeHTML`

- *Specify permission policy path.* If this setting is enabled, Office 2003 programs using RMS will scan the path provided in this registry entry to see if any permission policy templates exist. If they are there, the title for each is displayed in the Permission dialog box of the File menu.

  Value name: `Admintemplatepath`

Tip: The settings used to customize Windows RMS options are in the same location in the Microsoft Office 2003 tree in the CIW as they are in the Microsoft Office 2003 administrative template viewed in the Group Policy Editor.

6.4 Spam and other threats to incoming mail

Unwanted incoming mail and spam are among the largest productivity impediments faced by today's workforce. Symantec Corporation estimated in 2004 that 65 percent of all mail carried over the Internet was spam. Clearly, this is a growing problem for many organizations. Not only is spam a nuisance that must be dealt with before getting to actual business messages, but spam can also pose a threat as many viruses, fraudulent e-mails, and other potentially harmful messages come to users as spam. As a result of the growing spam problem, Microsoft has introduced a number of new or improved spam-fighting technologies in Outlook 2003, including the new Junk E-mail Filter and the disabling of automatic content download from external servers.

Outlook 2003 contains a new Junk E-mail Filter that replaces the rules used in previous versions of Microsoft Outlook. Outlook 2003 supports junk e-mail filtering for Exchange accounts configured in Cached Exchange mode or where mail is delivered to a Personal Folders .pst file. The Junk E-mail Filter feature is on by default, with the protection level set to low, which is designed to catch the most obvious junk e-mail messages. Any message that is caught by the Junk E-mail Filter is moved to a special Junk E-mail folder, where the user can retrieve or review it at a later time.

Note: As you learned in Chapter 5, a user who is not working in Cached Exchange mode can still benefit from Exchange 2003's server-side junk mail filtering by adding frequent correspondents to their Contacts folder and connecting to the mailbox with Outlook Web Access (OWA) to build up safe and blocked senders lists with OWA's Junk Mail feature. The Junk E-mail option in OWA must be enabled.

The junk filter technology, developed by Microsoft Research, uses advanced analysis of the message structure and content to determine the probability that it is a junk e-mail message. It does not do any "learning" from the user's designation of what is and is not spam. However, Microsoft does publish periodic updates to the spam filter based on analysis of the vast amount of data provide by the millions of messages received by its Hotmail and Microsoft Network mail servers.

Outlook 2003 helps reduce the risk presented by so-called Web beacons in e-mail messages by automatically blocking the downloading of pictures, sounds, and other content from links in HTML-format e-mail messages that point to external servers. Automatic content download is disabled by default. This feature can also help users avoid automatically downloading potentially offensive material. In addition, users can make their own decisions about the value of downloading an image. Users can view the blocked pictures by right-clicking any blocked image.

Additional protections that carry over from earlier versions of Outlook include the ability to force all messages to display in plain-text format and the blocking of potentially harmful attachments.

6.4.1   Configuring the Junk E-mail Filter

The new Junk E-mail Filter feature comprises two components:

- The Junk E-mail Filter itself evaluates messages to determine whether they should be treated as junk based on several factors, including the message content and whether the sender or recipient is included in one of the Junk E-mail Filter lists.

- The Junk E-mail Filter lists include safe senders, safe recipients, and blocked senders. E-mail from addresses or domain names in your Safe

Senders list will never be treated as junk e-mail. The same is true for any e-mail sent to addresses or domain names on the Safe Recipients list. E-mail from addresses or domain names on your Blocked Senders list will always be treated as junk e-mail. A separate option directs the Junk E-mail Filter to consider every entry in the user's Contacts folder as a safe sender.

The settings for the Junk E-mail Filter are associated with a user's Outlook profile. Administrators can configure both the Junk E-Mail Filter and the initial settings for the filter lists centrally using the CIW during a new installation or using GPOs or the CMW after deployment of Outlook 2003. The Safe Senders, Safe Recipients, and Blocked Senders lists that the administrator may deploy act only as defaults for the user, who can add or remove addresses and domains from the list by using the settings on the Tools | Options | Junk E-mail dialog in Outlook.

Note: When Outlook users upgrade to Outlook 2003 with the new Junk E-mail Filter, the rules that previously handled junk e-mail messages are removed. The existing rules and lists used by the old filter do not migrate to the new version of Outlook. However, if users have their old lists, which are stored as Junk Senders.txt and Adult Senders.txt in the %USERPRO-FILE%\Application Data\Microsoft\Outlook folder, they can import them through the Tools | Options | Junk E-mail | Blocked Senders dialog.

Outlook 2003 supports junk e-mail filtering for e-mail accounts in Cached Exchange mode or where mail is delivered to a Personal Folders .pst file. Outlook 2003 does not perform its junk e-mail content analysis for Exchange accounts in Classic Online mode or for server-based accounts exposed by third-party Messaging Application Programming Interface (MAPI) store providers. However, for users of Exchange 2003, the server also uses the Junk E-mail Filter lists managed by the user to evaluate mail, as described in Chapter 5. This means that if a sender is on a user's Blocked Senders list, mail is moved to the Junk E-mail folder on the Exchange 2003 server and is not evaluated by Outlook 2003.

Tip: If the Junk E-mail Filter on Exchange 2003 doesn't seem to be handling the user's junk e-mail lists, the user can use OWA to check the junk mail options.

To configure how the Junk E-mail Filter works for users, administrators can optionally do the following:

- Set the Junk E-mail Filter protection level.

- Permanently delete suspected junk e-mail messages or move them to the Junk E-mail folder.

- Trust e-mail messages from users' Contacts folder.

- Tell Outlook to add recipients to the Safe Senders list that the user sends messages to (added in Office 2003 Service Pack 1).

To configure Junk E-mail Filter settings with GPOs in the Group Policy Editor, go to User Configuration / Administrative Templates / Microsoft Office Outlook 2003 / Tools | Options / Preferences / Junk E-mail. (The Change Office User Settings hierarchy on screen 10 of the CIW and screen 7 of the CMW lists the corresponding settings in a similar location.) Table 6.2 shows the available settings, supported options, and the default setting that Outlook uses if the Group Policy setting or user preference is not configured, along with the corresponding registry values, all of which are REG_DWORD values. These registry values are set in HKEY_CURRENT_USER\Software\Policies\Microsoft\Office\11.0\Outlook\Options\Mail when they are controlled by GPOs and in HKEY_CURRENT_USER\Software\Microsoft\Office\11.0\Outlook\Options\Mail when they are set as user preferences with the CIW or CMW.

Table 6.2   *Junk E-mail Settings*

Setting	Registry Value	Possible Values
Junk e-mail protection level	JunkMailProtection	4294967295 = No Protection 6 = Low (default) 3 = High 2147483648 = Trusted lists only
Permanently delete junk mail	JunkMailPermDelete	1= Enabled 0 = Disabled (default)
Trust e-mail from Contacts	JunkMailTrustContacts	1 = Enabled (default) 0 = Disabled
Add people I e-mail to the Safe Senders list	JunkMailTrustOutgoingRecipients	1= Enabled 0 = Disabled (default)

The default values for the Junk E-mail Filter are designed to provide an acceptable level of security for most users.

Under Junk E-mail protection level, the Trusted Lists Only setting causes Outlook to skip its content analysis and to filter mail based only on the Safe Senders, Blocked Senders, and Safe Recipients lists.

6.4.2   Deploying Junk E-mail Filter lists

Outlook 2003 allows you to deploy initial lists of Safe Senders, Safe Recipients, and Blocked Senders. For example, you may want to distribute a Safe Senders list that contains the domains for your organization's prominent partners. If employees regularly receive mail from partner xyz.com, then you would want to put xyz.com on their initial Safe Senders lists to insure that mail from xyz.com is not misclassified as junk.

Note: You cannot lock down the users' junk filter lists with GPOs. Users will be able to edit the junk filter lists during their Outlook session.

You can deploy these junk filter lists when Outlook is installed by using the CIW. If you wish to modify the junk filter lists after Outlook has been deployed, you can use the CMW. Both the CIW and CMW can deploy the files used for the list, or you can maintain the junk filter lists on a network drive. Deploying junk filter lists requires several steps:

1. Preparing the junk filter lists themselves

2. Deploying the lists to a location where Outlook can access them

3. Setting registry values to tell Outlook where to look for the lists

4. Setting a registry value to direct Outlook to import the lists

A junk filter list for import should be a text file with each domain name or address on a separate line. An easy way to create a junk filter list for distribution is to run Outlook 2003, choose Tools | Options | Junk E-mail, add names to the desired list, then click the Export to File button.

You can use any of the following methods to deploy the junk filter lists:

- Place the files in a network folder that each user can access.
- Use screen 11 of the CIW to deploy the files to Outlook users' machines as part of the Outlook or Office installation.

- Use screen 8 of the CMW to deploy the files to Outlook users' machines after installation.

- Use any other technique you customarily employ to deploy files to users' machines.

Once you have deployed the files, you need to tell Outlook where to find them. You can do this with a user-preference setting in the CIW or CMW. On screen 10, Change Office User Settings, in the CIW (screen 7 in the CMW), navigate to Microsoft Office Outlook 2003 / Tools | Options / Preferences / Junk E-Mail. To specify a path to each filter list, double-click the settings corresponding to each list (e.g., "Specify path to Safe Senders list") and enter a path and file name in the box. The path must be exact, pointing to either a network folder or the location on the user's hard drive; you cannot use environment variables.

Note: You can also use GPO settings to provide the locations of the filter files for import. The settings are located under User Configuration / Administrative Templates / Microsoft Office Outlook 2003, in the same location in the hierarchy as in the CIW and CMW.

Finally, on the same Change Office User Settings screen in the CIW or CMW, double-click the Junk Mail Import List setting, choose Apply Changes, and ensure that the "Check to turn off import of Junk mail list"

Table 6.3   *Registry Settings Related to Importing Junk Filter Lists*

Setting	Registry Value	Type	Values
Junk Mail Import list	JunkMailImportLists	REG_DWORD	1 = Enabled 0 = Disabled (default)
Overwrite or append Junk Mail Import list	JunkMailImportAppend	REG_DWORD	1 = Disabled (append; default) 0 = Enabled (overwrite)
Specify path to Safe Senders list	JunkMailSafeSendersFile	REG_SZ	Path to list
Specify path to Safe Recipients list	JunkMailSafeRecipientsFile	REG_SZ	Path to list
Specify path to Blocked Senders list	JunkMailBlockedSendersFile	REG_SZ	Path to list

check box is cleared. By default, Outlook appends any imported junk filters to the user's existing lists. If you prefer to overwrite, double-click the Overwrite or Append Junk Mail Import List setting and select Apply Changes, and check the box for "Check to Overwrite list. Uncheck to Append." Table 6.3 summarizes the registry settings involved. These registry values are set in HKEY_CURRENT_USER\Software\Policies\Microsoft\Office\ 11.0\Outlook\Options\Mail when they are controlled by GPOs and in HKEY_CURRENT_USER\Software\Microsoft\Office\11.0\Outlook\ Options\Mail when they are set as user preferences with the CIW or CMW.

When you deploy the CIW's .mst file or the CMW's .cmw file, the registry value JunkMailImportLists in KEY_CURRENT_USER\Software\ Microsoft\Office\11.0\Outlook\Options\Mail will be set to 1. Outlook then will import the lists when it starts and set JunkMailImportLists to 0. The other registry values associated with the import are not reset.

Caution: The junk filter lists cannot be locked down with Group Policy settings, even though the administrative template for Outlook 2003 contains Group Policy settings that can control the path to junk filter lists for import and whether the imported lists overwrite the user's existing lists. You should not be tempted to try to enforce junk filter lists by adding a JunkMailImportLists value to the KEY_CURRENT_USER\Software\Policies\Microsoft\Office\11.0\Outlook\Options\Mail registry key. Microsoft cautions that doing so and setting JunkMailImportLists to 1 will cause excessive remote procedure call (RPC) traffic between Outlook and the Exchange Server.

However, a post-Service Pack 1 hotfix is available that changes both how Outlook handles the JunkMailImportLists registry value and when it performs the import. The result is that it becomes possible to use JunkMailImportLists as a policy setting without performance issues. The Microsoft Knowledge Base article 893057, "The JunkMailImportLists registry value may cause poor performance in Outlook 2003," provides details on this new behavior.

6.4.3 New Junk E-mail features in Outlook 2003 SP1

Microsoft made additional changes to the Junk E-mail feature in Office 2003 SP1 in the handling of outgoing mail recipients, the timing of the Junk E-mail filter, and the blocking of mail from specific countries.

In the original Outlook 2003 release, every entry in the user's Contacts folder was considered a safe sender by default. In Outlook 2003 SP1, a new setting allows the user to build the Safe Senders list from e-mail addresses of outgoing message recipients who are not in the Contacts folder. The user configures this setting in Tools | Options | Junk E-mail | Safe Senders by checking the "Automatically add people I e-mail to the Safe Senders List" check box. This setting is turned off by default. When it is turned on, if you send someone a message, any replies or future messages from that person will not be treated as junk. As you saw in Table 6.2, this setting (JunkMail-TrustOutgoingRecipients) can also be configured as a policy using the .adm administrative template for Office 2003 SP1 (see Appendix D for download location).

Note: As you'll see in Section 6.4.4, the Safe Senders list also affects the behavior of the Outlook feature that prevents external images and other content from downloading when the user views an HTML-format message. The default behavior is for messages from safe senders always to download external content. This is probably the main reason that the new SP1 option, "Add people I e-mail to the Safe Senders List," is turned off by default.

Starting with SP1, Outlook rules are designed to ignore messages that have been moved to the Junk E-mail folder. This keeps e-mail considered junk in the correct place rather than moving it to another folder according to the rule. On the other hand, it prevents users from creating their own content-based rules to try to sort out what's junk and what's not. Users can still use the Run Rules Now feature to run rules manually against the Junk E-mail folder.

Outlook 2003 SP1 also adds two settings that block unwanted e-mail messages that come from another country or region or appear in another language. Both are configurable by the user in the Tools | Options | Junk E-mail dialog in Outlook. However, the data is stored as part of the user's Outlook mail profile and cannot be configured through GPOs, the CIW, or the CMW.

The Blocked Top-Level Domains list enables users to block e-mail addresses that end in a specific domain. For example, selecting the CA (Canada), US (United States), and MX (Mexico) check boxes in the list blocks messages with e-mail addresses like someone@example.ca, someone@example.us, and someone@example.mx. Additional country codes appear in the list. This helps users eliminate unwanted e-mail messages they receive from specific countries or regions.

The Blocked Encodings list enables users to block all e-mail addresses in one or more specific language encodings. For example, if a user does no business with people in Korea but gets a lot of spam using the Korean-language character set, the user can add Korean to the list of language encodings to block.

Note: While the vast majority of junk e-mail is sent in the US-ASCII encoding, a lot of legitimate messages also use that encoding, so users will probably not want to block it.

6.4.4   Configuring automatic picture download

Another common e-mail security vulnerability that poses a threat to the user's privacy comes in the form of so-called Web beacons, which are links in HTML messages to external content. These links include more than just the URL to a picture or sound clip. Appended to a Web beacon URL is additional information that allows the sender of the message to log a report that a particular message was actually viewed. In the past, opening or previewing a message containing a Web beacon caused Outlook to send a request to the external Web server for the linked picture or sound from the Web server.

Note: Pictures that are embedded in a message as attachments—rather than referenced as links to external URLs—do not need to be downloaded and will appear in the message without any special action by the recipient. Also, in Exchange environments, any message originating from inside your own Exchange organization is considered safe and will download pictures linked to external URLs.

Web beacons have both legitimate and potentially malicious uses. An electronic newsletter publisher, for example, might use Web beacons to determine how many times a particular newsletter was read or to report to an advertiser the number of hits an ad received among the newsletter's audience. This can be done without collecting any personal information from the newsletter readers. However, spammers also use Web beacons to probe for valid e-mail addresses. When you open a message that contains an HTML link to the spammer's site and your mail program retrieves the content, you are, in essence, confirming that your e-mail address is valid. Now that they know your e-mail address really exists, the spammers may continue to send you spam and may sell your e-mail address to other e-mail marketers.

A new feature in Outlook 2003 can be used to block these beacons and is turned on by default. You can configure the default settings for automatic picture download by using the CIW or CMW, or you can enforce settings by configuring GPOs. To configure automatic picture download settings, in the Group Policy Editor go to User Configuration / Administrative Templates / Microsoft Office Outlook 2003 / Tools | Options / Security / Automatic Picture Download Settings, as shown in Figure 6.13.

Table 6.4 lists the registry entries for these settings, which are located in HKEY_CURRENT_USER\Software\Policies\Microsoft\Office\11.0\Outlook\Options\Mail when set with GPOs and HKEY_CURRENT_USER\ Software\Microsoft\Office\11.0\Outlook\Options\Mail when set as user preferences with the CIW or CMW. All are REG_DWORD values.

By default, Outlook does not download pictures or other content automatically, except when the external content comes from a Web site in the Trusted Sites zone, the picture is in a message from a sender in the Safe Senders list, or a message is sent to a recipient in the Safe Recipients list.

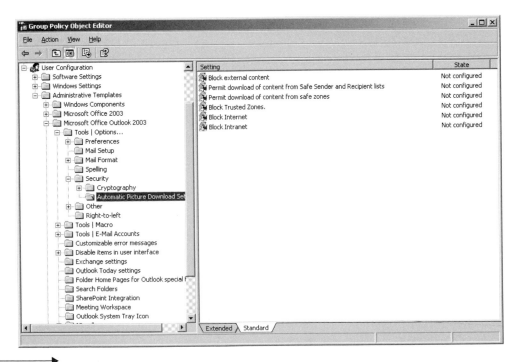

Figure 6.13   *Settings available for automatic picture download.*

Table 6.4 *Registry Settings Related to the External Content Block*

Setting	Registry Value	Values
Block external content	BlockExtContent	1 = Enabled (default) 0 = Disabled
Permit download of content from Safe Sender and Recipient lists	UnblockSpecificSenders	1 = Enabled (default) 0 = Disabled
Permit download of content from safe zones	UnblockSafeZone	1 = Enabled (default) 0 = Disabled
Block trusted zones	TrustedZone	1 = Disabled (default) 0 = Enabled
Block Internet	Internet	1 = Disabled 0 = Enabled (default)
Block intranet	Intranet	1 = Disabled 0 = Enabled (default)

Also, in Exchange environments, any message originating from inside your own Exchange organization is considered to be from a safe sender; therefore, pictures will be downloaded even if they are linked to external URLs.

As you can see from Table 6.4, you can change this behavior so that content from any of the zones (trusted sites, local intranet, and Internet) will be downloaded automatically or blocked automatically. However, enabling automatic content download to every site on the Internet is not recommended. Also note that the Intranet value appears to have no effect on external-content blocking.

Caution: Administrators should note that external content is automatically downloaded for messages from addresses in the Safe Senders list of the Junk E-mail Filter. If users do not wish to download content automatically, they should not enable the "Automatically add people I e-mail to the Safe Senders list" option in Outlook 2003 SP1, which is listed in Table 6.2. Alternatively, administrators may want to disable the connection between automatic picture downloading and the Safe Senders list by disabling the "Permit download of content from Safe Sender and Recipient lists" option listed in Table 6.4. When that option is disabled, Outlook uses solely the domain of the external content URL to determine whether the content should be downloaded.

Users can view the blocked pictures by right-clicking any blocked image and choosing Download Pictures from the pop-up contact menu. This will download all of the pictures in the message, not just the picture that was clicked on. Also, printing, replying to, or forwarding a message will force Outlook to download any external content, regardless of the automatic-content-download setting.

6.4.5   Forcing Outlook to read mail in plain text

As noted in the previous section, while it is possible to block Outlook from downloading external content, that block is ignored when the user prints, replies to, or forwards a message with such content. Outlook also does not block images embedded as attachments rather than linked to external sources. For organizations that want Outlook never to show pictures in messages, regardless of where they come from, a setting is available to force Outlook to read all messages in plain text. This will also cause all replies to be sent in plain-text format because Outlook always replies in the same format as the incoming message.

The "Read e-mail as plain text" option is located in the Microsoft Office Outlook 2003 administrative template, under Tools | Options / Preferences / E-mail options, and in a similar location in the user-settings screens in the CIW and CMW. This controls a registry value in HKEY_CURRENT_USER\Software\Policies\Microsoft\Office\11.0\Outlook\Options\Mail when managed with the GPOs and HKEY_CURRENT_USER\Software\Microsoft\Office\11.0\Outlook\Options\Mail when set as a user preference with the CIW or CMW:

```
Value name: ReadAsPlain
Value type: REG_DWORD
Values: 1 (enabled), 0 (disabled)
```

With ReadAsPlain set to 1, Outlook displays a plain-text version of all incoming messages that were originally in HTML or rich-text format. Any embedded images appear as separate attachments, as shown in Figure 6.14, while any <img> tags linking to external content are replaced with the URL to the linked image. When a user prints, replies to, or forwards a message that has been converted to plain text, no external content is downloaded, in contrast to the out-of-the-box behavior.

Outlook retains the original formatted content with the message; this allows the user to right-click the message "This message was converted to plain text" and choose Display as HTML (for an HTML-format message)

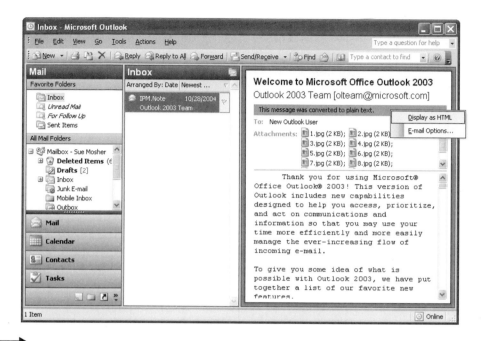

Figure 6.14   *An HTML-formatted message automatically converted to plain text.*

from the context menu to show the message as it was originally sent. At that point, an HTML-format message will be subject to the normal automatic-content-downloading restrictions described in Section 6.4.4.

6.4.6   Understanding the reading pane

Each version of Outlook is more secure than the previous. As you will see, administrators have little reason to want to disable the reading pane (known as the preview pane in previous versions) in Outlook 2003. In fact, Microsoft provides no policy setting or registry key to disable it, only a command-line switch discussed below.

The reading pane is a product of Microsoft's extensive research into how users manage their messages. It allows users to view the contents of the selected message quickly without having to open it. The default configuration on the right side of the main Outlook window, instead of the bottom as in previous versions, allows more of the message to show, making it more likely that the user can flag, delete, file, or respond to the message quickly without opening it or scrolling to see more text.

Note: Outlook 2003 includes no mechanism to configure global views to suppress the reading pane, put it on the bottom instead of the right, eliminate the Arrange By feature, or make other changes to the default views for all users in an organizations. For the time being, it remains up to each user to customize the Outlook interface to his or her preferences.

In Outlook 2003, the reading pane is on by default. When Outlook starts, if the Inbox is configured as the startup folder, Outlook will automatically display the contents of the user's first message in the Inbox. However, Outlook's basic security features keep this from being a threat, even if the message is a virus carrier message in HTML format with a malicious attachment:

- Outlook automatically blocks executables and other dangerous programs, as you'll see in Section 6.4.7.

- Outlook never loads or runs attached files automatically, except for pictures and sound files embedded in the message body.

As noted in the previous section, Outlook by default downloads external content in HTML-format messages only for pictures from Web sites in the Trusted Sites zone or in messages from people in the Safe Senders list or sent to people in the Safe Recipients list.

As always, it's best to stop infected messages at the server or gateway, which means few, if any, viruses should reach users' mailboxes. A responsible administrator will also remove executable file types from messages at the server level. When viruses don't make it to the mailbox, the reading pane is 100 percent safe.

There is no way to disable the reading pane. While you can start Outlook using the `/nopreview` command-line switch, this merely switches the reading pane off when Outlook starts. Users can turn the reading pane back on for any folder.

6.4.7   Attachment blocking

Due to the threat of viruses and, to a larger extent, worms (which spread themselves automatically via e-mail), Microsoft added attachment-blocking features to Outlook in 2000, beginning with a security update, then Office 2000 Service Pack 2.

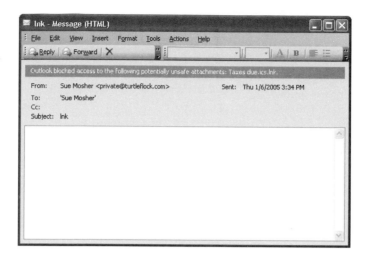

Figure 6.15
*Blocked files are
listed but not
accessible.*

Outlook offers two levels of attachment security. Outlook automatically blocks Level 1 attachments, which include more than 40 file types with the potential to run programs that can compromise the security of users' systems. Examples of Level 1 attachment types are .exe, .com, and .bat files. When users receive a Level 1 attachment, Outlook displays a message saying it has blocked potentially unsafe attachments, as shown in Figure 6.15. Users will not be able to open or save the attachment in Outlook.

When you try to send a Level 1 attachment, Outlook displays a warning (Figure 6.16) that other Outlook users might not be able to receive the attachment.

Note: Outlook does not actually block outgoing Level 1 files, although many users interpret the warning in Figure 6.16 to mean that they cannot send such files. Users will find, however, that if they open the sent message in their Sent Items folder, the file attachment will be blocked—even to the original sender.

Figure 6.16
*Blocked
attachment
warning for an
outgoing message.*

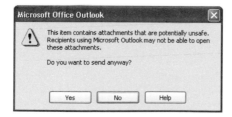

Users who receive an attachment with a Level 2 file type receive a warning that the attachment could be dangerous. The user will not be able to open the attachment but will be prompted to save the file to his or her hard disk. There are no default Level 2 files.

Administrators can add a file type to the Level 1 list or reduce a Level 1 file to Level 2 using GPOs. In the Group Policy Editor, under User Configuration Administrative Templates / Microsoft Office Outlook 2003 / Tools | Options / Security are two settings: "Allow access to e-mail attachments" and "Disallow access to e-mail attachments." (The second setting was added in Office 2003 SP1.) When each setting is enabled, it takes a semicolon-delimited list of file extensions as a parameter. For example, in order to allow users to access Microsoft Access .mdb files, the administrator enables the "Allow access to e-mail attachments" policy setting and enters MDB among the list of file extensions to allow, as shown in Figure 6.17.

Setting these policies results in two corresponding REG_SZ registry values in the HKEY_CURRENT_USER\Software\Policies\Microsoft\Office\11.0\Outlook\Security key: Level1Remove to unblock file extensions and Level1Add to add more extensions to the list of blocked files.

Note: The "Disallow access to e-mail attachments" Group Policy setting to set the Level1Add value was added to the Outlk11.adm administrative template for Office 2003 SP1. It does not appear in the original Outlk11.adm file. Also note that there are no corresponding Level2Add and Level2Remove registry values. To manage Level 2 attachments, you must use the Outlook Security Settings folder, as described in Chapter 7.

Administrators can also configure and control Level 1 and Level 2 file attachments via the Outlook Security Settings folder, which is discussed in the next chapter. Control of attachment security is much more granular via the Outlook Security Settings folder.

The Level1Remove and Level1Add policy settings also have analogous user-preference settings with the same names under HKEY_CURRENT_USER\Software\Microsoft\Office\11.0\Outlook\Security. If you are not using the Level1Remove and Level1Add policy settings, but you do want to block users from making changes to attachment blocking with the user-preference settings, you can do this with another policy setting under User Configuration / Administrative Templates / Microsoft Office Outlook 2003 / Tools | Options / Security. Enable "Prevent users from customizing attachment security settings." This controls the following registry value:

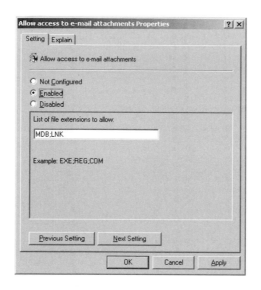

Figure 6.17
*Removing the
attachment block
from Microsoft
Access and
Windows shortcut
files.*

Key: HKEY_CURRENT_USER\Software\Policies\Microsoft\
Office\11.0\Outlook
Value name: DisallowAttachmentCustomization
Value type: REG_DWORD
Value: 1 (enabled), 0 (disabled)

6.5 Understanding the Object Model Guard

By default, Outlook blocks programming code that attempts to access certain Outlook features, making it much more difficult for malicious program to harvest addresses from Outlook or to send messages without the user's knowledge. Examples of blocked actions include accessing the address book, accessing an Outlook item's Send method, and accessing the HTML or plain-text body of a message. There is a price for such protection, however, and that price is that some applications may trigger security prompts to which the user must respond before the program can proceed.

Even other Microsoft Office programs are affected by these security prompts. For example, a user might want to perform a bulk mailing to Outlook contacts using Word's Mail Merge feature. If the user chooses to send the merged messages in plain-text format, after the user clicks the Merge to E-mail button in Word, the user will see the prompt in Figure 6.18. The user can choose to allow access to addresses for up to ten minutes, which is usually enough time to extract the e-mail addresses and construct the messages. However, for each individual message, the user will also

Figure 6.18
Users can allow applications to access address book information for up to ten minutes at a time.

see the prompt in Figure 6.19 and will need to wait five seconds for the Yes button to become available. (Yes, that's five seconds for each message.)

Tip: A Word mail merge to e-mail messages does not trigger either of these security prompts if the message format for the merge is set to HTML, which is Word 2003's default for a mail merge to e-mail.

This security feature is commonly known as the Outlook Object Model Guard. The object model is the hierarchy of objects, properties, methods, and events that make up the interface with which programmers create applications that interact with Outlook. Correctly constructed, Outlook VBA code and published Outlook custom forms generally have full access to the Outlook 2003 programming model without triggering the security prompts in Figures 6.19 and 6.20. For stand-alone users, Outlook also trusts all properly constructed Outlook COM add-ins (see sidebar "Building Outlook programs that avoid security prompts" on page 248) by default, and these, too, do not trigger security prompts.

Things get much more complicated in an Exchange environment. Whether Outlook trusts all or certain COM add-ins depends in part on whether the Outlook Security Settings folder, described in detail in Chapter 7, is being used to manage add-in security. The logic by which Outlook decides which COM add-ins to trust is very complex; you'll see a flow chart in Figure 7.4.

Figure 6.19
Users must wait five seconds before they can click Yes when this security prompt appears.

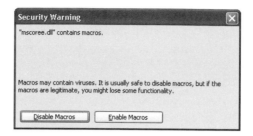

Figure 6.20
*Prompt from an
unsigned COM
add-in.*

The administrator can also control the COM add-in trust behavior with a GPO, using another setting under User Configuration / Administrative Templates / Microsoft Office Outlook 2003 / Tools | Options / Security. The Configure Add-In Trust Level setting controls the following registry value, with the possible values for AddinTrust shown in Table 6.5:

```
Key: HKEY_CURRENT_USER\Software\Policies\Microsoft\
Office\11.0\Outlook\Security
Value name: AddinTrust
Value type: REG_DWORD
```

You will see AddinTrust again in the flow chart in Figure 7.4, showing how Outlook determines which COM add-ins to trust.

As you learned earlier in in Section 6.4.7, Outlook supports control of attachment blocking though both settings administered through GPOs and local user-preference registry settings, which can be deployed with the CIW or CMW. However, there is no registry setting to suppress or otherwise control the Object Model Guard security prompts on untrusted COM add-ins or external programs. Microsoft Exchange Server administrators can exert some control over the security prompt behavior, however, through the use of a special folder in the Public Folders hierarchy on the Exchange server, as explained in Chapter 7.

Table 6.5   *Possible Values for AddinTrust to Control COM Add-in Behavior*

Option	Value
Trust all, use Exchange settings if present	0 (default)
Trust all loaded and installed COM add-ins	1
Do not trust loaded and installed COM add-ins	2

Building Outlook programs that avoid security prompts   You have read in this chapter about the concept of correctly constructed Outlook VBA code and VBScript code on published Outlook custom forms and the fact that this code doesn't trigger Object Model Guard security prompts. In this context, "correctly constructed" means that all Outlook objects are derived from the intrinsic Application object that those coding environments support. Similarly, in an Outlook COM add-in, which is a special type of application tightly integrated into Outlook, the OnConnection event in the IDTExtensibility2 interface passes as an argument an Application object that is "trusted." This trust means that all Outlook objects derived from that Application object will not trigger security prompts when other code in the COM add-in uses their address- or send-related properties or methods.

Ideally, all legitimate programs that access Outlook's address information and message-sending functionality should be constructed so that they produce no security prompts at all. Common programs like ActiveSync and other personal digital assistant synchronization tools accomplish this by using the more complex Extended MAPI programming interface instead of the Outlook object model. A method that can work well for in-house application developers is to build any Outlook functionality into an Outlook COM add-in that can be trusted, with public methods that other applications can call. For example, such a COM add-in might have a public method that sends an Outlook message. If the add-in is trusted, either by default for a stand-alone user or through the Outlook Security Settings folder for Exchange users (see Chapter 7), another program—even Access or Word VBA—can call that method to send a message without incurring a security prompt.

Yet another approach, not sanctioned by Microsoft but used by thousands of Outlook developers, is to use a third-party programming library called Redemption (http://www.dimastr.com/redemption), which provides a wrapper for Extended MAPI. Redemption works in Visual Basic, VBA, and even VBScript code behind custom Outlook forms, which makes it easier to use than Extended MAPI, which requires C++ or Delphi. As a COM component, Redemption can also be used in .NET applications through COM interop. In addition to avoiding the Object Model Guard security prompts, Redemption also exposes a great deal of programming functionality that Extended MAPI provides but the Outlook object model omits.

Note: COM is an application component and interface model common to the current generation of Windows operating systems and applications. Extended MAPI is a COM programming interface that provides access to the real guts of Outlook. However, because its structures and other parameters cannot be described in a type library, it cannot be used in languages like Visual Basic and is more difficult to implement

For .NET developers, MAPI33 (http://www.mapi33.freeservers.com/index.html) provides another Extended MAPI wrapper.

6.6   Other programmability security settings

The last security settings on our list to discuss in this chapter are all related to Outlook programmability and cover macro security in VBA, digitally signed COM add-ins, and a few options that affect custom Outlook forms.

6.6.1   VBA macro and add-in security

As with most other Office programs, Outlook supports the VBA programming environment where users can create macros and other procedures to automate their work. By default, VBA code will not run in Outlook 2003 because the setting in Tools | Macro | Security is set to High. The user normally can either set macro security to Medium, which will cause code to run with a prompt, or to Low, which will allow all VBA code to run with no prompt to enable macros. Alternatively, the user can leave macro security at the High level but digitally sign the VBA project with a certificate generated by the Selfcert.exe tool included with Office 2003. An additional setting can be invoked to require that all COM add-ins be digitally signed and their certificate trusted before they can run in Outlook.

Administrators using GPOs have several options with regard to VBA and COM add-ins:

- Disable VBA entirely for all Office applications.

- Mandate a certain macro security level in Outlook.

- Allow only digitally signed add-ins with trusted certificates to run in Outlook.

- Disable all COM add-ins.

Note: These settings are not at all related to the issue of trusted installed COM add-ins with regard to the Object Model Guard security prompts. Chapter 7 will show you how to trust a specific COM add-in in an Exchange environment.

To disable VBA for all Office programs, in the Group Policy Editor, go to User Configuration/Administrative Templates/Microsoft Office 2003/Security Settings. Under "Disable VBA for Office applications," select Enabled and check the box for "Disable VBA for Office applications." This setting corresponds to the following registry value:

```
Key: HKEY_CURRENT_USER\Software\Policies\Microsoft\
Office\11.0\Common
```
Value name: VbaOff
Value type: REG_DWORD
Value: 1 (VBA disabled), 0 (VBA enabled)

If you prefer to disable VBA on a per-machine rather than a per-user basis, you will find a similar policy setting under Computer Configuration / Administrative Templates / Microsoft Office 2003 / Security Settings, which sets a registry value in HKEY_LOCAL_MACHINE rather than HKEY_CURRENT_USER.

To configure Outlook-specific settings, in the Group Policy Editor, go to User Configuration / Administrative Templates / Microsoft Office Outlook 2003 / Tools | Macro / Security. To set the macro security level, enable the Security Level setting and set the security level to Very High, High, Medium, or Low. (The Very High setting, which disables all COM add-ins, was added in the Outlk11.adm file distributed after Office 2003 SP1 was released.) This policy setting controls the following registry value:

```
Key: HKEY_CURRENT_USER\Software\Policies\Microsoft\
Office\11.0\Outlook\Security
```
Value name: Level
Value type: REG_DWORD
Values: 1 (Low), 2 (Medium), 3 (High), 4 (Very High)

If the policy setting (or the corresponding user-preference registry value) is not present, Outlook uses a default value of 3 (high).

To allow only add-ins with trusted digital certificates to run, enable the setting for "Outlook: Trust all installed add-ins and templates" and clear the check box for "Check to Trust all installed add-ins and templates." This policy setting controls the following registry value:

```
Key: HKEY_CURRENT_USER\Software\Policies\Microsoft\
Office\11.0\Outlook\Security
```
Value name: DontTrustInstalledFiles
Value type: REG_DWORD
Values: 1 (enabled), 0 (disabled)

Clearing the "Check to Trust all installed add-ins and templates" check box in the group policy editor sets DontTrustInstalledFiles to 1. If the policy setting (or the corresponding user-preference registry value) is not present, Outlook uses a default value of 0 and trusts all installed add-ins.

Setting DontTrustInstalledFiles to 1 and Level to anything higher than 1 will cause the user to receive prompts when add-ins load that either don't

Table 6.6   *Add-in Behavior When DontTrustInstalledFiles = 1*

Macro Security Level Value	Behavior
1 (Low)	All COM add-ins load without security warning prompts.
2 (Medium)	User is prompted to enable or disable macros on unsigned add-ins and those from untrusted publishers. User has the option to trust publishers of signed add-ins and receive no further prompts for those publishers' add-ins.
3 (High)	User can enable macros only for signed add-ins from trusted publishers.
4 (Very High)	No COM add-ins load.

have digital certificates or have certificates from publishers that have not yet been trusted. (Trusted publishers are listed for the user on the Trusted Publishers tab of the Tools | Options | Macro | Security dialog.) Table 6.6 summarizes this behavior.

For example, if Level is set to 2 (medium) and an unsigned add-in tries to load, the user will see a prompt like that in Figure 6.20. The user can choose Enable Macros to allow the add-in to run or Disable Macros to block it.

This is a particularly problematic configuration with COM add-ins built with the Microsoft .NET Framework that use Mscoree.dll as their entry point to the Framework's Common Language Runtime. Since Mscoree.dll is a file used by all .NET programs, the Security Warning dialog provides the user with no information at all on what program might be involved. Ideally, a well-trained user will click Disable Macros because of the lack of information.

The Security Warning for a signed add-in, on the other hand, at least tells you the location of the file and its publisher. Figure 6.21 shows the prompt for the Microsoft Business Contact Manager (BCM) add-in for Outlook 2003. Although BCM was built as a .NET Outlook add-in, it was constructed in such a way that the entry point component (called a "shim" in this context) can be digitally signed.

In this case, the user has the same Disable Macros and Enable Macros options as in Figure 6.20 but can also check the "Always trust macros from this publisher" box so that other add-ins digitally signed with a certificate from Microsoft will not trigger this security warning.

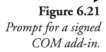

Figure 6.21
Prompt for a signed
COM add-in.

When the macro security level is set to high and the "Check to Trust all installed add-ins and templates" box is cleared, users affected by that GPO will be able to enable macros only for COM add-ins from trusted publishers. Note that this setting affects even VBA, which Office implements as a COM add-in, as users in this configuration see the prompt in Figure 6.22 when they to launch the VBA environment.

In order to use VBA, they will need to check the "Always trust macros from this publisher" box, then click Enable Macros, but they will need to do this only one time. Once the publisher has been trusted, add-ins from that publisher will load without prompts in subsequent Outlook sessions.

6.6.2   Blocked ActiveX controls in Outlook forms

One-off forms—those where the form definition is embedded in the item rather than drawn from a published form—present new problems in Outlook 2003. Not only is VBScript code behind the form blocked, but Outlook 2003 adds new restrictions on ActiveX controls. By default, only the

Figure 6.22
Prompt for a
digitally signed
COM add-in
(VBA).

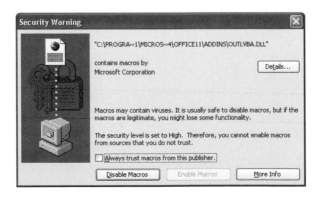

Table 6.7   *Values for AllowActiveXOneOffForms*

Setting	Value	Behavior
Allow all ActiveX controls	2	All ActiveX controls can run in one-off Outlook forms
Allow only safe controls	1	Only controls marked as "safe for initialization" may load
Load only Outlook controls (default)	0	Only the frm20.dll controls, the Outlook View Control, Outlook recipient control, and the docsite (message body) control may load

basic form controls (e.g., text box, combo box), message body control, recipient control, and Outlook View Control will load on a one-off form. If any other control is present, when users attempt to display the page showing that control, they'll see the error message "To help prevent malicious code from running, one or more objects in this form were not loaded. For more information, contact your administrator."

The ideal solution for this issue is to avoid one-off forms completely. If you must use a one-off form, you can control this behavior with GPOs, using the post-SP1 Outlk11.adm file. In the Group Policy Editor, go to User Configuration/Administrative Templates/Microsoft Office Outlook 2003/Security and enable the setting for Allow Active X One-Off Forms. This controls the following registry value:

```
Key: HKEY_CURRENT_USER\Software\Policies\Microsoft\
Office\11.0\Outlook\Security
Value name: AllowActiveXOneOffForms
Value type: REG_DWORD
```

Table 6.7 lists the supported values for AllowActiveXOneOffForms.

Note that published forms are not affected by this issue. If you're seeing the "To help prevent malicious code . . ." warning message, that's a certain indication that the form is now a one-off, which means the form definition is embedded in the item.

6.6.3   Forms in other mailboxes

Outlook 2003 includes a new setting—disabled by default—to allow forms in shared Exchange mailboxes to run script. Organizations that depend on custom Outlook forms in shared mailboxes will want to enable script to run on those forms, either through GPOs or with the corresponding user-preference registry setting.

To allow custom form scripts in shared mailboxes to run using GPO, in the Group Policy Editor, go to User Configuration/Administrative Templates/Microsoft Office Outlook 2003/Other/Advanced. Enable the setting for "Disable scripts in shared folders" and clear the check box for "Check to disable scripts in shared folders." This setting controls the following registry value:

```
Key: HKEY_CURRENT_USER\Software\Policies\Microsoft\
Office\11.0\Outlook\Security
Value name: SharedFolderScript
Value type: REG_DWORD
Values: 0 (default—disables scripts in shared folders), 1 (enables scripts in
shared folders)
```

There is a corresponding REG_DWORD value in the same security key named PublicFolderScript that similarly controls the behavior of scripts on custom forms in Public Folders.

6.7   Summary

This chapter has covered how to configure key security features and settings for Microsoft Outlook 2003. As discussed, threats to Outlook can be categorized into three main types. Network encryption techniques and S/MIME encryption of e-mail message can protect Outlook e-mail in transit. Enterprises can use the Microsoft Windows Server 2003 PKI to deploy the needed certificates more easily. To protect Outlook e-mail at rest, some administrators will choose to suppress the use of Personal Folders .pst files. To protect valuable digital information against unwanted dissemination, Microsoft provides support in Outlook 2003 for Windows Rights Management Services, an add-on for Windows Server 2003.

Threats to incoming e-mail, specifically spam and e-mail-borne viruses, create a security risk to enterprise e-mail environments and can be a distraction to employee productivity. Outlook 2003 includes a powerful Junk E-Mail filter that can be used to reduce spam. Administrators can use GPOs to initialize the filter lists used by the Junk E-mail Filter, as well as to control the overall level of protection. Outlook 2003 also, by default, blocks Web beacons, which are links to external content in HTML messages. Administrators will want to be aware of how this feature interacts with the user's Safe Senders list, Trusted Sites lists, and Outlook Contacts folder.

Finally, we have reviewed Outlook attachment blocking, the Outlook Object Model Guard, and other miscellaneous security settings related to Outlook programmability. In order to protect users from potentially dangerous attachments, it is recommended that administrators keep Level 1 attachment blocking in place and not allow users to demote attachments to Level 2.

In Chapter 7, Exchange administrators will learn how to manage attachment blocking, trusted COM add-ins, and programmatic security settings with the Outlook Security Settings folder. You'll also see that the interaction of those settings with policy or user-preference registry settings can sometimes be quite complex.

Managing the Outlook Security Settings Folder

As you saw in Chapter 6, Outlook 2003 blocks file attachments that could run code that might harm the user's machine. It also has features that make it much more difficult for a malicious program to harvest addresses from Outlook or to send messages without the user's knowledge.

Microsoft Exchange Server administrators can exert some control over both the attachment-blocking and the security-prompt behaviors through the use of a special folder in the Public Folders hierarchy on the Exchange server. This folder can contain both user-specific items for individual users and a default-settings item that applies to everyone else. In each security-settings item, the available options cover attachment blocking, COM add-in trusts, and programmatic access to properties and methods that a malicious program could use to harvest addresses from Outlook or send messages without the user's knowledge. With a Group Policy Object (GPO) setting or user-preference registry value (described in Section 7.3), Outlook can be directed to look to this folder to determine which security options should apply to the current user.

Note: The Security Settings folder is available only in Microsoft Exchange Server organizations and works with any version of Exchange. If your organization doesn't use Exchange, nothing in this chapter applies to you.

In this chapter, you will learn the following:

- Where to obtain and how to install the Outlook Administrator Pack, which contains the tools to administer the Outlook Security Settings folder

- How to set up the Outlook Security Settings folder, create individual security-settings entries, and modify the user's Outlook client so that it uses the settings defined in the folder

- What limitations affect the use of the Outlook Security Settings folder to control client security behavior

- What factors Outlook uses to decide whether to trust a particular Outlook COM add-in

- Why certain settings in the Outlook Security Settings folder may make client computers more vulnerable rather than more secure

7.1   Limitations of the Outlook Security Settings folder

Central management of Outlook security settings through an Exchange public folder sounds convenient, but it presents some significant limitations and risks. You might want to consider these issues before you embark on the process of creating and populating the Outlook Security Settings folder.

- The options that turn off security prompts not only affect useful external applications but also allow viruses and other malware to access address information or send messages with Outlook.

- As you saw in Chapter 6, central management of attachment blocking is already available through GPOs. If you are already managing attachment blocking with GPOs, then you will not want to manage it with the Outlook Security Settings folder too, and vice versa. The interaction of the security form's attachment-blocking settings with the Level1Remove and Level1Add policy and user-registry values is quite complex.

- Only Outlook COM add-ins can be trusted with full access to the Outlook object model, not external programs or even other Office programs like Access and Word. Therefore, even though the Outlook Security Settings folder gives you some control over when Outlook displays security prompts, that control may not be as granular as you want.

- Once an Outlook client is directed to look to the Outlook Security Settings folder, it will no longer trust any COM add-ins except those designated on the security-settings item that affects the user. This means that if you want to avoid security prompts on installed COM add-ins, you will need to trust *all* of them through the Security Settings folder.

- Only one version of a COM add-in can be trusted on any given security-settings item. You must repeat the trust process described Section 7.5.6 for each new version.

We'll discuss these limitations in more detail as we examine the different security options you can manage with the Outlook Security Settings folder.

7.2   Setting up the Outlook Security Settings folder

The Outlook Security Settings folder is part of the Public Folders hierarchy on any version of Microsoft Exchange Server. It uses a custom Outlook form to provide a management interface for the security-settings options that Outlook supports. Microsoft provides the custom form as part of an Outlook Administrator Pack in the Office 2003 Resource Kit. This package also includes components that allow an administrator to designate which Outlook COM add-ins can bypass the Object Model Guard (see Section 7.5.6) and thus avoid security prompts.

The process of setting up the folder and preparing a client workstation to manage it involves the following:

- Creating the public Outlook Security Settings folder

- Installing the Outlook Administrator Pack

- Publishing the custom form from the Administrator Pack to the folder

- Making the custom form the default form for that folder and setting folder permissions

- Installing components that allow the administrator to trust COM add-ins

After you finish the process, you will be ready to create new items in the folder using the custom form.

7.2.1   Creating the Outlook Security Settings folder

In order to create the Outlook Security Settings folder, you must start Outlook with a mail profile that does not use Cached Exchange mode. The profile also must connect to an Exchange mailbox that has permission to create top-level folders in the Public Folders hierarchy on the Exchange server.

► **Figure 7.1**

Create the Outlook
Security Settings
folder as a top-level
folder in Public
Folders.

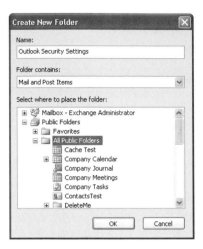

Tip: If you need to create a new profile for this purpose, you can either use the Mail applet in the Control Panel or click the New button on the Choose Profile dialog that appears when you start Outlook.

Use the File | New | Folder command in Outlook to create a new top-level public folder to hold mail and post items. If you want all versions of Outlook to use the same folder, name it "Outlook Security Settings," as shown in Figure 7.1. If you want to have Outlook 2000 use one Security Settings folder and to give Outlook 2002 and Outlook 2003 their own security settings, create two folders, one named "Outlook Security Settings" and the other named "Outlook 10 Security Settings." Note that the folder that a particular Outlook 2002 or Outlook 2003 user will use depends on how you set the CheckAdminSettings registry value on the client (as described in Section 7.3).

Note: The main difference between the Outlook 2000 security settings and those available to Outlook 2002 and Outlook 2003 is that the two newer programs support trusted COM add-ins. Outlook 2000 does not provide any way to trust specific Outlook COM add-ins. Throughout the rest of this chapter, references to the Outlook Security Settings folder apply to both folders unless otherwise specified.

7.2.2   Installing the Outlook Administrator Pack

To install the Outlook Administrator Pack, first download and install the latest version of the Office 2003 Resource Kit (Ork.exe) from http://www.microsoft.com/office/ork/2003/tools/ddl/default.htm onto any client workstation from which you plan to administer the Outlook Security Settings folder. Next, from the Program Files\ORKTools\ORK11\TOOLS\Outlook Administrator Pack folder, run the Admpack.exe program to extract the components for managing Outlook security settings. The location you choose as the destination for the Administrator Pack files doesn't matter. For convenience, you can specify the destination as the Program Files\ORKTools\ORK11\TOOLS\Outlook Administrator Pack folder.

After you run Admpack.exe to extract the files, you will see several files in the target folder:

- *OutlookSecurity.oft:* An Outlook form template file that you will use to publish the security custom form that administrators will use to create security-settings entries

- *Comdlg32.ocx and Hashctl.dll:* Two components used by the security form to trust Outlook COM add-ins

- *Readme.doc:* Documentation for the Security Settings form and folder

Microsoft does not provide a setup program for installing the various components in the Outlook Administrator Pack. You will need to install each one manually, as described in the following sections.

Note: It is not necessary to install any components from the Outlook Administrator Pack on nonadministrator client PCs. The only client change required is a registry value, which most organizations will manage with a GPO setting. This is covered in Section 7.3.

7.2.3   Publishing the custom form

You will use the OutlookSecurity.oft file that you unpacked from the Outlook Administrator Pack, as described in the previous section, to set up the form with which administrators will create security-settings items in the Outlook Security Settings folder. Follow these steps to publish the form to the Outlook Security Settings folder:

1.   Double-click the OutlookSecurity.oft form template file.

2.   When you see the Select Folder prompt, choose the Outlook Security Settings folder you created earlier. After that, a new Outlook item will open, using the custom form, with the window caption "Default Security Settings."

3.   From the Default Security Settings item's menu, choose Tools | Forms | Publish Form.

4.   In the Look In drop-down list at the top of the Publish Form As dialog (Figure 7.2), choose Outlook Folders.

5.   Click the Browse button and, in the Go to Folder dialog, select the Outlook Security Settings folder from the Public Folders hierarchy, then click OK.

6.   Enter a display name and form name. You can use any display name and form name that you prefer.

7.   Click Publish to publish the form.

8.   Close the item, and choose No when you're prompted to save changes. (You created a new item only for the purpose of publishing the form associated with that item. This step discards that item, which you do not need to save.)

The form that you have published to the folder is now a template that you can use to create new security-settings items in the folder.

Figure 7.2
Publish the form for managing Outlook security settings to the Outlook Security Settings public folder.

7.2.4   **Managing Security Settings folder options**

Next, you need to work with the options for the Outlook Security Settings folder to make the published form the default for the folder and to set user permissions for the folder.

Return to the main Outlook 2003 window, and click the Folder List button at the bottom of the Navigation pane to display all of the available folders. Expand the Public Folders\All Public Folders hierarchy until you see the Outlook Security Settings folder. Right-click on the Outlook Security Settings folder, choose Properties, and on the General tab under "When posting to this folder, use," choose the security form that you just published. This will make it the default form for the folder so that whenever an administrator clicks the New button in that folder, a new item using the security form will appear.

On the Permissions tab of the folder's Properties dialog, adjust the folder permissions as needed. The role for the default user should be Reviewer since each user must be able to read his or her settings from the folder. Grant the Editor permission to any administrators who will add, delete, and modify security-settings items in the folder, as shown in Figure 7.3.

Figure 7.3
*Typical permissions
for the Outlook
Security Settings
folder.*

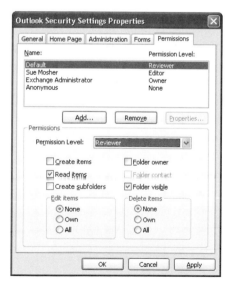

If you are also using the Outlook 10 Security Settings folder, repeat the procedures in this and the previous section to publish the form to that folder, make it the default, and set that folder's permissions.

7.2.5 Installing COM add-in trust components

You also need to install two helper components on the client machine(s) where you plan to administer the Outlook Security Settings folder. If you don't install these components on your administrative client, you'll get a warning message, "Could not load an object because it is not available on this machine," each time you open a security-settings item. You do not need to install them on users' machines because users will not be creating or opening security-settings items directly.

From the Program Files\ORKTools\ORK11\TOOLS\Outlook Administrator Pack folder, copy Hashctl.dll to your Windows\System32 or Winnt\System32 folder, whichever is appropriate for that computer. (You may need to be logged in as an administrator to perform this operation.) Choose Start | Run, and type this command line into the Run box:

```
regsvr32 hashctl.dll
```

Click OK to register the control. Repeat the copy-and-registration procedure with the Comdlg32.ocx file. If you can't copy it because it's already in use, that's OK. That just means that the control is already installed on that system; therefore, you won't need to register it.

7.3 Configuring Outlook to use the Security Settings folder

Outlook pays no attention to the entries in the Outlook Security Settings folder until you set a value in the user's Windows registry, preferably through a GPO. In the Group Policy Editor, under User Configuration / Administrative Templates / Microsoft Office Outlook 2003 / Tools | Options / Security, configure the setting named "Outlook virus security settings." For reference, it should be noted that this policy setting creates and sets a new DWORD value named CheckAdminSettings in the HKEY_CURRENT_USER\Software\Policies\Microsoft\Security key. Table 7.1 shows the options that you'll see in the Group Policy Editor and the corresponding values for CheckAdminSettings.

Table 7.1   *Supported Values for CheckAdminSettings*

Policy Setting Option	CheckAdminSettings Value	Outlook Uses . . .
Use default administrative settings	0 or not present	Default attachment-blocking and Object Model Guard behavior (all Outlook COM add-ins are trusted)
Look in the Outlook Security Settings folder	1	Settings defined in Outlook Security Settings folder
Look in the Outlook 10 Security Settings folder	2	Settings defined in Outlook 10 Security Settings folder
—	Any other value	Default attachment-blocking and Object Model Guard behavior (no Outlook COM add-ins are trusted)

Note: Once you point a user to the Outlook Security Settings folder by setting CheckAdminSettings to 1 or 2, Outlook 2003 will no longer trust COM add-ins by default. It will trust only those listed on the Trusted Code page of the Security Settings form. If CheckAdminSettings has any other nonzero value, no Outlook COM add-ins are trusted.

One ingenious feature of the Outlook Security Settings folder is that Outlook automatically makes it available for offline use and keeps it synchronized. The user does not need to add it to Public Folders\Favorites as would normally be required to make a folder available offline. (In fact, the user can't add it to Favorites.) For users connecting with Cached Exchange mode, Outlook automatically caches the Outlook Security Settings folder. Users who normally operate in Classic Offline mode will need to connect to the server in online mode and synchronize Outlook twice—once so that Outlook can create a hidden instance of the folder under Favorites and a second time to populate that folder with the actual security-settings items.

7.4   **Understanding how Outlook uses the Security Settings folder**

Once the Outlook Security Settings folder and the CheckAdminSettings registry value described in the previous section are in place, Outlook will look to the appropriate Security Settings folder at startup to determine what security options to apply to the current user. The folder may contain two types of items. One item—and one only—represents the default security settings. Other items may also be present to apply custom settings to specific individuals or groups. Section 7.5 explains how to create both types of items.

Through the items in the Outlook Security Settings folder, an administrator can do the following:

- Block access to certain file types beyond those that Outlook blocks by default

- Require users to save certain file attachments to disk before opening them

- Allow users to open certain file attachments without saving them to disk

- Prevent users from making changes to the blocked attachments list

- Designate certain COM add-ins as trusted, giving them full access to the Outlook programming model without triggering prompts

- Adjust the behavior of the security prompts that appear when external programs—those other than trusted COM add-ins, Outlook Visual Basic for Applications, and published Outlook forms—access blocked Outlook properties and methods

To help you understand how Outlook applies programming modal security settings from the Outlook Security Settings folder, Figure 7.4 illustrates the process that occurs at Outlook startup to determine which security options related to COM add-ins and other applications should apply to the current user. The AddinTrust policy is the setting discussed in Chapter 6 for controlling whether all COM add-ins will be trusted, none of them will, or only those trusted with an Outlook Security Settings folder item will. As Figure 7.4 shows, both the AddinTrust setting and the Check-AdminSettings setting can have an impact on which add-ins are trusted. Note that there are four scenarios in which all COM add-ins are trusted and three in which none are trusted.

The process for determining which attachments Outlook will block for the current user is even more complex because the registry may also contain Level1Remove and Level1Add Group Policy settings, user-preference settings, or both. You'll see how Outlook coordinates those managed and user settings later, in Section 7.5.3.

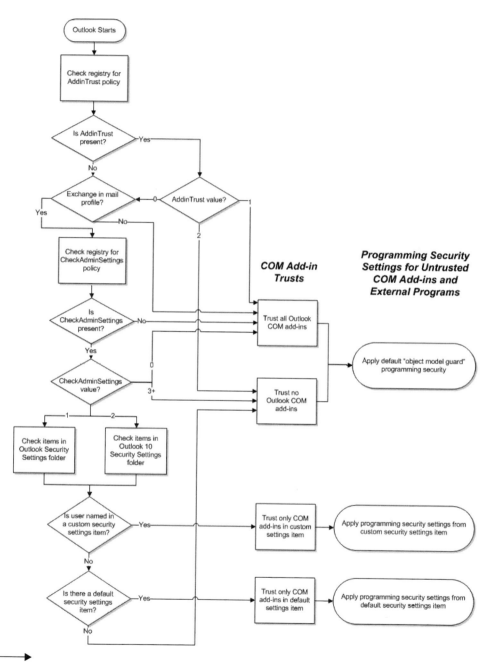

Figure 7.4   *Outlook uses a combination of a policy and entries in the Outlook Security Settings folder to determine which security options related to programming methods and properties should apply to the user.*

7.5   Creating security-settings items

To create a security-settings item, use the Folder List navigation pane in Outlook 2003 to switch to the Outlook Security Settings folder, then click New. For the default settings item, select Default Security Settings for All Users (see Figure 7.5). For a custom item, select Security Settings for Exception Group, then type the names of the individual users or Active Directory mail-enabled security groups to whom the custom settings should apply, separating the names with semicolons. You cannot use the Address Book to select names. However, you can type in a partial name and then press Ctrl+K to invoke Outlook's name-resolution feature, which will display matching names in the Check Names dialog if it finds more than one match.

Note: If you are using Exchange 5.5 or an earlier version, you can enter only names, not security groups, for the members of a custom security-settings item.

Caution: If a user is listed as a member in more than one security-settings item, the settings from the most recently modified item will apply. You should be careful, therefore, not to include a user in more than one security-settings item.

To save and close the new item, either choose File | Post or click the Close button, then respond Yes to the "Do you want to save changes?" prompt. If you are running Outlook with a profile that points to a mailbox other than the mailbox for the Windows account that you are logged in under (for example, an Exchange administrator's mailbox that you manage separately from the mailbox for your personal mail), you will be prompted for your network credentials the first time you create a security-settings item during a given Outlook session. Use the credentials for the mailbox whose Outlook profile you are using.

If you need to modify a custom security-settings item, open the item, then choose Edit | Revise Contents. If you make a change to the members of the item, be sure to make some other change in the item—perhaps toggling a setting on and off. Otherwise, Outlook may not save the change to the member list. To save the changes to the item, choose File | Post.

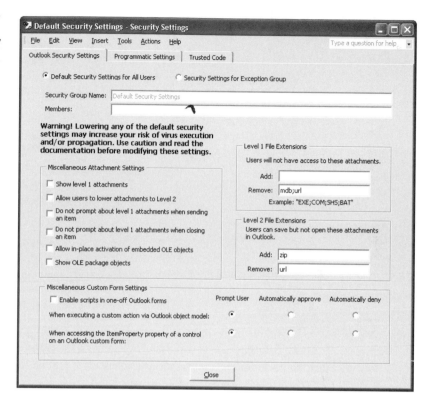

Figure 7.5
*Attachment and
miscellaneous
security settings.*

Note: If you simply open the item, make changes without choosing Edit |
Revise Contents, then save the item or click the Close button and choose
Save Changes, you may receive a mail message in your Inbox that a conflict
has occurred because multiple edits were made to the item. As a result of
the conflict, the security item's settings may not be applied as you intended.
Using Edit | Revise Contents, then File | Post, avoids this problem.

Table 7.2   *Outlook Security Settings Form Pages*

Page	Options
Outlook Security Settings	Attachment blocking, miscellaneous custom form settings
Programmatic Settings	Programmatic access to properties and methods
Trusted Code	Trusted COM add-ins

Changes made to a security-settings item do not affect any users who are currently running Outlook. The settings are loaded once at startup and are not checked dynamically during the Outlook session.

The Security Settings form consists of three pages of options, listed in Table 7.2. You can set as many or as few as you need.

The next few sections discuss the details of each page's options.

7.5.1   Managing attachment-block settings

As you learned in Chapter 6, Outlook has two levels of attachment security—Level 1 and Level 2—organized by file extension (e.g., .exe for executable files). Level 1 files are those to which Outlook allows no access. The list of Level 1 file types that are blocked by default expands with almost every Outlook service pack and includes most files that could potentially cause malicious code to run on the user's machine. The current list of more than 40 file types is available on Microsoft's Web site. Normally, the name of a blocked attachment is shown in a gray info bar at the top of an Outlook item (see Figure 6.16).

Level 2 files are those that must be saved to disk before they can be opened. Out-of-the-box, Outlook designates no files as Level 2. An administrator can manage Level 2, as well as Level 1, file types with the Security Settings form. The Security Settings form offers more control than the technique you saw in Chapter 6 of using GPOs to set the Level1Remove and Level1Add registry values.

To use the Security Settings form to add more file types to the Level 1 blocked list, enter the extensions for the types you want to add, separated by semicolons, in the Add box under Level 1 File Extensions on the first page of the Security Settings form. To move a file type from Level 1 to Level 2, enter the extensions for the types you want to unblock, separated by semicolons, in the Remove box under Level 1 File Extensions.

To change a file type that is completely blocked (Level 1) so that it becomes accessible without saving it to disk, enter its extension in the Remove box under Level 1 File Extensions and also in the Remove box under Level 2 File Extensions.

To force the user to save certain file types to disk before opening them, enter the extensions for those types, separated by semicolons, in the Add box under Level 2 File Extensions.

An example should help you understand the different options available. Figure 7.5 shows a default security-settings item that changes the behavior for .url (Internet Explorer shortcut), .mdb (Microsoft Access database), and .zip (Zip archive) files. When a user starts Outlook, Microsoft Access database files, normally blocked, will now be accessible but must be saved to disk first. Zip files, which normally can be opened directly, now also must be saved to disk first. Because .url is entered in the Remove box for both Level 1 and Level 2, .url files become accessible. If the user double-clicks a .url shortcut file, it will either open immediately or display a prompt asking whether the user wants to save or open the item. Whether the prompt appears depends on Windows' setting for .url files, not Outlook's.

7.5.2 Managing miscellaneous attachment-block settings

Under Miscellaneous Attachment Settings in Figure 7.5, the "Show level 1 attachments" option removes the blocking from all Level 1 attachments and makes Outlook treat them as Level 2 attachments. Even though users would have to save such attachments before opening them, enabling this setting presents a great security risk and is therefore not recommended.

If Outlook is set (with the CheckAdminSettings registry value) to look for settings in the Outlook Security Settings folder, users normally cannot demote file types from Level 1 to Level 2 using the user's Level1Remove registry key (HKEY_CURRENT_USER\Software\Microsoft\Office\11.0\ Outlook\Security\Level1Remove). You can grant the user that ability by checking the "Allow users to lower attachments to Level 2" box on the first page of the security form, but again, that would increase the security risk.

The attachment-blocking settings include not just what files will be blocked or available but how Outlook will present information about blocked attachments to the user. The two "Do not prompt . . ." settings control what Outlook does when the user sends or saves an item that contains a blocked file type.

By default, when the user sends a message that contains a blocked attachment, Outlook displays the warning shown in Figure 6.17. Note that Outlook does not actually prevent the user from sending a blocked attachment; it only issues a warning. To turn off this warning, check the "Do not prompt about level 1 attachments when sending an item" box. Since most recipients probably will not be able to access the attachment, we recommend that you leave the box unchecked so that the default setting applies.

By default, when the user saves an item that contains a blocked attachment, Outlook displays the warning message in Figure 7.6. To turn off this warning, check the "Do not prompt about level 1 attachments when clos-

Figure 7.6
Blocked-attachment warning for an item being saved.

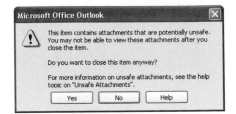

ing an item" box. Since the user will not be able to remove a blocked attachment after saving the item, we recommend that you leave the box unchecked so that the default setting applies.

The "Allow in-place activation of embedded OLE objects" and the "Show OLE package objects" settings control how content added with the Insert | Object command is handled. The default settings hide OLE packages and prevent users from opening OLE objects, such as embedded Excel worksheets, in rich-text messages and other items. These are the most secure and recommended settings.

7.5.3 Understanding managed versus user attachment-block settings

As mentioned in Chapter 6, Outlook supports three possible ways to manage attachment-blocking settings:

- Using the Outlook Security Settings folder

- Using GPO settings that set Level1Remove and Level1Add values in HKEY_CURRENT_USER\Software\Policies\Microsoft\Office\11.0\ Outlook\Security

- Allowing users to create their own custom Level1Remove and Level1Add settings in HKEY_CURRENT_USER\Software\Microsoft\Office\11.0\Outlook\Security

If a security-settings item lists a file type as Level 1 but a Group Policy setting designates it as Level 2, which setting wins? In other words, given the different ways to manage attachment blocking, which takes precedence? Under what conditions are the user's settings used, even if administrative settings are present in the Security Settings form or a Group Policy setting?

Let's look first at how you can control whether Outlook will ignore any user-preference settings for attachment blocking. There are three ways to accomplish this, one through the Outlook Security Settings folder and two through GPO settings.

Using the Security Settings form, if you leave the "Allow users to lower attachments to Level 2" box clear, which is the default setting, Outlook will ignore the user's changes to the Level1Remove and Level1Add registry values.

You'll find the Group Policy setting to suppress all user attachment-block customizations in the Group Policy Editor under User Configuration / Administrative Templates / Microsoft Office Outlook 2003 / Tools | Options / Security. The "Prevent users from customizing attachment security settings" setting controls a DWORD value named DisallowAttachmentCustomization in the registry under HKEY_CURRENT_USER\Software\Policies\Microsoft\Office\11.0\Outlook. If this registry value is present, Outlook ignores the user's changes to the Level1Remove and Level1Add values. The actual value for DisallowAttachmentCustomization does not matter.

The policy setting takes precedence over the Security Settings form. If the DisallowAttachmentCustomization value is present, Outlook will ignore the user's changes to the Level1Remove and Level1Add registry values, even if the "Allow users to lower attachments to Level 2" box on the Security Settings form is checked.

In addition, if the Level1Remove or Level1Add policy value is present in HKEY_CURRENT_USER\Software\Microsoft\Office\11.0\Outlook\Security, Outlook will ignore the corresponding user-preference value.

Table 7.3 summarizes how these settings work in combination. Note that if the security form is not being used, the Group Policy settings control whether Outlook ignores or applies the user's settings, just as if the form

Table 7.3 *How Administrative Settings Affect User Settings for Attachment Blocking*

Security Form	Group Policy Settings			User Settings	
Allow Users to Lower Attachments to Level 2	DisallowAttachmentCustomization	Level1Remove	Level1Add	Level1Remove	Level1Add
Off				Ignored	Ignored
On	Not present			Applied	Applied
On	Present			Ignored	Ignored
On	Not present	Present	Not present	Ignored	Applied
On	Not present	Not present	Present	Applied	Ignored
On		Present	Present	Ignored	Ignored

were present and the "Allow users to lower attachments to Level 2" box were checked.

For example, for greatest control over end-user attachment security, you can completely block users from customizing attachment blocking. Either use the security form and check the "Allow users to lower attachments to Level 2" box or deploy the DisallowAttachmentCustomization policy setting. You can also deploy both the Level1Remove and Level1Add Group Policy settings and leave the values blank.

However, you might have a situation where you don't want users to be able to customize their Level1Remove setting, but you don't mind if they block additional file types by adding them with their own Level1Add value. In that case, you would add the Level1Remove setting using GPOs but not the Level1Add setting. You would not add the DisallowAttachmentCustomization policy setting, and if you were using the Security Settings form, you would check the "Allow users to lower attachments to Level 2" box.

Let's look at a case where the same file type is configured on both the Security Settings form and in the Level1Add or Level1Remove Group Policy setting and see how different combinations of settings would make those file attachments available or leave them blocked. As you can see from Table 7.4, the highest security setting always wins. If either the security form or the Group Policy setting blocks the file type by specifying it as a Level 1 file, Outlook will always block that file type. If, however, neither the form nor the policy enforces the Level 1 setting, either the form or the policy setting can move it to Level 2.

How might these settings be used in combination? Consider a scenario in which a few users occasionally need to exchange a Microsoft Access data-

Table 7.4   *Using the Security Form and Group Policy Settings to Control Attachment Blocking*

| Security Form | | Group Policy Setting | | |
Level 1 Add	Level 1 Remove	Level 1 Add	Level 1 Remove	Result
	X			Available
			X	Available
	X		X	Available
X			X	Blocked
	X	X		Blocked

base by e-mail and also need to run code in the database that generates electronic mailings. You could set up a custom security-settings item form for that group of people to loosen programmatic security (as described in Section 7.5.5) so that the code could run without prompts. In addition, you could add "mdb" to the Level 1 Remove text box on the Security Settings form. To ensure that the form could not also unblock .exe files, you could use the Level1Add Group Policy setting with "exe" as its value, along with the extensions for other files that you don't ever want the Security Settings form to unblock.

If you find the different combinations of settings confusing, here's the key point to remember: a higher administrative setting always wins over a lower user attachment-block setting. If the security form or a GPO specifies a file as Level 1, the user cannot lower it to Level 2. The user will be able to lower a file type to Level 2 only if all of these conditions are met:

- The Level1Remove Group Policy setting is not present.

- The DisallowAttachmentCustomizations policy setting is not present.

- The CheckAdminSettings policy setting is either not present or set to 0, or the file type is not listed on the security form under Level 1 Add.

- If CheckAdminSettings is present and set to 1 or 2, the security form has the option for "Allow users to lower attachments to level 2" checked, and the file type is not listed on the security form under Level 1 Add.

As you can see, the interaction among the security form settings and Group Policy settings for attachment blocking can be quite complex. If you plan to use both approaches to control attachment blocking, you should test the results carefully before deploying widely. You might also choose to keep things simple and pick just one of these methods to control attachment blocking.

7.5.4 Managing form-related security settings

The Outlook Security Settings tab of the security form (Figure 7.5) has several other settings that are related to custom Outlook forms.

The "Enable scripts in one-off Outlook forms" setting is either on or off. One-off forms are forms embedded in the actual Outlook items, either because those items were created from unpublished forms or perhaps because form code performed operations that caused the form to be one-off. Off is the default for this setting. If you turn this setting on, users will be prompted to enable or disable macros whenever they open a one-off form that contains VBScript code. This behavior is the same as that of Outlook 2000 and other versions that predate the Outlook E-mail Security Update. In an Exchange environment, there are few situations where a one-off form with code behind it is preferred over a properly published form. Therefore, you will probably want to leave this setting disabled.

For the "When executing a custom action via Outlook object model" setting, it's helpful to understand that voting buttons are a type of custom action. Such actions are constructed on a custom form's (Actions) page and can include an option to send a response item immediately. Because executing a custom action can result in an item being sent, it's treated as a special case of the restriction on sending items via the Outlook object model and thus normally triggers a security prompt. You can control that behavior with the "When executing a custom action via Outlook object model" setting.

The final setting on the first tab of the form, "When accessing the Item-Property property of a control on an Outlook custom form," is intended to thwart attempts to gain access to address information by programmatically setting a control on an Outlook form to a property that may contain address information.

The "Automatically deny" setting is the most secure for these two options.

7.5.5   Managing programmatic settings

The options on the Programmatic Settings page of the security form (Figure 7.7) govern the Object Model Guard, Outlook's security feature that restricts access by programming code to properties and methods that could be used to harvest addresses or send messages. While you can trust a single COM add-in, as described in the next section, there is no way to loosen programmatic access for a single external application. Any change affects all applications. Therefore, we recommend that you change the programmatic access settings only when absolutely necessary. The Security Settings form provides separate options for three different programming interfaces, listed in Table 7.5.

Figure 7.7 shows the programmatic settings available. For each option, the default is to prompt the user, but you can change that to "Automatically approve" or "Automatically deny."

Table 7.5   *Programming Interfaces Controlled by Outlook Security Settings*

Interface	Description
Outlook object model	Programming interface built into Outlook for automating all kinds of Outlook functions, including creating items and sending messages
Collaboration Data Objects (CDO)	Collaboration Data Objects, an optional programming library included with Outlook, can perform many operations that Outlook cannot, such as retrieving information from the Address Book, retrieving Internet message headers, and displaying an address-resolution dialog
Simple Messaging Application Programming Interface (MAPI)	The simple version of the Messaging Application Programming Interface allows programs to read messages from an Inbox and create and send messages

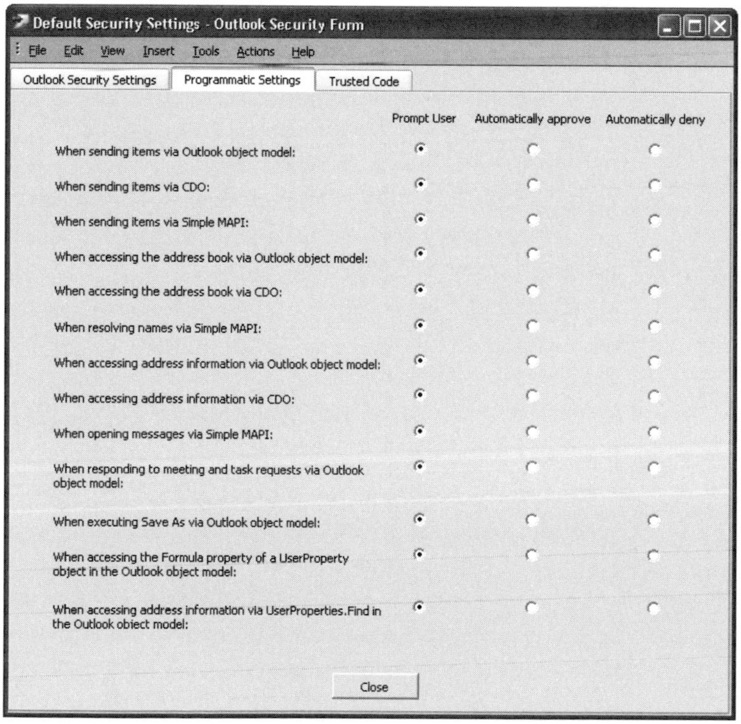

Figure 7.7
Default settings for the Outlook Object Model Guard.

Note: Some of the properties associated with accessing address information may surprise you. For security purposes, the HTMLBody, HTMLEditor, Body, and WordEditor properties all are subject to address-information security prompts because the body of a message often contains the sender's or other people's e-mail addresses.

If you are trying to loosen security to the minimum amount needed for a particular application to run without prompts and you do not have access to the source code for the application, you may not know which settings to change. You may need to change the settings, restart Outlook, then run the application—and repeat this sequence several times in order to determine which settings suppress the prompts that the application triggers.

Tip: An application that displays the Address Book where users can choose names may be using Collaboration Data Objects (CDO) since Outlook has no comparable method in its object model.

It is very important to understand that the Outlook Security Settings folder does not provide any granularity for suppressing security prompts for programs that are external to Outlook, for example, a database program that creates and sends Outlook messages. You cannot say that Program A can send e-mail messages but not look up addresses, while Program B can look up addresses but not send mail. If you want Program A to be able to use the Outlook programming model to send e-mail messages without prompts and Program B to look up addresses, you will have to loosen the security for sending mail messages programmatically and looking up addresses for *all* external programs, including not just both Program A and Program B but also any malicious programs that might find their way onto the user's machine.

The security implications should be clear: if you loosen programmatic security for the sake of an in-house external program, you've also loosened it for every other program, including viruses and other malware. Therefore, you should keep programmatic security as tight as possible in your default security-settings item and loosen it only where absolutely necessary in custom security-settings items for people who need a less secure environment to run programs important to your organization.

On the other hand, if you keep programmatic security tight so that users need to respond to Outlook security prompts at least occasionally, you may be creating a security vulnerability of a different sort. If users become accustomed to automatically clicking the Yes button when they see Outlook security prompts, there's a higher risk that one day they'll click Yes and allow a virus or other malicious code to go to work. To reduce that risk, you may need to replace external programs that trigger security prompts with other applications that don't (see sidebar in Chapter 6, "Building Programs That Don't Trigger Security Prompts"). You may also want to migrate functionality to Outlook COM add-ins, which can be trusted so that they do not trigger security prompts.

7.5.6 **Trusting COM add-ins**

As you saw in Figure 7.4, the default behavior is for properly constructed Outlook COM add-ins to have full access to the Outlook 2003 object model without triggering security prompts. However, when the Check-AdminSettings policy setting is present and its value is 1 or 2, the only Outlook COM add-ins that are trusted are those specified in the security-settings item relevant to the user (or in the default security-settings item). If you want to trust an Outlook COM add-in, use the Trusted Code page of the Security Settings form (Figure 7.8). You will need access to the primary .dll file for each COM add-in, but the full add-in does not actually need to be installed on your administrative client machine.

Note: Outlook does not require a COM add-in to have a digital signature in order to be trusted with regard to the Object Model Guard. However, as discussed in Chapter 6, a separate security setting in the DontTrust-InstalledAddins controls whether unsigned COM add-ins are allowed to run at all.

For each add-in you want to trust, click Add, then select the .dll file registered for the add-in. If a new version of the add-in is deployed (even if the .dll is recompiled without a new version number), you will need to remove the add-in from the list with the Remove button and add the new version of the .dll to the trusted list. The inability to trust multiple versions of Outlook COM add-ins simultaneously makes this feature less useful than it could be.

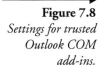

Figure 7.8
*Settings for trusted
Outlook COM
add-ins.*

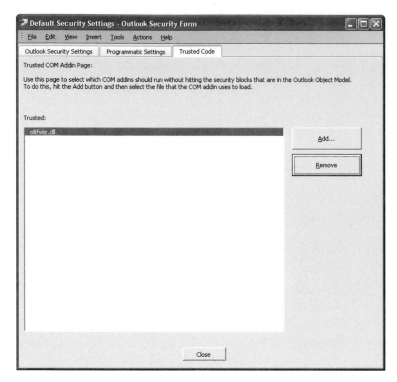

The easiest way to learn which .dll should be trusted may be to ask the developer. If that is not feasible, you can install the add-in, then look in the HKEY_CURRENT_USER\Software\Microsoft\Office\Outlook\Addins or HKEY_LOCAL_MACHINE\Software\Microsoft\Office\Outlook\Addins

Figure 7.9
*ProgID values for
Outlook COM
add-ins.*

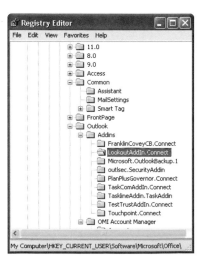

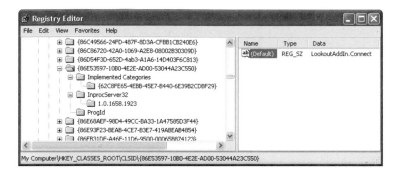

Figure 7.10
*The matching
entry in HKEY_
CLASSES_
ROOT\CLSID for
a COM add-in.*

registry key, depending on where the particular add-in installs. Each add-in will have its own key, as shown in Figure 7.9. For example, the Lookout search add-in for Outlook has a key named LookoutAddIn.Connect. This is also the name of a property of the add-in known as its ProgID.

You can search the registry to locate a reference to this ProgID in the HKEY_CLASSES_ROOT\CLSID portion of the registry, as show in Figure 7.10.

Once you locate the add-in's globally unique identifier (GUID), which is {86E53597-10B0-4E2E-AD00-53044A23C550} in this case, look at the default value of the InProcServer32 key under HKEY_CLASSES_ROOT\CLSID\{Add-in GUID} to determine the full path to the .dll that can be trusted.

In this case, because Lookout is a COM add-in built with the .NET Framework, the name of the .dll is Mscoree.dll, as shown in Figure 7.11. Therefore, to add the Lookout COM add-in to the Trusted Code page of the Security Settings form, you'd browse to \Windows\System32 and select the Mscoree.dll file. For other add-ins, you may find the main .dll in the add-in's installation folder.

Figure 7.11
*The COM add-in
.dll that can be
trusted, located
under the
InprocServer32
key.*

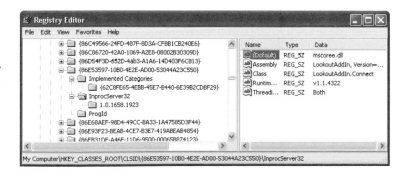

Note: Only one copy of Mscoree.dll resides on the user's machine in the \Windows\System32 folder. When you use the security settings form to trust Mscoree.dll, you are applying that trust to all COM add-ins that use Mscoree.dll as their entry point. Any such add-in will be exempt from Outlook "object model guard" security prompts.

7.6   Summary

In this chapter, you've learned how to use the Outlook Security Settings folder in an Exchange environment to manage attachment blocking, COM add-in trusts, and other programmatic settings. Administrators need to be aware of the complex interaction between the settings in the Outlook Security Settings folder and the policy and user-registry settings for managing attachment blocking, especially if you allow users to downgrade file types from Level 1 to Level 2.

With regard to the Object Model Guard security prompts, it may be difficult to achieve a balance between the desired level of security and the need for programs that interface with Outlook to operate smoothly and without interruption. Ultimately, you may need to develop or purchase replacement programs that avoid Outlook security prompts.

8

Special Configuration Scenarios

The previous chapters have discussed the basics of how to configure Outlook options as part of a new installation or with a post-setup update using the Custom Maintenance Wizard (CMW) or Group Policy Objects (GPOs) and how to change certain Outlook settings, especially mail profiles. In many cases, though, you need to get beyond the basics to deal with a configuration scenario that has special requirements.

Also, your work as an administrator doesn't stop once the deployment is complete and the users are up and running with Outlook 2003. Supporting Outlook with service packs and hotfixes is just as crucial as a good initial deployment. This chapter also covers special tasks that you, as an administrator, need to keep up regularly.

We will go into more detail about the following configuration scenarios:

- Deploying on a terminal server

- Moving a user to a new machine

- Managing multilanguage installations

- Upgrading from Outlook 2000 or 2002

- Deploying hotfixes and service packs

8.1   Deploying on Terminal Server

The combination of Office 2003 and Windows Server 2003 Terminal Server has made Terminal Server installations easier than ever. The installation process and the ability to update the configuration after installation don't differ much from a normal Office or Outlook installation. While this section focuses on Windows Server 2003, it also largely applies to other terminal server environments, such as Citrix.

8.1.1   Benefits of Office on a terminal server

The key benefit of deploying Office on a terminal server is that by configuring just one server, you can serve many users without the need to deploy and configure each separate client machine. This enables you to create a standard environment in a short amount of time. The fact that it is a single installation also makes it easy to update all of your users at once.

A terminal server is even accessible with ancient hardware and non-Windows operating systems. Microsoft provides the Remote Desktop Connection tool for making connections from everything from Windows 95 to Windows Server 2003. You can download the tool from http://www.microsoft.com/downloads/details.aspx?FamilyID=80111f21-d48d-426e-96c2-08aa2bd23a49. The download is the same version built into Windows XP Service Pack 2.

Besides ancient hardware and non-Windows operating systems, mobile devices, such as PDAs, can also access a terminal server. This enables your users to enjoy the full Office suite. Microsoft Knowledge Base article 314537, "How to Use a Handheld PC or a Pocket PC as a Mobile Terminal," explains how to install and configure the client software and make the connection.

8.1.2   Drawbacks of Office on a terminal server

While there are many benefits to creating a standard environment by means of a terminal server, you should be well aware of the downside as well. The most important drawback is that using a terminal server creates a single point of failure. If the terminal server goes down, all users will be disconnected and any unsaved changes might get lost.

Office on a Terminal server also requires a lot of server resources. You should plan for the following:

- 10 MB of memory per connection

- At least 8 MB of memory per Office application per user

- Additional memory and CPU cycles to process application usage

- Sufficient network bandwidth

- A fast hard-disk configuration

The Windows Server Resource Kit provides Terminal Server scaling tools to help you make an accurate calculation of your server needs.

8.1.3 Installing Office on a terminal server

Once Terminal Server is configured on the Windows 2003 server, you can install Office 2003 on the server. Unlike previous versions of Office, Office 2003 will detect that it is being installed on a terminal server. This removes the need to place the terminal server in Install mode or the modify the Office installer with a special transform .mst file.

During the installation, you'll notice that you have the same setup options as when doing a normal client installation. The biggest difference is with what components are being installed and the way they are installed. Since many users will be using the terminal server and they won't be able to modify the installation on the server, all components that are normally set to install on first use are now installed by default. Components that are hard to interact with on a terminal server are disabled by default. This means that Outlook 2003 installed on a terminal server also doesn't include sound and won't display some icon animations; also high-resolution images are substituted with low-resolution images. The following shared Office functions are also disabled:

Office Shared Features

- Alternative Input (speech and handwriting)
- Additional True Type Fonts
- International Support (Universal font and Syriac font)
- New and Open Office Documents Shortcuts (Start menu)

Office Tools

- HTML Source Editing (Web debugging)

Warning: The above features can be enabled, but this can result in poor performance, high network usage, or some options not working as expected due to Terminal Server interaction limitations.

8.1.4 Things to consider with Outlook and Office on a terminal server

Since all users share the same hardware resources on a terminal server, you might want to limit the resources used by each user by disabling Word as

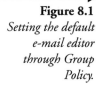

Figure 8.1
*Setting the default
e-mail editor
through Group
Policy.*

the e-mail editor. You can force Outlook as the e-mail editor with GPOs. You can find this setting under User Configuration / Administrative Templates / Microsoft Office Outlook 2003 / Tools | Options / Mail Format / Message Format. Figure 8.1 shows the available options. This policy setting controls the following registry value; Outlook refers to the built-in e-mail editor:

> Key: `HKEY_CURRENT_USER\Software\Policies\Microsoft\Office\11.0\Outlook\Options\Mail`
> Value name: `EditorPreference`
> Value type: `REG_DWORD`
> Value data: `131072` = HTML/Outlook
> `131073` = HTML/Microsoft Word
> `196610` = Rich Text/Outlook
> `196609` = Rich Text/Microsoft Word
> `65536` = Plain Text/Outlook
> `65537` = Plain Text/Microsoft Word

When most users always run both Outlook and Word on the terminal server, there is no direct need to force a particular editor because the server should already be configured with sufficient resources to allow all users to run Outlook and Word concurrently.

For users who only read and send e-mail, having the full Outlook version available might be overkill; they may be able to use the improved Outlook Web Access (OWA) of Exchange 2003 for all of their e-mail needs. Therefore, you may want to limit which users can actually start Outlook on the terminal server. To accomplish this, you can set appropriate NTFS permissions on the Outlook.exe file itself. Create a security group called "No Outlook" in Active Directory Users and Computers and assign that group Deny permissions on Outlook.exe. A cleaner approach is possible when you have multiple terminal servers available. Then you can choose not to install Outlook on a specific terminal server, direct that group of users to that server, and have them use OWA instead.

8.1.5   Terminal server issues with Outlook

While Outlook installed on a terminal server generally works just as it would when installed on a normal client, there are several special features that a terminal server installation does not support.

Cached Exchange mode or Classic Offline mode can't be enabled when creating a new profile. If you deploy mail profiles by using a .prf file and configure it to enable Cached Exchange mode or Classic Offline mode, Outlook running on a terminal server will ignore those settings and will always configure the profile for Classic Online mode. This makes sense because having Cached Exchange mode or Classic Offline mode enabled on a Terminal server could severely impact the server's performance and take up a lot of hard-disk space. There would also be a need to recreate the offline cache on multiple machines for users who don't always log on to the same terminal server. Because Cached Exchange mode can't be enabled, the Outlook Junk E-mail Filter doesn't work either, because it requires Cached Exchange mode.

Custom Outlook forms that require VBScript do not work automatically when Outlook is used on a terminal server. This is because Outlook VBScript support is not installed in this configuration. If VBScript is required on the terminal server, you can enable it by manually copying Outlvbs.dll from the installation CD to C:\Program Files\Microsoft Office\Office11.

Custom Messaging Application Programming Interface (MAPI) forms also do not work when Outlook is installed on a terminal server. To enable this, terminal server users must have Query Value, Set Value, and Create Subkey special permissions on the HKEY_CLASSES_ROOT\CLSID registry key.

Time zone settings can't be changed from within Outlook as these are system settings only administrators can change. Since terminal server users might log on from different time zones, the Outlook Calendar could appear quite confusing to them. To handle this scenario, you can deploy Outlook with a second time zone setting. From a computer that already has a second time zone configured, export the registry key HKEY_CURRENT_USER\Soft-ware\Microsoft\Office\11.0\Outlook\Options\TimeZone. You can import its settings into the CMW or deploy the .reg file settings using a login script.

As an alternative, you can configure the Windows 2003 Terminal Server to allow time zone redirection. Time zone redirection is only supported, how-ever, when clients logon with a remote desktop connection or Windows CE 5.1. You can manage this setting with GPOs. It is available under Computer Configuration / Administrative Templates / Windows Components / Termi-nal Services / Client\Server Data Redirection / Allow Time Zone Redirection. This policy setting controls the following registry value:

```
Key: HKEY_LOCAL_MACHINE\Software\Policies\Microsoft\
Windows NT\Terminal Services
Value name: fEnableTimeZoneRedirection
Value type: REG_DWORD
Value data: 1 = Enabled, 0 = Disabled (default)
```

8.2   Moving a user to a new machine

Moving a user to a new machine is never a pleasant thing to do. Most of the time, users have been working on the old machine for years. In practically all cases, this means that they have stored a lot of data locally and have made changes to the settings for their favorite applications. While you can often move the data easily between the two machines (assuming you can find it all), changes to the working application environment are harder to transfer, especially when you are in an environment where roaming profiles are not configured or when you are moving the user to Outlook 2003 from a machine running an older version of Outlook.

If you are using roaming profiles, then users' settings will travel with them to the new machine, and all of their data should be in their home folder on the server or in folders that roam. If not, Microsoft provides two tools to assist with data and settings transfers:

- *In Office:* Save My Settings Wizard, also known as the Office Profile Wizard (OPW), which you learned about in Chapter 2.

- *In Windows XP:* Files and Settings Transfer Wizard

Note: Another Microsoft tool is the User State Migration Tool, which we'll touch on briefly in Section 8.2.3. It's probably overkill, however, to use it just for transferring Outlook files and settings.

A key first step in preparing for a transfer is to determine what files and settings in what locations need to move to the other machine.

8.2.1 Files and settings to transfer

As you learned in Chapter 1, the personalized environment for each Outlook user involves many different registry and file locations. Table 8.1 summarizes the most important keys and locations and types of settings or files you should include when manually moving a user to a new machine.

Table 8.1 *Registry and File Locations of Outlook Data and Settings to Transfer to a New Machine*

Location	Settings/Files Included	Examples
HKEY_CURRENT_USER\Software\Microsoft\Office\11.0	This registry key holds the main part of all of the settings for Office. Outlook stores most of its settings in the Outlook subkey but also stores several in the Common subkey.	Practically everything that can be set through Tools | Options in Outlook
HKEY_CURRENT_USER\Software\Microsoft\Windows NT\CurrentVersion\Windows Messaging Subsystem	This registry key holds all of the mail profiles configured for Outlook.	(See Chapter 1 for a detailed description of this key.)
%USERPROFILE%\Application Data\Microsoft\Outlook	This file location holds specific mail profile and other settings that can't be stored in the registry, such as Send/Receive settings, navigation pane settings, toolbar customizations, and the nickname cache.	.srs, .xml, .nk2, Outcmd.dat files
%USERPROFILE%\Application Data\Signatures	This file location holds all of the user's signatures. The actual name of the Signatures folder might be translated to your locale through a registry REG_SZ (string) registry value named Signatures in the (HKEY_CURRENT_USER\Software\Microsoft\Office\11.0\Common\General key.	Signatures are stored in three file formats: .txt, .htm, .rtf vCard (.vcf) files to attach as part of signatures
%USERPROFILE%\Local Settings\Application Data\Microsoft\Outlook	This file location holds all information that is not being transferred by Windows roaming profiles either because the files are too large or because they will automatically be recreated from the original source.	.pst (can be very big) .ost, .oab (recreated from Exchange) Extend.dat (recreated from registry)

8.2.2   Save My Settings Wizard

The Save My Settings Wizard is an end-user Office tool that is installed by default when you install any Office application. It can be found on the Microsoft Office Tools menu, which is a submenu of the Microsoft Office folder in the Start menu. When you run this tool, you will have the choice either to save the settings or to restore the settings from a single .ops file. When saving the settings, the wizard stores settings for all of the Office applications installed on the computer. At first, that makes it look like the Save My Settings Wizard is not very flexible at all. However, as you saw in Chapter 2, the Save My Settings Wizard is really the same tool as the Office Profile Wizard (OPW) and can be controlled with command-line switches and .ini files.

When the user runs the Save My Settings Wizard from the Start menu, the wizard loads the Opw11usr.ini file (from C:\Program Files\Microsoft Office\Office11) to determine what settings to store to the .ops file. You can open the Opw11usr.ini file in Notepad to view or change its settings. Chapter 2 explains in detail what each section does. One strategy, if you want to migrate only certain settings for specific applications, would be to deploy a customized Opw11usr.ini file, then have the user run the wizard normally on the old machine to make an .ops file and store it in a network volume. When the user is up and running on the new machine, run the Save My Settings Wizard again to reverse the process and copy the settings from the .ops file to the new machine.

To start the tool with command-line switches and invoke other options, you must start it from the Run command or a command prompt, rather than from the Save My Settings Wizard menu command on the Start menu. By default the location of the executable of the tool is C:\Program Files\Microsoft Office\Office11\Proflwiz.exe.

Tip: To get the Save My Settings Wizard user interface when you run Proflwiz.exe from a command prompt or the Run command, use the /u switch. To get the administrator interface but store only the Outlook settings, you can give it the /ol command-line switch. To store as well the settings of common Office applications (like Microsoft Office Picture Manager and Clip Organizer), you can add the /common command-line switch. Table 2.5 has the full list of command-line settings.

When you start the tool with the administrator interface, you can specify for what application(s) you want to save your settings. To start the Save My Settings Wizard with the administrator interface, either start the tool from the Run command or a command prompt without any command-line switch or use the /a switch. It will look for a file named Opw11adm.ini to determine what settings to store to the .ops file. This file is not normally installed on the client, but it is included in the Office Resource Kit (ORK). You can also create your own .ini file by making a copy of either Opw11adm.ini or Opw11usr.ini and modifying it to handle the settings you are interested in, as explained in Chapter 2.

When you take a look at the [ExcludeFiles] section in the .ini file, you'll notice that by default .ost, .pst, and .pab files are excluded. This is because these files are considered to be data, not settings, just like Word and Excel document and worksheet files. While .pst files technically can be included in the .ops file by modifying the .ini file, it is best to move them manually since they can become quite large. Also, since an .ost file is nothing more than a local copy of the Exchange mailbox, you should resynchronize with the Exchange server instead of moving the file. As for .pab files, these continue to be supported primarily for backward compatibility. Unless there is a specific need to retain the .pab file, it's usually preferable to import its data into the Contacts folder. (The Custom Installation Wizard [CIW] walk-through in Chapter 2 covered the ImportPAB registry value.)

If you decide to include .pst files within the .ops file, you should also consider whether to overwrite the files when restoring the settings. This feature is controlled in the [ExcludeFilesToRemoveToResetToDefaults] section of the .ini file. Note that when you are using the restore option only to restore settings because they have become corrupted, you'll also replace those files and might lose e-mail messages by restoring an old pst-file.

Once you have run the wizard and saved your setting to an .ops file, you can use the OPS File Viewer included in the ORK to view its contents, as discussed in Chapter 2.

On the new machine, you can restore the settings captured in the .ops file either through the Save My Settings Wizard or by running Proflwiz.exe with the /r switch, specifying the location of the .ops file. When restoring, you have the option to first reset all settings to their defaults before restoring from the .ops file. This will make sure that any options already set on the local machine and not specified in the .ops file will return to the default state. This behavior can be specified with the /d switch.

8.2.3 Files and Settings Transfer Wizard

The Files and Settings Transfer Wizard is a graphical-user-interface-based tool included in Windows XP and is installed by default. It can be found in the System Tools folder, which is a subfolder of the Accessories folder in the Start menu. Since this tool is very generic, we will only discuss what to modify in the wizard in relation to Outlook to stay on the topic of the book.

When you start this tool, you'll have to specify whether you're on the old or the new computer. After specifying a path, you'll get an overview of files and settings to transfer to the new computer. Make sure "Both Files and Settings" and "Let me select a custom list of files and settings when I click Next" are selected. Depending on whether you installed the stand-alone version of Outlook or you installed Outlook from one of the Office suites, you'll either see Office or Outlook listed in the application list. You can now choose to exclude other applications and files. For Outlook you'll need to include the folder where you keep your .pst files and the .pst file type or add these files individually.

Tip: If Office or Outlook is not included in the list, download the latest version of the User State Migration Tool (USMT) from http://www.microsoft.com/downloads/details.aspx?familyid=4AF2D2C9-F16C-4C52-A203-8DAF944DD555&displaylang=en. The USMT is a command-line version of the Files and Settings Transfer Wizard. This download includes a file called Migapp.inf. Copy this file to C:\WINDOWS\system32\usmt, and restart the Wizard.

The File and Settings Transfer Wizard is very much like the Save My Settings Wizard as it will also save all settings to a single file that you then restore on the new computer. The biggest differences between the two tools are as follows:

- The Save My Settings Wizard is limited to Office applications. The File and Settings Transfer Wizard can (in theory) handle all files and settings on the computer. For more info to add additional applications, see the help included with the USMT download.

- The Files and Settings Transfer Wizard supports various methods to transfer the file to the new computer or get the settings from the old computer. Available transfer methods are direct cable, network, removable media, or to file (for dual boot machines).

Keep in mind that both tools will have the best results when the machines are identical in software installation. Since the migrated keys also hold information and references to the installed Outlook add-ins, Outlook can produce errors or even fail to start completely when not all add-ins from the old machine are installed on the new machine. Also, any corrupt registry settings will be transferred to the new machine. For these reasons, it's best to remove all add-ins first that you won't be using on the new machine before running any of the tools.

8.3 Upgrading from earlier Outlook versions

A very common scenario in a corporate network is to upgrade from Outlook 2000 or 2002 to Outlook 2003. While this is largely a straightforward process, it is important to know what settings will migrate and to understand some issues that can arise.

8.3.1 What migrates?

Most of a user's settings in earlier versions of Outlook will migrate to Outlook 2003. Since Outlook 2003 adds functionality but also drops or changes other features, whether or not settings will migrate depends on whether they are still compatible with Outlook 2003. An additional factor if you are migrating from Outlook 2000 is whether Outlook was configured for Internet Mail Only (IMO) or Corporate/Workgroup mode.

Here are the major settings that migrate when you upgrade from an older version to Outlook 2003:

- *Send/Receive groups:* Outlook 2002 Send/Receive groups are migrated and settings will be maintained. (Outlook 2000 does not use Send/Receive groups.)

- *Outlook Bar shortcuts:* The Outlook Bar has been replaced with the Shortcuts navigation pane in Outlook 2003. When upgrading Outlook 2002 to Outlook 2003, all custom shortcuts from the Outlook Bar will be migrated to the Shortcuts navigation pane.

- *Rules Wizard rules:* When rules exist that are specific for an Outlook version, Outlook 2003 will prompt the user to upgrade the rules. This could lead to broken rules that need to be recreated. All rules get upgraded to Unicode format unless you are working with an Outlook 97 to 2002 .pst file or are connected to a Exchange 5.5 server. Since Unicode rules take up more space, the number of rules you can have enabled might be smaller. This is because when you are using an Exchange mailbox, Outlook can have only up to 32 KB of rules active at a time. This is a limitation imposed by the Exchange store; the available size for rules cannot be expanded.

Tip: Because of the 32-KB rule limit, it is crucial to do as much as you can with the fewest rules. For tips to reduce the size of your rules, see Microsoft Knowledge Base Article 886616, "Some Rules Are Disabled, and You Receive an Error Message When You Try to Enable Them after You Upgrade to Outlook 2003."

- *Rules location store:* When Outlook 2003 detects an Exchange account in the profile, even when it is not the default delivery location, it will prompt you to keep either client- or server-based rules. This is because Outlook 2002 and 2003, unlike 2000, store rules in the default delivery store.

- *Junk senders:* Junk senders specified in a Junk Senders.txt or Adult Senders.txt list do not get imported automatically in the new Junk E-mail Filter. At the same time, the Outlook 2000 and 2002 junk and adult senders rules are automatically removed. You can use the CIW to configure Outlook to import the Junk Senders.txt file during installation (see Figure 8.2). The user can also import either list manually. Alternatively, you can deploy companywide black lists and white lists, as described in Chapter 6.

- *Mail profiles:* Mail-profile information from Outlook 2002 and from Outlook 2000 Corporate/Workgroup mode—including not just account settings but also such settings as default stationery, default signature, and startup folder—migrates intact. Since Outlook 2000 IMO does not have mail profiles, when you migrate from that configuration to Outlook 2003, the user will see a default mail profile named Microsoft Outlook Internet Settings, which will have the correct account and other settings migrated from IMO mode.

Outlook 2003 does not convert an Outlook 2000 .nick nickname file to the newer .nk2 nickname file format.

Outlook 2003 does not include support for the following features found in earlier versions:

- cc:Mail mail accounts

- Microsoft Mail mail accounts

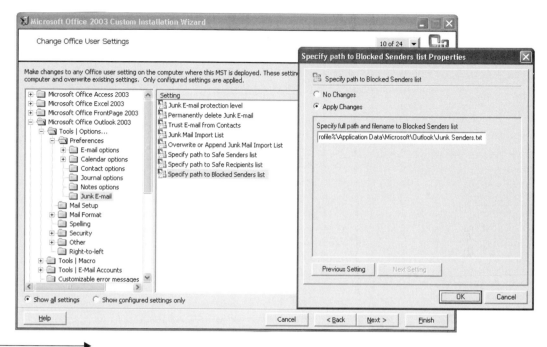

Figure 8.2   *Setting a path to import Junk Senders.txt in the CIW. The same option can be found in the Group Policy template.*

- Sharing with Net Folders
- Microsoft Fax
- WinFax Starter Edition (SE)
- Browsing system files and folders
- Outlook Bar (replaced with the shortcuts navigation pane)

Note that migrated settings will take precedence after any other user-preference settings specified in the CIW. This is because the settings are migrated when the user first runs an Office 2003 application.

8.3.2   Archive.pst file type for Exchange 2003: Unicode or ANSI

As described in Chapter 1, a major new feature in Outlook 2003 is support for Unicode .pst and .ost files that enable you store a virtually unlimited amount of data. If your organization encourages users to maintain their archives in Personal Folders .pst files, this increased capacity is great news.

However, when you upgrade any version of Outlook to Outlook 2003, the archive .pst files will still be in the old format. Unfortunately, there is no way to convert existing .pst files to the Unicode format. If you want a Unicode archive, you must create a new archive .pst file. Chapter 4 shows how you can use a .prf file to change the default archive .pst file to a Unicode-format file.

Note: If users have folder-specific archive settings that point to .pst files other than the default file, archiving to those files will continue. If you change the default archive .pst file to a new Unicode-format file, you may want to advise users to check the archive settings at the folder level to make sure those folders are archiving to a Unicode-format .pst file.

There is another important reason to move to a Unicode archive .pst file: By default, Outlook will not provide full Unicode support unless both the offline folders .ost file and the archive .pst file are in Unicode format. However, you can use a policy setting to tell Outlook to disregard the format of the archive file. In the Group Policy Editor, under User Configuration/Administrative Templates/Microsoft Office Outlook 2003/Exchange Settings, enable the setting Exchange Unicode Mode—Ignore Archive Format and check the "Ignore existing format of the Archive PST" box. This setting controls this registry value:

```
Key: HKEY_CURRENT_USER\Software\Policies\Microsoft\
Office\11.0\Outlook\EMSP
Value name: IgnoreArchiveFormat
Value type: REG_DWORD
Value data: 1 = Enabled, 0 = Disabled
```

Tip: When you create a new Outlook profile using an Exchange account and Cached Exchange mode, Outlook automatically creates a new .ost file in Unicode format, along with a new archive .pst file in Unicode format.

Once the new Unicode archive .pst file is in place, users can then either import or move data from old archive .pst files into that new archive or just leave the old files as they are and open them in Outlook only when needed. There is, however, no automatic import process. The user needs to run File | Import and Export or drag folders or items between files to move them.

> **Tip:** Microsoft now offers a free COM add-in called Lookout to help users search Outlook data faster, including data in multiple .pst files. If Lookout is installed, the user really shouldn't need to import data from old .pst files into the new Unicode .pst file. See Appendix D for download information.

If users continue to use an older .pst file for archiving, they may complain that AutoArchive no longer works for them, even when they are well below the 2-GB file limit. This is because of issues related to archiving from a Unicode store, usually Exchange 2000 or 2003, to an ANSI store. Apart from migrating the users to a Unicode archive .pst file, you can obtain and apply the hotfix described in Microsoft Knowledge Base article 888089, "You Receive an 'Error While Archiving Folder' Error Message When You Try to AutoArchive Your Outlook Data in Outlook 2003." This update adds support for a new registry value that allows Outlook to archive from a Unicode account to an ANSI .pst file:

Key: `HKEY_CURRENT_USER\Software\Microsoft\Office\11.0\Outlook`
Value name: `AllowUnicodeToAnsiArchiveDataLoss`
Value type: `REG_DWORD`
Value: `1` to allow archiving from Unicode to ANSI; `0` to block it (default)

8.3.3 Loss of Outlook Address Book from Outlook 2000 IMO mode

Upgrading from Outlook 2000 configured in IMO to Outlook 2003 often results in a mail profile that is missing the Outlook Address Book, which is essential for displaying contact information for use in addressing messages. This is a side effect of the fact that Outlook 2000 IMO does not store the mail profile in the Windows Messaging Subsystem registry key, as Outlook 2000 in Corporate/Workgroup mode and Outlook 2003 do. When Outlook 2000 IMO is upgraded to Outlook 2003, if no .prf file is invoked, Outlook will construct a new mail profile from the information stored about the IMO mode Internet mail accounts and .pst file(s). However, this may lead to errors, such as the Outlook Address Book not installing correctly or not having the default Contacts folder marked to display as an Outlook Address Book. The user may be able to add the service manually and enable the folder to display as in Outlook Address Book, but a good administrator will want to automate the job by building a new mail profile with a .prf file, as discussed in Chapters 3 and 4.

8.3.4　Configuring a new mail profile

As you saw in the previous section, upgrading from Outlook 2000 IMO mode to Outlook 2003 presents one situation in which creating a new mail profile gives you a chance to get the settings right the first time Outlook starts. For an Exchange 2000 or 2003 user, a new profile will automatically create a new offline folders .ost file and a new archive .pst file using the Unicode format. You might want to consider deploying not just Outlook but a new profile when the following are true:

- Most users have the same type of mail account and the Windows login name and the user's e-mail account name are the same.

- Exchange users know how to add additional mailboxes they might need.

- Users know how to open their old Personal Folders .pst files.

Even if the user's Windows login name and e-mail account name are not the same, you can still consider deploying a new profile with a .prf file by using a script to personalize the .prf file with the correct mail-account settings for the user. Chapter 4 has an example of such a script.

Tip: You also might want to create a special .prf file for users with a complex profile configuration and store it locally so that you can easily recreate that mail profile if disaster strikes and the original profile becomes damaged.

8.3.5　Moving to a New Version of Outlook on a New Machine

If you need to move a user's settings and data from a machine running Outlook 2003 to a newer machine, you can use the procedure described in the Section 8.2. However, the process of migrating data and settings from a machine with an earlier version of Office to a new machine running Outlook 2003 is more involved. Settings are migrated not when Office is installed, but when each Office program runs for the first time. Therefore, the process involves these steps:

1. Collect the user's settings and data in an .ops file, using the version of Proflwiz.exe for that older version of Office and a customized .ini file.

2. Install Office 2003 or Outlook 2003 on the new machine with specific setup properties that will enable the migration to occur, even though the new machine has never had a previous version of Outlook on it.

3. Copy the .ops file to the new machine and apply it using the version of Proflwiz.exe for Outlook 2003 and the customized .ini file that you used in Step 1.

4. Run Outlook 2003 on the new machine for the first time;

A detailed description of each step follows:

Step 1: Collect the user's old settings and data in an .ops file

To capture the user's settings from a machine running Outlook/Office 2000 or Outlook 2002/Office XP, you will need the Proflwiz.exe file appropriate to that version of Office. Office XP installs Proflwiz.exe in the \Program Files\Microsoft Office\Office 10 folder. For Office/Outlook 2000, it is included in the Office 2000 Resource Kit. From the downloads page at http://www.microsoft.com/office/orkarchive/2000ddl.htm, download and install the Office Resource Kit core tool set, then look under \Program Files\ ORKTOOLS\ToolBox\Tools\Office Profile Wizard for the Proflwiz.exe application.

As described in Chapter 2, you can control what settings and data are captured by using a customized.ini file. The .ini file also controls what registry entries and data files are removed when the .ops file is applied. In particular, to ensure that settings are migrated, under the [RegistryTreesToRemoveToResetToDefaults] section, you must add this line to your customized .ini file:

```
HKCU\Software\Microsoft\Office\11.0\Common\Migration
```

This will ensure that if the Migration key already exists on the new machine that's running Outlook 2003, it will be deleted so that the Office 2003 applications will perform migration when they first run.

Run Proflwiz.exe with the customized .ini file to create the .ops file. You can use the command-line switches described in Chapter 2. For example, if you have customized an .ini file named MigrateXP.ini to capture settings and data for an Office XP user (and placed it in a folder named C:\Cust\), you could create an .ops file named MigrateXP.ops with this command:

```
"C:\ \Program Files\Microsoft Office\Office 10\
Proflwiz.exe" /i C:\Cust\ MigrateXP.ini /s C:\Cust\
MigrateXP.ops
```

Tip: If you want to migrate only Outlook settings, append these switches to the ProflWiz.exe command: `/ol /common`.

Step 2: Install Office 2003 or Outlook 2003 on the new machine

Use the Custom Installation Wizard to build the .mst transform file for the installation, as described in Chapter 2. Before saving the .mst file, on Screen 23, Modify Setup Properties (Figure 8.3), click the Add button to add the properties listed in Table 8.2. You only need to add the properties corresponding to the products whose settings you are migrating with the .ops file. If your local language version is not English (U.S.), then instead of 1033, use the appropriate locale identifier (LCID), found in Table 8.3 later in this chapter.

Alternatively, instead of using the CIW to add these properties to the .mst transform file, you can add them to the Setup.ini file. Complete instructions for working with setup properties and the Setup.ini file are available in the Office Resource Kit.

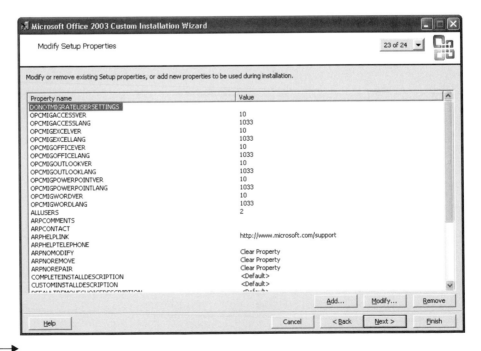

Figure 8.3   *Custom Installation Wizard with migration properties added.*

Table 8.2   *Setup Properties for Settings Migration*

Property Name	Value
DONOTMIGRATEUSERSETTINGS	" "
OPCMIGACCESSVER	9, if migrating from Office 2000
	10, if migrating from Office XP
OPCMIGACCESSLANG	1033, for English (U.S.), or other LCID
OPCMIGEXCELVER	9 or 10
OPCMIGEXCELLANG	1033, for English (U.S.), or other LCID
OPCMIGOFFICEVER	9 or 10
OPCMIGOFFICELANG	1033, for English (U.S.), or other LCID
OPCMIGOUTLOOKVER	9 or 10
OPCMIGOUTLOOKLANG	1033, for English (U.S.), or other LCID
OPCMIGPOWERPOINTVER	9 or 10
OPCMIGPOWERPOINTLANG	1033, for English (U.S.), or other LCID
OPCMIGWORDVER	9 or 10
OPCMIGWORDLANG	1033, for English (U.S.), or other LCID

Click Finish to save the .mst transform file. Complete this step by installing Office or Outlook 2003 on the new machine using the .mst file.

Step 3: Copy and apply the .ops file and customized .ini file

After you have installed Office or Outlook 2003, copy to the new machine both the .ops file created in Step 1 and the customized .ini file that you used to create the .ops file. We'll assume that those files are in a folder named C:\ Cust\. Run Proflwiz.exe with this command:

```
"C:\Program Files\Microsoft Office\OFFICE11\ProflWiz.exe"
/r C:\Cust\MigrateXP.ops /i C:\Cust\ MigrateXP.ini
```

After you run ProflWiz.exe, you can run Regedit.exe and examine the Windows registry to confirm that the user's settings have been copied to the HKEY_CURRENT_USER\Software\Microsoft\Office\10.0\ key if the migration is from Office XP or Outlook 2002 and to the HKEY_CURRENT_USER\Software\Microsoft\Office\9.0\if the migration is from Office or Outlook 2000.

Step 4: Start Outlook 2003

When Outlook starts for the first time, it will migrate the settings to the HKEY_CURRENT_USER\Software\Microsoft\Office\11.0\ key. You confirm this with the registry editor.

8.4   Managing multilanguage installations

When your environment supports different languages, you are most likely better off deploying Office with the Multilingual User Interface (MUI) pack than deploying several translated versions of Office (localized versions).

The MUI allows you to choose what language Outlook uses to show most of the menus, dialogs, and help files through the Microsoft Office 2003 Language Settings dialog box shown in Figure 8.4. When you want to deploy Office with an MUI, you must deploy the English version of Office. Then, with the deployment of the MUI, you can choose what languages are available or what language will be applied.

One key benefit of deploying Office with an MUI rather than with several localized versions of Office is that you need to maintain only one installation source. Deploying updates is easier, too, because you don't have to determine the language first and then deploy a localized update. Instead, you only have to deploy a single MUI update.

Tip: When you are deploying different localized versions of Office throughout your organization or branch offices, you might want to consider deploying Office with an MUI to your support personnel. This way they can switch (easily) between user-interface languages and help users in their native language.

The MUI has only one real disadvantage over the localized version of Outlook: not all components are translated by the MUI pack. This means that in some cases, users will still be confronted with an English-language user interface or help screen.

8.4.1   MUI contents

In addition to a localized version of the user interface, the MUI also contains proofing tools for over 50 languages. (A localized version usually contains support for two to six languages.) Proofing tools contain fonts,

Figure 8.4
*Japanese has only
limited support
because support for
Japanese must also
be installed in
Windows.*

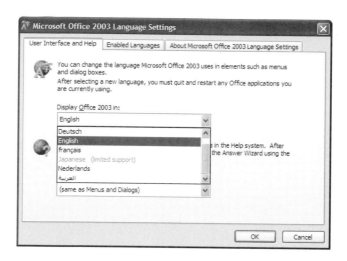

AutoCorrect lists, and spell- and grammar-checkers specific for a certain language.

The MUI pack cannot be bought as a separate product in stores. It is only available bundled with the English version of Office 2003 Standard or Professional. These special bundles can only be obtained when you are a Volume License customer.

The full Office 2003 Professional MUI pack consists of six CDs and applies to Access, Excel, FrontPage, InfoPath, OneNote, Outlook, Power-Point, Publisher, and Word. On the CDs, you'll find folders with names that each consist of four-digit numbers called locale identifiers (LCIDs). Each corresponds to a certain language. In Table 8.3, you can look up the language and corresponding LCID.

8.4.2 **MUI deployment**

You can automate deployment of the MUI pack in much the same ways as you can deploy Office. You can create an administrative installation point by running Muisetup.exe from the CD with the /a command-line switch. During setup, you can choose what languages will be installed at the installation point. Languages that are not on the CD will be disabled, as shown in Figure 8.5. You can add those languages to the installation point by inserting the corresponding CD, running Muisetup.exe with the /a switch again, and pointing it to the same location on the server. By using the CIW from the ORK, you can modify the way each MUI pack is installed. Note that you cannot create a general transform .mst file that applies to all MUI

Table 8.3   *Languages Supported by Office 2003 MUI Pack and Their Corresponding LCIDs*

Language	LCID	Language	LCID
Arabic	1025	Latvian	1062
Basque	1069	Lithuanian	1063
Bulgarian	1026	Marathi	1102
Chinese (simplified)	2052	Norwegian (Bokmål)	1044
Chinese (traditional)	1028	Norwegian (Nynorsk)	2068
Croatian	1050	Polish	1045
Czech	1029	Portuguese (Brazil)	1046
Danish	1030	Portuguese (Portugal)	2070
Dutch	1043	Punjabi	1094
English (U.S.)	1033	Romanian	1048
Estonian	1061	Russian	1049
Finnish	1035	Serbian (Latin)—includes Serbian (Cyrillic) proofing tools	2074
French	1036		
Gaelic (Ireland)	2108		
Galician	1110	Slovak	1051
German	1031	Slovenian	1060
Greek	1032	Spanish	3082
Gujarati	1095	Swedish	1053
Hebrew	1037	Tamil	1097
Hindi	1081	Telugu	1098
Hungarian	1038	Thai	1054
Icelandic	1039	Turkish	1055
Indonesian	1057	Ukrainian	1058
Italian	1040	Urdu	1056
Japanese	1041	Vietnamese	1066
Kannada	1099	Welsh	1106
Korean	1042		

Figure 8.5
MUI packs that have already been installed will be checked and disabled; MUI packs not on the current CD will be disabled as well.

packs. Instead, you must create a separate transform .mst file based on the Mui.msi file in each LCID folder. The 2003 ORK provides more details on this process.

To deploy the MUI directly with the deployment of Office or Outlook, you can chain the MUI to the Office or Outlook installation manually or by using the CIW, as discussed in the ORK.

Note: When using the German MUI, you will need to follow the instructions in Microsoft Knowledge Base article 831030, "Cannot Install German Language MUI Files in Office 2003."

8.5 Hotfixes and service packs

Keeping desktop systems up-to-date is critical in today's Internet environment. Due to the quick proliferation of viruses, worms, and other security threats, enterprises must update their desktop systems in order to protect their critical infrastructure. An infection of a single system can quickly spread to the whole corporate network, bringing it to its knees and causing the interruption of critical information technology services. Microsoft provides three types of patches to maintain the maximum protection and stability of the desktop environment—hotfixes, updates, and service packs.

A *hotfix* is a patch to a software product that is released as required to fix bugs or security vulnerabilities. A hotfix package is composed of one or more files used to address a specific problem. A hotfix is sometimes also referred to as a QFE or patch. (Quick Fix Engineering, or QFE, is a team within Microsoft that produces hotfixes.) Most hotfixes are built to correct security vulnerabilities, but Microsoft also provides hotfixes to correct critical stability or performance issues. Some hotfixes address a specific customer situation and may not be distributed outside the customer organization. Others are documented in Microsoft Knowledge Base articles and can be obtained by any organization experiencing the same problem by contacting Microsoft Product Support Services.

Microsoft refers to an *update* as a broadly released fix for a specific problem addressing a noncritical, nonsecurity-related bug. A security update is a broadly released fix for a product-specific, security-related vulnerability. For the remainder of this chapter, we will use the term *update* or *patch* to refer generically to a hotfix, update, or QFE. We will use the term *security update* to refer to a specific update that addresses a security vulnerability.

An update or security update typically addresses only one issue and will be applied to fix a particular stability, performance, or security issue. Because updates and security updates address only one issue, customers can be choosy about the updates they deploy. Generally, every update or security update is accompanied by a bulletin that explains exactly what problems will be fixed or the risks the security vulnerability might pose. In addition, the bulletin will indicate exactly what versions of software are affected. If the vulnerability doesn't apply to your environment, you don't have to worry about applying the patch. This makes life easier for administrators and users.

Microsoft releases many types of security updates that address a broad range of issues. To make it easier for customers to prioritize security updates, Microsoft provides the following categories as guidance:

- *Critical:* Exploitation of the vulnerability could allow the propagation of an Internet worm without user action.

- *Important:* Exploitation of the vulnerability could compromise the confidentiality, integrity, or availability of user data or the integrity or availability of processing resources.

- *Moderate:* Exploitability is mitigated to a significant degree by factors such as default configuration, auditing, or difficulty of exploitation.

- *Low:* Exploitation of the vulnerability is extremely difficult or would have minimal impact.

When a new security update is released, administrators should evaluate the update according to the risk the vulnerabilities pose. If the vulnerability poses a serious risk to their organization, administrators should apply the security update right away. For lower-priority patches, administrators should put in place a regularly scheduled update process that allows them to install several patches at once.

Microsoft defines a *service pack* as a tested, cumulative set of all hotfixes, security updates, critical updates, and other updates created, since the release of the software. Service packs may also contain a limited number of customer-requested design changes or features plus other fixes not previously released. Another thing to remember is that service packs are cumulative. Every service pack is a roll-up of all previous service packs for that product. For example, Windows XP Service Pack 2 includes every change made in Windows XP Service Pack 1.

Service packs are typically planned well in advance and are released at regular intervals after considerable testing. Updates, on the other hand, are released as bugs or security vulnerabilities are encountered. Another difference between a service pack and an update is that service packs address both minor and major issues. Because frequent updates are difficult for customers to deploy, Microsoft usually develops updates only for issues that are fairly major. The last major difference between a service pack and an update is that service packs must meet a higher category of quality. Service packs will undergo weeks of rigorous final testing, including testing in conjunction with hundreds or thousands of third-party products. The quality is on par with the quality assurance done on a new release of the product itself. Because updates generally need to be released quickly to address a critical issue or security vulnerability, their quality is not as high, and they are more likely to contain regression errors than service packs are.

Microsoft Office updates are released in two forms:

- Full-file patches, or administrative patches, completely replace all files modified by an update. Typically, in the past, full-file patches were used exclusively to update an administrative installation point, from which clients then recached and reinstalled Office to get the updated version. With Office 2003, you can apply full-file patches directly to client computers. Because complete files are installed, full-file patches typically do not require access to the original Office installation source.

- Binary patches, or client patches, replace only portions of the files that have been updated. For this reason, they are smaller and more efficient to distribute than full-file patches; however, they typically require that clients have access to the original installation source. Binary patches cannot be applied to an administrative image.

8.5.1   Deploying updates

Since there are many different ways in which the base Office and Outlook software can be installed, there are also many alternatives for deploying updates to the Office suite. Depending on the original method of deployment, a customer may have limited deployment options for updates. Microsoft's recommended update strategy for corporations is as follows:

- To perform the original deployment of Office from a compressed CD image, with clients maintaining a Local Installation Source (LIS), and

- To distribute either full-file or binary updates directly to clients

This method uses less network bandwidth for updates and allows distribution of smaller binary patches. If you are using this method, and you then want to deploy a new Outlook 2003 client from the compressed image, you must include all current patches to ensure that the user has all of the latest updates. You can chain client updates to the core Office 2003 installation by adding the appropriate files to the [ChainedInstall_*n*] sections of the Setup settings file (Setup.ini), as discussed in the ORK.

If the LIS method is not feasible because, for instance, Office has already been deployed from an administrative distribution point or the desktop hard disks are not big enough for the LIS, Microsoft recommends that you do the following:

- Deploy Office from an uncompressed administrative installation point.

- Use full-file patches to keep the administrative point up-to-date.

- Have the clients recache and reinstall promptly.

In order to apply an update when using the administrative distribution point, you must use administrative updates (.msp files). To apply an update, run Windows Installer with options to specify the path to the Windows Installer package (.msi file) from your original administrative image and the name and path of the .msp file. The update instructs Windows Installer to add, update, or remove files in the administrative image; for example:

1.   Download the self-extracting executable file for the update and run the following command line to extract the MSP file:

```
[path\name of .exe file] /c /t:[location for extracted
MSP file]
```

2.   Connect to the server share for your administrative installation point. You must have write access to the administrative installation point on the server and the appropriate privileges to carry out the task.

3.   On the Start menu, click Run, and then type

```
msiexec.exe /p [path\name of .msp file]/a [path\name
of MSI file] /qb /lv* [path\name of log file]
```

If an update contains multiple .msp files, you must run the command line separately for each .msp file that you apply to the administrative installation point.

To update an existing client installation from an administrative installation point, users need only rerun the Setup.exe file from the administrative installation point. Administrators can also distribute the following command line to clients to run in quiet mode and generate log files:

```
[path]setup.exe REINSTALL=[list of features modified by
the update] /qb
```

8.5.2   Update tools

There are also many tools that can be used to deploy updates. Use of certain tools may be limited based on the original method chosen to install the base Outlook software. The following are tools that can be used to obtain and deploy Microsoft Office 2003 and Outlook 2003 updates:

- *Office Update.* Office Update is a Web site (http://office.microsoft.com/en-us/officeupdate/default.aspx) that allows users of Office 2003 to obtain updates and service packs for their software. Office Update provides a detection service at the Web site that will examine your system and determine if it requires any Office updates or service packs. Office Update is primarily for home or small-business users who manage their own systems. If the Office Update detects that your system is missing certain updates, it will display any updates that you don't have, describe them, and inform you if they are considered critical. Users then have the option of accepting or rejecting individual updates based on their usage patterns and the vulnerability of their systems. Once accepted, the updates are downloaded to a user's system and an automatic install takes place. Depending on the update, a reboot may be necessary after the install.

In large corporate environments, where administrators manage the configuration of desktop systems from a central location, other methods of obtaining and installing updates are preferable. In these environments, administrators may wish to turn off the users' ability to use Office Update using a Group Policy setting. To do this, go to User Configuration/Administrative Templates/Microsoft Office 2003/ Miscellaneous in the Group Policy Editor and select the "Block Updates from the Office Update site from applying" setting. Select the Enable setting and check the box to disable updates from the Office Update site. This sets the following registry value:

```
Key: HKEY_CURRENT_USER\Software\Policies\Microsoft\
Office\Common\OfficeUpdate
Value name: BlockUpdates
Value type: REG_DWORD
Value: 1 to disable updates, 0 to allow them
```

If this policy is enforced by administrators, users will receive an error message when they attempt to update their computers on the Office Update site. Figure 8.6 shows the error message received by users.

- *Windows Server Update Servises (WSUS).* Introduced in June 2005, WSUS is a free add-in component for Windows 2000 (with Service Pack 4) and Windows Server 2003 and for client computers running Windows 2000 (with Service Pack 3 or later), Windows XP, and Windows Server 2003. It is designed to help corporate administrators manage desktop computers and servers by allowing centralized control of the installation of critical updates, security updates, and service packs for the Windows operating system, Microsoft Office 2003, Microsoft Exchange Server 2003, and other Microsoft applications. WSUS is the successor to Software Update Services (SUS), which will no longer be supported after June 6, 2006, and will probably become the preferred solution for distributing Office updates to corporate desktops.

- *Systems Management Server (SMS) or similar software deployment tools.* Microsoft SMS is a software-deployment, inventory-tracking and remote-troubleshooting tool for large organizations. The goal of the tool is to reduce the cost of managing the desktop environment in large distributed enterprises. SMS can also be used to deploy Office updates automatically to the desktop. SMS will work in environments where Active Directory has not been deployed. Other vendors such as IBM Tivoli and Hewlett-Packard also offer tools that assist in software deployment.

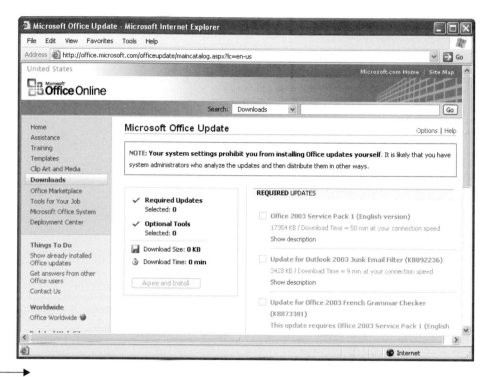

Figure 8.6 *Message displayed to users when administrator has disallowed Office Update via policy.*

SMS 2003 now gives you the option of installing the Installation Local Source (LIS) for Office 2003. These source files can be downloaded in the background, and if the download is interrupted, it will pick up where it left off the next time the connection is made. SMS also allows you to download from a compressed source—a copy of the CD on the network. This download will proceed even more quickly. Having the Office source available allows administrators to deploy new features or repairs quickly, without having to prompt the user for a CD or network source. The LIS also allows deployment of smaller Office updates. If the source is required, it is already available on the local computer, and users can apply the update even when they are not connected to the network.

SMS administrators can use the Microsoft Office Inventory Tool for Updates, which is provided in the Software Update Management feature of SMS 2003. This tool extends the SMS hardware inventory to report on the software updates required to keep Office current. The Office Update Inventory Tool uses the same tools as would be available via Office Update, except in this case the tools are run via

SMS. SMS uses the Office Update Database (Invcif.exe) to analyze client computers for applicable Office updates. The Office Update Inventory Tool will compare what has been installed against the contents of the latest Office Update Database (Invcif.exe) file. The data gathered by the Office Update Inventory Tool is then stored in the SMS site database. The Office Update Sync Tool automatically downloads the latest version of the tool on a regular basis and distributes it to the computers in an enterprise by using SMS distribution points.

Once the Office Update Inventory Tool has been run, administrators will know which desktops are missing key Office updates. With this inventory information, SMS administrators can then deploy the updates to the desktop using the software deployment capabilities of SMS.

■ *Group Policy Objects.* You can also deploy Outlook and updates by using GPOs. Group Policy bypasses Office Setup.exe and Setup.ini. As a result, although you can use Group Policy to deploy Office from a compressed CD image, you cannot take advantage of new setup functionality to create a LIS on users' computers.

8.6   Summary

This chapter has discussed five special configuration situations for Outlook.

Deploying Outlook or Office with an MUI has several benefits over deploying several localized versions of Outlook or Office within a network and changes your update strategy.

Moving a user to a new machine is easier with special tools like the Save My Settings Wizard and the Files and Settings Transfer Wizard. Although these tools can transfer just about anything, it is still important to know what files and settings are involved and to be able to determine if the settings of the source computer are compatible with the target computer.

Using Outlook or Office on a terminal server differs in several ways from using Outlook or Office directly from a client. Important benefits include the flexibility of clients able to connect to the terminal server and the ability to control settings and updates directly on the server instead of addressing the individual clients. Important drawbacks are that you'll need a lot of available server resources and that you create a single point of failure.

When upgrading from a previous version of Outlook to Outlook 2003 you should be aware of how the new, changed, and dropped functionality in Outlook 2003 will be handled. The new format of the .ost and .pst files is also an important change that should be taken in account when mailboxes are being switched from an Exchange 5.5 server to an Exchange 2000 or 2003 server.

Last but certainly not least, we addressed methods to keep the deployed environment up-to-date. It is important to know the differences between the available updates and when they should be applied. There are various ways to deploy the updates. The methods available heavily depend on the way Outlook originally was deployed.

9

Configuring Other Outlook Options

As you've seen in the preceding chapters, you can deploy and manage many key Outlook settings with such tools as the Custom Installation Wizard (CIW) and Group Policy Objects (GPOs). Appendixes A, B, and C list many additional policy and registry settings for Outlook 2003. However, there are many options that are not directly (at least, not obviously) addressed by policies, registry entries, .prf files, or settings files. This chapter shows you how to add such enhancements to Outlook, including the following:

- COM add-ins

- Custom stationery

- Custom signatures

- A custom Outlook Today page

- Custom categories

- Custom calendar color labels

In addition, administrators commonly ask for a number of other modifications that are not possible by any obvious means. We'll review why and suggest workarounds.

9.1   COM add-ins and VBA code

COM add-ins are a type of application that integrates tightly with Outlook to add new functionality. (Other Office programs also support COM add-ins.) There are both commercial and shareware COM add-ins, and many organizations have their own in-house COM add-ins to enhance business processes that use Outlook.

COM add-ins for Outlook have proliferated in part because good samples are available for programmers to learn from and because they can be built with Visual Basic. Typically, a COM add-in will provide a custom toolbar to invoke its functionality and set its options. It may also monitor specific "events" in order to respond when certain actions happen in Outlook, such as new mail arriving or being sent. A good example would be an add-in that combines all attachments in an outgoing message into a .zip file to reduce the overall size of the message.

A COM add-in's setup program will register the add-in either in the HKEY_LOCAL_MACHINE\Software\Microsoft\Office\Outlook\Addins key of the Windows registry or in the HKEY_CURRENT_USER\Software\Microsoft\Office\Outlook\Addins key. Add-ins registered in HKLM are not visible to the user in the Tools | Options | Other | Advanced Options | COM Add-ins dialog (Figure 9.1).

Often power users or administrators develop code that they want to deploy to other users in the organization in Visual Basic for Applications (VBA). Outlook provides no robust way to deploy Outlook VBA code to other users. As you saw in Chapter 1, the user's VBA code project resides in the Vbaproject.otm file in the user's Application Data\Microsoft\Outlook folder. You can deploy a Vbaproject.otm file containing macros to other users by using the CIW, Custom Maintenance Wizard (CMW), Office Profile Wizard (OPW), or a login script. (Chapter 2 showed you how to build an .ops file with the OPW that does nothing but install a Vbaproject.otm file.) However, deploying a new Vbaproject.otm file to the user will overwrite any Outlook VBA macros the user has already created. Furthermore, if the user has not previously used VBA, any event-handler code, such as a procedure to scan outgoing messages to make sure they don't go out with blank subject lines, will not run until the user manually starts the VBA

Figure 9.1   *Users see only COM add-ins registered in HKEY_CURRENT_USER.*

development environment. Finally, VBA project files do occasionally become corrupted, in which case the code won't be available at all.

For these reasons, organizations generally should not attempt to deploy Outlook VBA code to multiple users. Instead, the same functionality should be built into an Outlook COM add-in. Most of the VBA code can often transfer directly into the COM add-in with little or no modification.

9.2   Group Policy and user-preference settings

As you saw in Chapters 1 and 2, the Windows registry contains two kinds of settings for Outlook—mandatory settings usually maintained with GPOs and user-preference settings that the user can modify. While the administrative template .adm files that control Group Policy settings and the .opm files that manage user-preference settings through the CIW and CMW contain many options, they don't contain all of them. This section highlights some of the key registry settings that are not exposed by these tools. You can use any of the methods in Chapter 2 to deploy these settings—adding them in the CIW or CMW or building a supplementary administrative template .adm file to manage them with GPOs.

9.2.1   Master category list

When the user clicks the Categories button on any Outlook item, a list of categories appears from which the user may choose. The user can also remove or add categories. This list, which is specific to each user, is kept in the following registry entry:

```
Key: HKEY_CURRENT_USER\Software\Microsoft\Office\11.0\
Outlook\Categories
Value name: MasterList
Value type: REG_BINARY
```

The MasterList registry value will be present only if the user has added or removed categories from the default master category list. The value data for MasterList is binary because it supports multilingual entries through Unicode. Therefore, it is not possible just to type in the desired values in screen 12 of the CIW or screen 9 of the CMW. It is possible, however, to import a default category list. Use the Categories dialog on a machine running Outlook 2003 to modify the master list for the current user. Then, run Regedit.exe and export the HKEY_CURRENT_USER\Software\Microsoft\Office\11.0\Outlook\Categories key to a .reg file. On CIW screen

12 or CMW screen 9, you can then import the .reg file to add MasterList to the list of values that will be deployed with either a transform .mst file or a .cmw file.

The MasterList registry value will also be included if you use the OPW to create an .ops file, then deploy it using any of the methods discussed in Chapter 2.

Note that Outlook does not offer any kind of central master category list that can be applied to all users. Each user can add or remove categories from his or her own personal master list at any time. Furthermore, the master list is just a convenience to the user. An Outlook item may have categories that are not listed in the master list.

9.2.2 Default mail font

The default mail font is another option that you cannot set by simply typing some values into the Group Policy Editor, the CIW, or the CMW. One way to set a default font for new messages is to use custom stationery, as

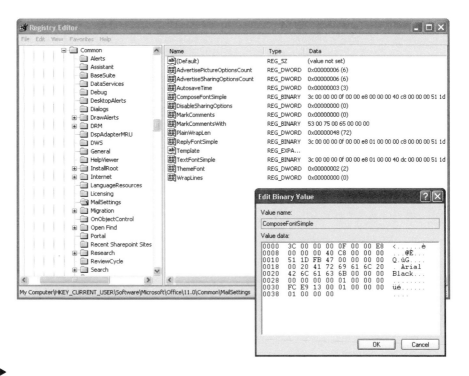

Figure 9.2   *Font and other mail-format options.*

you'll see in Section 9.2.3, but this affects only HTML-format messages. The other method is to set the appropriate registry values, but as with the master category list, the font registry settings are not something you can just type in. In fact, they are not even found in the Outlook portion of the registry! Instead, as you can see in Figure 9.2, Outlook's font settings are located in the HKEY_CURRENT_USER\Software\Microsoft\Office\11.0\Common\MailSettings key, probably because this information is shared by Outlook and Word, when Word is used as the e-mail editor (a configuration known as WordMail).

Note: The font stored in the ComposeFontSimple value is used not just for new messages but also for the body of all new Outlook items—Contacts, Appointments, Tasks, and so on. Setting the default font for new HTML messages with stationery means that you can have separate default fonts for messages and other Outlook items.

As with the master category list, you can either export the MailSettings key from the registry of a machine that is configured the way you want it to be, then import that .reg file into the CIW or CMW, or you can use the OPW to capture these settings.

9.2.3 Default stationery

If you want everyone in your organization to be "on the same page" when they send messages, you may want to deploy stationery or signatures that use your logo, motto, contact information, or corporate disclaimer. We'll cover signatures a bit later in Section 9.3.2. Let's first consider stationery, which is a feature specifically of messages composed in HTML format and that does not apply to messages created in rich-text or plain-text format.

Note: The other approach to this type of content control—and the one we recommend for disclaimers and other mandatory text—is to insert the disclaimer or other content into the outgoing message at the server level. If you add the text at the server level, you avoid the problem of the user deleting it before the message is sent. Microsoft offers sample code for how to do this with an Exchange Server event sink, and at least a dozen companies offer add-ins for Exchange Server and Simple Mail Transfer Protocol (SMTP) gateways to insert disclaimers.

As you learned in Chapter 1, custom Outlook stationery files for HTML-format messages are stored in the user's Application Data\ Microsoft\Stationery folder. You can deploy a custom .htm file to the Stationery folder either as part of Outlook setup, using the CIW; later, using the CMW; or with a login script, copying the file from a central location.

The registry value that controls the default stationery for the user:

```
Key: HKEY_CURRENT_USER\Software\Microsoft\Office\11.0\
Common\MailSettings
Value name: NewStationery
Value type: REG_EXPAND_SZ
Value: Name of the HTML file, without the .htm tag
```

For example, if the name of the stationery file is Company Letterhead.htm, the value for NewStationery would be Company Letterhead.

Similarly, a value called NewTheme controls the default theme for messages created using WordMail.

You can also enforce a mandatory stationery file by creating a NewStationery value in the HKEY_CURRENT_USER\Software\Policies\Microsoft\Office\11.0\Common\MailSettings key. You can even create that value and leave it blank as part of a strategy to prevent the user from using any HTML stationery at all. (The additional settings for that strategy are covered in Section 9.2.4.)

Note: Because the Stationery folder resides in the user's own Windows profile folders, a clever user who wants to avoid using the company stationery can simply replace the mandated stationery file with one of the same name. This is yet another example of the fact that a technological solution isn't always the sole answer. You need to couple software-policy settings with clear employee policies that explain the company's rules for e-mail use.

9.2.4   Blocking stationery use

While some organizations want to use signatures or stationery to give all messages the same look and feel or to provide standard information, others may want to prohibit all use of HTML stationery, perhaps because they find it unprofessional and a waste of bandwidth and storage space. You saw in the previous section how you could create a NewStationery value in the HKEY_CURRENT_USER\Software\Policies\Microsoft\Office\11.0\

Table 9.1 *Outlook and Word Commands to Disable to Prevent Stationery Use*

Outlook Menu	Command	ID
Actions | New Message Using	More Stationery	5611

Word Menu	Command	ID
Format	Background	30403
Format	Theme	3623
Format | Background	Standard Colors	3224
Format | Background	More Colors	2857
Format | Background	Fill Effects	2858
Format | Background	Printed Watermark	4003
View	HTML Source	3902

Common\MailSettings key and leave it blank to prevent users from choosing any default stationery. You will also need to prevent users from choosing stationery on a per-message basis, both with the regular editor and with Word-Mail. This process involves disabling certain toolbar commands using GPOs, as described in Appendix C. The key information you need to disable a toolbar command is the command's ID. Table 9.1 lists the Outlook and Word commands that should be disabled if you want to prevent stationery use.

9.2.5 Outlook Today settings

Outlook Today is a feature that presents the user with a combined view of data from key Outlook folders whenever the user clicks on the root folder of the default information store. The default is to show upcoming appointments for the next five days, a list of tasks, plus the number of unread messages in the Inbox, Outbox, and Drafts folders. The user can configure these options but, as you'll see, they can also be preset for the user.

The Outlk11.adm administrative template includes two Group Policy settings to turn Outlook Today off or on and to display a specific URL instead of the built-in Outlook Today page. Look under User Configuration/Administrative Templates/Microsoft Office Outlook 2003/Outlook Today Settings for the following policy settings, which control registry values in the HKEY_CURRENT_USER\Software\Policies\Microsoft\Office\11.0\Outlook\Today key:

Policy setting: Outlook Today availability
Value name: `Disable`
Value type: `REG_DWORD`
Value: `0` to enable Outlook Today (default), `1` to disable Outlook Today

Policy setting: URL for custom Outlook Today
Value name: `Url`
Value type: `REG_SZ`
Value: URL for custom Outlook Today page, up to 129 characters

Similar settings are available in the CIW and CMW, setting corresponding registry keys in HKEY_CURRENT_USER\Software\Microsoft\Office\ 11.0\Outlook\Today. For example, if you are using SharePoint Portal Server or some other corporate portal, especially one that displays some of the user's Outlook information, you might want to show the portal instead of Outlook Today. In that case, you'd add a policy setting or user preference to set the URL value described above.

If you don't choose to show a custom Web page instead of Outlook Today, you can customize the options that the user sees. Figure 9.3 shows the default settings, and Table 9.2 describes each option.

Remember that the user can also change all of the settings in Table 9.2 through the Outlook Today page itself, which has a Customize Outlook Today button.

One enhancement that you might want to deploy for the Outlook Today page is to add more folders. For example, if you have a public folder

Figure 9.3   *User-preference settings for Outlook Today.*

Table 9.2 *Outlook Today Options*

Option	Description
CalDays	This represents the number of days' worth of appointments to show from the default Calendar folder.
CustomURL	This is the name of the page used for the design, which corresponds to the choice for Style. For example, if Style is set to Style3, CustomURL should be set to Outlook3.htm.
IncNoDueDate	This is set as TRUE to include tasks with no due date, FALSE to exclude them.
Sort1	This is the sort field for the first task-sorting group. Allowable values are tilde (~), [CreationTime], [Importance], [DueDate], or [StartDate]. Use the tilde when you want no sorting.
Sort1Asc	This is set to TRUE to sort in ascending order, FALSE to sort in descending order.
Sort2	This represents the same values as Sort1.
Sort2Asc	This represents the same values as Sort1Asc.
Style	One of these values corresponding to the built-in styles: ■ Style0—Standard ■ Style1—Standard (two column) ■ Style2—Standard (one column) ■ Style3—Summer ■ Style4—Winter
TaskFilter	This is the filter to apply to the tasks. Allowable values are All, to show all tasks, and Today, to show today's tasks.

that users should monitor for unread items, you can add that folder by adding a new entry to the HKEY_CURRENT_USER\Software\Microsoft\Office\11.0\Outlook\Today\Folders key. As noted above, by default, Outlook shows the unread items count from three folders. The Folders key shown in FIgure 9.4 contains three REG_SZ (string) values, named 0, 1, and 2, each pointing to one of those folders. To add another folder, add a value with the next highest number to the Folders key. For example, to add a Public Folder named Inquiries that resides under the top-level Sales folder, you would add a new value 3 and enter for its data the full path to the Inquiries folder—\\Public Folders\All Public Folders\Sales\Inquiries.

You probably noticed that the first three values in the Folders key, the ones that Outlook adds by default, use the literal mailbox name as part of the folder path. If the Windows login name and the mailbox name are the same, you can also use an expandable string value (REG_EXPAND_SZ)

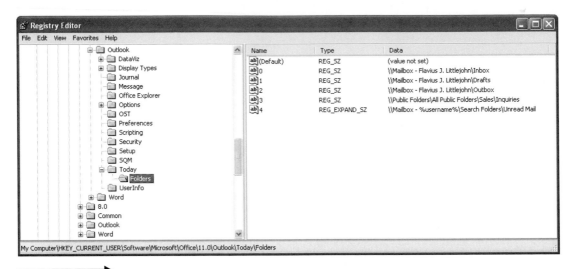

Figure 9.4   *Additional folders to be listed in Outlook Today.*

and have Outlook automatically build the correct path to a mailbox folder. The value for 4 in Figure 9.4 shows the Unread Mail search folder set up as one of the folders shown on the Outlook Today screen. Using an expandable string value makes it possible to deploy a registry value in the Folders key to show a mailbox folder without the need for a script or some other mechanism to build the literal mailbox name.

Tip: If you are deploying Outlook in an environment without Exchange, the default path to the Unread Mail search folder will be \\Personal Folders\ Search Folders\Unread Mail.

9.2.6   Startup navigation pane

One of the major changes in Outlook 2003, compared with earlier versions, is the new user interface with a navigation pane that groups folders by type—all mail folders, all calendar folders, and so on. As you learned in Chapter 1, Outlook 2003 stores its navigation pane settings for each mail profile in an .xml file with the file name matching the profile name. The format of the .xml file is not documented, and the navigation pane itself is a little bit fragile, at least in versions through Service Pack 1; it sometimes loses its settings. Therefore, we don't recommend that you try to configure the navigation pane details by editing the .xml file directly.

Similarly, while it is possible for the user to select which folder to show when Outlook starts, this information is specific to the mail profile and is in an undocumented format. Thus, it cannot be configured with a simple registry entry.

It is possible, however, to force Outlook to open with a particular navigation pane displayed by adding the following registry entry and setting the appropriate value:

Key: HKEY_CURRENT_USER\Software\Microsoft\Office\11.0\
Outlook\Options\WunderBar
Value name: BootModule
Value type: REG_DWORD
Value: 0 to show the Mail folders, 5 to show the folder list, and 6 to show the Shortcuts pane. (The Shortcuts pane needs to have the Inbox folder in it, if the Inbox is the user's startup folder.)

For example, if you have users who make heavy use of the folders in the Exchange server's Public Folders\All Public Folders hierarchy, these folders do not appear on any of the type-specific navigation panes. (Users will see nonmail folders from the Public Folders\Favorites hierarchy, though.) Therefore, it might be appropriate to have those users start in the Folder List by setting BootModule to 5, at least until they become accustomed to the new interface.

9.2.7 Mail-alert duration

Another new feature in Outlook is the system-tray mail alert that appears briefly when a message arrives, allowing the user to open, flag, or delete the message; it fades after a few seconds. To help users get to know this feature, you may want to make the alert stay on the screen longer. It is not possible to make it stay permanently. The maximum time is approximately 50 days, which should be long enough for just about everyone!

Set the alert-display duration in the following registry key:

Key: HKEY_CURRENT_USER\Software\Microsoft\Office\11.0\
Common\DesktopAlerts
Value name: TimeOn
Value type: REG_DWORD
Value: Number of milliseconds to display the alert; maximum is 4,294,967,295.

Notice that this is another case where an Outlook feature is controlled by a registry value outside the main Outlook registry hierarchy.

> **Tip:** A free command-prompt tool to convert minutes, hours, or days into milliseconds and vice versa is available at http://www.howto-outlook.com/ Downloads/TimeOnConverter.zip.

9.2.8   New-mail notification sound

Does your organization have its own "You've got mail" sound? By default, in Windows XP, the Windows XP Notify.wav file plays whenever Outlook gets new mail. You can, of course, deploy .wav sound files as part of your Office installation or at a later time. Place the sound file in the %SYSTEM-ROOT%\Media folder. To change the new-mail notification sound, change the following registry entry:

> Key: `HKEY_CURRENT_USER\AppEvents\Schemes\Apps\.Default\`
> `MailBeep\.Current`
> Value name: (Default)
> Value type: `REG_SZ`
> Value: Name of the .wav file to play

9.2.9   Viewing Internet message parts

The Options dialog for any message received in Outlook from a POP3 or IMAP4 account by default shows only the Internet message headers. It is possible to have Outlook show the full message source by adding the following registry value:

> Key: `HKEY_CURRENT_USER\Software\Microsoft\Office\11.0\`
> `Outlook\Options\Mail`
> Value name: `SaveAllMIMENotJustHeaders`
> Value type: `REG_DWORD`
> Value: `0` to show only the headers (default); `1` to show the full message including all MIME message parts

This setting may be most useful for troubleshooting, for example, when you are trying to determine why a message body appears to be missing.

9.2.10   Wrapping lines in plain-text messages

By default, Outlook 2003 inserts a hard return at the end of each line in a plain-text message. This renders long URLs unusable in the received message. If you prefer to use quoted-printable encoding, which allows soft returns and doesn't break URLs, configure the following two registry entries:

Key: `HKEY_CURRENT_USER\Software\Microsoft\Office\11.0\`
`Common\MailSettings`
Value name: `WrapLines`
Value type: `REG_DWORD`
Value: `0` to turn off hard line returns; `1` to insert hard line returns (default)

Key: `HKEY_CURRENT_USER\Software\Microsoft\Office\11.0\`
`Outlook\Options\Mail`
Value name: `InternetMailTextEncoding`
Value type: `REG_DWORD`
Value: `0` to apply the optimal encoding automatically (default);
`1` to use quoted-printable encoding; `2` to use Base64 encoding;
`3` to use 8-bit encoding

If WrapLines is set to 0 and InternetMailTextEncoding is set to 0 or 1, Outlook will generate plain-text messages with the encoding set to quoted-printable and will insert soft, instead of hard, returns so that long URLs don't break.

Note: Microsoft Knowledge Base article 823921, "BUG: Line Wrapping Does Not Appear as Expected When You Send E-mail Messages in Outlook 2003," explains how Outlook determines what encoding to use when InternetMailTextEncoding is set to 0 and also explains how to set the line length when WrapLines is set to 1.

9.2.11   Additional journal types

The Outlook journal form includes an Entry Type drop-down list (Figure 9.5) from which the user can choose what type of Journal entry to make. Unlike many other drop-down lists on Outlook forms, the user cannot simply type any text into the Entry Type box but must instead choose an item from the list.

If your organization wants users to make manual journal entries for other types of activities, you will need to add the corresponding types to the Entry Type drop-down list by updating the registry. For each new entry type that you want to add, create a new key in the HKEY_CURRENT_USER\Software\Microsoft\Shared Tools\Outlook\Journaling key, giving it a short name that describes the entry type, then add the following values for that key:

Value name: `Description`
Value type: `REG_SZ` (string)
Value data: Display name that you want to appear in the Entry Type drop-down list

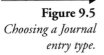

Figure 9.5
*Choosing a Journal
entry type.*

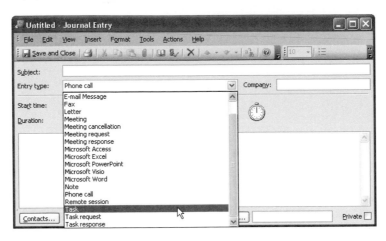

Value name: `Large Icon`
Value type: `REG_SZ`
Value data: A number in brackets indicating the icon to display and ranging
from `1` to at least `24`

Figure 9.6 shows the available, known icons. Outlook does not use icons
[5], [22], or [24] for any of its entry types. (Icon [23] is the same as [22].) If
you do not specify a value for Large Icon, Outlook uses the blank paper
icon shown at the top of Figure 9.6. You can also enter a Small Icon value; if
you do, set it to the same value as Large Icon.

For example, if you wanted to add an entry type for the time that users
spend in training sessions (e.g., classroom, online, self-paced), you would
create a new key, perhaps called Training Session, and populate it with the
values shown in Figure 9.7.

You can also remove the keys for Journal entry types that you do not use,
but do not delete the Phone Call key. Outlook uses the Phone Call key to
determine what Journal entry to show as the default. If that key is not
present, Outlook will show Phone Call as the default entry anyway.

If you want the default Journal entry to be something other than Phone
Call, the solution is to edit the information in the Phone Call key, then cre-
ate a separate new key (call it Phone Call 2) for the actual Phone Call entry.
Follow these steps:

1.   In the Phone Call key, rename the DescriptionID field xDescrip-
      tionID.

2.   Still in the Phone Call key, add a new REG_SZ value named
      Description; for its value, type in the Journal entry type that you

Figure 9.6
*Icons available for
Journal entry types.*

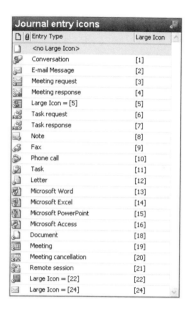

want the user to see when a new Journal entry opens. Change the Large Icon to a more appropriate icon from the list in Figure 9.6.

3. In the Journal key, create a new key named Phone Call 2, and add Description and Large Icon values as described above.

Figure 9.7
*Adding a new
Journal entry type
for training
sessions.*

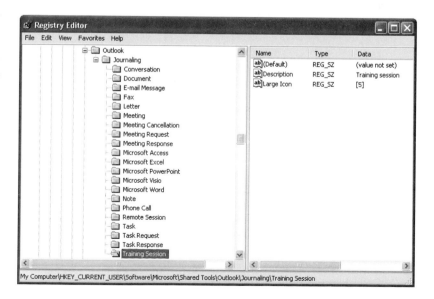

9.2.12 **Outlook desktop icon**

For compliance with Windows XP user-interface requirements, Outlook 2003 does not install a desktop icon, as previous versions did. You can add such an icon, though, by adding a new registry key. Under the key HKEY_ LOCAL_MACHINE\SOFTWARE\Microsoft\Windows\CurrentVersion\ Explorer\Desktop\NameSpace, insert a new key named {00020D75-0000-0000-C000-000000000046}. You do not need to add any values under that key. The next time Windows starts, a desktop icon for Microsoft Office Outlook will appear. The user can double-click it to run Outlook or can right-click it and choose Properties to modify the mail-profile settings.

9.3 **Mail-profile-specific settings**

As you learned in Chapters 3 and 4, Outlook stores settings, many of them undocumented, for mail profiles in the HKEY_CURRENT_USER\Soft-ware\Microsoft\WindowsNT\CurrentVersion\Windows Messaging Sub-system\Profiles key. Only a few of the settings reside in keys that remain the same from profile to profile and, thus, can be managed relatively easily with a .prf file. Some other settings, however, can be controlled with a script. In this section, we'll look at two different scripting techniques for working with Outlook profile settings—Windows Management Instrumentation (WMI) and a third-party library called Profman.

9.3.1 **Outlook Address Book order**

As you saw in Chapter 4, if you export the Profile key from the registry before and after making a change to the Outlook user interface, you can compare those snapshots to discover what registry value(s) have changed. Through that process, you can discover that changing the Outlook Address Book order from First Last (default) to File As (normally Last, First) changes a binary registry value (000b6602) from 00 00 to 01 00, and vice versa. The problem is that this value won't be in the same key for each profile!

The VBScript code in Listing 9.1 solves this problem by looping through all of the keys in a profile looking for the one that contains settings for the Outlook Address Book by examining the value of another key, 001f300a, which holds the name of the .dll associated with a particular account or service. The particular scripting interface that Listing 9.1 uses is called WMI and offers a key advantage over some other Windows scripting techniques: it allows you to iterate all of the subkeys in a registry key, in this case all of the service keys under a particular Profile key.

Listing 9.1   *Setting the Outlook Address Book Display Order*

```
' Use this version to set the default profile
Call SetOABLastFirst(True, "")

' Use this version (and comment the other) to
' set a named profile.
' Call SetOABLastFirst(True, "profilename")

Sub SetOABLastFirst(blnLastFirst, strProfile)
    ' If blnLastFirst = True, set OAB order to
    ' File As (Last, First)
    ' If blnLastFirst = False, set OAB order to
    ' First Last
    ' strProfile can be a named profile or blank.
    ' If blank, set the order on the default profile.
    On Error Resume Next
    Const HKEY_CURRENT_USER = &H80000001
    strComputer = "."
    blnFoundKey = False

    If Not IsOutlookRunning Then
        Set objreg = GetObject _
          ("winmgmts:{impersonationLevel=impersonate}!\\" _
          & strComputer & "\root\default:StdRegProv")
        strKeyPath = "Software\Microsoft\Windows NT\" & _
                    "CurrentVersion\" & _
                    "Windows Messaging Subsystem\Profiles\"
        ' get string for service DLL file
        strServDLL = StringToHex4("contab.dll")
        ' get profile name
        If strProfile = "" Then
            objreg.GetStringValue HKEY_CURRENT_USER, _
                                strKeyPath, _
                                "DefaultProfile", _
                                strProfile
        End If
        If strProfile <> "" Then
            strKeyPath = strKeyPath & strProfile
            objreg.EnumKey HKEY_CURRENT_USER, strKeyPath, _
                        arrProfileKeys
            For Each subkey In arrProfileKeys
                strSubkeyPath = strKeyPath & "\" & subkey
                ' 001f300a value contains
                ' name of the service DLL file
                objreg.GetBinaryValue HKEY_CURRENT_USER, _
                                    strSubkeyPath, _
                                    "001f300a", _
                                    arrKeyValue
```

Listing 9.1 *Setting the Outlook Address Book Display Order (continued)*

```
                If Not IsNull(arrKeyValue) Then
                    For i = 0 To UBound(arrKeyValue)
                        ' build string from hex values
                        strhexkeyvalue = strhexkeyvalue & _
                                    HexByte(arrKeyValue(i))

                    Next
                    ' compare with service name
                    If InStr(strhexkeyvalue, _
                            strServDLL) = 1 Then
                        blnFoundKey = True
                        ' we have the right key,
                        ' so change the value
                        If blnLastFirst Then
                            arrBinary = Array(1, 0)
                        Else
                            arrBinary = Array(0, 0)
                        End If
                        objreg.SetBinaryValue _
                            HKEY_CURRENT_USER, _
                            strSubkeyPath, _
                            "000b6602", arrBinary
                        Exit For
                    End If
                End If
            Next
            If blnFoundKey = False Then
                strMsg = "Could not find Outlook " & _
                        "Address Book in the " & _
                        strProfile & " mail profile."
                MsgBox strMsg, vbExclamation, _
                        "SetOABLastFirst"
            End If
        Else
            strMsg = "Please run Outlook once before " & _
                    "running this script. "
            MsgBox strMsg, vbExclamation, "SetOABLastFirst"
        End If
    Else
        strMsg = "Please shut down Outlook before " & _
                "running this script."
        MsgBox strMsg, vbExclamation, "SetOABLastFirst"
    End If
End Sub

Function IsOutlookRunning()
    strComputer = "."
    Set objWMIService = GetObject("winmgmts:" _
        & "{impersonationLevel=impersonate}!\\" _
        & strComputer & "\root\cimv2")
```

Listing 9.1 *Setting the Outlook Address Book Display Order (continued)*

```
    strQuery = "Select * from Win32_Process Where " & _
            "Name = 'Outlook.exe'"
    Set colProcesses = objWMIService.ExecQuery(strQuery)
    For Each objProcess In colProcesses
        If UCase(objProcess.Name) = "OUTLOOK.EXE" Then
            IsOutlookRunning = True
        Else
            IsOutlookRunning = False
        End If
    Next
End Function

Function HexByte(b)
    HexByte = Right("0" & Hex(b), 2)
End Function

Public Function StringToHex4(Data)
    ' Input: normal text
    ' Output: four-character strings for each character,
    ' e.g. "3204" for lower-case Russian B,
    ' "6500" for ASCII e
    Dim strChar
    Dim strAll

    For i = 1 To Len(Data)
        ' get the four-character hex for each character
        strChar = Mid(Data, i, 1)
        strTemp = Right("00" & Hex(AscW(strChar)), 4)
        strAll = strAll & Right(strTemp, 2) & _
                Left(strTemp, 2)
    Next
    StringToHex4 = strAll
End Function
```

Note: Modifying profile settings through direct registry manipulation is not a procedure that Microsoft supports. As Microsoft Knowledge Base article 266352 ("INFO: MAPI Is the Only Way to Programmatically Change Profiles") explains, the only supported way to modify mail profiles programmatically is with Extended Messaging Application Programming Interface (MAPI).

You can use this code either in a stand-alone VBScript file with a .vbs extension or as part of a larger login script. See Appendix D for resources on WMI scripting.

9.3.2   Default signatures

Signatures in Outlook 2003 are account specific. When the user creates a new message, Outlook automatically appends the automatic signature for the default mail account, assuming the user set a default. When the user replies or forwards a message, Outlook automatically appends the reply/forward signature associated with the account that the message arrived in. In addition, if the user has WordMail as his or her editor, when the user switches the sending account for a message, Outlook automatically replaces the existing signature with the signature for the newly selected account. (This feature works only if all accounts have default new message and reply/forward signatures associated with them.)

These per-account signature settings are buried very deeply in the Windows registry, in the HKEY_CURRENT_USER\Software\Microsoft\Windows NT\CurrentVersion\Windows Messaging Subsystem\Profiles key. Each Outlook mail profile has its own key, and each mail-profile key has a subkey named 9375CFF0413111d3B88A00104B2A6676. Under this key are a number of undocumented settings, including those for per-account signatures. If the user has set up signatures for the account, they'll be listed in the New Signature and Reply-Forward Signature entries, both REG_BINARY to provide Unicode support.

The VBScript code in Listing 9.2 takes something of a brute-force approach and sets or modifies the signature for each service in the profile, even those that are not mail accounts. (This does no harm since the signature entries for nonmail accounts are simply ignored.) Like Listing 9.1, it uses WMI scripting.

9.3.3   Adding a secondary Exchange mailbox

One of the most common profile configuration tasks that you cannot automate with a simple .prf file is the addition of a secondary Exchange mailbox to the mail profile. For example, many organizations have a help desk that multiple support employees need to access. They add the help desk mailbox to their Outlook configuration through the Tools | E-mail Accounts dialog by changing the properties of the Exchange account. It is possible to script this procedure with a tool called Profman, which is included with the distributable version of Outlook Redemption (http://www.dimastr.com/redemption). Redemption, as you saw in Chapter 6, is a third-party

Listing 9.2 *Setting the Default Signature for All Accounts*

```
' Use this version to set all accounts
' in the default mail profile
' to use a previously created signature
Call SetDefaultSignature("Signature Name", "")

' Use this version (and comment the other) to
' modify a named profile.
'Call SetDefaultSignature _
'  ("Signature Name", "Profile Name")

Sub SetDefaultSignature(strSigName, strProfile)
    Const HKEY_CURRENT_USER = &H80000001
    strComputer = "."

    If Not IsOutlookRunning Then
        Set objreg = GetObject("winmgmts:" & _
          "{impersonationLevel=impersonate}!\\" & _
          strComputer & "\root\default:StdRegProv")
        strKeyPath = "Software\Microsoft\Windows NT\" & _
                     "CurrentVersion\Windows " & _
                     "Messaging Subsystem\Profiles\"
        ' get default profile name if none specified
        If strProfile = "" Then
            objreg.GetStringValue HKEY_CURRENT_USER, _
                strKeyPath, "DefaultProfile", strProfile
        End If
        ' build array from signature name
        myArray = StringToByteArray(strSigName, True)
        strKeyPath = strKeyPath & strProfile & _
                     "\9375CFF0413111d3B88A00104B2A6676"
        objreg.EnumKey HKEY_CURRENT_USER, strKeyPath, _
                arrProfileKeys
        For Each subkey In arrProfileKeys
            strsubkeypath = strKeyPath & "\" & subkey
            ' On Error Resume Next
            objreg.SetBinaryValue HKEY_CURRENT_USER, _
              strsubkeypath, "New Signature", myArray
            objreg.SetBinaryValue HKEY_CURRENT_USER, _
              strsubkeypath, "Reply-Forward Signature", myArray
        Next
    Else
        strMsg = "Please shut down Outlook before " & _
                 "running this script."
        MsgBox strMsg, vbExclamation, "SetDefaultSignature"
    End If
End Sub
```

Listing 9.2   *Setting the Default Signature for All Accounts (continued)*

```
Function IsOutlookRunning()
    strComputer = "."
    strQuery = "Select * from Win32_Process " & _
               "Where Name = 'Outlook.exe'"
    Set objWMIService = GetObject("winmgmts:" _
        & "{impersonationLevel=impersonate}!\\" _
        & strComputer & "\root\cimv2")
    Set colProcesses = objWMIService.ExecQuery(strQuery)
    For Each objProcess In colProcesses
        If UCase(objProcess.Name) = "OUTLOOK.EXE" Then
            IsOutlookRunning = True
        Else
            IsOutlookRunning = False
        End If
    Next
End Function


Public Function StringToByteArray _
                 (Data, NeedNullTerminator)
    Dim strAll
    strAll = StringToHex4(Data)
    If NeedNullTerminator Then
        strAll = strAll & "0000"
    End If
    intLen = Len(strAll) \ 2
    ReDim arr(intLen - 1)
    For i = 1 To Len(strAll) \ 2
        arr(i - 1) = CByte _
                ("&H" & Mid(strAll, (2 * i) - 1, 2))
    Next
    StringToByteArray = arr
End Function


Public Function StringToHex4(Data)
    ' Input: normal text
    ' Output: four-character string for each character,
    ' e.g. "3204" for lower-case Russian B,
    ' "6500" for ASCII e
    ' Output: correct characters
    ' needs to reverse order of bytes from 0432
    Dim strAll
    For i = 1 To Len(Data)
        ' get the four-character hex for each character
        strChar = Mid(Data, i, 1)
        strTemp = Right("00" & Hex(AscW(strChar)), 4)
        strAll = strAll & Right(strTemp, 2) & Left(strTemp, 2)
    Next
    StringToHex4 = strAll
End Function
```

programming library that brings Extended MAPI functionality within the reach of average Outlook programmers. Profman is an extension of the same Extended MAPI techniques, aimed specifically at Outlook mail-profile management.

To use the Profman library in a script to configure a user's profile, you will need to install the Profman.dll file on the user's machine and register it with the following command:

```
regsvr32.exe <path>\Profman.dll
```

where `<path>` is the path to the location where the Profman.dll file is installed. You can use the CIW, CMW, or other installation tools to perform these installation tasks.

The Redemption Web site includes documentation for the objects, properties, and methods for the Profman library. As an example of what you can do with Profman, the VBScript code in Listing 9.3 adds a mailbox with the alias "helpdesk" to the user's default profile, assuming that the profile contains the Exchange service.

Listing 9.3 *Adding a Secondary Exchange Mailbox*

```
' Name of user profile to modify
' Leave blank to modify default profile
strProfileName = "Flavius"

' Alias of mailbox to add to the profile
strMailbox = "helpdesk"

' Constants for MAPI properties
Const PR_STORE_PROVIDERS = &H3D000102
Const PR_PROVIDER_UID = &H300C0102
Const PR_DISPLAY_NAME = &H3001001E
Const PR_PROFILE_MAILBOX = &H660B001E
Const PR_PROFILE_SERVER = &H660C001E
Const PR_PROFILE_SERVER_DN = &H6614001E
Const PR_EMAIL_ADDRESS = &H3003001E


'get PR_PROFILE_SERVER and PR_PROFILE_SERVER_DN
'It is assumed that the mailbox to add is on the
'same server as the current user's mailbox
MAPI_STORE_PROVIDER = 33
On Error Resume Next
Set profiles = CreateObject("ProfMan.Profiles")
On Error GoTo 0
```

Listing 9.3   *Adding a Secondary Exchange Mailbox (continued)*

```
If Err = 0 Then
    If strProfileName = "" Then
        Set profile = profiles.DefaultProfile
    Else
        For i = 1 To profiles.Count
            Set profile = profiles.Item(i)
            If profile.Name = strProfileName Then
                Exit For
            End If
        Next
    End If
    If profile.Name = strProfileName Then
        Set Services = profile.Services
        For i = 1 To Services.Count
            Set Service = Services.Item(i)
            If Service.ServiceName = "MSEMS" Then
                Set Providers = Service.Providers
                For j = 1 To Providers.Count
                    Set Provider = Providers.Item(j)
                    If Provider.ResourceType = _
                       MAPI_STORE_PROVIDER Then
                        Set ProfSect = Provider.ProfSect
                        strProfileServer = _
                          ProfSect.Item(PR_PROFILE_SERVER)
                        strProfileServerDN = _
                          ProfSect.Item(PR_PROFILE_SERVER_DN)
                    End If
                Next
            End If
        Next

        ' use CDO 1.21 to obtain the AddressEntry for the
        ' desired mailbox alias
        Set myCDOSession = CreateObject("MAPI.Session")
        myCDOSession.Logon strProfileName, "", False, True
        ' Next statement is subject to Outlook security
        ' prompts; the user must click Yes for the script to
        ' complete.
        Set cdoAddrEntry = GetAddressEntry _
                              (strMailbox, myCDOSession)
        If Not cdoAddrEntry Is Nothing Then
            ' add the mailbox to the profile
            Call AddMailBox(strProfileName, _
                    "Mailbox - " & _
                      cdoAddrEntry.Fields(PR_DISPLAY_NAME).Value, _
                    cdoAddrEntry.Fields(PR_EMAIL_ADDRESS).Value, _
                    strProfileServer, _
                    strProfileServerDN)
        End If
```

Listing 9.3   *Adding a Secondary Exchange Mailbox (continued)*

```
            myCDOSession.Logoff
        Else
            strMessage = "No profile named " & strProfileName & _
                         " was available."
            MsgBox strMessage, vbExclamation, "Script halted"
        End If
    Else
        strMessage = "Please install the Profman library " & _
                     "before running the AddMailbox script."
        MsgBox strMessage, vbExclamation, "Script halted"
    End If


    Sub AddMailBox(strProfile, strDisplayName, _
                 strMailboxDN, strServer, strServerDN)
        Set profiles = CreateObject("ProfMan.Profiles")
        If strProfile = "" Then
            Set profile = profiles.DefaultProfile
        Else
            For i = 1 To profiles.Count
                Set profile = profiles.Item(i)
                If profile.Name = strProfile Then
                    Exit For
                End If
            Next
        End If

        If profile.Name = strProfile Then
            ' find the Exchange service
            Set Services = profile.Services
            For i = 1 To Services.Count
                Set Service = Services.Item(i)
                If Service.ServiceName = "MSEMS" Then
                    ' Add "EMSDelegate" provider
                    Set Properties = _
                      CreateObject("ProfMan.PropertyBag")
                    Properties.Add _
                      PR_DISPLAY_NAME, strDisplayName
                    Properties.Add _
                      PR_PROFILE_MAILBOX, strMailboxDN
                    Properties.Add _
                      PR_PROFILE_SERVER, strServer
                    Properties.Add _
                      PR_PROFILE_SERVER_DN, strServerDN
                    Set Provider = _
                      Service.Providers.Add _
                        ("EMSDelegate", Properties)
```

Listing 9.3 *Adding a Secondary Exchange Mailbox (continued)*

```
                        ' update the old value of PR_STORE_PROVIDERS
                        ' so that Outlook will show the mailbox in
                        ' the list in Tools | E-mail Accounts
                        Set GlobalProfSect = profile.GlobalProfSect
                        OldProviders = _
                           GlobalProfSect.Item(PR_STORE_PROVIDERS)
                        strUID = Provider.UID
                        GlobalProfSect.Item(PR_STORE_PROVIDERS) = _
                           OldProviders & strUID
                    End If
                Next
            Else
                strMessage = "No profile named " & strProfileName & _
                             " was available."
                MsgBox strMessage, vbExclamation, "Script halted"
            End If
End Sub

Function GetAddressEntry(strAlias, mySession)
    Dim objMsg
    Dim objRecip
    Set objMsg = mySession.Outbox.Messages.Add
    Set objRecip = objMsg.Recipients.Add("=" & strAlias)
    objRecip.Resolve True
    If Left(objRecip.Address, 3) = "EX:" Then
        Set GetAddressEntry = objRecip.AddressEntry
    Else
        Set GetAddressEntry = Nothing
    End If
End Function
```

After you run this script, Outlook may initially display "Exchange Message Store" as the name of the root folder of the added mailbox. Eventually, it will change that to the expected display name, "Mailbox—*<user name>*."

9.4   Folder-related settings

As you'll recall from Chapter 1, some options that users can set are stored not in the Windows registry, but in Outlook as properties or hidden items in individual Outlook folders. In this section, we'll look at scripts that you can use to set various folder-specific options, including calendar color labels and permissions. You'll also see how to create a search folder with a script.

Some of these procedures require the use of Collaboration Data Objects (CDO) 1.21, which is an optional component of the Outlook 2003 installation.

9.4.1 Calendar color labels

The color-coded calendar labels introduced in Outlook 2002 have turned into a popular feature. Some organizations ask whether they can deploy a consistent set of color labels to all of their users. Before you consider whether this is something you want to do, take a moment to understand how Outlook stores the label settings.

Each Calendar folder where the user has customized the labels has a special property (MAPI property tag 0x36DC0102, which is not exposed in the Outlook object model for programmers). This property stores the text that corresponds to each color whose label has been customized. Since this property is folder specific, each folder can have its own set of label customizations. The only thing stored in an appointment itself is a number corresponding to the selected color label. If you copy an appointment from one folder to another, that item will appear labeled with the same color in both folders, but the text associated with that color will depend on which folder the item is in.

Furthermore, Outlook does not transmit the color label as part of a meeting request. Any time you get a meeting request—whether from an Exchange user or an Internet correspondent—it will not contain any calendar color label information.

As a practical matter, therefore, there are probably only a few scenarios in which you might want to start users off with a specific set of default calendar color labels in their own Calendar folders. But if that is something you need to do, you can accomplish it with a script that uses CDO 1.21, an optional component that you can install during Outlook or Office setup or later with the CMW.

Note: The user must have run Outlook at least once before running this script. Otherwise, the Calendar folder will not exist yet.

The VBScript code in Listing 9.4 modifies the calendar color labels in the default Calendar folder either for the user's default profile or for a specific named profile. It does not matter whether this code runs when Outlook is running.

Running the script in Listing 9.4 sets the color labels to the values shown in Figure 9.8. Notice that the fourth and seventh labels, which were left blank in strLabelList are set to their default localized values.

Listing 9.4   *Setting Color Labels for the Default Calendar Folder*

```
' Set the 10-element list of color labels here,
' separating each pair with a semicolon.
' To use the default label for a color,
' leave the element blank.
' To convert non-ASCII characters, use
' ChrW(CLng(<hex value of character>)
strLabelList = "red;blue;green;;orange;aqua;;" & _
               "purple;;" & _
               ChrW(CLng(&H436)) & ChrW(CLng(&H451)) & _
               ChrW(CLng(&H43B)) & ChrW(CLng(&H442)) & _
               ChrW(CLng(&H44B)) & ChrW(CLng(&H439))

' To reset the color label list to localized defaults,
' comment out the strLabelList statement above
' and use this one instead.
'strLabelList = ";;;;;;;;;"

' Use this version to modify the labels in the
' Calendar folder in the default mail profile.
'Call SetDefaultCalLabels(strLabelList, "")

' Use this version (and comment the other out) to
' modify the labels in a particuilar profile
Call SetDefaultCalLabels(strLabelList, "Flavius")


Sub SetDefaultCalLabels(strLabelNames, strProfile)
    Const CdoDefaultFolderCalendar = 0
    On Error Resume Next
    If strProfile = "" Then
        strProfile = GetDefaultMailProfileName()
    End If
    ' Start CDO session
    Set cdoMySession = CreateObject("MAPI.Session")
    cdoMySession.Logon strProfile, "", False, True
    Set cdocalendar = cdoMySession.GetDefaultFolder _
                    (CdoDefaultFolderCalendar)
    res = SetCalendarLabels(cdocalendar, strLabelNames)
    cdoMySession.Logoff
    Set cdoMySession = Nothing
End Sub

Function SetCalendarLabels(cdoFolder, strLabels)
    ' Return True if successful, False if not.
    On Error Resume Next
    ' build string for properties
    ' need 10 labels, can be blank between ;
    strAllLabels = "0000"
    arr = Split(strLabels, ";")
```

Listing 9.4 *Setting Color Labels for the Default Calendar Folder (continued)*

```
        For j = 0 To 9
            strLabelName = arr(j)
            strAllLabels = strAllLabels & _
                        StringToHex4(strLabelName) & "0000"
        Next
        Set cdoMyField = cdoFolder.Fields(&H36DC0102)
        If cdoMyField Is Nothing Then
            Set cdoMyField = cdoFolder.Fields.Add _
                        (&H36DC0102, strAllLabels)
        Else
            cdoMyField.Value = strAllLabels
        End If
        cdoFolder.Update True, True

        If Err = 0 Then
            SetCalendarLabels = True
        Else
            SetCalendarLabels = False
        End If
End Function

Function StringToHex4(Data)
    ' Input: normal text
    ' Output: four-character string for each character,
    ' e.g. "3204" for lower-case Russian B,
    ' "6500" for ASCII e
    ' Output: correct characters
    ' needs to reverse order of bytes from 0432
    Dim strAll
    For i = 1 To Len(Data)
        ' get the four-character hex for each character
        strChar = Mid(Data, i, 1)
        strTemp = Right("00" & Hex(AscW(strChar)), 4)
        strAll = strAll & _
                Right(strTemp, 2) & Left(strTemp, 2)
    Next
    StringToHex4 = strAll
End Function

Function GetDefaultMailProfileName()
    Const HKEY_CURRENT_USER = &H80000001
    strComputer = "."
    Set objreg = GetObject("winmgmts:" & _
            "{impersonationLevel=impersonate}!\\" & _
            strComputer & "\root\default:StdRegProv")
    strKeyPath = "Software\Microsoft\Windows NT\" & _
                "CurrentVersion\Windows " & _
                "Messaging Subsystem\Profiles\"
    objreg.GetStringValue HKEY_CURRENT_USER, _
            strKeyPath, "DefaultProfile", strProfile
    GetDefaultMailProfileName = strProfile
End Function
```

Figure 9.8
*Calendar color
labels customized
with a script.*

The last label, which is the Russian word for yellow, was constructed from this complicated looking string:

```
ChrW(CLng(&H436)) & ChrW(CLng(&H451)) & _
ChrW(CLng(&H43B)) & ChrW(CLng(&H442)) & _
ChrW(CLng(&H44B)) & ChrW(CLng(&H439))
```

Each of the hex values, such as &H436, represents a different letter in the Cyrillic alphabet. You would need to use a similar technique to handle any other character that you can't input in the editor you use to edit the script and set the value for `strLabelList`.

Tip: To look up the hex value of a character, you can use the Insert | Symbol dialog in Word.

9.4.2 Custom search folders

One of the most exciting new features in Outlook 2003 is the concept of search folders—virtual folders that display messages meeting your search criteria in one or more folders. Several search folders—For Follow Up, Large Messages, and Unread Mail—are preconfigured for the user. To create more, the user can right-click on the Search Folders folder in the Mail or Folder List navigation pane and choose New Search Folder.

Note: The folders searched by a search folder must all be either in the user's own Exchange mailbox or in the same Personal Folders .pst file.

There are scenarios, however, when you may want to create a new search folder for the user. For example, if your company does business with one partner, you might want users to have a search folder that shows all mail from that company in the Inbox and any Inbox subfolders. The VBScript code in Listing 9.5 is intended to run in a stand-alone VBScript .vbs file and will create a search folder showing messages from a particular domain.

With microsoft.com set as the domain for the search folder, `MakeDomainSearchFolder()` performs a search using this search query:

```
"http://schemas.microsoft.com/mapi/proptag/0x0065001f"
LIKE '%microsoft.com%'
```

The `LIKE '%microsoft.com%'` expression should be familiar to you if you've done any work with SQL or Access databases. It's a typical "contains"

Listing 9.5 *Creating a Search Folder for All Inbox Messages from a Domain*

```
' Name of the domain you want to filter
' with a search folder
strDomain = "microsoft.com"

Call MakeDomainSearchFolder(strDomain, True)

Sub MakeDomainSearchFolder(SearchDomain, SearchSubfolders)
    schemaFromName = "urn:schemas:httpmail:fromname"
    schemaFromAddress = _
      "http://schemas.microsoft.com/mapi/proptag/0x0065001f"

    SearchDomain = "%" & SearchDomain & "%"
    strSearch = Quote(schemaFromAddress) & _
                " LIKE " & SQLQuote("%microsoft.com%")
    Set olApp = CreateObject("Outlook.Application")
    Set olSearch = olApp.AdvancedSearch _
                    ("Inbox", strSearch, SearchSubfolders)
    olSearch.Stop
    Set olFolder = _
      olSearch.Save("Messages from " & SearchDomain)
    Set olFolder = Nothing
    Set olSearch = Nothing
    Set olApp = Nothing
End Sub

Function Quote(Data)
    Quote = Chr(34) & Data & Chr(34)
End Function

Function SQLQuote(Data)
    SQLQuote = Chr(39) & Data & Chr(39)
End Function
```

search string. The `http://schemas.microsoft.com/mapi/proptag/` `0x0065001f` expression looks like a Web page address, doesn't it? Well, it's not. It's actually the name of a property of a mail message expressed in the syntax of a query language called DAV Searching and Locating (DASL). In particular, it's the property representing the sender's address. So, the entire query string simply searches for items in which the sender's e-mail address contains microsoft.com.

At this point, you're probably wondering how anyone could possibly know that `http://schemas.microsoft.com/mapi/proptag/0x0065001f` is the expression to use if you want to search the sender's address. The secret lies on the dialog used to create a filter for a folder.

To view a mail folder's filter, choose View | Arrange By | Current View | Customize Current View, then click Filter. On the Messages tab, type a domain name into the box next to the From button, then switch to the SQL tab. Check the "Edit these criteria directly" box to make it easier to see the SQL query for the folder, as shown in Figure 9.9.

You should recognize the expression after the OR as the same one that Listing 9.5 uses. A little manual editing and testing of the search query in the SQL tab will show you that the first expression—`"urn:sche-mas:httpmail:fromname"` `LIKE` `'%microsoft.com%'`—searches only for the text "microsoft.com" in the sender's display name, not in the e-mail address. It's the second expression that performs the address search, so that's all we need to use in Listing 9.5.

Figure 9.9
Viewing the SQL query for a folder filter.

Figure 9.10
*Constructing a
filter with the
Query Builder.*

Look closely at Figure 9.9, and you'll see a tab in the Filter dialog that is not normally present, the one named Query Builder. To add it, add a new registry subkey named QueryBuilder to the registry key HKEY_CURRENT_USER\Software\Microsoft\Office\11.0\Outlook. You do not need to set the default value or add any other values to the QueryBuilder key.

As Figure 9.10 shows, you can use the Query Builder to construct more complex searches than would be possible using the first three tabs of the Filter dialog. You can then inspect the results on the SQL tab and use that information to write more scripts to create more search folders.

The search depicted in Figure 9.10 results in the following query string:

```
("urn:schemas:httpmail:importance" = 2 OR "urn:schemas-
microsoft-com:office:office#Keywords" LIKE '%Key
Customer%')
```

9.4.3 Adding Public Folders to Favorites

Outlook 2003 makes two significant changes to the way public folders are handled. If the mail profile is using Cached Exchange mode and is set to download Public Folders\Favorites, Outlook will cache all folders in the Public Folders\Favorites hierarchy in the local offline folders .ost file, both for quicker access and for offline use.

Note: Remember that the option to download Public Folders\Favorites is one that you can choose as part of the mail-profile settings.

Furthermore, only folders in Public Folders\Favorites can be added to the Favorite Folders list in the Mail navigation pane, the Other Calendars list in the Calendar pane, the Other Contacts list in the Contacts pane, and so forth. Some users may have a hard time finding important Public Folders if the only place they can see them is in the Folder List navigation pane. Therefore, you may want to use a script to place certain key folders in user's Public Folders\Favorites hierarchy.

For example, let's say that your human-resources department has its own branch in the Public Folders hierarchy and adds a Company Events calendar that lists holidays, important company meetings, and other events crucial to your business. Listing 9.6, which is designed to run as a stand-alone VBScript .vbs file after Outlook has started, adds the Company Events folder to the user's Public Folders\Favorites. Note that the folder path needs to include the top two levels of the Public Folder hierarchy—Public Folders\All Public Folders.

The `AddFolderToFavorites` subroutine in Listing 9.6 includes an argument to add a contact folder not just to Public Folders\Favorites but also to the Outlook Address Book.

9.4.4 Folder permissions

When it comes to calendars, many organizations using Microsoft Exchange want people not only to see each other's free/busy times but also to be able to view everyone's appointment details. Therefore, they want to set the permission on the mailbox Calendar folder to use Reviewer as the default role. This can be done with a script, but it requires CDO 1.21, which is an optional component in the Outlook installation, plus an additional file—the access control list (ACL) component from the platform software development kit. You can obtain Acl.dll from Microsoft's Web site (see Appendix D). After you run the self-extracting download file and extract the Acl.dll file, you will need to register Acl.dll with the following command:

```
regsvr32 <path>\acl.dll
```

where `<path>` is the full path to the folder where you extracted Acl.dll.

Information on how to use Acl.dll is available on Microsoft's Web site (see Appendix D). As an example, the VBScript code in Listing 9.7 is intended to run on the local user's machine and sets Reviewer as the default role on the Calendar folder. Outlook does not need to be running when you run this script.

Listing 9.6 *Adding a Public Folder to Favorites*

```
' Path to public folder; should be similar to
' "Public Folders\All Public Folders\Company\Sales"
strFolder = "Public Folders\All Public Folders\" & _
            "Human Resources\Company Events"
Call AddFolderToFavorites(strFolder, True)

Sub AddFolderToFavorites(strPath, AddToAddressBook)
    Const olContactItem = 2
    Set myFolder = GetFolder(strPath)
    If Not myFolder Is Nothing Then
        myFolder.AddToPFFavorites
        ' if contacts folder,
        ' optionally add new Favorite to OAB
        If myFolder.DefaultItemType = olContactItem Then
            If AddToAddressBook = True Then
                strFavFolder = _
                  "Public Folders\Favorites\" & _
                  myFolder.Name
                Set myFavFolder = GetFolder(strFavFolder)
                If Not myFavFolder Is Nothing Then
                    myFavFolder.ShowAsOutlookAB = True
                End If
            End If
        End If
    End If
    Set myFolder = Nothing
End Sub

Public Function GetFolder(strFolderPath)
  On Error Resume Next
  strFolderPath = Replace(strFolderPath, "/", "\")
  arrFolders = Split(strFolderPath, "\")
  Set objApp = CreateObject("Outlook.Application")
  Set objNS = objApp.GetNamespace("MAPI")
  Set objFolder = objNS.Folders.Item(arrFolders(0))
  If Not objFolder Is Nothing Then
    For I = 1 To UBound(arrFolders)
      Set colFolders = objFolder.Folders
      Set objFolder = Nothing
      Set objFolder = colFolders.Item(arrFolders(I))
      If objFolder Is Nothing Then
        Exit For
      End If
    Next
  End If
  Set GetFolder = objFolder
  Set colFolders = Nothing
  Set objNS = Nothing
  Set objApp = Nothing
End Function
```

Listing 9.7 *Setting the Default Calendar Role to Reviewer*

```
Dim cdoMyCalendar
Const CdoDefaultFolderCalendar = 0
'On Error Resume Next
strProfileName = GetDefaultMailProfileName()
' Start CDO session
Set cdoMySession = CreateObject("MAPI.Session")
cdoMySession.Logon strProfileName, "", False, True
Set cdoMyCalendar = cdoMySession.GetDefaultFolder _
                   (CdoDefaultFolderCalendar)
If Not cdoMyCalendar Is Nothing Then
    ' make sure Calendar is an Exchange folder
    strStoreID = cdoMyCalendar.StoreID
    Set cdoMyStore = _
      cdoMySession.GetInfoStore(strStoreID)
    If cdoMyStore.ProviderName = _
      "Microsoft Exchange Server" Then
        Call SetDefaultACLReviewer(cdoMyCalendar)
    End If
End If
Set cdoMyCalendar = Nothing
cdoMySession.Logoff
Set cdoMySession = Nothing

Sub SetDefaultACLReviewer(thisFolder)
    Const ROLE_REVIEWER = &H401
    ' get ACL & bind to folder
    Set objCalACL = CreateObject("MSExchange.ACLObject")
    objCalACL.CDOItem = thisFolder
    Set colACEs = objCalACL.ACEs
    ' get the Default user's Access Control Entry
    Set objACE = colACEs.Item("ID_ACL_DEFAULT")
    If objACE Is Nothing Then
        Set objACE = CreateObject("MSExchange.ACE")
        objACE.ID = "ID_ACL_DEFAULT"
    End If
    ' set ReadItems and update ACL
    objACE.Rights = ROLE_REVIEWER
    objCalACL.Update
End Sub

Function GetDefaultMailProfileName()
    Const HKEY_CURRENT_USER = &H80000001
    strComputer = "."
    Set objreg = GetObject("winmgmts:" & _
          "{impersonationLevel=impersonate}!\\" & _
          strComputer & "\root\default:StdRegProv")
    strKeyPath = "Software\Microsoft\Windows NT\" & _
                "CurrentVersion\Windows " & _
                "Messaging Subsystem\Profiles\"
    objreg.GetStringValue HKEY_CURRENT_USER, _
        strKeyPath, "DefaultProfile", strProfile
    GetDefaultMailProfileName = strProfile
End Function
```

The heart of Listing 9.7 is the `SetDefaultACLReviewer` subroutine, which takes as its argument a folder returned with the CDO object model. That procedure creates an ACLObject, binds it to the folder, gets the default users access control entry, and updates it to the Reviewer role.

9.5 Some configuration challenges

Despite the best efforts of administrators, power users, and developers, it simply is not possible to manage some Outlook configuration options either through GPOs, scripts, or any other means. This concluding section of the book discusses some of these configuration challenges, why they're difficult—if not impossible—and what workarounds might be available.

9.5.1 Custom views

Perhaps the biggest challenge is to create custom views that capture particular settings and to make them available to users the first time they start Outlook 2003. Since Outlook 2003 makes some big changes in the user interface, some administrators worry that users' productivity will suffer and, therefore, wish they could turn off the new Arrange By grouping in all views or make other global changes.

That's not possible for several reasons. If the user has ever used Outlook with the mailbox previously, chances are that the user has customized the view for each folder without even knowing it. Each time you click a column heading to sort a view, for example, Outlook creates a copy of the current named view as a hidden item and uses that view's settings rather than the master settings for the named view. This means that you can't just change the settings for the default Messages view. To have the new settings for that named view apply, you also need to remove all of the hidden copies of the Messages view that are associated with each message folder where the view has been modified on the fly. Starting Outlook with the `/cleanviews` switch will remove those copies, but it will also remove all of the user's named custom views.

A further obstacle is that not all view settings are exposed in a manner that makes them programmatically accessible. The Outlook object model does have a View object with an XML property that represents most view settings, but it omits all automatic formatting rules.

9.5.2   Disabling the reading pane

As discussed earlier in Chapter 6, administrators frequently ask how to disable the Outlook 2003 reading pane, presumably because they perceive it to be a security threat. Given that Microsoft does not consider the reading pane a security vulnerability, it's not surprising that Outlook offers no way to turn it off with a policy setting. You can disable the View | Reading Pane menu with a policy setting (as described in Appendix C). However, this doesn't affect existing views, especially the default Messages view; nor does it disable the reading pane options in the Other Settings view customization dialog.

Even starting Outlook with the `/nopreview` switch doesn't disable the reading pane permanently. The user can turn it back on.

9.5.3   Global rules

Some server-based spam applications mark spam with "[Spam]" in the subject line or with a custom property. Many administrators wonder if they can deploy a rule to all users to have Outlook move such items to the Junk E-mail folder that Outlook 2003 creates.

There is no policy setting or other mechanism built into Outlook to accomplish this. However, in an Exchange Server environment, it is possible to create certain types of very simple server-side rules programmatically using CDO 1.21 and Rule.dll, another downloadable component. (See Appendix D for references on how to obtain and use it.)

Such rules may raise more support issues than they resolve, however. For one thing, it's difficult to control the relative order of such rules compared with the user's own rules. Also, rules created with Rule.dll do not appear in the Rules Wizard. This can lead to a situation where the user sees items moving to the Junk E-mail folder, for example, but can't explain why.

9.5.4   Welcome message

Microsoft eliminated the customizable welcome message in Outlook 2002, replacing it with a message that cannot be customized. Many administrators work around this issue for new users by sending a regular e-mail message to each newly created mailbox. That way, the message is already there and waiting when the user first uses Outlook to access a new account.

In Outlook 2003 with Service Pack 1, a welcome message no longer appears automatically when the user starts Outlook for the first time. If you do want users to get the standard Outlook welcome message, which includes information on new features, add this registry value:

```
Key: HKEY_CURRENT_USER\Software\Microsoft\Office\11.0\
Outlook\Setup
Value name: CreateWelcome
Value type: REG_DWORD
Value data: 1
```

You will also need to remove this registry entry (or set its value to 0), which denotes that Outlook has completed starting up for the first time:

```
HKEY_CURRENT_USER\Software\Microsoft\Office\11.0\
Outlook\Setup\First-Run
```

9.6   Summary

In this chapter, you have learned about many settings that can be customized either with various registry values or with scripts using several different programming libraries. The WMI and Profman interfaces are particularly useful for working with Outlook profiles. CDO 1.21 offers the ability to change the color labels on a Calendar folder or, with the help of an additional component, to change the permissions on a folder.

Other commonly requested Outlook configuration settings can be accomplished with a combination of registry settings or with registry entries that reside outside the normal key uses for Outlook settings. Some of the most practical changes you can make are to deploy a starter list of categories and add new types of items to the list of entry types available on the Journal form.

Making it easy for users to transition to the Outlook 2003 user interface is a high priority for many organizations. While it's simple to change the navigation pane so that it starts in the Folder List pane rather than the Mail pane, Outlook provides no easy way to turn off the reading pane, eliminate the new type of grouping, or deploy a customized view that will apply to every mail folder.

In the appendices that follow, you'll get a complete list of Outlook settings in the administrative template used by the Group Policy Editor, see some other Outlook-related settings that we have not yet covered in this book, and learn how to disable toolbar and menu commands with GPOs. Finally, you'll get a list of resources for your further exploration of Outlook configuration issues.

Outlook 2003 Policy Settings

This appendix provides a list of all the policy settings exposed in the group policy editor through the Outlk11.adm administrative template. (See Chapter 2, *Outlook Configuration Techniques*, for details on how to install the template and use the group policy editor.) The settings are presented in the same order that you would see them in the group policy editor. HKCU is used as an abbreviation for the HKEY_CURRENT_USER registry hive.

Most of these options also exist as user preference settings in the Custom Installation Wizard and Custom Maintenance Wizard tools, in which case the registy values would reside in the HKEY_CURRENT_USER\Software\ Microsoft key instead of the HKEY_CURRENT_USER\Software\Policies\ Microsoft key.

All the settings discussed in this appendix are located in the group policy editor under User Configuration/Administrative Templates/Microsoft Office Outlook 2003, as shown in Figure A.1. We will walk through each node of the hierarchy in sequence, starting with Tools | Options or rather with Tools | Options/Preferences/E-mail options, since neither the Tools | Options node nor the Preferences subnode contains any individual settings.

In the case of multipart policy settings, applying the setting sets the registry value for *every* option in the setting. For example, Figure A.1 shows the first setting under Tools | Options/Preferences/E-mail options—the "Message handling" policy setting. This setting consists of six separate options, each controlling a different registy value. When you apply this policy setting, you set all six registry values.

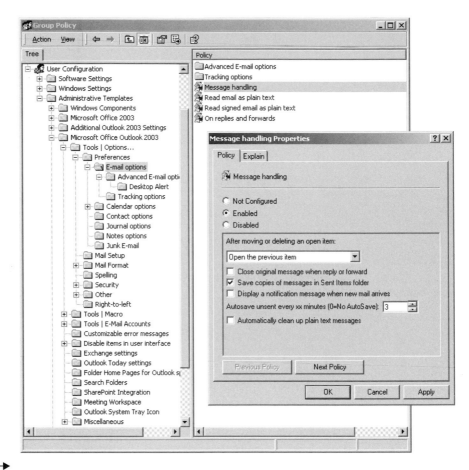

Figure A.1   *Enabling a multipart policy setting applies all the options for that setting.*

Tools | Options / Preferences / E-mail options

Message handling (multipart policy setting)

After moving or deleting an open item

Key: HKCU\Software\Policies\Microsoft\Office\11.0\
Outlook\Preferences

Value name: AfterMove

Value type: REG_DWORD

Value data: 0 = Open the next item
              1 = Return to the Inbox
              2 = Open the previous item (default)

Close original message when reply or forward

Key: HKCU\Software\Policies\Microsoft\Office\11.0\Outlook\Preferences

Value name: CloseOrig

Value type: REG_DWORD

Value data: 1 = Enabled, 0 = Disabled

Save copies of messages in Sent Items folder

Key: HKCU\Software\Policies\Microsoft\Office\11.0\Outlook\Preferences

Value name: SaveSent

Value type: REG_DWORD

Value data: 1 = Enabled (default), 0 = Disabled

Display a notification message when new mail arrives

Key: HKCU\Software\Policies\Microsoft\Office\11.0\Outlook\Preferences

Value name: Notification

Value type: REG_DWORD

Value data: 1 = Enabled, 0 = Disabled

Autosave unsent every xx minutes

Key: HKCU\Software\Policies\Microsoft\Office\11.0\Common\MailSettings

Value name: AutosaveTime

Value type: REG_DWORD

Value data: 0 to 99, 0 = no AutoSave (default = 3)

Automatically clean up plain text messages

Key: HKCU\Software\Policies\Microsoft\Office\11.0\Outlook\Options\Mail

Value name: AutoFormatPlainText

Value type: REG_DWORD

Value data: 1 = Enabled, 0 = Disabled

Read email as plain text

Key: HKCU\Software\Policies\Microsoft\Office\11.0\Outlook\Options\Mail

Value name: ReadAsPlain

Value type: REG_DWORD

Value data: 1 = Enabled, 0 = Disabled (default)

Read signed email as plain text

Key: HKCU\Software\Policies\Microsoft\Office\11.0\Outlook\
Options\Mail

Value name: ReadSignedAsPlain

Value type: REG_DWORD

Value data: 1 = Enabled, 0 = Disabled (default)

On replies and forwards (multipart policy setting)

When replying to a message

Key: HKCU\Software\Policies\Microsoft\Office\11.0\
Outlook\Preferences

Value name: ReplyStyle

Value type: REG_DWORD

Value data: 0 = Do not include original message
           1 = Attach original message
           2 = Include original message text
           3 = Include and indent orginal message text (default)
  1000 = Prefix each line of the orginal message

When forwarding a message

Key: HKCU\Software\Policies\Microsoft\Office\11.0\
Outlook\Preferences

Value name: ForwardStyle

Value type: REG_DWORD

Value data: 1 = Attach original message
           2 = Include original message text (default)
           3 = Include and indent orginal message text
  1000 = Prefix each line of the orginal message

Prefix each line with

Key: HKCU\Software\Policies\Microsoft\Office\11.0\
Outlook\Preferences

Value name: PrefixText

Value type: REG_SZ

Value data: text for prefix (default = ">")

Allow user's comments to be marked

Key: HKCU\Software\Policies\Microsoft\Office\Common\
mailsettings

Value name: MarkComments

Value type: REG_DWORD

Value data: 1 = Enabled, 0 = Disabled

Tools | Options / Preferences / E-mail options / Advanced E-mail options

Save Messages—Save unsent items in this folder

Key: HKCU\Software\Policies\Microsoft\Office\11.0\Outlook\Options\General

Value name: SAVE_LOC

Value type: REG_DWORD

Value data: 4 = Outbox
5 = Sent Items
6 = Inbox
16 = Drafts (default)

More save messages (multipart policy setting)

Key: HKCU\Software\Policies\Microsoft\Office\11.0\Outlook\Preferences

In folders other than the Inbox, save replies with original message

Value name: SaveReplies

Value type: REG_DWORD

Value data: 1 = Enabled, 0 = Disabled (default)

Save forwarded messages

Value name: SaveFW

Value type: REG_DWORD

Value data: 1 = Enabled, 0 = Disabled (default)

When new items arrive (multipart policy setting)

Key: HKCU\Software\Policies\Microsoft\Office\11.0\Outlook\Preferences

Play a sound

Value name: PlaySound

Value type: REG_DWORD

Value data: 1 = Enabled (default), 0 = Disabled

Briefly change the mouse cursor

Value name: ChangePointer

Value type: REG_DWORD

Value data: 1 = Enabled (default), 0 = Disabled

Show an envelope icon in the system tray

Value name: `ShowEnvelope`

Value type: `REG_DWORD`

Value data: `1` = Enabled (default), `0` = Disabled

When sending a message (multipart policy setting)

Set importance

Key: `HKCU\Software\Policies\Microsoft\Office\11.0\Outlook\Preferences`

Value name: `Importance`

Value type: `REG_DWORD`

Value data: `0` = Low
             `1` = Normal (default)
             `2` = High

Set sensitivity

Key: `HKCU\Software\Policies\Microsoft\Office\11.0\Outlook\Preferences`

Value name: `Sensitivity`

Value type: `REG_DWORD`

Value data: `0` = Normal (default)
             `1` = Personal
             `2` = Private
             `3` = Confidential

Messages expire after (days)

Key: `HKCU\Software\Policies\Microsoft\Office\11.0\Outlook\Options\General`

Value name: `NumDaysExpire`

Value type: `REG_DWORD`

Value data: `0` to `3652` (default = 0)

Allow commas as address separator

Key: `HKCU\Software\Policies\Microsoft\Office\11.0\Outlook\Options\General`

Value name: `AllowCommasInRecip`

Value type: `REG_DWORD`

Value data: `1` = Enabled, `0` = Disabled (default)

Automatic name checking

Key: `HKCU\Software\Policies\Microsoft\Office\11.0\Outlook\Options\General`

Value name: `AutoNameCheck`

Value type: `REG_DWORD`

Value data: `1` = Enabled (default), `0` = Disabled

Delete meeting request from Inbox when responding

Key: `Software\Policies\Microsoft\Office\11.0\Outlook\Options\General`

Value name: `DeleteWhenRespond`

Value type: `REG_DWORD`

Value data: `1` = Enabled (default), `0` = Disabled

Suggest names while completing To, Cc, and Bcc fields

Key: `HKCU\Software\Policies\Microsoft\Office\11.0\Outlook\Preferences`

Value name: `ShowAutoSug`

Value type: `REG_DWORD`

Value data: `1` = Enabled (default), `0` = Disabled

Add properties to attachments to enable Reply with Changes

Key: `HKCU\Software\Policies\Microsoft\Office\11.0\Outlook\Options\Mail`

Value name: `AdHocReviewBehavior`

Value type: `REG_DWORD`

Value data: `0` = Enabled, `1` = Disabled (default)

Note: Note that this policy's possible values are the reverse of the usual meaning for 1 and 0.

Tools | Options / Preferences / E-mail options / Advanced E-mail options / Desktop Alert

Check to disable New Mail Desktop Alert; Uncheck to enable

Key: HKCU\Software\Policies\Microsoft\Office\11.0\Outlook\ Preferences

Value name: NewmailDesktopAlerts

Value type: REG_DWORD

Value data: 0 = Alerts are enabled (default), 1 = Alerts are disabled

Specify duration of fade in

Key: HKCU\Software\Policies\Microsoft\Office\11.0\Common\ DesktopAlerts

Value name: TimeIn

Value type: REG_DWORD

Value data: 0 to 25000 milliseconds, 1000 = default

Specify duration of Desktop Alert before fade

Key: HKCU\Software\Policies\Microsoft\Office\11.0\Common\ DesktopAlerts

Value name: TimeOn

Value type: REG_DWORD

Value data: 0 to 1,000,000,000 milliseconds, 4000 = default

Specify duration of Desktop Alert on mouse over

Key: HKCU\Software\Policies\Microsoft\Office\11.0\Common\ DesktopAlerts

Value name: TimeFocus

Value type: REG_DWORD

Value data: 0 to 250,000 milliseconds, 60,000 = default

Specify duration of fade out

Key: HKCU\Software\Policies\Microsoft\Office\11.0\Common\ DesktopAlerts

Value name: TimeOut

Value type: REG_DWORD

Value data: 0 to 25,000 milliseconds, 2000 = default

Specify opacity of Desktop Alert

Key: HKCU\Software\Policies\Microsoft\Office\11.0\Common\
DesktopAlerts

Value name: Opacity

Value type: REG_DWORD

Value data: 0 to 255, 51 = default

Specify opacity at start of fade in

Key: HKCU\Software\Policies\Microsoft\Office\11.0\Common\
DesktopAlerts

Value name: FirstOpacity

Value type: REG_DWORD

Value data: 0 to 255, 0 = default

Specify default location of Desktop Alert (multipart policy setting)

Key: HKCU\Software\Policies\Microsoft\Office\11.0\Common\
DesktopAlerts

Corner

Value name: Corner

Value type: REG_DWORD

Value data: 0 = upper left quadrant of screen
             1 = upper right
             2 = lower left
             3 = lower right (default)

XOffset

Value name: XOffset

Value type: REG_DWORD

Value data: 44 = default

Note: Horizontal distance from the selected corner.

YOffset

Value name: YOffset

Value type: REG_DWORD

Value data: 42 = default

Note: Vertical distance from the selected corner.

Tools | Options / Preferences / E-mail options / Tracking options

Options (multipart policy setting)

Process requests and responses on arrival

Key: HKCU\Software\Policies\Microsoft\Office\11.0\
Outlook\Options\General

Value name: AutoProcReq

Value type: REG_DWORD

Value data: 1 = Enabled (default), 0 = Disabled

Note: This value governs Outlook's ability to process incoming meeting requests and responses automatically, when the system is idle.

Process receipts on arrival

Key: HKCU\Software\Policies\Microsoft\Office\11.0\
Outlook\Options\General

Value name: AutoProcRcpts

Value type: REG_DWORD

Value data: 1 = Enabled (default), 0 = Disabled

Delete blank voting and meeting responses after processing

Key: HKCU\Software\Policies\Microsoft\Office\11.0\
Outlook\Options\General

Value name: AutoDelRcpts

Value type: REG_DWORD

Value data: 1 = Enabled, 0 = Disabled (default)

Request a read receipt for all messages a user sends

Key: HKCU\Software\Policies\Microsoft\Office\11.0\
Outlook\Preferences

Value name: ReadReceipt

Value type: REG_DWORD

Value data: 1 = Enabled, 0 = Disabled (default)

Request delivery rcpt for all msgs a user sends (Exchange only)

Key: HKCU\Software\Policies\Microsoft\Office\11.0\
Outlook\Preferences

Value name: DeliveryReceipt

Value type: REG_DWORD

Value data: 1 = Enabled, 0 = Disabled (default)

> **Note:** Despite the name of the policy, delivery receipt requests are not an Exchange-only feature.

When Outlook is asked to respond to a read receipt request

Key: HKCU\Software\Policies\Microsoft\Office\11.0\Outlook\Options\Mail

Value name: Receipt Response

Value type: REG_DWORD

Value data: 0 = Always send a response
1 = Never send a response
2 = Ask before sending a response (default)

Tools | Options / Preferences / Calendar options

Reminders on Calendar items

Key: HKCU\Software\Policies\Microsoft\Office\11.0\Outlook\Preferences

Value name: ApptReminders

Value type: REG_DWORD

Value data: 1 = Enabled, 0 = Disabled (default)

Calendar Item Defaults: Show reminders <x> minutes before the event starts

Key: HKCU\Software\Policies\Microsoft\Office\11.0\Outlook\Options\Calendar

Value name: RemindDefault

Value type: REG_DWORD

Value data: 0 to 2880, 15 = default

Work week

Key: HKCU\Software\Policies\Microsoft\Office\11.0\Outlook\Options\Calendar

Value name: Workday

Value type: REG_DWORD

Value data: 124 = Monday to Friday (default)
120 = Monday to Thursday
60 = Tuesday to Friday

<pre>
126 = Monday to Saturday
 30 = Wednesday to Saturday
142 = Thursday to Sunday
252 = Sunday to Friday
254 = All seven days
</pre>

First day of the week

Key: `HKCU\Software\Policies\Microsoft\Office\11.0\Outlook\Options\Calendar`

Value name: `FirstDOW`

Value type: `REG_DWORD`

Value data: 0 = Sunday (default)
<pre>
1 = Monday
2 = Tuesday
3 = Wednesday
4 = Thursday
5 = Friday
6 = Saturday
</pre>

First week of year

Key: `HKCU\Software\Policies\Microsoft\Office\11.0\Outlook\Options\Calendar`

Value name: `FirstWOY`

Value type: `REG_DWORD`

Value data: 0 = Starts on Jan. 1 (default)
<pre>
2 = First full week
3 = First four-day week
</pre>

Working hours (multipart policy setting)

Key: `HKCU\Software\Policies\Microsoft\Office\11.0\Outlook\Options\Calendar`

Start Time

Value name: `CalDefStart`

Value type: `REG_DWORD`

Value data: Time in minutes representing the start of the work day, e.g., `0` =12:00 A.M., `480` = 8:00 A.M., (default), `960` = 4:00 P.M.

End Time

Value name: CalDefEnd

Value type: REG_DWORD

Value data: Time in minutes representing the end of the work day,
e.g., 480 = 8:00 A.M., 1020 = 5:00 P.M. (default), 1320 = 10:00 P.M.

Calendar week numbers

Key: HKCU\Software\Policies\Microsoft\Office\11.0\Outlook\
Options\Calendar

Value name: WeekNum

Value type: REG_DWORD

Value data: 1 = display week numbers in calendar
             0 = don't display week numbers (default)

Meeting Requests using iCalendar

Key: HKCU\Software\Policies\Microsoft\Office\11.0\Outlook\
Options\Calendar

Value name: SendMtgAsICAL

Value type: REG_DWORD

Value data: 1 = send meeting requests using iCalendar by default (default)
             0 = don't use iCalendar by default

Allow attendees to propose new times for meetings you organize

Key: HKCU\Software\Policies\Microsoft\Office\11.0\Outlook\
Options\Calendar

Value name: AllowPropose

Value type: REG_DWORD

Value data: 1 = Enabled, 0 = Disabled (default)

Use this response when you propose new meeting times

Key: HKCU\Software\Policies\Microsoft\Office\11.0\Outlook\
Options\Calendar

Value name: Propose Response Type

Value type: REG_DWORD

Value data: 2 = Tentative
             3 = Accept (default)
             4 = Decline

Table A.1   *Secondary Calendar Language Registry Value*

Language	Alter Calendar Lang	Alter Calendar Type
Chinese Lunar (Simplified Chinese)	2052	15
Chinese Lunar (Traditional Chinese)	1028	15
Gregorian (Arabic)	1025	10
Gregorian (Transliterated English)	1025	11
Gregorian (Transliterated French)	1025	12
Hebrew Lunar (English)	1033	8
Hebrew Lunar (Hebrew)	1037	8
Hijri (Arabic)	1025	6
Hijri (English)	1033	6
Japanese Lunar (Japanese)	1041	14
Korean Lunar (Korean)	1042	14
Rokuyou (Japanese)	1041	19
Zodiac (Japanese)	1041	18
Zodiac (Korean)	1042	18
Zodiac (Simplified Chinese)	2052	17
Zodiac (Traditional Chinese)	1028	17

Secondary calendar settings (multipart policy setting)

Key: `HKCU\Software\Policies\Microsoft\Office\11.0\Outlook\Options\Calendar`

Use secondary calendar

Value name: `Show BothCal`

Value type: `REG_DWORD`

Value data: `1` = Enabled, `0` = Disabled (default)

Set secondary calendar language

Selecting a secondary calendar language changes two registry values, both REG_DWORD – Alter Calendar Lang and Alter Calendar Type, as shown in Table A.1.

Hide lucky days when using Rokuyou (Japanese) calendar

Key: HKCU\Software\Policies\Microsoft\Office\11.0\Outlook\Options\Calendar

Value name: LunarRokuyou

Value type: REG_DWORD

Value data: 0 = Enabled, 1 = Disabled (default)

Note: This policy setting's possible values are the reverse of the usual meaning for 1 and 0.

Tools | Options / Preferences / Calendar options / Planner options

Meeting Planner (multipart policy setting)

Key: HKCU\Software\Policies\Microsoft\Office\11.0\Outlook\Options\Calendar

Show popup calendar details

Value name: MeetMode Show popup details

Value type: REG_DWORD

Value data: 1 = Enabled, 0 = Disabled

Show calendar details in the grid

Value name: MeetMode Show details in grid

Value type: REG_DWORD

Value data: 1 = Enabled, 0 = Disabled

Group Calendar (multipart policy setting)

Key: HKCU\Software\Policies\Microsoft\Office\11.0\Outlook\Options\Calendar

Show popup calendar details

Value name: GroupCalMode Show popup details

Value type: REG_DWORD

Value data: 1 = Enabled, 0 = Disabled

Show calendar details in the grid

Value name: GroupCalMode Show details in grid

Value type: REG_DWORD

Value data: 1 = Enabled, 0 = Disabled

Tools | Options / Preferences / Calendar options / Free/Busy options

Disable the Microsoft Office Internet Free/Busy Service

Key: HKCU\Software\Policies\Microsoft\Office\11.0\Outlook\
Options\Calendar\Internet Free/Busy

Value name: NoService

Value type: REG_DWORD

Value data: 1 = Enabled, 0 = Disabled

Options (multipart policy setting)

Months of free/busy information published

Key: HKCU\Software\Policies\Microsoft\Office\11.0\
Outlook\Preferences

Value name: FBPublishRange

Value type: REG_DWORD

Value data: 0 to 12, 2 = default

Prevent users from changing Months of Free/Busy information

Key: HKCU\Software\Policies\Microsoft\Office\11.0\
Outlook\Options\Calendar\Internet Free/Busy

Value name: Lock FB Range

Value type: REG_DWORD

Value data: 1 = Enabled, 0 = Disabled

Free/Busy updated on the server every xxx seconds

Key: HKCU\Software\Policies\Microsoft\Office\11.0\
Outlook\Options\Calendar\Internet Free/Busy

Value name: FBUpdateSecs

Value type: REG_DWORD

Value data: 0 to 86400, 900 = default

Internet Free/Busy Options (multipart policy setting)

Key: HCKUSoftware\Policies\Microsoft\Office\11.0\Outlook\
Options\Calendar\Internet Free/Busy

Publish free/busy information

Value name: Publish to Internet

Value type: REG_DWORD

Value data: 1 = Enabled, 0 = Disabled

Publish at this URL

Value name: `Write URL`

Value type: `REG_SZ`

Value data: Path to location where Outlook should publish free/busy information

Search at this URL

Value name: `Read URL`

Value type: `REG_SZ`

Value data: Path to location where Outlook should look for free/busy information

Tools | Options / Preferences / Contact options

Select the default setting for how to file new contacts (multipart policy setting)

Key: `HKCU\Software\Policies\Microsoft\Office\11.0\Outlook\Contact`

Note: The last two settings in this policy have nothing to do with how to file new contacts. Instead, they control the tab settings on address card views.

Default Full Name order

Value name: `NameParserStyle`

Value type: `REG_SZ`

Value data: `E` = First (Middle) Last (default)
            `H` = Last First
            `S` = First Last1 Last2

Default Flle As order

Value name: `FileAsOrder`

Value type: `REG_DWORD`

Value data: `32791` = Last, First (default)
            `32823` = First Last
            `14870` = Company
            `32793` = Last, First (Company)
            `32792` = Company (Last, First)

Check for duplicate contacts

Value name: ConfirmDuplicates

Value type: REG_DWORD

Value data: 1 = Enabled, 0 = Disabled

Show an additional Contacts Index

Value name: IndexTabsOn

Value type: REG_DWORD

Value data: 1 = Enabled, 0 = Disabled

Additional Contacts Index

Value name: IndexTabsScript

Value type: REG_DWORD

Value data: 2 = Arabic
              7 = Cyrillic
             15 = Greek
             16 = Hebrew
             28 = Thai
             30 = Vietnamese

Tools | Options / Preferences / Journal options

Disable journaling of these Outlook items (multipart policy setting)

E-mail Message

Key: HKCU\Software\Policies\Microsoft\Shared Tools\
Outlook\Journaling\E-mail Message

Value name: AutoJournaled

Value type: REG_DWORD

Value data: 1 = Enabled, 0 = Disabled

Meeting cancellation

Key: HKCU\Software\Policies\Microsoft\Shared Tools\
Outlook\Journaling\Meeting Cancellation

Value name: AutoJournaled

Value type: REG_DWORD

Value data: 1 = Enabled, 0 = Disabled

Meeting request

Key: HKCU\Software\Policies\Microsoft\Shared Tools\
Outlook\Journaling\Meeting Request

Value name: AutoJournaled

Value type: REG_DWORD

Value data: 1 = Enabled, 0 = Disabled

Meeting response

Key: HKCU\Software\Policies\Microsoft\Shared Tools\
Outlook\Journaling\Meeting Response

Value name: AutoJournaled

Value type: REG_DWORD

Value data: 1 = Enabled, 0 = Disabled

Task request

Key: HKCU\Software\Policies\Microsoft\Shared Tools\
Outlook\Journaling\Task Request

Value name: AutoJournaled

Value type: REG_DWORD

Value data: 1 = Enabled, 0 = Disabled

Task response

Key: HKCU\Software\Policies\Microsoft\Shared Tools\
Outlook\Journaling\Task Response

Value name: AutoJournaled

Value type: REG_DWORD

Value data: 1 = Enabled, 0 = Disabled

Automatically journal these items (multipart policy setting)

E-mail Message

Key: HKCU\Software\Policies\Microsoft\Shared Tools\
Outlook\Journaling\E-mail Message

Value name: Enabled

Value type: REG_DWORD

Value data: 1 = Enabled, 0 = Disabled

Meeting cancellation

Key: HKCU\Software\Policies\Microsoft\Shared Tools\
Outlook\Journaling\Meeting Cancellation

Value name: Enabled

Value type: REG_DWORD

Value data: 1 = Enabled, 0 = Disabled

Meeting request

Key: HKCU\Software\Policies\Microsoft\Shared Tools\
Outlook\Journaling\Meeting Request

Value name: Enabled

Value type: REG_DWORD

Value data: 1 = Enabled, 0 = Disabled

Meeting response

Key: HKCU\Software\Policies\Microsoft\Shared Tools\
Outlook\Journaling\Meeting Response

Value name: Enabled

Value type: REG_DWORD

Value data: 1 = Enabled, 0 = Disabled

Task request

Key: HKCU\Software\Policies\Microsoft\Shared Tools\
Outlook\Journaling\Task Request

Value name: Enabled

Value type: REG_DWORD

Value data: 1 = Enabled, 0 = Disabled

Task response

Key: HKCU\Software\Policies\Microsoft\Shared Tools\
Outlook\Journaling\Task Response

Value name: Enabled

Value type: REG_DWORD

Value data: 1 = Enabled, 0 = Disabled

Note: If any of the above policy settings is set to 1 (Enabled), then the policy setting below is also set to 1 (Enabled).

Key: `HKCU\Software\Policies\Microsoft\Office\11.0\Outlook\Options\Journal`

Value name: `EnableJournal`

Value type: `REG_DWORD`

Value data: 1 = Enabled, 0 = Disabled

Journal entry options

Key: `HKCU\Software\Policies\Microsoft\Office\11.0\Outlook\Options\Journal`

Value name: `Journal Open Assoc Item`

Value type: `REG_DWORD`

Value data: 0 = Opens the journal entry (default)
            1 = Opens the associated item

Tools | Options / Preferences / Notes options

Notes appearance (multipart policy setting)

Key: `HKCU\ Software\Policies\Microsoft\Office\11.0\Outlook\Options\Note`

Color

Value name: `NoteColor`

Value type: `REG_DWORD`

Value data: 3 = Yellow (default)
            0 = Blue
            1 = Green
            2 = Pink
            4 = White

Size

Value name: `NoteSize`

Value type: `REG_DWORD`

Value data: 1 = Medium (default)
            0 = Small
            2 = Large

Tools | Options / Preferences / Junk E-mail

Junk E-mail protection level

Key: HKCU\Software\Policies\Microsoft\Office\11.0\Outlook\Options\Mail

Value name: JunkMailProtection

Value type: REG_DWORD

Value data: 4294967295 = No protection
                       6 = Low (default)
                       3 = High
              2147483648 = Trusted Lists Only

Permanently delete Junk E-mail

Key: HKCU\Software\Policies\Microsoft\Office\11.0\Outlook\Options\Mail

Value name: JunkMailPermDelete

Value type: REG_DWORD

Value data: 1 = Enabled, 0 = Disabled

Trust E-mail from Contacts

Key: HKCU\Software\Policies\Microsoft\Office\11.0\Outlook\Options\Mail

Value name: JunkMailTrustContacts

Value type: REG_DWORD

Value data: 1 = Enabled (default), 0 = Disabled

Add people I e-mail to the Safe Senders List

Key: HKCU\Software\Policies\Microsoft\Office\11.0\Outlook\Options\Mail

Value name: JunkMailTrustOutgoingRecipients

Value type: REG_DWORD

Value data: 1 = Enabled, 0 = Disabled (default)

Note: This setting was added to the Outlook 2003 administrative template in Office 2003 Service Pack 1.

Overwrite or Append Junk Mail Import List

Key: HKCU\Software\Policies\Microsoft\Office\11.0\Outlook\
Options\Mail

Value name: JunkMailImportAppend

Value type: REG_DWORD

Value data: 1 = Append (default), 0 = Overwrite

Specify path to Safe Senders list

Key: HKCU\Software\Policies\Microsoft\Office\11.0\Outlook\
Options\Mail

Value name: JunkMailSafeSendersFile

Value type: REG_SZ

Value data: Path to text file containing safe senders and domains, one per line

Specify path to Safe Recipients list

Key: HKCU\Software\Policies\Microsoft\Office\11.0\Outlook\
Options\Mail

Value name: JunkMailSafeRecipientsFile

Value type: REG_SZ

Value data: Path to text file containing safe recipients and domains, one per line

Specify path to Blocked Senders list

Key: HKCU\Software\Policies\Microsoft\Office\11.0\Outlook\
Options\Mail

Value name: JunkMailBlockedSendersFile

Value type: REG_SZ

Value data: Path to text file containing blocked recipients and domains, one per line

Tools | Options / Mail Setup

Mail Account Options: Send messages immediately

Key: HKCU\Software\Policies\Microsoft\Office\11.0\Outlook\
Options\Mail

Value name: Send Mail Immediately

Value type: REG_DWORD

Value data: 1 = Enabled, 0 = Disabled

Dial-up options (multipart policy setting)

Key: `HKCU\Software\Policies\Microsoft\Office\11.0\Outlook\Options\Mail`

Warn before switching dial-up connection

Value name: `Warn on Dialup`

Value type: `REG_DWORD`

Value data: `1` = Enabled (default), `0` = Disabled

Hang up when finished sending, receiving, or updating

Value name: `Hangup after Spool`

Value type: `REG_DWORD`

Value data: `1` = Enabled (default), `0` = Disabled

Automatically dial during a background Send/Receive

Value name: `Poll on DUN`

Value type: `REG_DWORD`

Value data: `1` = Enabled, `0` = Disabled

Tools | Options / Mail Format / Message format

Message format/editor (multipart policy setting)

Key: `Software\Policies\Microsoft\Office\11.0\Outlook\Options\Mail`

Use the following Format/Editor for e-mail messages

Value name: `EditorPreference`

Value type: `REG_DWORD`

Value data:
- `131072` = HTML/Outlook (default if Word is installed
- `131073` = HTML/Microsoft Word (default if Word is not installed
- `196610` = Rich Text/Outlook
- `196609` = Rich Text/Microsoft Word
- `65536` = Plain Text/Outlook
- `65537` = Plain Text/Microsoft Word

Note: "Outlook" here refers to the built-in Outlook message editor. "Microsoft Word" refers to WordMail or Word used as the Outlook message editor.

Use Microsoft Word to read rich text e-mail messages

Value name: `UseWordMail`

Value type: `REG_DWORD`

Value data: `1` = Enabled, `0` = Disabled

Tools | Options / Mail Format / Internet Formatting

HTML Options

Key: `HKCU\Software\Policies\Microsoft\Office\11.0\Outlook\Options\Mail`

Value name: `Send Pictures With Document`

Value type: `REG_DWORD`

Value data: `1` = Send linked pictures as part of the message and change links to point to the embedded pictures
`0` = Leave picture links as-is

Outlook Rich Text options

Key: `HKCU\Software\Policies\Microsoft\Office\11.0\Outlook\Options\Mail`

Value name: `Message RTF Format`

Value type: `REG_DWORD`

Value data: `0` = Convert to HTML format
`1` = Convert to Plain Text format
`2` = Send using Outlook Rich Text format

Note: This setting controls what format Outlook will use to send messages composed in rich-text format. The format that the recipient ultimately receives may also depend on any per-recipient format setting and on how the mail server handles outgoing rich-text messages.

Plain text options (multipart policy setting)

Key: `HKCU\Software\Policies\Microsoft\Office\11.0\Common\MailSettings`

Automatically wrap text at <x> characters

Value name: `PlainWrapLen`

Value type: `REG_DWORD`

Value data: `30` to `132`, `76` = default

Encode attachments in UUENCODE format when sending a plain text message

Value name: `Message Plain Format MIME`

Value type: `REG_DWORD`

Value data: `0` = Enabled, `1` = Disabled

Note: This policy's possible values are the reverse of the usual meaning for 1 and 0. See Chapter 9 for more infomation on this setting.

Tools | Options / Mail Format / International Options

English message headers and flags (multipart policy setting)

Key: `HKCU\Software\Policies\Microsoft\Office\11.0\Outlook\Preferences`

Use English for message headers on replies or forwards

Value name: `ENMessageHeaders`

Value type: `REG_DWORD`

Value data: `1` = Enabled, `0` = Disabled

Use English for message flags

Value name: `ENMessageFlags`

Value type: `REG_DWORD`

Value data: `1` = Enabled, `0` = Disabled

Euro encoding for outgoing messages

Key: `HKCU\Software\Policies\Microsoft\Office\11.0\Outlook\Options\MSHTML\International`

Value name: `Autodetect_IgnoreEuro`

Value type: `REG_DWORD`

Value data: `0` = send messages as UTF-8
              `1` = ignore euro

Auto-select encoding for outgoing messages

Key: HKCU\Software\Policies\Microsoft\Office\11.0\Outlook\Options\MSHTML\International

Value name: Autodetect_CodePageOut

Value type: REG_DWORD

Value data: 1 = Enabled, 0 = Disabled

Encoding for outgoing messages

Key: HKCU\Software\Policies\Microsoft\Office\11.0\Outlook\Options\MSHTML\International

Value name: Default_CodePageOut

Value type: REG_DWORD

Value data:
```
28596 = Arabic (ISO)
 1256 = Arabic (Windows)
28594 = Baltic (ISO)
 1257 = Baltic (Windows)
28592 = Central European (ISO)
 1250 = Central European (Windows)
  936 = Chinese Simplified (GB2312)
52936 = Chinese Simplified (HZ)
  950 = Chinese Traditional (Big5)
28595 = Cyrillic (ISO)
20866 = Cyrillic (KOI8-R)
21866 = Cyrillic (KOI8-U)
 1251 = Cyrillic (Windows)
28597 = Greek (ISO)
 1253 = Greek (Windows)
38598 = Hebrew (ISO-Logical)
 1255 = Hebrew (Windows)
51932 = Japanese (EUC)
50220 = Japanese (JIS)
50221 = Japanese (JIS-Allow 1 byte Kana)
  932 = Japanese (Shift-JIS)
  949 = Korean
51949 = Korean (EUC)
28593 = Latin 3 (ISO)
28605 = Latin 9 (ISO)
  874 = Thai (Windows)
28599 = Turkish (ISO)
 1254 = Turkish (Windows)
65000 = Unicode (UTF-7)
65001 = Unicode (UTF-8)
20127 = US-ASCII
50000 = User Defined
```

```
 1258 = Vietnamese (Windows)
28591 = Western European (ISO)
 1252 = Western European (Windows)
```

Tools | Options / Mail Format / Stationery and Fonts

Stationery font options

Key: HKCU\Software\Policies\Microsoft\Office\11.0\Common\
MailSettings

Value name: ThemeFont

Value type: REG_DWORD

Value data: 0 = Use the font specified in Stationery
              1 = Use user's font on replies and fwds
              2 = Always use user's fonts

Note: See Chapter 9 for techniques for setting or blocking the stationery employed by the user.

Tools | Options / Mail Format / Signature

Note: While the next two policy settings appear in the administrative template for Outlook 2003, they do not work unless you apply the Outlook and Word hotfixes described in Microsoft Knowledge Base article 898076, "Description of the Outlook 2003 and Word 2003 post-Service Pack 1 hotfix package: April 28, 2005." Chapter 9 includes a script for settings the user's default signature.

Disable signatures for new messages

Key: HKCU\Software\Policies\Microsoft\Office\11.0\Common\
MailSettings

Value name: NewSignature

Value type: REG_SZ

Value data: <blank> = no signature

Disable signatures for replies and forwards

Key: HKCU\Software\Policies\Microsoft\Office\11.0\Common\
MailSettings

Value name: ReplySignature

Value type: REG_SZ

Value data: <blank> = no signature

Tools | Options / Spelling

General (multipart policy setting)

Always suggest replacements for misspelled words

Key: HKCU\Software\Policies\Microsoft\Office\11.0\
Outlook\Options\Spelling

Value name: SpellAlwaysSuggest

Value type: REG_DWORD

Value data: 1 = Enabled, 0 = Disabled

Always check spelling before sending

Key: HKCU\Software\Policies\Microsoft\Office\11.0\
Outlook\Options\Spelling

Value name: Check

Value type: REG_DWORD

Value data: 1 = Enabled, 0 = Disabled

Ignore words in UPPERCASE

Key: HKCU\Software\Policies\Microsoft\Office\11.0\
Outlook\Options\Spelling

Value name: SpellIgnoreUpper

Value type: REG_DWORD

Value data: 1 = Enabled, 0 = Disabled

Ignore words with numbers

Key: HKCU\Software\Policies\Microsoft\Office\11.0\
Outlook\Options\Spelling

Value name: SpellIgnoreNumbers

Value type: REG_DWORD

Value data: 1 = Enabled, 0 = Disabled

Ignore original message text in reply or forward

Key: HKCU\Software\Policies\Microsoft\Office\11.0\Common\
MailSettings

Value name: IgnoreReplySpelling

Value type: REG_DWORD

Value data: 1 = Enabled, 0 = Disabled

Use AutoCorrect in Rich Text and plain text messages

Key: HKCU\Software\Policies\Microsoft\Office\11.0\
Outlook\Options\Spelling

Value name: UseAutoCorrect

Value type: REG_DWORD

Value data: 1 = Enabled, 0 = Disabled

Tools | Options / Security

Note: The next five settings are explained in more detail in Chapters 6 and 7.

Prevent users from customizing attachment security settings

Key: HKCU\Software\Policies\Microsoft\Office\11.0\Outlook

Value name: DisallowAttachmentCustomization

Value type: REG_DWORD

Value data: 1 = Enabled, 0 = Disabled

Allow access to e-mail attachments

Key: HKCU\Software\Policies\Microsoft\Office\11.0\Outlook\
Security

Value name: Level1Remove

Value type: REG_SZ

Value data: Semicolon delimited string of file extensions that should not be
blocked, e.g., EXE;REG;COM

Disallow access to e-mail attachments

Key: HKCU\Software\Policies\Microsoft\Office\11.0\Outlook\Security

Value name: Level1Add

Value type: REG_SZ

Value data: Semicolon delimited string of file extensions that should be blocked, e.g., ZIP;EXE;REG;COM

Note: This setting was added to the Outlook 2003 administrative template in Office 2003 Service Pack 1.

Outlook virus security settings

Key: HKCU\Software\Policies\Microsoft\Security

Value name: CheckAdminSettings

Value type: REG_DWORD

Value data: 0 = Uses default administrative settings
              1 = Look in the Outlook Security Settings folder
              2 = Look in the Outlook 10 Security Settings folder

---

Note: As explained in Chapter 7, this setting has nothing to do with any anti-virus program, as we normally think of such applications. Instead, in an Exchange environment (and only in an Exchange environment), it controls whether Outlook uses its built-in attachment and automation security settings or looks to a security settings folder in the Public Folders hierarchy to locate the settings that Outlook should use.

Configure Add-In Trust Level

Key: HKCU\Software\Policies\Microsoft\Office\11.0\Outlook\Security

Value name: AddinTrust

Value type: REG_DWORD

Value data: 0 = Trust all, or use Exchange settings if present (default)
              1 = Trust all loaded and installed COM addins
              2 = Do NOT trust loaded and installed COM add-ins

Security Zone for loaded Messages

Key: HKCU\Software\Policies\Microsoft\Office\11.0\Outlook\
Options\General

Value name: Security Zone

Value type: REG_DWORD

Value data:　0　=　Local Machine
　　　　　　　1　=　Intranet
　　　　　　　2　=　Trusted
　　　　　　　3　=　Internet
　　　　　　　4　=　Untrusted　(default)

Note: The zone corresponding to a value of 4 is more commonly known as the Restricted Sites zone. This setting partially controls what Web-page operations an HTML-format message will support. For example, if Security Zone = 2, a message will be able to perform the operations allowed for sites in the Trusted Sites security zone in Internet Explorer. (The two separate settings below, EnableItemScript and EnablePreviewScript, respectively control whether the message can run scripts when open in its own window and when viewed in the reading pane.) The most secure Security Zone setting is the default, 4 (Untrusted). However, this setting still allows the user to open the message and choose View | View in Internet Zone. Therefore, you may also want to block that menu command, using the technique discussed in Appendix C. This setting was added to the Outlook 2003 administrative template in Office 2003 Service Pack 1.

Item Scripting

Key: HKCU\Software\Policies\Microsoft\Office\11.0\Outlook\
Scripting

Value name: EnableItemScript

Value type: REG_DWORD

Value data:　0　=　Disable Item Scripts (default)
　　　　　　　1　=　Uses IE Settings
　　　　　　　2　=　Always warns

Note: This setting controls whether an HTML format message can run script when it is open in its own window. If EnableItemScript = 1, the message will be able to run script if the Internet Explorer security zone for messages (see above setting for Security Zone) allows it. If EnableItemScript = 2, the user will see a prompt and will be able to choose Disable Script or Run Script, regardless of the value for Security Zone. This setting was added to the Outlook 2003 administrative template in Office 2003 Service Pack 1.

Scripting

Key: `HKCU\Software\Policies\Microsoft\Office\11.0\Outlook\Scripting`

Value name: `EnablePreviewScript`

Value type: `REG_DWORD`

Value data   `0` = Disable Scripts (default)
               `1` = Uses IE Settings to decide

Note: This setting controls whether an HTML format message can run script when it is viewed in the reading (preview) pane. If EnablePreview-Script = 1, the message will be able to run script if the Internet Explorer security zone for messages (see above setting for Security Zone) allows it. This setting was added to the Outlook 2003 administrative template in Office 2003 Service Pack 1.

Allow Active X One Off Forms

Key: `HKCU\Software\Policies\Microsoft\Office\11.0\Outlook\Security`

Value name: `AllowActiveXOneOffForms`

Value type: `REG_DWORD`

Value data: `0` = Load only Outlook Controls (default)
              `1` = Allows only Safe Controls
              `2` = Allows all ActiveX Controls

Note: This setting is explained in more detail in Chapter 6. This setting was added to the Outlook 2003 administrative template in Office 2003 Service Pack 1.

Disable 'Remember Password' checkbox for Internet E-mail settings dialog

Key: `HKCU\Software\Policies\Microsoft\Office\11.0\Outlook\Security`

Value name: `EnableRememberPwd`

Value type: `REG_DWORD`

Value data: 0 = "Remember Password" check box is disabled
              1 = "Remember Password" check box is available

Note: This setting affects POP3, IMAP4, and HTTP e-mail accounts.

Prompt user to choose security settings if default settings fail

Key: `HKCU\Software\Policies\Microsoft\Office\11.0\Outlook\Security`

Value name: `ForceDefaultProfile`

Value type: `REG_DWORD`

Value data: 1 = Prompt the user
              0 = Automatically select

Do not automatically sign replies

Key: `HKCU\Software\Policies\Microsoft\Office\11.0\Outlook\Security`

Value name: `NoSignOnReply`

Value type: `REG_DWORD`

Value data: 1 = Automatic signing is disabled
              0 = Automatic signing is enabled

Tools | Options / Security / Cryptography

Required Certificate Authority

Key: HKCU\Software\Policies\Microsoft\Office\11.0\Outlook\Security

Value name: RequiredCA

Value type: REG_SZ

Value data: X.509 issued DN that restricts choice of certifying authorities

Minimum encryption settings

Key: HKCU\Software\Policies\Microsoft\Office\11.0\Outlook\Security

Value name: MinEncKey

Value type: REG_DWORD

Value data: 1 to 9999, 40 = default

Note: Minimum key size in bits.

S/MIME interoperability with external clients

Key: HKCU\Software\Policies\Microsoft\Office\11.0\Outlook\Security

Value name: ExternalSMime

Value type: REG_DWORD

Value data: 0 = Handle internally
1 = Handle externally
2 = Handle if possible

Outlook Rich Text in S/MIME messages

Key: HKCU\Software\Policies\Microsoft\Office\11.0\Outlook\Security

Value name: ForceTNEF

Value type: REG_DWORD

Value data: 1 = Always send Outlook Rich Text formatting in
S/MIME messages
0 = Don't send Rich Text formatting

S/MIME password settings (multipart policy setting)

Key: HKCU\Software\Policies\Microsoft\Cryptography\Defaults\
Provider\Microsoft Exchange Cryptographic Provider v1.0

Default S/MIME password time (minutes)

Value name: DefPwdTime

Value type: REG_DWORD

Value data: 1 to 9999, 30 = default

Maximum S/MIME password time (minutes)

Value name: MaxPwdTime

Value type: REG_DWORD

Value data: 1 to 9999, 300 = default

Enable fix for reference count problem causing CopyTo Operations to fail

Key: HKCU\Software\Policies\Microsoft\Office\11.0\Outlook\
Security

Value name: EMSMDBMsgRefCnt

Value type: REG_DWORD

Value data: 1 = Enabled, 0 = Disabled

Note: Do not use this setting for clients running against Exchange versions earlier than Exchange 5.5 Service Pack 3.

Message Formats

Key: HKCU\Software\Policies\Microsoft\Office\11.0\Outlook\
Security

Value name: MsgFormats

Value type: REG_DWORD

Value data: 1 = S/MIME
              2 = Exchange
             20 = Fortezza
              3 = S/MIME and Exchange
             21 = S/MIME and Fortezza
             22 = Exchange and Fortezza
             23 = S/MIME, Exchange, and Fortezza

Note: Sets the secure message formats that Outlook supports.

Message when Outlook cannot find the digital ID to decode a message

Key: HKCU\Software\Policies\Microsoft\Office\11.0\Outlook\Security

Value name: NeedEncryptionString

Value type: REG_SZ

Value data: Text of the desired error message

Disable Continue button on all Encryption warning dialogs

Key: HKCU\Software\Policies\Microsoft\Office\11.0\Outlook\Security

Value name: DisableContinueEncryption

Value type: REG_DWORD

Value data: 1 = Enabled, 0 = Disabled

Run in FIPS compliant mode

Key: HKCU\Software\Policies\Microsoft\Office\11.0\Outlook\Security

Value name: FIPSMode

Value type: REG_DWORD

Value data: 1 = Enabled, 0 = Disabled

Do not check e-mail address against address of certificates being used

Key: HKCU\Software\Policies\Microsoft\Office\11.0\Outlook\Security

Value name: SupressNameChecks

Value type: REG_DWORD

Value data: 1 = Enabled, 0 = Disabled

Encrypt all e-mail messages

Key: HKCU\Software\Policies\Microsoft\Office\11.0\Outlook\Security

Value name: AlwaysEncrypt

Value type: REG_DWORD

Value data: 1 = Enabled, 0 = Disabled (default)

Sign all e-mail messages

Key: HKCU\Software\Policies\Microsoft\Office\11.0\Outlook\Security

Value name: AlwaysSign

Value type: REG_DWORD

Value data: 1 = Enabled, 0 = Disabled (default)

Send all signed messages as clear signed messages

Key: HKCU\Software\Policies\Microsoft\Office\11.0\Outlook\Security

Value name: ClearSign

Value type: REG_DWORD

Value data: 1 = Enabled, 0 = Disabled

Request an S/MIME receipt for all S/MIME signed messages

Key: HKCU\Software\Policies\Microsoft\Office\11.0\Outlook\Security

Value name: RequestSecureReceipt

Value type: REG_DWORD

Value data: 1 = Enabled, 0 = Disabled

URL for S/MIME certificate

Key: HKCU\Software\Policies\Microsoft\Office\11.0\Outlook\Security

Value name: EnrollPageURL

Value type: REG_SZ

Value data: URL where the user can obtain an S/MIME certificate

---

Note: The URL can contain %1, %2, and %3, which will be replaced by the user's name, e-mail address, and language, respectively. Chapter 6 has more information on this setting.

Ensure all S/MIME signed messages have a label

Key: HKCU\Software\Policies\Microsoft\Office\11.0\Outlook\
Security

Value name: ForceSecurityLabel

Value type: REG_DWORD

Value data: 1 = Enabled, 0 = Disabled

Disable 'Publish to GAL' button

Key: HKCU\Software\Policies\Microsoft\Office\11.0\Outlook\
Security

Value name: PublishToGalDisabled

Value type: REG_DWORD

Value data: 1 = Enabled, 0 = Disabled

Signature Warning

Key: HKCU\Software\Policies\Microsoft\Office\11.0\Outlook\
Security

Value name: WarnAboutInvalid

Value type: REG_DWORD

Value data: 0 = Let user decide if they want to be warned
              1 = Always warn about invalid signatures
              2 = Never warn about invalid signatures

S/MIME receipt requests

Key: HKCU\Software\Policies\Microsoft\Office\11.0\Outlook\
Security

Value name: RespondToReceiptRequests

Value type: REG_DWORD

Value data: 0 = Open message if receipt can't be sent
              3 = Don't open message if receipt can't be sent
              1 = Always prompt before sending receipt
              2 = Never send S/MIME receipts

Fortezza certificate policies

Key: HKCU\Software\Policies\Microsoft\Office\11.0\Outlook\
Security

Value name: Fortezza_Policies

Value type: REG_SZ

Value data: List of policies that can be in the policies extension of a certificate indicating it's a Fortezza certificate. The list should be separated by semicolons, e.g., policy1;policy2;policy3

Enable Cryptography Icons

Key: HKCU\Software\Policies\Microsoft\Office\11.0\Outlook\
Security

Value name: ConvertSMIMEBlobSignedIcons

Value type: REG_DWORD

Value data: 1 = Enabled, 0 = Disabled

Tools | Options / Security / Cryptography / Signature Status Dialog

Retrieving CRLs (Certificate Revocation Lists)

Key: HKCU\Software\Policies\Microsoft\Office\11.0\Outlook\
Security

Value name: UseCRLChasing

Value type: REG_DWORD

Value data:　0 = Use system Default
　　　　　　1 = When online always retreive the CRL
　　　　　　2 = Never retreive the CRL

Missing CRLs

Key: HKCU\Software\Policies\Microsoft\Office\11.0\Outlook\
Security

Value name: SigStatusNoCRL

Value type: REG_DWORD

Value data:　0 = Indicate a missing CRL as a warning
　　　　　　1 = Indicate a missing CRL as an error

Missing root certificates

Key: HKCU\Software\Policies\Microsoft\Office\11.0\Outlook\Security

Value name: SigStatusNoTrustDecision

Value type: REG_DWORD

Value data: 0 = Indicate a missing root certificate as neither error nor warning
1 = Indicate a missing root certificate as a warning
2 = Indicate a missing root certificate as an error

Promoting errors as warnings

Key: HKCU\Software\Policies\Microsoft\Office\11.0\Outlook\Security

Value name: PromoteErrorsAsWarnings

Value type: REG_DWORD

Value data: 1 = Enabled, 0 = Disabled

Attachment Secure Temporary Folder

Key: HKCU\Software\Policies\Microsoft\Office\11.0\Outlook\Security

Value name: OutlookSecureTempFolder

Value type: REG_SZ

Value data: Path to the folder where Outlook stores temporary copies of files when users open attachments

---

Note: Outlook automatically creates such a folder in the user's folders. The default location is %USERPROFILE%\Local Settings\Temporary Internet Files\OLKxxx, where OLKxxx is a folder name that Outlook generates. Microsoft Knowledge Base article 817878, "Attachments remain in the Outlook Secure Temporary File folder when you exit Outlook 2003," explains this setting. This setting was added to the Outlook 2003 administrative template in Office 2003 Service Pack 1.

Tools | Options / Security / Automatic Picture Download Settings

Block external content

Key: HKCU\Software\Policies\Microsoft\Office\11.0\Outlook\
Options\Mail

Value name: BlockExtContent

Value type: REG_DWORD

Value data: 1 = Enabled (default), 0 = Disabled

Note: As explained in Chapter 6, this setting has no effect on images or other content that is embedded in the message. It blocks only external content.

Tools | Options / Other

Empty Deleted Items Folder

Key: HKCU\Software\Policies\Microsoft\Office\11.0\Outlook\
Preferences

Value name: EmptyTrash

Value type: REG_DWORD

Value data: 1 = Empty the Deleted Items folder upon exiting Outlook
             0 = Don't empty the Deleted Items folder on exit

Make Outlook the default program for E-mail, Contacts, and Calendar

Key: HKCU\Software\Policies\Microsoft\Office\11.0\Outlook\
Options\General

Value name: Check Default Client

Value type: REG_DWORD

Value data: 1 = Enabled, 0 = Disabled

Preview pane (multipart policy setting)

Mark messages as read in preview window

Key: HKCU\Software\Policies\Microsoft\Office\11.0\
Outlook\Preferences

Value name: PreviewMarkMessage

Value type: REG_DWORD

Value data: 1 = Enabled, 0 = Disabled

Wait xxx seconds before marking items as read

Key: HKCU\Software\Policies\Microsoft\Office\11.0\Outlook\Preferences

Value name: PreviewWaitSeconds

Value type: REG_DWORD

Value data: 1 to 999, 5 = default

Mark item as read when selection changes

Key: HKCU\Software\Policies\Microsoft\Office\11.0\Outlook\Preferences

Value name: PreviewDontMarkUntilChange

Value type: REG_DWORD

Value data: 1 = Enabled, 0 = Disabled

Single key reading using spacebar

Key: HKCU\Software\Policies\Microsoft\Office\11.0\Outlook\Options\General

Value name: SingleKeyReading

Value type: REG_DWORD

Value data: 1 = Enabled, 0 = Disabled

Tools | Options / Other / Advanced

Minimize Outlook to the system tray

Key: HKCU\Software\Policies\Microsoft\Office\11.0\Outlook\Preferences

Value name: MinToTray

Value type: REG_DWORD

Value data: 1 = Enabled, 0 = Disabled

General

Key: HKCU\Software\Policies\Microsoft\Office\11.0\Outlook\Preferences

Value name: WordSelect

Value type: REG_DWORD

Value data: 1 = When selecting text, automatically select entire word

0 = Don't select entire word

More Options

Key: HKCU\Software\Policies\Microsoft\Office\11.0\
Outlook\Options\General

Value name: WarnDelete

Value type: REG_DWORD

Value data: 1 = Warn before permanently deleting items (default)

             0 = Don't warn

Enable mail logging (troubleshooting)

Key: HKCU\Software\Policies\Microsoft\Office\11.0\
Outlook\Options\Mail

Value name: EnableLogging

Value type: REG_DWORD

Value data: 1 = Enabled, 0 = Disabled

Note: Starting with Outlook 2003 Service Pack 1, turning on logging will cause the title bar of the main Outlook window to display the text "[Logging Enabled]." Because logging can be an intense operation, you should leave this setting enabled only for a short period of time, as needed for troubleshooting. The log files are stored in the current user's Temp folder, by default, %USERPROFILE%\Local Settings\Temp.

Disable 'Add-In Manager . . .' button

Key: HKCU\Software\Policies\Microsoft\Office\11.0\
Outlook\Preferences

Value name: DisableAddinBtns

Value type: REG_DWORD

Value data: 1 = Enabled, 0 = Disabled

Note: This setting disables both the Add-in Manager and COM Add-ins buttons on the Tools | Options | Advanced Options dialog, as well as the COM Add-ins toolbar button.

Disable scripts for shared folders

Key: HKCU\Software\Policies\Microsoft\Office\11.0\
Outlook\Security

Value name: SharedFolderScript

Value type: REG_DWORD

Value data: 0 = Do not run scripts on custom forms used by items
accessed from other Exchange users' mailboxes
(default)
1 = Allow scripts on custom forms to run for items
accessed from other Exchange users' mailboxes

Disable scripts for public folders

Key: HKCU\Software\Policies\Microsoft\Office\11.0\
Outlook\Security

Value name: PublicFolderScript

Value type: REG_DWORD

Value data: 0 = Do not run scripts on custom forms used by items
accessed from Exchange public folders
1 = Allow scripts on custom forms to run for items
accessed from other Exchange public folders (default)

Tools | Options / Other / Advanced / Reminder Options

Reminders (multipart policy setting)

Key: HKCU\Software\Policies\Microsoft\Office\11.0\Outlook\
Options\Reminders

Display the reminder

Value name: Type

Value type: REG_DWORD

Value data: 1 = Enabled (default), 0 = Disabled

Play reminder sound

Value name: PlaySound

Value type: REG_DWORD

Value data: 1 = Enabled (default), 0 = Disabled

More reminders

Key: `HKCU\AppEvents\Schemes\Apps\Office97\Office97-Reminder\`
`.Current`

Value name: (default)

Value type: `REG_DWORD`

Value data: Path and .wav file to play for reminder. Default = `reminder.wav`

Tools | Options / Other / AutoArchive

AutoArchive Settings (multipart policy setting)

Key: `HKCU\Software\Policies\Microsoft\Office\11.0\Outlook\`
`Preferences`

Turn on AutoArchive

Value name: `DoAging`

Value type: `REG_DWORD`

Value data: `1` = Enabled (default), `0` = Disabled

Run AutoArchive every <x> days

Value name: `EveryDays`

Value type: `REG_DWORD`

Value data: `1` to `60`, `14` = default

Prompt before AutoArchive runs

Value name: `PromptForAging`

Value type: `REG_DWORD`

Value data: `1` = Enabled (default), `0` = Disabled

Delete expired items (e-mail folders only)

Value name: `DeleteExpired`

Value type: `REG_DWORD`

Value data: `1` = Enabled (default), `0` = Disabled

Archive or delete old items

Value name: `ArchiveOld`

Value type: `REG_DWORD`

Value data: `1` = Enabled (default), `0` = Disabled

Show archive folder in folder list

Value name: `ArchiveMount`

Value type: `REG_DWORD`

Value data: `1` = Enabled (default), `0` = Disabled

Clean out items older than

Value name: `ArchivePeriod`

Value type: `REG_DWORD`

Value data: `1` to `60`, `6` = default

Value name: `ArchiveGranularity`

Value type: `REG_DWORD`

Value data: `0` = Months (default)
              `1` = Weeks
              `2` = Days

Note: The two above settings work together to allow the user to set the item retention period from as short as 1 day to as long as 60 months.

Permanently delete old items

Value name: `ArchiveDelete`

Value type: `REG_DWORD`

Value data: `1` = Enabled, `0` = Disabled

Retention Settings (multipart policy setting)

Key: `HKCU\Software\Policies\Microsoft\Office\11.0\Outlook\Preferences`

Note: Retention policies work with the AutoArchive feature to override the user's settings for how long to keep items. If you turn on retention policies, you should also enable the DoAging policy setting above.

Turn Retention Policies On

Value name: `RetentionOn`

Value type: `REG_DWORD`

Value data: `1` = Enabled, `0` = Disabled (default)

Maximum number of days to retain items in Inbox

Value name: `RetentionInbox`

Value type: `REG_DWORD`

Value data: `0` to `30`

Maximum number of days to retain items in all mail folders excluding Inbox

Value name: `RetentionMail`

Value type: `REG_DWORD`

Value data: `0 to 30`

Maximum number of days to retain Calendar items in any folder

Value name: `RetentionCalendar`

Value type: `REG_DWORD`

Value data: `0 to 30`

Maximum number of days to retain items in all other folders being AutoArchived

Value name: `RetentionOther`

Value type: `REG_DWORD`

Value data: `0 to 30`

For items not being retained

Value name: `RetentionDelete`

Value type: `REG_DWORD`

Value data: `0` = move to Deleted Items folder

`1` = permanently delete

URL with corporate retention policy information

Value name: `RetentionPath`

Value type: `REG_SZ`

Value data: URL for a Web page that you have created to explain the corporate retention policy

Tools | Options / Other / Person Names

Enable the Person Names Smart Tag

Key: `HKCU\Software\Policies\Microsoft\Office\11.0\Outlook\IM`

Value name: `Enabled`

Value type: `REG_DWORD`

Value data: `0` = Enabled, `1` = Disabled

Display Messenger Status in the From field

Key: `HKCU\Software\Policies\Microsoft\Office\11.0\Outlook\IM`

Value name: `EnablePresence`

Value type: `REG_DWORD`

Value data: `0` = Enabled, `1` = Disabled

Note: The above two policy settings' possible values are the reverse of the usual meaning for 1 and 0.

Tools | Options / Other / Right-to-left

Layout Options (multipart policy setting)

Key: `HKCU\Software\Policies\Microsoft\Office\11.0\Outlook\Options\Calendar`

Set layout direction

Value name: `Calendar Direction`

Value type: `REG_DWORD`

Value data: `0` = Left to Right (default)

`1` = Right to Left

Set global text direction

Value name: `Text Direction`

Value type: `REG_DWORD`

Value data: `0` = Context-based

`1` = Left to Right (default)

`2` = Right to Left

Tools | Macro / Security

Note: See Chapter 6 for more information on these settings.

Security Level

Key: `HKCU\Software\Policies\Microsoft\Office\11.0\Outlook\Security`

Value name: `Level`

Value type: `REG_DWORD`

Value data: 4 = Very High

               3 = High (default)

               2 = Medium

               1 = Low

Note: As you will see in Appendix B, the Office administrative template also includes this setting as a machine-level policy, which means it would apply to all users on a machine.

Outlook: Trust all installed add-ins and templates

Key: `HKCU\Software\Policies\Microsoft\Office\11.0\Outlook\Security`

Value name: `DontTrustInstalledFiles`

Value type: `REG_DWORD`

Value data: 0 = Trust Outlook add-ins (default)

               1 = Don't trust Outlook add-ins

Tools | E-mail Accounts / Exchange over the Internet

Enable Exchange Over Internet User Interface

Key: `HKCU\Software\Policies\Microsoft\Office\11.0\Outlook\RPC`

Value name: `EnableRPCTunnelingUI`

Value type: `REG_DWORD`

Value data: 0 = RPC over HTTP user interface is hidden

               1 = All RPC over HTTP settings can be configured by the user

               2 = User can enable or disable RPC over HTTP, but not configure it

               3 = User can make changes to pre-deployed RPC over HTTP settings

               4 = User can see all settings but not make changes

Tools | E-mail Accounts / Cached Exchange Mode

Disable Cached Exchange Mode on new profiles

Key: HKCU\Software\Policies\Microsoft\Office\11.0\Outlook\Cached Mode

Value name: Enable

Value type: REG_DWORD

Value data: 0 = Enable Cached Exchange Mode (default)

1 = Disable Cached Exchange Mode

In Cached Exchange, make Send/Receive F9 null operation

Key: HKCU\Software\Policies\Microsoft\Office\11.0\Outlook\Cached Mode

Value name: NoManualOnlineSync

Value type: REG_DWORD

Value data: 1 = Skip synchronization commands containing more than one folder

0 = Perform send/receive normally

Enter seconds to wait to upload changes to server

Key: HKCU\Software\Policies\Microsoft\Office\11.0\Outlook\Cached Mode

Value name: Upload

Value type: REG_DWORD

Value data: 0 to 86400, 15 = default

Enter seconds to wait to download changes from server

Key: HKCU\Software\Policies\Microsoft\Office\11.0\Outlook\Cached Mode

Value name: Download

Value type: REG_DWORD

Value data: 0 to 86400, 30 = default

Enter maximum seconds to wait to sync changes

Key: HKCU\Software\Policies\Microsoft\Office\11.0\Outlook\Cached Mode

Value name: Maximum

Value type: REG_DWORD

Value data: 0 to 86400, 60 = default

Cached Exchange Mode

Key: HKCU\Software\Policies\Microsoft\Office\11.0\Outlook\ Cached Mode

Value name: CachedExchangeMode

Value type: REG_DWORD

Value data: Cached Exchange Mode setting for new profiles:
>   1 = Download Headers
>   2 = Download Full Items
>   3 = Download Headers and then Full Items

Note: The next settings control which Cached Exchange Mode options users will be able to choose.

Disallow Download Full Items

Key: HKCU\Software\Policies\Microsoft\Office\11.0\Outlook\ Cached Mode

Value name: NoFullItems

Value type: REG_DWORD

Value data: 1 = Enabled, 0 = Disabled

Disallow Download Headers then Full Items

Key: HKCU\Software\Policies\Microsoft\Office\11.0\Outlook\ Cached Mode

Value name: NoDrizzle

Value type: REG_DWORD

Value data: 1 = Enabled, 0 = Disabled

Disallow Download Headers

Key: HKCU\Software\Policies\Microsoft\Office\11.0\Outlook\ Cached Mode

Value name: NoHeaders

Value type: REG_DWORD

Value data: 1 = Enabled, 0 = Disabled

Disallow On Slow Connections Only Download Headers

Key: HKCU\Software\Policies\Microsoft\Office\11.0\Outlook\Cached Mode

Value name: NoSlowHeaders

Value type: REG_DWORD

Value data: 1 = Enabled, 0 = Disabled

Download Public Folder Favorites

Key: HKCU\Software\Policies\Microsoft\Office\11.0\Outlook\Cached Mode

Value name: SyncPFFav

Value type: REG_DWORD

Value data: 1 = Enabled, 0 = Disabled

Customizable error messages

List of error messages to customize

Key: HKCU\Software\Policies\Microsoft\Office\11.0\Outlook\CustomizableAlerts

Note: This policy creates new registry values with data type REG_SZ (string) corresponding to the error IDs that you want to customize. For each error value, you enter the message you want users to see. The Office Resource Kit article "Customizing Error Messages" at http://office.microsoft.com/en-us/assistance/HA011362701033.aspx explains how to create a Web page to display the error messages. Although it was written for Office XP, the information should also apply to Outlook and Office 2003.

Disable items in user interface / Predefined

Disable command bar buttons and menu items (multipart policy setting)

All folders and items: Tools | Speech

Key: HKCU\Software\Policies\Microsoft\Office\11.0\
Outlook\DisabledCmdBarItemsCheckBoxes

Value name: ToolsSpeech

Value type: REG_DWORD

Value data: 5764 = Commands disabled, 0 = Commands enabled

All folders and items: Tools | Tools on the Web

Key: HKCU\Software\Policies\Microsoft\Office\11.0\
Outlook\DisabledCmdBarItemsCheckBoxes

Value name: ToolsontheWeb

Value type: REG_DWORD

Value data: 7032 = Commands disabled, 0 = Commands enabled

All folders and items: Tools | Customize

Key: HKCU\Software\Policies\Microsoft\Office\11.0\
Outlook\DisabledCmdBarItemsCheckBoxes

Value name: ToolsCustomize

Value type: REG_DWORD

Value data: 797 = Commands disabled, 0 = Commands enabled

All folders and items: Tools | Forms | Design Options

Key: HKCU\Software\Policies\Microsoft\Office\11.0\
Outlook\DisabledCmdBarItemsCheckBoxes

Value name: NoForms3Design

Value type: REG_DWORD

Value data: 1 = Commands disabled, 0 = Commands enabled

All folders and items: Help | Microsoft Office Online

Key: HKCU\Software\Policies\Microsoft\Office\11.0\
Outlook\DisabledCmdBarItemsCheckBoxes

Value name: HelpOfficeWeb

Value type: REG_DWORD

Value data: 3775 = Commands disabled, 0 = Commands enabled

All folders and items: Help | Activate Product

Key: `HKCU\Software\Policies\Microsoft\Office\11.0\Outlook\DisabledCmdBarItemsCheckBoxes`

Value name: `HelpRegistration`

Value type: `REG_DWORD`

Value data: `5933` = Commands disabled, `0` = Commands enabled

All folders and items: Help | Detect and Repair

Key: `HKCU\Software\Policies\Microsoft\Office\11.0\Outlook\DisabledCmdBarItemsCheckBoxes`

Value name: `HelpRepair`

Value type: `REG_DWORD`

Value data: `3774` = Commands disabled, `0` = Commands enabled

All folders: Go menu

Key: `HKCU\Software\Policies\Microsoft\Office\11.0\Outlook\DisabledCmdBarItemsCheckBoxes`

Value name: `WebGo`

Value type: `REG_DWORD`

Value data: `30328` = Commands disabled, `0` = Commands enabled

All folders: Go | Internet Call

Key: `HKCU\Software\Policies\Microsoft\Office\11.0\Outlook\DisabledCmdBarItemsCheckBoxes`

Value name: `GoInternetCall`

Value type: `REG_DWORD`

Value data: `31123` = Commands disabled, `0` = Commands enabled

Inbox: Tools | E-mail Accounts

Key: `HKCU\Software\Policies\Microsoft\Office\11.0\Outlook\DisabledCmdBarItemsCheckBoxes`

Value name: `ToolsServices`

Value type: `REG_DWORD`

Value data: `6863` = Commands disabled, `0` = Commands enabled

Mail item: View | Bcc Field

Key: HKCU\Software\Policies\Microsoft\Office\11.0\ Outlook\DisabledCmdBarItemsCheckBoxes

Value name: ViewBccField

Value type: REG_DWORD

Value data: 1860 = Commands disabled, 0 = Commands enabled

Key: HKCU\Software\Policies\Microsoft\Office\11.0\ Outlook\Preferences

Value name: ShowBcc

Value type: REG_DWORD

Value data: 0 = Command disabled

Note: If the check box for the Mail item: View | Bcc Field policy is checked, the ShowBcc value is deleted from the registry. This policy setting does not prevent the user from adding Bcc recipients to a message. The user can still click the To or Cc button on a message and add Bcc recipients using the Address Book dialog. Once a message has a Bcc recipient, the Bcc box will be displayed, regardless of the state of this policy setting.

Mail item: View | From Field

Key: HKCU\Software\Policies\Microsoft\Office\11.0\ Outlook\DisabledCmdBarItemsCheckBoxes

Value name: ViewFromField

Value type: REG_DWORD

Value data: 1867 = Commands disabled, 0 = Commands enabled

Key: HKCU\ Software\Policies\Microsoft\Office\11.0\ Outlook\Preferences

Value name: ShowFrom

Value type: REG_DWORD

Value data: 0 = Command disabled

Note: If the check box for the Mail item: View | From Field policy is checked, the ShowFrom value is deleted from the registry.

Contact item: Actions | Display Map of Address

Key: HKCU\Software\Policies\Microsoft\Office\11.0\
Outlook\DisabledCmdBarItemsCheckBoxes

Value name: ActionDisplayMap

Value type: REG_DWORD

Value data: 5602 = Command disabled, 0 = Command enabled

Web toolbar: Refresh Current Page

Key: HKCU\Software\Policies\Microsoft\Office\11.0\
Outlook\DisabledCmdBarItemsCheckBoxes

Value name: WebRefreshCurrentPage

Value type: REG_DWORD

Value data: 1020 = Command disabled, 0 = Command enabled

Web toolbar: Start Page

Key: HKCU\Software\Policies\Microsoft\Office\11.0\
Outlook\DisabledCmdBarItemsCheckBoxes

Value name: WebStartPage

Value type: REG_DWORD

Value data: 1016 = Command disabled, 0 = Command enabled

Web toolbar: Search the Web

Key: HKCU\Software\Policies\Microsoft\Office\11.0\
Outlook\DisabledCmdBarItemsCheckBoxes

Value name: WebSearchTheWeb

Value type: REG_DWORD

Value data: 1922 = Commands disabled, 0 = Commands enabled

Key: HKCU\Software\Policies\Microsoft\Office\11.0\
Outlook\Preferences

Value name: FileOpenSearchTheWeb

Value type: REG_DWORD

Value data: 4087 = Command disabled

Note: If the check box for the Web toolbar: Search the Web policy is checked, the FileOpenSearchTheWeb value is deleted from the registry.

Web toolbar: Address

Key: `HKCU\Software\Policies\Microsoft\Office\11.0\`
`Outlook\DisabledCmdBarItemsCheckBoxes`

Value name: `WebAddress`

Value type: `REG_DWORD`

Value data: `1740` = Command disabled, `0` = Command enabled

Disable shortcut keys

Key: `HKCU\Software\Policies\Microsoft\Office\11.0\Outlook\`
`DisabledShortcutKeysCheckBoxes`

Value name: `CtrlEnter`

Value type: `REG_SZ`

Value data: `13,8` = Disable Ctrl+Enter (Send in a Mail item)
             `0` = Enable Ctrl+Enter

Disable items in user interface / Custom

Disable command bar buttons and menu items

Disable shortcut keys

Note: See Appendix C for a complete description of how to use these policy settings.

Exchange settings

Exchange view information (multipart policy setting)

Key: `HKCU\Software\Policies\Microsoft\Office\11.0\Outlook`

Publish Exchange views in Public Folders

Value name: `ExchVwPub`

Value type: `REG_DWORD`

Value data: `1` = Enabled, `0` = Disabled

Publish Exchange views in Personal (non-public) Folders

Value name: `ExchVwPsnl`

Value type: `REG_DWORD`

Value data: `1` = Enabled, `0` = Disabled

Folder size display

Key: HKCU\Software\Policies\Microsoft\Office\11.0\Outlook

Value name: ChkFldrSize

Value type: REG_DWORD

Value data: 1 = Enabled, 0 = Disabled

OST Creation

Key: HKCU\Software\Policies\Microsoft\Office\11.0\Outlook\OST

Value name: NoOST

Value type: REG_DWORD

Value data: 2 = Prevent creation of offline folders .ost files
0 = Disabled

Personal distribution lists (Exchange only)

Key: HKCU\Software\Policies\Microsoft\Office\11.0\Outlook\Options\Mail

Value name: ExpandPDLUsingCache

Value type: REG_DWORD

Value data: 0 = Always validate personal DLs when sending mail
1 = Don't validate personal DLs

Exchange Unicode Mode - Prefer ANSI

Key: HKCU\Software\Policies\Microsoft\Office\11.0\Outlook\EMSP

Value name: PreferANSI

Value type: REG_DWORD

Value data: 1 = Prefer ANSI format for offline folders .ost files
0 = Do not prefer ANSI

Note: ANSI is the legacy format for offline folders .ost files. It does not have multilanguage support and is limited in size to just under 2GB.

Exchange Unicode Mode - Ignore Archive Format

Key: HKCU\Software\Policies\Microsoft\Office\11.0\Outlook\
EMSP

Value name: IgnoreArchiveFormat

Value type: REG_DWORD

Value data: 1 = Enabled, 0 = Disabled

Note: This setting is discussed in Chapter 5.

Exchange Unicode Mode - Ignore OST Format

Key: HKCU\Software\Policies\Microsoft\Office\11.0\Outlook\
EMSP

Value name: IgnoreOSTFormat

Value type: REG_DWORD

Value data: 0 = OST Format determines mailbox mode
             1 = Create new OST if format doesn't match mailbox mode
             2 = Prompt to create new OST if format doesn't match
                 mailbox mode

Note: For more information on this setting, consult these two Microsoft Knowledge Base articles:

- 841207, "An Outlook 2003 cached offline folder file is created in ANSI format instead of in Unicode format in Exchange 2003 or in Exchange 2000"

- 892089, "An Outlook 2003 Group Policy setting that forces Outlook clients to only use a Unicode offline folder is not applied correctly." This describes a hotfix required to make the IgnoreOSTFormat detection logic work properly. Also describes a new SilentOST-FormatChange policy setting, which is covered in Appendix B.

Offline Address Book: Enable Send/Receive Group Download

Key: HKCU\Software\Policies\Microsoft\Exchange\Exchange Provider

Value name: Allow SRS Full OAB Download

Value type: REG_DWORD

Value data: 1 = Allow full download of the Offline Address Book in Cached Exchange mode send/receive groups
                0 = Don't allow full OAB downloads in send/receive groups

Offline Address Book: Limit number of full OAB downloads

Key: HKCU\Software\Policies\Microsoft\Exchange\Exchange Provider

Value name: Allow SRS CE Full OAB Download

Value type: REG_DWORD

Value data: Number of full Outlook Address Book downloads allowed per 13-hour period (default = 1)

Offline Address Book: Limit number of incremental OAB downloads

Key: HKCU\Software\Policies\Microsoft\Exchange\Exchange Provider

Value name: Limit SRS Incremental Download

Value type: REG_DWORD

Value data: Number of incremental Outlook Address Book downloads allowed per 13-hour period

Offline Address Book: Limit manual OAB downloads

Key: HKCU\Software\Policies\Microsoft\Exchange\Exchange Provider

Value name: Manual OAB Download

Value type: REG_DWORD

Value data: Number of manual Outlook Address Book downloads allowed per 13-hour period

Offline Address Book: Prompt before Downloading Full OAB

Key: HKCU\Software\Policies\Microsoft\Exchange\Exchange Provider

Value name: Allow Full OAB Prompt

Value type: REG_DWORD

Value data: 1 = Enabled, 0 = Disabled

Cached Exchange low bandwidth threshold

Key: HKCU\Software\Policies\Microsoft\Office\11.0\Outlook\RPC

Value name: SlowBitRate

Value type: REG_DWORD

Value data: 0 to 10000000. Bit rate, in kbps, that Outlook will use to determine whether it is running on "low" bandwidth.

Note: For example, enter 128 to use a bit rate of 128 kbps.

Authentication with Exchange Server

Key: HKCU\Software\Policies\Microsoft\Office\11.0\Outlook\Security

Value name: AuthenticationService

Value type: REG_DWORD

Value data: 9 = Kerberos/NTLM Password Authentication (default)
            16 = Kerberos Password Authentication
            10 = NTLM Password Authentication

Use legacy Outlook authentication dialogs

Key: HKCU\Software\Policies\Microsoft\Office\11.0\Outlook\RPC

Value name: DisableCredUI

Value type: REG_DWORD

Value data: 1 = Use legacy Outlook authentication dialogs with Change Password
             0 = Don't use legacy dialogs

Outlook Today Settings

Outlook Today availability

Key: HKCU\Software\Policies\Microsoft\Office\11.0\Outlook\Today

Value name: Disable

Value type: REG_DWORD

Value data: 0 = Outlook Today is available
             1 = Outlook Today is not available

URL for custom Outlook Today

Key: HKCU\Software\Policies\Microsoft\Office\11.0\Outlook\Today

Value name: Url

Value type: REG_SZ

Value data: URL pointing to custom Outlook Today Web page or .htm file

Folder Home Pages for Outlook special folders

> **Note:** Note that all on/off options for individual folder home pages are REG_SZ (string) values, not the usual REG_DWORD values.

Inbox Folder Home Page (multipart policy setting)

Key: HKCU\Software\Policies\Microsoft\Office\11.0\Outlook\Webview\Inbox

Show associated web page

Value name: Show

Value type: REG_SZ

Value data: yes = Enabled, no = Disabled

URL address of associated web page

Value name: Url

Value type: REG_SZ

Value data: URL for folder home page

Turn off Internet Explorer security checks for this web page

Value name: Security

Value type: REG_SZ

Value data: yes = Enabled, no = Disabled

Disable Folder Home Pages

Key: HKCU\Software\Policies\Microsoft\Office\11.0\Outlook\Webview

Value name: Disable

Value type: REG_DWORD

Value data: 1 = Disable folder home pages, 0 = Allow folder home page

Note: Disabling folder home pages with the previous setting does not affect
Outlook Today.

Calendar Folder Home Page (multipart policy setting)

Key: `HKCU\Software\Policies\Microsoft\Office\11.0\Outlook\Webview\Calendar`

Show associated web page

Value name: `Show`

Value type: `REG_SZ`

Value data: `yes` = Enabled, `no` = Disabled

URL address of associated web page

Value name: `Url`

Value type: `REG_SZ`

Value data: URL for folder home page

Turn off Internet Explorer security checks for this web page

Value name: `Security`

Value type: `REG_SZ`

Value data: `yes` = Enabled, `no` = Disabled

Contacts Folder Home Page (multipart policy setting)

Key: `HKCU\Software\Policies\Microsoft\Office\11.0\Outlook\Webview\Contacts`

Show associated web page

Value name: `Show`

Value type: `REG_SZ`

Value data: `yes` = Enabled, `no` = Disabled

URL address of associated web page

Value name: `Url`

Value type: `REG_SZ`

Value data: URL for folder home page

Turn off Internet Explorer security checks for this web page

Value name: `Security`

Value type: `REG_SZ`

Value data: `yes` = Enabled, `no` = Disabled

Deleted Items Folder Home Page (multipart policy setting)

Key: `HKCU\Software\Policies\Microsoft\Office\11.0\Outlook\Webview\Deleted Items`

Show associated web page

Value name: `Show`

Value type: `REG_SZ`

Value data: `yes` = Enabled, `no` = Disabled

URL address of associated web page

Value name: `Url`

Value type: `REG_SZ`

Value data: URL for folder home page

Turn off Internet Explorer security checks for this web page

Value name: `Security`

Value type: `REG_SZ`

Value data: `yes` = Enabled, `no` = Disabled

Drafts Folder Home Page (multipart policy setting)

Key: `HKCU\Software\Policies\Microsoft\Office\11.0\Outlook\Webview\Drafts`

Show associated web page

Value name: `Show`

Value type: `REG_SZ`

Value data: `yes` = Enabled, `no` = Disabled

URL address of associated web page

Value name: `Url`

Value type: `REG_SZ`

Value data: URL for folder home page

Turn off Internet Explorer security checks for this web page

Value name: `Security`

Value type: `REG_SZ`

Value data: `yes` = Enabled, `no` = Disabled

Journal Folder Home Page (multipart policy setting)

Key: `HKCU\Software\Policies\Microsoft\Office\11.0\Outlook\Webview\Journal`

Show associated web page

Value name: Show

Value type: REG_SZ

Value data: yes = Enabled, no = Disabled

URL address of associated web page

Value name: Url

Value type: REG_SZ

Value data: URL for folder home page

Turn off Internet Explorer security checks for this web page

Value name: Security

Value type: REG_SZ

Value data: yes = Enabled, no = Disabled

Notes Folder Home Page (multipart policy setting)

Key: HKCU\Software\Policies\Microsoft\Office\11.0\Outlook\
Webview\Notes

Show associated web page

Value name: Show

Value type: REG_SZ

Value data: yes = Enabled, no = Disabled

URL address of associated web page

Value name: Url

Value type: REG_SZ

Value data: URL for folder home page

Turn off Internet Explorer security checks for this web page

Value name: Security

Value type: REG_SZ

Value data: yes = Enabled, no = Disabled

Outbox Folder Home Page (multipart policy setting)

Key: HKCU\Software\Policies\Microsoft\Office\11.0\Outlook\
Webview\Outbox

Show associated web page

Value name: Show

Value type: REG_SZ

Value data: yes = Enabled, no = Disabled

URL address of associated web page

Value name: Url

Value type: REG_SZ

Value data: URL for folder home page

Turn off Internet Explorer security checks for this web page

Value name: Security

Value type: REG_SZ

Value data: yes = Enabled, no = Disabled

Sent Items Folder Home Page (multipart policy setting)

Key: HKCU\Software\Policies\Microsoft\Office\11.0\Outlook\ Webview\Sent Mail

Show associated web page

Value name: Show

Value type: REG_SZ

Value data: yes = Enabled, no = Disabled

URL address of associated web page

Value name: Url

Value type: REG_SZ

Value data: URL for folder home page

Turn off Internet Explorer security checks for this web page

Value name: Security

Value type: REG_SZ

Value data: yes = Enabled, no = Disabled

Tasks Folder Home Page (multipart policy setting)

Key: HKCU\Software\Policies\Microsoft\Office\11.0\Outlook\ Webview\Tasks

Show associated web page

Value name: Show

Value type: REG_SZ

Value data: yes = Enabled, no = Disabled

URL address of associated web page

Value name: Url

Value type: REG_SZ

Value data: URL for folder home page

Turn off Internet Explorer security checks for this web page

Value name: Security

Value type: REG_SZ

Value data: yes = Enabled, no = Disabled

Search Folders

Keep search folders offline

Key: HKCU\Software\Policies\Microsoft\Office\11.0\Outlook\
Options\General

Value name: SearchOfflineKeepAliveDays

Value type: REG_DWORD

Value data: 0 to 999, days to keep folders alive in offline or cached mode. 60 = default.

Keep search folders in Exchange online

Key: HKCU\Software\Policies\Microsoft\Office\11.0\Outlook\
Options\General

Value name: SearchOnlineKeepAliveDays

Value type: REG_DWORD

Value data: 0 to 1000, days to keep folders alive in offline or cached mode. 60 = default.

Default search folders at startup

Key: HKCU\Software\Policies\Microsoft\Office\11.0\Outlook\Setup

Value name: SearchNoCreateDefaults

Value type: REG_DWORD

Value data: 1 = Do not create default search folders when Outlook 2003 runs for the first time

0 = Create default search folders

Note: The three default search folders are For Follow Up, Large Messages, and Unread Mail. See Chapter 9 for a script that adds a search folder for all messages from a particular domain.

Maximum Number of Online Search Folders per mailbox

Key: HKCU\Software\Policies\Microsoft\Office\11.0\Outlook\Options\General

Value name: SearchMaxNumberOnline

Value type: REG_DWORD

Value data: 0 to 999, maximum number of search folders for Exchange Server to run

SharePoint Integration

Note: See Appendix B for additional SharePoint integration policies that are covered in the administrative template for Office 2003.

Disable Sharepoint integration in Outlook

Key: HKCU\Software\Policies\Microsoft\Office\11.0\Outlook\Preferences

Value name: DisallowSTS

Value type: REG_DWORD

Value data: 1 = Disable SharePoint integration in Outlook
0 = Enable SharePoint integration in Outlook

Sharepoint folder sync interval

Key: HKCU\Software\Policies\Microsoft\Office\11.0\Outlook\
Preferences

Value name: STSSyncInterval

Value type: REG_DWORD

Value data: 0 to 1440, interval in minutes to update SharePoint folder data in
Outlook; 20 = default

Note: SharePoint integration is one-way, from the SharePoint server to
Outlook.

Meeting Workspace

Disable Meeting Workspace button

Key: HKCU\Software\Policies\Microsoft\Office\11.0\
Meetings\Profile

Value name: EntryUI

Value type: REG_DWORD

Value data: 1 = Disable the Meeting Workspace button
              0 = Enable the Meeting Workspace button

Disable user entries to server list

Key: HKCU\Software\Policies\Microsoft\Office\11.0\
Meetings\Profile

Value name: ServerUI

Value type: REG_DWORD

Value data: 1 = Publish default, allow others
              2 = Publish default, disallow others

Default servers and data for Meeting Workspaces

Key: HKCU\Software\Policies\Microsoft\Office\11.0\
Meetings\Profile

Value name: MRUInternal

Value type: REG_SZ

Value data: Delimited list of up to five servers where users can create meeting
workspace sites.

Note: The Office Resource Kit article "Configuring Meeting Workspace Options in Outlook 2003," at http://office.microsoft.com/en-us/assistance/HA011402651033.aspx explains the necessary format for each server's information. Each server must be added as a pipe delimited list, a total of 6 pipes per record. (The OrganizerName field should be left blank.) The Office Resource Kit article "Configuring Meeting Workspace Options in Outlook 2003," at http://office.microsoft.com/en-us/assistance/HA011402651033.aspx explains the necessary format for each server's information. Example:

> http://server1 | Friendly name for server 1 | templateLCID | templateID | TemplateName | OrganizerName | http://server2 | Friendly name for server 2 | templateLCID | templateID | TemplateName | OrganizerName |

Outlook System Tray Icon

Time before notifying of pending RPC via balloon (multipart policy setting)

Key: `HKCU\Software\Policies\Microsoft\Office\11.0\Outlook\Display Types`

Time to wait if a high bandwidth connection is detected

Value name: `TimetoShowRPCMessageHighBandwidth`

Value type: `REG_DWORD`

Value data:
```
 15000 = 15 seconds
 30000 = 30 seconds  (default)
 60000 =  1 minute
120000 =  2 minutes
300000 =  5 minutes
600000 = 10 minutes
```

Time to wait if a low bandwidth connection is detected

Value name: `TimetoShowRPCMessageLowBandwidth`

Value type: `REG_DWORD`

Value data:
```
 15000 = 15 seconds
 30000 = 30 seconds
 60000 =  1 minute
120000 =  2 minutes  (default)
300000 =  5 minutes
600000 = 10 minutes
```

Time before notifying of pending RPC via notifications tray icon (multipart policy setting)

Key: HKCU\Software\Policies\Microsoft\Office\11.0\Outlook\Display Types

Time to wait if a high bandwidth connection is detected

Value name: TimeToUpdateTrayIconHighBandwidth

Value type: REG_DWORD

Value data:
```
    3000 =  3 seconds (default)
    5000 =  5 seconds
   10000 = 10 seconds
   15000 = 15 seconds
   30000 = 30 seconds
   60000 =  1 minute
  120000 =  2 minutes
```

Time to wait if a low bandwidth connection is detected

Value name: TimeToUpdateTrayIconLowBandwidth

Value type: REG_DWORD

Value data:
```
    3000 =  3 seconds
    5000 =  5 seconds
   10000 = 10 seconds (default)
   15000 = 15 seconds
   30000 = 30 seconds
   60000 =  1 minute
  120000 =  2 minutes
```

Miscellaneous

Disable VLV Browsing on LDAP servers

Key: HKCU\Software\Policies\Microsoft\Office\11.0\Outlook\LDAP

Value name: DisableVLVBrowsing

Value type: REG_DWORD

Value data: 1 = Disable virtual list view browsing
             0 = Enable VLV browsing

Do not download permission for e-mail during offline Exchange folder sync

Key: HKCU\Software\Policies\Microsoft\Office\11.0\Common\Drm

Value name: DoNotAcquireDRMLicenseOnSync

Value type: REG_DWORD

Value data: 1 = Disable downloading of Rights Management licenses
during offline folder synchronization

0 = Download Rights Management licenses during offline
folder synchronization

Auto-repair of MAPI32.DLL

Key: HKCU\Software\Policies\Microsoft\Office\11.0\Outlook\

Value name: FixMapi

Value type: REG_DWORD

Value data: 5 = Ask the user before running Fixmapi.exe
6 = Do not ask; automatically repair

Note: Outlook requires the correct version of Mapi32.dll be installed for it to function properly. Sometimes other programs install a version that is incompatible with Outlook. Rather than prompt the user to run the Fixmapi.exe utility, Outlook can run it automatically any time it detects a problem.

Prevent users from adding e-mail account types (multipart policy setting)

Key: HKCU\Software\Policies\Microsoft\Office\11.0\Outlook\
Options

Prevent users from adding HTTP e-mail accounts

Value name: DisableHTTP

Value type: REG_DWORD

Value data: 1 = Disable account type
0 = Allow account type

Prevent users from adding Exchange e-mail accounts

Value name: DisableExchange

Value type: REG_DWORD

Value data: 1 = Disable account type
0 = Allow account type

Prevent users from adding POP3 e-mail accounts

Value name: `DisablePOP3`

Value type: `REG_DWORD`

Value data: `1` = Disable account type
             `0` = Allow account type

Prevent users from adding IMAP e-mail accounts

Value name: `DisableIMAP`

Value type: `REG_DWORD`

Value data: `1` = Disable account type
             `0` = Allow account type

Prevent users from adding other types of e-mail accounts

Value name: `DisableOtherTypes`

Value type: `REG_DWORD`

Value data: `1` = Disable account type
             `0` = Allow account type

Prevent users from making changes to Outlook profiles

Key: `HKCU\Software\Policies\Microsoft\Office\11.0\Outlook\Setup`

Value name: `ModifyAccounts`

Value type: `REG_DWORD`

Value data: `1` = Prevent users from modifying accounts through
                 Tools | Options, Tools | E-mail Accounts, or the
                 Mail applet in Control Panel
             `0` = Allow users to modify accounts

Note: As explained in Chapter 6, even with ModifyAccounts = 1, the user still will be able to add and remove secondary Exchange mailboxes

Disable Windows Friendly Logon Mail Query

Key: `HKCU\Software\Policies\Microsoft\Office\11.0\Outlook`

Value name: `DontUpdateFriendlyLogon`

Value type: `REG_DWORD`

Value data: `1` = Disable Windows Friendly Logon Mail Query
             `0` = Enable Windows Friendly Logon Mail Query

Disable Dual Font Support

Key: HKCU\Software\Policies\Microsoft\Office\11.0\Outlook\Preferences

Value name: DontUseDualFont

Value type: REG_DWORD

Value data: 1 = Disable Dual Font Support
0 = Enable Dual Font Support

Offline Address Book exact alias matching

Key: HKCU\Software\Policies\Microsoft\Exchange\Exchange Provider

Value name: OAB Exact Alias Match

Value type: REG_DWORD

Value data: 1 = Force alias to do exact match
0 = Don't force alias to do exact match

Automatically show the Outlook Attachment pane when adding attachment

Key: HKCU\Software\Policies\Microsoft\Office\11.0\Common\MailSettings

Value name: SharingOptionsCount

Value type: REG_DWORD

Value data: 1 = Enabled, 0 = Disabled

Miscellaneous/PST Settings

Default location for PST files

Key: HKCU\Software\Policies\Microsoft\Office\11.0\Outlook

Value name: ForcePSTPath

Value type: REG_EXPAND_SZ (expandable string value)

Value data: Path to default location where you want Outlook to create .pst and .ost files.

Note: Environment variables such as %userprofile% are supported. If you do not enable this policy, Outlook automatically creates .pst and .ost files in the %userprofile%\Local Settings\Application Data\Microsoft\Outlook\ folder. Appendix B has information on a new registry value, ForceOST-Path, that allows you to specify a different default location for offline folders .ost files.

Preferred PST Mode (Unicode/ANSI)

Key: `HKCU\Software\Policies\Microsoft\Office\11.0\Outlook`

Value name: `NewPSTFormat`

Value type: `REG_DWORD`

Value data: `0` = Prefer Unicode PST (default)

`1` = Prefer ANSI PST

`2` = Enforce Unicode PST

`3` = Enforce ANSI PST

Note: Unicode and ANSI here refer respectively to the new, "large" .pst files supported in Outlook 2003 (up to 20 GB by default) and the older, "legacy" .pst files that can grow to slightly less than 2 GB.

Large PST: Absolute maximum size

Key: `HKCU\Software\Policies\Microsoft\Office\11.0\Outlook\PST`

Value name: `MaxLargeFileSize`

Value type: `REG_DWORD`

Value data: `0` to `4294967295`, maximum size in megabytes, up to 4,294,967,295mb

Large PST: Size to disable adding new content

Key: `HKCU\Software\Policies\Microsoft\Office\11.0\Outlook\PST`

Value name: `WarnLargeFileSize`

Value type: `REG_DWORD`

Value data: `0` to `4294967295`, size to disable adding new content, in megabytes, up to 4,294,967,295 mb

Legacy PST: Absolute maximum size

Key: HKCU\Software\Policies\Microsoft\Office\11.0\Outlook\ PST

Value name: MaxFileSize

Value type: REG_DWORD

Value data: 0 to 2075149312, maximum size in bytes, up to 2,075,149,312 bytes

Legacy PST: Size to disable adding new content

Key: HKCU\Software\Policies\Microsoft\Office\11.0\Outlook\ PST

Value name: WarnFileSize

Value type: REG_DWORD

Value data: 0 to 2075149312, size to disable adding new content, in bytes, up to 2,075,149,312 bytes

Permanently remove all deleted items

Key: HKCU\Software\Policies\Microsoft\Office\11.0\Outlook\ PST

Value name: PSTNullFreeOnClose

Value type: REG_DWORD

Value data: 1 = Outlook complete removes all deleted data from.pst and .ost files on shutdown
0 = Some traces of deleted data may remain

Note: This setting was added to the Outlook 2003 administrative template in Office 2003 Service Pack 1.

Miscellaneous/Online Meeting Settings

Online Meetings

Key: HKCU\Software\Policies\Microsoft\Office\11.0\Outlook

Value name: DisableOnlineMeetings

Value type: REG_DWORD

Value data: 1 = Disable all online meeting options
0 = Enable online meeting options

Microsoft Exchange Conferencing

Key: HKCU\Software\Policies\Microsoft\Office\11.0\Outlook\
ExchangeConferencing

Value name: ExchangeConferencing

Value type: REG_DWORD

Value data: 1 = Enable Exchange Conferencing options

           0 = Disable Exchange Conferencing options

Windows Media Services Meeting

Key: HKCU\Software\Policies\Microsoft\Office\11.0\Outlook\
WindowsMediaMeeting

Value name: WindowsMediaMeeting

Value type: REG_DWORD

Value data: 1 = Enable Windows Media Services options

           0 = Disable Windows Media Services options

B

Additional Outlook Registry Settings

In Appendix A, you saw all the settings included in the Outlk11.adm administrative template file for Outlook 2003 with Office 2003 Service Pack 1. In this appendix, we cover three other types of policy and user preference settings:

- Settings available through the group policy editor as options for Office in general, but particularly relevant to Outlook

- Settings added to Outlook by hotfixes released after Office 2003 Service Pack 1

- Other Outlook settings of interest, including confirmation dialogs

Presumably Microsoft will include the hotfix settings in a new Outlk11.adm administrative template file released when Office 2003 Service Pack 2 becomes available. In the meantime, if you want to manage these settings through the group policy editor, you can create a new .adm file, as described in Chapter 2.

The Office settings discussed in this appendix are located in the group policy editor under Computer Configuration/Administrative Templates or User Configuration/Administrative Templates and are presented in the same order that you would see them in the group policy editor. The user options generally also exist as user preference settings in the Custom Installation Wizard (CIW) and Custom Maintenance Wizard (CMW) tools, in which case the registy values would reside in the HKEY_CURRENT_USER\Software\Microsoft key instead of the HKEY_CURRENT_USER\Software\Policies\Microsoft key.

Hotfix settings can also be deployed with the CIW or CMW, using the screen for adding registry values.

HKCU is used throughout as an abbreviation for the HKEY_
CURRENT_USER registry hive, and HKLM for the HKEY_LOCAL_
MACHINE hive.

B.1   Office administrative template settings

The Office11.adm administrative template file includes both computer-
related policy settings and user-related policy settings.

B.1.1   Computer configuration policy settings

These settings related to Outlook are located in the group policy editor
under Computer Configuration/Administrative Templates/Microsoft
Office 2003.

Security settings

Note that all three of these settings are also available as user settings in
HKCU, the first two through the Office administrative template, as you'll
see below and the third through the Outlook administrative template, as
listed in Appendix A.

Disable VBA for Office applications

Key: `HKLM\Software\Policies\Microsoft\Office\11.0\Common`

Value name: `VbaOff`

Value type: `REG_DWORD`

Value data: `1` = Disable Visual Basic for Applications
                    `0` = Enable VBA

Automation Security

Key: `HKLM\Software\Policies\Microsoft\Office\11.0\Common\`
`Security`

Value name: `AutomationSecurity`

Value type: `REG_DWORD`

Value data: `3` = Disable macros
                    `2` = Use application macro security level
                    `1` = Macros enabled

Outlook: Macro Security Level

Key: `HKLM\Software\Policies\Microsoft\Office\11.0\Outlook\Security`

Value name: `Level`

Value type: `REG_DWORD`

Value data: 4 = Very High
             3 = High (default)
             2 = Medium
             1 = Low

As you saw in Appendix A, the Outlook administrative template also includes this setting as a user-level policy.

B.1.2   User configuration policy Settings

These settings related to Outlook are located in the group policy editor under User Configuration/Administrative Templates/Microsoft Office 2003.

Tools | Customize | Options

Always show full menus

Key: `HKCU\Software\Policies\Microsoft\Office\11.0\Common\Toolbars`

Value name: `AdaptiveMenus`

Value type: `REG_DWORD`

Value data: 0 = Always show full menus
             1 = Show adaptive menus

You may want to set AdaptiveMenus to 0, either as a policy setting or as a user preference setting with the CIW or CMW, so that users can see all the available commands and not have to hunt for them.

Show full menus after a short delay

Key: `HKCU\Software\Policies\Microsoft\Office\11.0\Common\Toolbars`

Value name: `AutoExpandMenus`

Value type: `REG_DWORD`

Value data: 1 = Enabled, 0 = Disabled

Tools | Options | General | Web Options / General

Rely on CSS for font formatting (multipart policy setting)

Key: HKCU\Software\Policies\Microsoft\Office\11.0\Common\
Internet

Rely on CSS for font formatting

Value name: DoNotRelyOnCSS

Value type: REG_DWORD

Value data: 1 = Enforce CSS off, 0 = Enforce CSS on

CSS stands for "cascading style sheets," a technique used to transmit formatting information as part of a Web page or HTML-format e-mail message.

Use the CSS setting for Word as an E-mail editor

Key: HKCU\Software\Policies\Microsoft\Office\11.0\Common\
Internet

Value name: UseRelyOnCSSForMail

Value type: REG_DWORD

Value data: 1 = Enabled, 0 = Disabled

Setting UseRelyOnCSSForMail = 1 will produce a more compact HTML message when Word is used as the e-mail editor.

Tools | Options | General | Service Options / Online Content

Online content options

Key: HKEY_CURRENT_USER\Software\Microsoft\Office\11.0\
Common\Internet

Value name: UseOnlineContent

Value type: REG_DWORD

Value data: 0 = Never show Office Online content or entry points
              1 = Use only offline content whenever available,
                  for example, .chm Help files
              2 = Use Office Online content whenever available (default)

Use a value of 1 if you want Office programs, including Outlook, to search local Help files by default but still retain the option to search Microsoft's online Office content. The online content is likely to be more up-to-date, but users may get answers to their most common questions faster if they search the local Help files first.

Tools | Options | General | Service Options / Shared Workspace

Disable the Shared Attachments option in Outlook mail messages

Key: HKCU\Software\Policies\Microsoft\Office\11.0\Common\MailSettings

Value name: DisableSharingOptions

Value type: REG_DWORD

Value data: 1 = Disable the ability to share attachments through a Windows SharePoint Services document workspace
0 = Enable SharePoint attachment sharing

Security Settings

Disable VBA for Office applications

Key: HKCU\Software\Policies\Microsoft\Office\11.0\Common

Value name: VbaOff

Value type: REG_DWORD

Value data: 1 = Disable Visual Basic for Applications
0 = Enable VBA

Automation Security

Key: HKCU\Software\Policies\Microsoft\Office\11.0\Common\Security

Value name: AutomationSecurity

Value type: REG_DWORD

Value data: 3 = Disable macros
2 = Use application macro security level
1 = Macros enabled

Collaboration Settings

Outlook: 'send for review'

Key: HKCU\Software\Policies\Microsoft\Office\11.0\Outlook\Options\Mail

Value name: ExplicitReviewBehavior

Value type: REG_DWORD

Value data: 0 = Enable 'send for review'
2 = Exclude author's e-mail in documents
1 = Disable 'send for review'

Outlook: Ad hoc reviewing

Key: `HKCU\Software\Policies\Microsoft\Office\11.0\Outlook\Options\Mail`

Value name: `AdHocReviewBehavior`

Value type: `REG_DWORD`

Value data: `0` = Enable ad hoc reviewing
`2` = Exclude author's e-mail in documents
`1` = Disable ad hoc reviewing

Services/Fax

Disable Fax Over Internet feature

Key: `HKCU\Software\Policies\Microsoft\Office\11.0\Common\Services\Fax`

Value name: `NoFax`

Value type: `REG_DWORD`

Value data: `1` = Disable fax over the Internet
`0` = Enable fax over the Internet

B.2   Outlook hotfix settings

As discussed in Chapter 8, Microsoft frequently releases "hotfixes" that resolve issues reported by one or more organizations. Sometimes these include support for new registry values. This section lists those new values in alphabetically order, according to their position in the registry hierarchy, and includes a reference to the relevant Microsoft Knowledge Base (MSKB) article, which you can find at http://support.microsoft.com. It should be possible to implement these new values as policy settings by creating the value in the HKCU\Software\Policies\Microsoft hiearchy, even though that possibility may not be mentioned explicitly in the MSKB articles. Be sure to test thoroughly. In some cases, you will need to create a new registry key, as well as the new registry value.

You receive an "Error while archiving folder" error message when you try to AutoArchive your Outlook data in Outlook 2003 (MSKB 888089)

Key: `HKCU\Software\Microsoft\Office\11.0\Outlook`

Value name: `AllowUnicodeToAnsiArchiveDataLoss`

Value type: `REG_DWORD`

Value data: `1` = Enable setting, `0` = Disable setting

Setting `AllowUnicodeToAnsiArchiveDataLoss` = 1 allows Outlook to archive data from a Unicode information store (such as an Exchange 2000 or 2003 mailbox) to a Personal Folders .pst file in the older ANSI or legacy format for Outlook 97-2002. Some data loss may occur since the ANSI format does not have the same multilanguage capabilities as the newer Unicode format .pst file.

You receive an "An error occurred adding the following Windows SharePoint Services folder to Outlook" error message when you link a Windows SharePoint Services Calendar or Events list to Outlook 2003 (MSKB 897658)

Key: `HKEY_LOCAL_MACHINE\Software\Microsoft\Office\11.0\Outlook`

Value name: `AlwaysAllowSharePointPST`

Value type: `REG_DWORD`

Value data: `1` = Enabled, `0` = Disabled

Enabling `AlwaysAllowSharePointPST` permits Outlook to link to Windows SharePoint Services contacts and events lists, even if `DisablePST` = 1 (see next setting).

A network administrator can add the DisablePST registry value to a registry key so that all the users of a computer cannot create or access Outlook .pst files in Outlook (MSKB 896515)

Key: `HKCU\Software\Microsoft\Office\11.0\Outlook or HKCU\Software\Policies\Microsoft\Office\11.0\Outlook`

Value name: `DisablePST`

Value type: `REG_DWORD`

Value data: `1` = Enable setting, `0` = Disable setting

As described in Chapter 6, setting `DisablePST` = 1 is the strongest available option to prevent users from accessing most Personal Folders .pst files. This hotfix makes DisablePST available either as a user preference or user policy setting. Previously, it was available only as a per-machine setting and not as a policy or user preference setting.

You cannot specify a separate folder to store the .ost file when you use the ForcePSTPath value in Outlook 2003 (MSKB 896591)

Key: HKCU\Software\Microsoft\Office\11.0\Outlook

Value name: ForceOSTPath

Value type: REG_EXPAND_SZ (expandable string value)

Value data: Path to default location where you want Outlook to create .ost files. Environment variables such as %userprofile% are supported.

If you do not enable this setting, Outlook automatically creates .ost files in the %userprofile%\Local Settings\Application Data\Microsoft\Outlook\ folder or in the path set for the ForcePSTPath registry value, which is listed in Appendix A.

An Outlook 2003 Group Policy setting that forces Outlook clients to only use a Unicode offline folder is not applied correctly (MSKB 892089)

Key: HKCU\Software\Policies\Microsoft\Office\11.0\Outlook\ EMSP

Value name: SilentOSTFormatChange

Value type: REG_DWORD

Value data: 1 = Enable setting, 0 = Disable setting

Setting SilentOSTFormatChange = 1 allows Outlook to switch the user from an ANSI to a Unicode offline folders .ost file without prompting the user.

It takes longer than expected to synchronize an IMAP mailbox store in Outlook 2003 (MSKB 896006)

Key: HKCU\Software\Microsoft\Office\11.0\Outlook\OutlookBar

Value name: DisableStoreCrawling

Value type: REG_DWORD

Value data: 1 = Enable setting, 0 = Disable setting

Setting DisableStoreCrawling = 1 prevents Outlook from crawling the entire public folder hierarchy when synchronizing an IMAP4 mailbox, an operation that could make it take longer than expected to get mail from an IMAP4 mailbox.

Outlook 2003 stops responding when you try to plan a meeting that contains users who are behind a firewall (MSKB 843191)

Key: HKCU\Software\Microsoft\Office\11.0\Outlook\Preferences

Value name: IgnoreServerConnection

Value type: REG_SZ

Value data: Semicolon-delimited list of server names to ignore

Without this setting, Outlook may appear to hang when you attempt to get details about meeting attendees whose information is stored on a server that is behind a firewall.

Duplicate entries are rendered in the Mail Folder view when you group by a multi-value field in Outlook 2003 (MSKB 843489)

Key: HKCU\Software\Microsoft\Office\11.0\Outlook\PST

Value name: RemoveDuplicatesFromMviView

Value type: REG_DWORD

Value data: 1 = Enable setting, 0 = Disable setting

Setting RemoveDuplicatesFromMviView = 1 solves a problem with multi-valued fields in Cached Exchange mode that may result in duplicate entries appearing in the list of items in the folder.

B.3   Additional CIW/CMW settings

The settings in this section are exposed by the Custom Installation Wizard and/or Custom Maintenance Wizard, but are not included in the administrative template for the group policy editor. (There probably is a reason why —often it's performance related.) These are user preference settings, therefore, and the user can change them while running Outlook. They are listed in the order in which they appear in the CIW or CMW.

Tools | Options / Preferences / Junk E-mail

Junk Mail Import List

Key: HKCU\Software\Microsoft\Office\11.0\Outlook\Options\Mail

Value name: JunkMailImportLists

Value type: REG_DWORD

Value data: 1 = Enable junk mail list import, 0 = Disable junk mail list import

As explained in Chapter 6, this setting should not be deployed as a policy setting unless you also install a hotfix (see MSKB article 893057) that changes the import behavior. It is, however, fine to use the CIW or CMW to deploy this setting as a user preference.

MSG Unicode format when dragging to the file system

Key: `HKEY_CURRENT_USER\Software\Microsoft\Office\11.0\Outlook\Options\General`

Value name: `MSGFormat`

Value type: `REG_DWORD`

Value data: `1` = Use Unicode format for .msg files, `0` = Use ANSI format for .msg files

If `MSGFormat` = `1`, users will not be able to open the saved .msg files in Outlook 2002 or earlier versions.

Outlook System Tray Icon

Show Network Warnings

Key: `HKCU\Software\Microsoft\Office\11.0\Outlook\Display Types\Balloons`

Value name: `NetWarn`

Value type: `REG_DWORD`

Value data: `1` = Enable, `0` = Disable

Show Exchange Server Messages

Key: `HKCU\Software\Microsoft\Office\11.0\Outlook\Display Types\Balloons`

Value name: `Exchange`

Value type: `REG_DWORD`

Value data: `1` = Enable, `0` = Disable

Show Network Connectivity Changes

Key: `HKCU\Software\Microsoft\Office\11.0\Outlook\Display Types\Balloons`

Value name: `NetConn`

Value type: `REG_DWORD`

Value data: `1` = Enable, `0` = Disable

Miscellaneous

Send immediately when Offline

Key: HKCU\Software\Microsoft\Office\11.0\Outlook\Preferences

Value name: SendImmediatelyOffline

Value type: REG_DWORD

Value data: 1 = Enable, 0 = Disable

Remember that "offline" does not refer to the state of the network connection but to the state of the Outlook application. It is certainly possible to be working offline while fully connected to the Internet.

Allow Third Party Transports to send immediately when Offline

Key: HKCU\Software\Microsoft\Office\11.0\Outlook\Preferences

Value name: PollTransportOffline

Value type: REG_DWORD

Value data: 1 = Enable, 0 = Disable

Load Transports immediately after startup

Key: HKCU\Software\Microsoft\Office\11.0\Outlook\Preferences

Value name: LoadTransportProviders

Value type: REG_DWORD

Value data: 1 = Enable, 0 = Disable

Date Picker/Calendar behavior

Key: HKCU\Software\Microsoft\Office\11.0\Outlook\Options\
Calendar

Value name: CalendarTaskpadOn

Value type: REG_DWORD

Value data: 1 = Show the TaskPad along with the default Calendar
            0 = Don't show the TaskPad

Disable Show in Groups and new style arrangements on old views

Key: HKCU\Software\Microsoft\Office\11.0\Outlook\Setup

Value name: AutoArrangeViews

Value type: REG_DWORD

Value data: 1 = Use Show in Groups on old views
            0 = Disable Show in Groups on old views

B.4   Confirmation dialogs

Often, after users check the "Don't show this message again" box on a dialog, they want to get that dialog back. The following registry entries govern that behavior. Set the value to 1 or delete the registry value to restore the confirmation dialog.

Show "Check Full Name" dialog when contact name is incomplete or unclear

Key: `HKCU\Software\Microsoft\Office\11.0\Outlook\Contact`

Value name: `ConfirmName`

Value type: `REG_DWORD`

Value data: `1` = Show dialog, `0` = Don't show dialog

Show "Check Address" dialog when address is incomplete or unclear

Key: `HKCU\Software\Microsoft\Office\11.0\Outlook\Contact`

Value name: `ConfirmAddress`

Value type: `REG_DWORD`

Value data: `1` = Show dialog, `0` = Don't show dialog

B.5   Other Outlook settings

Besides the settings you've seen so far, both in the appendices and in earlier chapters, there are many other Outlook settings in the Windows registry. In this section, we highlight a few that are particularly interesting but have not been covered elsewhere, giving MSKB references where appropropriate.

How to use the Outlook 2003 forms cache and to troubleshoot forms cache problems (MSKB 839804)

Key: `HKLM\Software\Microsoft\Office\11.0\Outlook`

Value name: `ForceFormReload`

Value type: `REG_DWORD`

Value data: `1` = Enable setting, `0` = Disable setting

Setting `ForceFormReload` = `1` changes the behavior of the forms cache, which normally stores a local copy of each custom form that the user runs. With the ForceFormReload setting enabled, Outlook resolves problems that it encounters with custom forms by clearing the old version from the cache and attempting to open the item again. This will force Outlook to download a new copy of the original form from its published location.

Multiple signatures added on a custom multi-page form in Outlook 2003 (MSKB 840393)

Key: HKCU\Software\Microsoft\Office\11.0\Outlook\Options

Value name: NoAutosigOnCustomForms

Value type: REG_DWORD

Value data: 1 = Do not use automatic signature on custom form messages
              0 = Include automatic signature on custom form messages

This setting was added in Office 2003 Service Pack 1. Previously, Outlook 2003 did not include automatic signatures on messages created with custom forms. Setting NoAutosigOnCustomForms = 1 makes Outlook keep the pre-SP1 behavior.

Items deleted from a shared mailbox go to the wrong folder in Outlook (MSKB 202517)

Key: HKCU\Software\Microsoft\Office\11.0\Outlook\Options\ General

Value name: DelegateWastebasketStyle

Value type: REG_DWORD

Value data: 8 = Store all deleted items in the user's Deleted Items folder
              4 = Store items deleted from another mailbox in that mailbox's
                  Deleted Items folder

If you set DelegateWastebasketStyle = 4, items deleted from User A's mailbox by User B will go into User A's Deleted Items folder. However, for this to work, User B, the user deleting the items, needs at least the Author role on the User A's Deleted Items folder. Otherwise, the item will be either deleted permanently or User B will get an error message.

Deleted items are not available after you use "Recover Deleted Items" in Outlook 2003 (MSKB 886205)

Key: HKLM\Software\Microsoft\Exchange\Client\Options

Value name: DumpsterAlwaysOn

Value type: REG_DWORD

Value data: 1 = Allow the user to recover deleted items
              0 = Don't allow the user to recover deleted items

This setting affects only Exchange folders. After setting Dumpster-AlwaysOn = 1, the user will be able to recover items deleted from that point forward, but not items already deleted. Deleted item recovery is disabled by default if Outlook connects to Exchange using RPC over HTTP.

You cannot connect over the Internet to Exchange Server 2003 from Outlook 2003 (MSKB 831060)

Key: `HKEY_CURRENT_USER\Software\Microsoft\Office\11.0\Outlook\RPC`

Outlook uses the following three registry values to determine how long to wait for a connection when using RPC over HTTP (see Chapter 5). If a value is not set, the default timeout is 45 seconds.

Value name: `ConnectTimeout`

Value type: `REG_DWORD`

Value data: Timeout value, in milliseconds, for RPC over HTTP operations when Outlook detects a connection on a network adapter that is functioning at greater than 128 kbps.

Value name: `ConnectTimeoutLow`

Value type: `REG_DWORD`

Value data: Timeout value, in milliseconds, for RPC over HTTP operations when Outlook detects a connection on a network adapter that is functioning at less than 128 kbps.

Value name: `RFRTimeout`

Value type: `REG_DWORD`

Value data: Timeout value, in milliseconds, for a direct server referral (e.g., to connect to the global catalog server, to another user's mailbox, or to an uncached public folder), regardless of the network adapter speed.

User name of the last user who logged on to Exchange Server is not displayed in the logon dialog box when you start Outlook 2003 or Outlook 2002 SP3 (MSKB 841300)

Key: `HKLM\Software\Microsoft\Windows\CurrentVersion\Policies\System`

Value name: `DontDisplayLastUserName`

Value type: `REG_DWORD`

Value data: `0` = Display the last Exchange user name in the Connect to
                 <server> dialog
            `1` = Don't display the last Exchange user name

Setting `DontDisplayLastUserName = 0` also causes the last Windows user's name to appear in the Windows login box.

C

Disabling Menu and Toolbar Commands and Shortcut Keys

A common Outlook configuration task is to disable certain menu and toolbar commands and shortcut keys in order to prevent users from using those features. This is yet another task that you can accomplish with Group Policy Objects, as described in Chapter 2, using the options listed in the Group Policy Editor under User Configuration/Administrative Templates/ Microsoft Office Outlook 2003/Disable items in user interface.

Under Predefined, the Group Policy Editor lists just 17 predefined menu/toolbar commands (see Figure C.1) and only one predefined shortcut key, Ctrl+Enter. This appendix explains how to disable others and provides a comprehensive list of the menu/toolbar command IDs required for the procedure.

C.1   Disabling menu and toolbar commands

To disable a menu or toolbar command that is not on the predefined list, navigate in the Group Policy Editor to the User Configuration/Administrative Templates/Microsoft Office Outlook 2003/Disable items in user interface/Custom node and open the "Disable command bar buttons and menu items" policy, then click Show. As you can see in Figure C.2, the interface for this policy setting is quite simple. To disable a particular command, click Add, type in the numeric ID for the command you want to disable, and then click OK. Repeat for any additional commands you want to disable.

In Figure C.2, the commands with IDs 355 and 6908 are set to be disabled. These are, respectively, the command to Reply to All and the View in Internet Zone command that would allow an HTML format message to be viewed with the same security as a Web page, which is normally much less strict than that on Outlook messages.

Figure C.1
*Predefined
command bar
button and menu
commands that you
can disable with
Group Policy
Objects.*

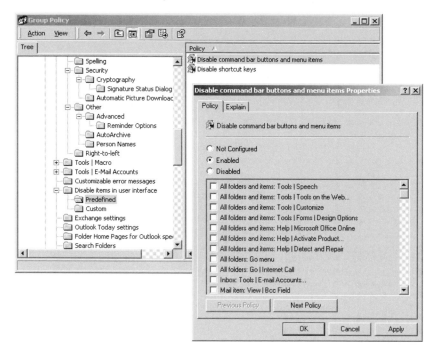

Note that a single policy setting—Disable command bar buttons and menu items—disables multiple commands. On users affected by this policy, each disabled command will be listed in the registry, under the HKEY_CURRENT_USERS\Software\Policies\Microsoft\Office\11.0\Outlook\DisabledCmdBarItemsList key as a separate REG_SZ (string) registry value with the name TCID# where # is some number and a data value of the command bar ID, as shown in Figure C.3.

Also note that the ID for the Reply to All command, 355, is listed only once, even though it appears on the toolbar on both folder and item windows. If a command appears on both the folder window and also on the individual item window in Outlook, the same ID applies to both commands.

Table C.2 later in this appendix provides a convenient list of the Outlook menu and toolbar command IDs that you can use with this policy setting.

To disable a feature completely, you may need to disable both the toolbar/menu command and the shortcut key corresponding to the command. Shortcut keys are also listed in Table C.2. Instructions on how to disable them appear in Section C.3.

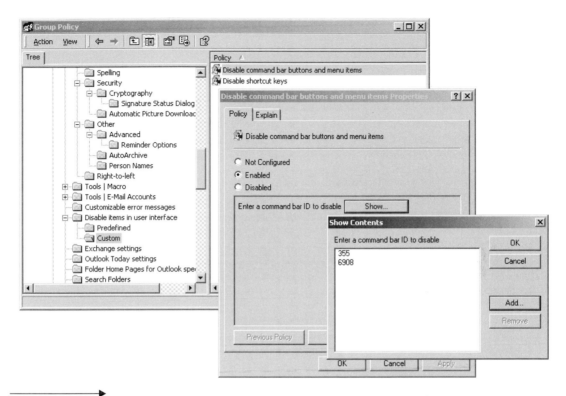

Figure C.2   *To disable a toolbar or menu command, you must know its numeric ID.*

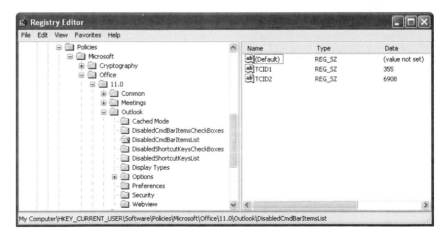

Figure C.3   *Custom disabled commands are listed in the DisabledCmdBarItemsList registry key.*

In some cases, you will need to disable not only commands in Outlook, but also some commands in Word. When Word is used as the e-mail editor (a configuration known as WordMail), the Word toolbar and menu commands can affect an Outlook message. You saw a good example of this in Chapter 9, with stationery, where it is necessary to disable certain Word features if you don't want users to create HTML-format messages with backgrounds, themes, or other stationery features.

The behavior of commands on the toolbar that appears on a new message when WordMail is the editor is inconsistent. Some, such as the From command, apparently can be disabled with a group policy setting. Others, such as the Address Book button, can't. You will want to test any settings to disable mail message toolbar commands in both the regular mail editor and WordMail.

C.2   Providing user feedback on disabled commands

If you disable a command using either the Predefined or Custom policy setting, users will see that command disabled on the toolbar or menu. When they hover the mouse over the toolbar button, a tooltip will explain that the command was disabled by the system administrator, as shown in Figure C.4.

You can use another policy setting to customize the text that the user sees in the tooltip. In the Group Policy Editor, navigate to User Configuration/Administrative Templates/Microsoft Office 2003/Disable items in user interface. Enable the policy setting for "Tooltip for disabled toolbar buttons and menu items" and type in the text you want to display. This sets the following registry value, which affects all Office programs, not just Outlook:

Key: `HKEY_CURRENT_USER\Software\Policies\Microsoft\Office\11.0\Common\Toolbars`

Value Name: `AttemptDisabledActionMessage`

Value Type: `REG_SZ`

Value: Text, up to 80 characters that you want to display as the tooltip for disabled menu and toolbar items.

Figure C.4   *Tooltip explaining a disabled command*

C.3   Disabling shortcut keys

As noted in the introduction to this appendix, the only predefined Outlook shortcut key for which there is a group policy setting is Ctrl+Enter, the key combination that sends a message. As with toolbar and menu commands, you can also apply a group setting to disable other shortcut keys, but you will first need to know the code for each key.

Each shortcut key is represented by a two-part code. For example, the code for Ctrl+Shift+R, the shortcut key for Reply to All is 82,12.

The first part is the numeric value of the uppercase letter, number, or symbol key. If you have macro security set to Low or Medium in Outlook, you can check this value in the Immediate window of the Visual Basic for Applications environment. Press Alt+F11 to start VBA, then Ctrl+G to display the Immediate window. Type in **? Asc("R")** and then press Enter to get the return value of that function, which will be 82.

Another way to look up character codes is with the Insert | Symbol dialog in Word. As shown in Figure C.5, you will need to set the value of the "from" dropdown list at the lower right of that dialog to "ASCII (decimal)." You can then click on any character to see its numeric code in the "Character code" box.

You probably won't need to do this, though, because Table C.2 provides a comprehensive listing of the shortcut keys in Outlook.

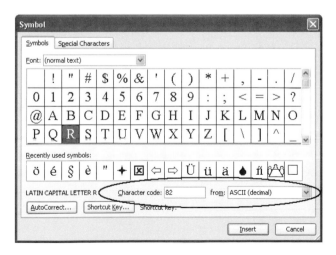

Figure C.5   *Using Word to look up key codes.*

Table C.1 *Code Values for Shortcut Key Modifiers*

Modifier	Code Value
Alt	16
Ctrl	8
Shift	4
Ctrl+Alt	24
Alt+Shift	20
Ctrl+Shift	12

The second part of the key code comes from the optional modifier, which can be any combination of the Alt, Ctrl, and Shift keys. Each modifier key has its code value. As you can see in Table C.1, if more that one modifier key is used, you add all the corresponding code values to get the code value for the second part of the shortcut key. For example, the second

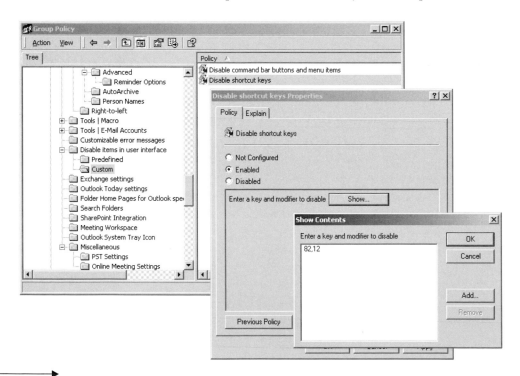

Figure C.6 *Disabling a shortcut key with the Group Policy Editor.*

part of the code for the Reply to All shortcut key is 12, because that shortcut uses Ctrl+Shift as the modifier.

Once you know the code, you can proceed to disable any shortcut key using a process similar to that for disabling toolbar and menu commands. Navigate in the Group Policy Editor to the User Configuration/Administrative Templates/Microsoft Office Outlook 2003/Disable items in user interface/Custom node and open the "Disable shortcut keys" policy, then click Show. Click Add and type in the key and modifier codes, separated by a comma, as shown in Figure C.6. Click OK, and repeat for any additional shortcut keys that you want to disable.

On users affected by this policy, each disabled command will be listed in the registry, under the HKEY_CURRENT_USERS\Software\Policies\ Microsoft\Office\11.0\Outlook\DisabledShortcutKeysList key as a separate REG_SZ (string) registry value with the name KeyMod# where # is some number and a data value of the shortcut key code.

C.4   Command and shortcut key IDs

Table C.2 lists all the Outlook toolbar/menu commands and shortcut keys that you are likely to want to disable. It omits some basic formatting commands and a few commands related to Outlook form design.

Some items that appear in this listing may not actually be used by Outlook 2003, but may be holdovers from previous versions. In a few cases, there may be two or more menu or toolbar commands with the same name but different IDs; you should plan to disable all of them.

Table C.2   *Command and Shortcut Key IDs for Outlook 2003*

Command	Menu/Toolbar Command ID	Shortcut Key	Shortcut Key ID
About Microsoft Office Outlook	927		
About this Form	2503		
Activate Product	5933		
Add Folder to Favorites	5627		
Add or Remove Attendees	5430		
Add Picture to Contact	7899		
Add Recipient to Safe Recipients List	9788		

Table C.2   *Command and Shortcut Key IDs for Outlook 2003 (continued)*

Command	Menu/Toolbar Command ID	Shortcut Key	Shortcut Key ID
Add Reminder to Message	7478		
Add Sender to Blocked Senders List	9786		
Add Sender to Safe Senders List	9787		
Add Sender's Domain to Safe Senders List	10028		
Add to Internet Explorer Favorites	6844		
Address Book	353	Ctrl+Shift+B	66,12
Advanced Find	5505	Ctrl+Shift+F	70,12
Allow New Meeting Request Time Proposals	6848		
Always Show Unread and Flagged Messages	9730		
Archive	1886		
Arrange By Attachments	7619		
Arrange By Categories	7620		
Arrange By Conversation	7621		
Arrange By Custom	7622		
Arrange By Date	7623		
Arrange By E-mail Account	9284		
Arrange By Flag	7624		
Arrange By Folder	7625		
Arrange By From	7626		
Arrange By Importance	7628		
Arrange By Size	7629		
Arrange By Subject	7630		
Arrange By To	7631		
Arrange By Type	7632		
Assign Task	1976		
AutoCorrect Options	793		

Table C.2 *Command and Shortcut Key IDs for Outlook 2003 (continued)*

Command	Menu/Toolbar Command ID	Shortcut Key	Shortcut Key ID
AutoPreview On/Off	1744		
Background Color	401		
Background Picture	5562		
Bcc Field On/Off	1860		
Blue Flag as Default	7473		
Blue Flag Follow Up	7467		
Call Using NetMeeting	5597		
Cancel Meeting Invitation	2487		
Cancel Task Assignment	2004		
Categories	1888		
Change Picture on Contact	7900		
Check for Updates	9340		
Check Names	361		
Choose Form	1910		
Clear Flag	2776		
Clear Selected Text	47	Del	
Close	2011	Alt+F4	
Close All Items	722		
Collapse All Groups	1917		
Collapse This Group	1870		
COM Add-Ins	3754		
Connect to Server	9441		
Contact Us	7903		
Copy Folder	2499		
Copy Folder Design	5629		
Copy Selected Text or Item	19	Ctrl+C	67,8

Table C.2   *Command and Shortcut Key IDs for Outlook 2003 (continued)*

Command	Menu/Toolbar Command ID	Shortcut Key	Shortcut Key ID
Copy to Folder	1676		
Copy to Personal Calendar	2572		
Copy to Personal Contacts	695		
Create Rule	721		
Current View	1893		
Customer Feedback Options	7714		
Customize Current View	1861		
	5590		
Customize Search Folder	7794		
Customize Toolbars	797		
Cut Selected Text or Item	21	Ctrl+X	88,8
Data File Management	7091		
Define Print Styles	1894		
Define Send/Receive Groups	6901	Ctrl+Alt+S	83,24
Define Views	1862		
Delete	478	Ctrl+D	68,8
Delete Folder	2500		
Design a Form	5617		
Design This Form	2519		
Detect and Repair	3774		
Dial-up Connection Location Settings	4394		
Digitally Sign Message	719		
Disable Scheduled Send/Receive	6867		
Display InfoBar Menu		Ctrl+Shift+W	87,12
Display Map of Address	5602		
Download Address Book	5658		

Table C.2   *Command and Shortcut Key IDs for Outlook 2003 (continued)*

Command	Menu/Toolbar Command ID	Shortcut Key	Shortcut Key ID
Download Full Items (Cached Exchange Mode)	9410		
Download Headers (Cached Exchange Mode)	9411		
Download Headers and then Full Items (Cached Exchange Mode)	10002		
Download Headers in This Folder	6904		
Draft Font On/Off	6868		
Edit Appointment Series	2010		
Edit Message	5604		
E-mail Accounts	6863		
Empty Deleted Items Folder	1671		
Encrypt Message Contents and Attachments	718		
Exit Outlook	1891		
Expand All Groups	1916		
Expand This Group	1884		
Explore Contact's Web Page	2497	Ctrl+Shift+X (in contact window)	88,12
Export to vCard File in Signatures Folder	5572		
Field Chooser On/Off	1748		
Find	5592	Ctrl+E	69,8
Find a Contact	5454		
Find Messages from Sender	2607		
Find Next Text in an Item	570	Shift+F4	
Find People	5581	Ctrl+Shift+P (in contact window)	80,12
Find Public Folder	5438		
Find Related Messages	2684		
Find Text in an Item	141	F4	

Table C.2   *Command and Shortcut Key IDs for Outlook 2003 (continued)*

Command	Menu/Toolbar Command ID	Shortcut Key	Shortcut Key ID
First Item in Folder	1865		
Flag Complete	1907		
Folder Properties	2502		
Follow Up	1678	Ctrl+Shift+G	71,12
Font Color	2611		
Font Format	253		
Font Size	5571		
Font Size Larger	5567		
Font Size Largest	5566		
Font Size Medium	5568		
Font Size Smaller	5569		
Font Size Smallest	5570		
Format as HTML	5564		
Format as Plain Text	5563		
Format Columns	1898 5591		
Format Paragraph	779		
Forward	356	Ctrl+F	70,8
Forward as iCalendar	5459		
Forward as vCard	5573		
Free/Busy Information	5619		
From Field On/Off	1867		
Go Back to Previous Folder or Web Page	6881		
Go Forward to Next Folder or Web Page	6882		
Go to Calendar Navigation Pane	7262	Ctrl+2	50,8
Go to Contacts Navigation Pane	7263	Ctrl+3	51,8
Go to Deleted Items	3134		

Table C.2 *Command and Shortcut Key IDs for Outlook 2003 (continued)*

Command	Menu/Toolbar Command ID	Shortcut Key	Shortcut Key ID
Go to Drafts	52		
Go to Folder	1868	Ctrl+Y (in folder window)	89,8
Go to Folder List Navigation Pane	7267	Ctrl+6	54,8
Go to Inbox	3127	Ctrl+Shift+I	73,12
Go to Journal Navigation Pane	7270	Ctrl+8	56,8
Go to Mail Navigation Pane	7261	Ctrl+1	49,8
Go to My Computer Window	3135		
Go to My Documents Window	3136		
Go to News Reader	5672		
Go to Notes Navigation Pane	7265	Ctrl+5	53,8
Go to Outbox	3171	Ctrl+Shift+O	79,12
Go to Outlook Today	5599		
Go to Sent Items	3133		
Go to Shortcuts Navigation Pane	9650	Ctrl+7	55,8
Go to Start Page (Web)	1016		
Go to Tasks Navigation Pane	7264	Ctrl+4	52,8
Go to Web Address	1740		
Go to Web Browser	5673		
Green Flag as Default	7475		
Green Flag Follow Up	7469		
Group By Box On/Off	1750		
Help	984 32794	F1	
Import and Export	2577		
Importance: High	1074		
Importance: Low	1075		

Table C.2   *Command and Shortcut Key IDs for Outlook 2003 (continued)*

Command	Menu/Toolbar Command ID	Shortcut Key	Shortcut Key ID
Inbox Assistant	32789		
Insert File	777		
	1079		
Insert Horizontal Line	5555		
Insert Hyperlink	1576		
Insert Item	2505		
Insert Object	546		
Insert Picture	5612		
Insert Signature	31145		
Internet Call	5674		
Invite Attendees	1086		
Join Conference	5596		
Join NetMeeting	5618		
Junk E-mail Options	9790		
Last Item in Folder	1991		
Letter Wizard	796		
Link File to Contact	5418		
Link Items to Contact	5419		
Macro Security	3627		
Macros	186	Alt+F8	
Mailbox Cleanup	7092		
Make This Folder Available Offline	7093		
Mark All as Read	1906		
Mark as Not Junk	9789	Ctrl+Alt+J	74,24
Mark as Read	1674	Ctrl+Q	81,8
Mark as Unread	1675	Ctrl+U	85,8
Mark Task Complete	2985		

Table C.2   *Command and Shortcut Key IDs for Outlook 2003 (continued)*

Command	Menu/Toolbar Command ID	Shortcut Key	Shortcut Key ID
Mark to Download Message Copy	1753		
Mark to Download Message(s)	1104	Ctrl+Alt+M	77,24
Message Header On/Off	1751		
Message Options	5598		
Microsoft Office Online	3775		
More Signatures	5609		
More Stationery	5611		
Move Folder	2506		
Move to Folder	1679	Ctrl+Shift+V	86,12
Navigation Pane	2515	Alt+F1	
New All Day Event	5498		
New Appointment	1106 1992	Ctrl+Shift+A	65,12
New Appointment with Contact	5433		
New Call to Contact	2501	Ctrl+Shift+D	68,12
New Contact	1099 1993	Ctrl+Shift+C	67,12
New Contact from Same Company	1908		
New Distribution List	5434 5435 5436	Ctrl+Shift+L	76,12
New Folder	1660 1755	Ctrl+Shift+E	69,12
New HTML Message Using WordMail or the Built-in Editor (whichever is not currently active)	5660		
New Instant Message	6880		
New Internet Fax	9409	Ctrl+Shift+X (in folder window)	88,12

Table C.2   *Command and Shortcut Key IDs for Outlook 2003 (continued)*

Command	Menu/Toolbar Command ID	Shortcut Key	Shortcut Key ID
New Item in This Folder		Ctrl+N	78,8
New Journal Entry	1990	Ctrl+Shift+J	74,12
New Journal Entry for Contact	5677		
New Letter to Contact	2498		
New Mail Message	1757 2986	Ctrl+Shift+M	77,12
New Mail Message Using HTML (No Stationery)	5610		
New Mail Message Using Plain Text	5422		
New Mail Message Using Rich Text	5421		
New Meeting Request	1754 2777	Ctrl+Shift+Q	81,12
New Meeting Request to Contact	1980		
New Message to Contact	1978		
New Navigation Pane Shortcut	5507		
New Note	1758	Ctrl+Shift+N	78,12
New Office Document	2576	Ctrl+Shift+H	72,12
New Outlook Data File	5575		
New Post in This Folder	2687	Ctrl+Shift+S	83,12
New Recurring Appointment	2608 2610		
New Search Folder	7790	Ctrl+Shift+P (in folder window)	80,12
New Task	1100 1997	Ctrl+Shift+K	75,12
New Task for Contact	1979		
New Task Request	2006	Ctrl+Shift+U	85,12
Next Flagged Message	1999		
Next High Importance Item	1871		

Table C.2   *Command and Shortcut Key IDs for Outlook 2003 (continued)*

Command	Menu/Toolbar Command ID	Shortcut Key	Shortcut Key ID
Next Incomplete Task	1899		
Next Item	360	Ctrl+>	62,8
Next Item from Sender	1901		
Next Item in Conversation Topic	1903		
Next Unread Item	2000		
Office Clipboard	809		
On Slow Connections Download Only Headers (Cached Exchange Mode)	9413		
Open Other User's Folder	1863		
Open Outlook Data File	5576		
Open Selected Items	5476	Ctrl+O	79,8
Options	522		
Orange Flag as Default	7476		
Orange Flag Follow Up	7470		
Organize	5593		
Organize Internet Explorer Favorites	6845		
Out of Office Assistant	5621		
Paste	22	Ctrl+V	86,8
Paste Special	755		
Permission	9925		
Plan a Meeting	1084		
Post Reply to Folder	1985		
Previous Flagged Message	1998		
Previous High Importance Item	1872		
Previous Incomplete Task	1900		
Previous Item	359	Ctrl+<	60,8
Previous Item from Sender	1902		

Table C.2   *Command and Shortcut Key IDs for Outlook 2003 (continued)*

Command	Menu/Toolbar Command ID	Shortcut Key	Shortcut Key ID
Previous Item in Conversation Topic	1904		
Previous Unread Item	2001		
Print	4	Ctrl+P	80,8
Print All Fields	6891		
Print Preview	109		
Process All Marked Headers	10031		
Process Marked Headers in This Folder	6903		
Properties for Item	750		
Protect Document	336		
Publish Form	1913		
Publish Form As	5616		
Purple Flag as Default	7477		
Purple Flag Follow Up	7471		
Reading Pane Bottom	7222		
Reading Pane Off	7223		
Reading Pane On/Off	5514		
Reading Pane Right	7221		
Recall This Message	2511		
Record in Journal	1672	Ctrl+J	74,8
Recover Deleted Items	5654		
Recurrence	1977	Ctrl+G	71,8
Red Flag as Default	7472		
Red Flag Follow Up	7466		
Redial	30147		
Redo	129	Ctrl+Y (in item window)	89,8
Refresh	9729	F5	.

Table C.2 *Command and Shortcut Key IDs for Outlook 2003 (continued)*

Command	Menu/Toolbar Command ID	Shortcut Key	Shortcut Key ID
Refresh Web Page	1020		
Reminders Window	6894		
Remove Hyperlink	3626		
Remove Picture from Contact	7901		
Rename Folder	2512		
Reply	354	Ctrl+R	82,8
Reply to All	355	Ctrl+Shift+R	82,12
Request Meeting Request Responses	1881		
Research	7343		
Resend This Message	3165		
Rich Text	5565		
Rules and Alerts	10012		
Run Rules Now	5450		
Save	3	Ctrl+S	83,8
Save and Close	1975 5645		
Save and New Contact	1665		
Save and New in Company	1915		
Save As	748		
Save Attachments	3167		
Save Stationery	5666		
Script Debugger	5557		
Search the Web	1922		
Select All	756	Ctrl+A	65,8
Send	2617 3037	Ctrl+Enter	13,8
Send All	5577		

Table C.2   *Command and Shortcut Key IDs for Outlook 2003 (continued)*

Command	Menu/Toolbar Command ID	Shortcut Key	Shortcut Key ID
Send Link to This Folder	5449		
Send Pictures from the Internet	5669		
Send Status Report	1760		
Send/Receive All	7095	F9	
Send/Receive This Folder	5657	Shift+F9	
Share Calendar	5646		
Share Contacts	5648		
Share Tasks	5647		
Share This Folder	5649		
Sharing	32811		
Show Day Calendar	1094		
Show in Groups	7627		
Show Month Calendar	1096		
Show Send/Receive Progress	6902		
Show the Office Assistant	1004		
Show Views In Navigation Pane	9387		
Sign out of Microsoft .NET Passport	5950		
Skip Task Occurrence	1919		
Speech	5764		
Speed Dial	30144		
Spelling	2	F7	
Start NetMeeting	5681		
Status Bar On/Off	850		
Stop Web Page Loading	1019		
Translate	7021		
Undo	128	Ctrl+Z	90,8

Table C.2   *Command and Shortcut Key IDs for Outlook 2003 (continued)*

Command	Menu/Toolbar Command ID	Shortcut Key	Shortcut Key ID
Unmark All Headers	1105		
Unmark Selected Headers	1921	Ctrl+Alt+U	85,24
Unwrap Text	6906		
Use Existing Connection (LAN)	5455		
View - Automatic Formatting	5561		
View - Filter	1752		
View - Group By	1666		
View - Other Settings	1875		
View - Show Fields	2009		
View - Sort	2916		
View Calendar (in new window if not already displayed)	1987		
View Folder Up One Level	1762		
View Group Schedules	7001 7002		
View Message in Internet Zone	6908		
View Today's Calendar	5497		
View Week Calendar	1095		
View Windows Media	5417		
View Work Week Calendar	5556		
Visual Basic Editor	1695	Alt+F11	
Work Offline	5613		
Yellow Flag as Default	7474		
Yellow Flag Follow Up	7468		

D

Other Resources

The resources listed in this appendix are just a selection of what was available from Microsoft and other sources at press time. Other resources may become available, and these URLs may change. We may publish updates from time to time online at http://www.turtleflock.com/olconfig/.

The latest version of the Office 2003 Resource Kit tools and documentation are available online at http://office.microsoft.com/en-us/FX011511471033.aspx. Articles of particular interest include:

Office 2003 Resource Kit Downloads

http://www.microsoft.com/office/orkarchive/2003ddl.htm

Includes all the ORK tools and the updated administrative template .adm files for Service Pack 1 and later service packs

Planning an Outlook 2003 Deployment

http://office.microsoft.com/en-us/assistance/HA011402511033.aspx

Office 2003 Resource Kit Toolbox

http://office.microsoft.com/en-us/assistance/HA011401681033.aspx

Whitepaper: Configuring Outlook Profiles by Using a PRF File

http://office.microsoft.com/en-us/assistance/HA011403051033.aspx

Office Profile Wizard Reference

http://office.microsoft.com/en-us/assistance/HA011513701033.aspx

Customizing and Installing Office 2003 Multilingual User Interface Packs

http://office.microsoft.com/en-us/assistance/HA011402171033.aspx

Deploying Office and Other Products Together

http://office.microsoft.com/en-us/assistance/HA011402051033.aspx

For links to third-party components to connect Outlook to different types of mail, calendar, and other collaboration servers or even directly to databases, see:

Enterprise Mail Services

http://www.slipstick.com/addins/services/enterprise.htm

Connecting Outlook and Exchange to Databases

http://www.outlookcode.com/d/database.htm

These tools can help you drill down into Outlook's folder structure to discover hidden settings:

MFCMAPI

http://support.microsoft.com/?kbid=291794

Outlook Spy

http://www.dimastr.com/outspy/

For information on Group Policy, see:

Windows Server 2003 Technical Reference—Group Policy

http://www.microsoft.com/technet/prodtechnol/
windowsserver2003/library/TechRef/6d7cb788-b31d-4d17-9f1e-
b5ddaa6deecd.mspx

Office 2003 Resource Kit—How Policies Work

http://office.microsoft.com/en-us/assistance/HA011403201033.aspx

Managing Users' Configurations by Policy (Office 2003)

http://office.microsoft.com/en-us/assistance/HA011402401033.aspx

Office 2003 Policy Template Files and Deployment Planning Tools

http://office.microsoft.com/en-us/assistance/HA011513711033.aspx

Managing Group Policy Interactive Simulation

http://www.microsoft.com/windowsserver2003/evaluation/demos/
sims/gpmc/viewer.htm

Applying WMI Filters

http://www.microsoft.com/technet/prodtechnol/
windowsserver2003/library/DepKit/7cae3dab-b973-4905-9e47-
00a638241da9.mspx

Group Policy Administrative Template File Format

http://msdn.microsoft.com/library/en-us/policy/policy/template_
file_format.asp

Micky Balladelli and Jan De Clerq, *Mission-Critical Active Directory*
(Digital Press, 2001). Chapter 7 provides a good foundation on
group policy design.

Group Policy Resource Center

http://www.gpanswers.com

The last site includes a Group Policy Solutions Guide. Among those
solutions, Policy Maker (http://www.desktopstandard.com) is of particular
interest, because it offers the ability to manage Outlook mail profile settings
through Group Policy objects, including not just basic accounts, but also
secondary Exchange mailboxes and address book search order.

In addition to Policy Maker, other tools that can help deploy and manage Outlook mail profiles include:

OProfile

http://www.imanami.com

Outlook Profiler

http://goff.nu/products/windows/profiler/index.html

Priasoft Migration Suite for Exchange—Outlook Profile Update Manager

http://www.priasoft.com/exchangemigration/products.asp

Profiles.exe

http://www.smtechnologies.com/Help/Profiles/Profiles.htm

ProfMan (programming library included with Outlook Redemption)

http://www.dimastr.com/redemption/profiles.htm

ScriptLogic

http://www.scriptlogic.com/

For information on configuring Cached Exchange mode, RPC over HTTP, and other new Exchange-related features in Outlook 2003, see:

Exchange Server 2003 Client Access Guide

http://www.microsoft.com/downloads/details.aspx?
familyid=847774d9-db4a-444b-a5c9-d0b01958f6b7

Enabling a Superior Client Experience with Outlook 2003

http://www.microsoft.com/office/outlook/prodinfo/enabling.mspx

Description of Outlook 2003 with Cached Exchange Mode in an Exchange Server 2003 Environment

http://support.microsoft.com/?kbid=870926

Exchange Server 2003 RPC over HTTP Deployment Scenarios

http://www.microsoft.com/technet/prodtechnol/exchange/2003/
library/ex2k3rpc.mspx

RPC over HTTP Reloaded

http://mcpmag.com/columns/article.asp?EditorialsID=758

Using Exchange Server 2003 Recovery Storage Groups

http://www.microsoft.com/technet/prodtechnol/exchange/guides/
UseE2k3RecStorGrps/6923d327-f5a1-48a6-bfdb-
1ef9ef9a928c.mspx

Administering the Offline Address Book in Outlook 2003

http://support.microsoft.com/?kbid=841273

Offline Address Book Best Practices Guide

http://www.microsoft.com/downloads/details.aspx?
familyid=19b69064-81b8-419e-aae9-612dceb98aeb

Includes information on manually deploying Offline Address Book files, as well as Exchange Server configuration details.

How to deploy the .oab files and the .ost files for use with Outlook 2003 in Cached Exchange Mode

http://support.microsoft.com/?kbid=872930

Description of Offline Address Book logging in Outlook 2003 Service Pack 1

http://support.microsoft.com/?kbid=843483

For information on Windows Server 2003 and Exchange Server security, see:

Windows Server 2003 Security Guide

http://www.microsoft.com/technet/security/prodtech/win2003/w2003hg/sgch01.mspx

Microsoft Exchange Server 2003 Security Hardening Guide

http://www.microsoft.com/technet/prodtechnol/exchange/2003/library/exsecure.mspx

Paul Robichaux, *Secure Messaging with Microsoft® Exchange Server 2003*. (Microsoft Press, 2004)

Exchange Security

http://www.e2ksecurity.com

For information on Windows Rights Management see:

Windows Rights Management Services

http://www.microsoft.com/windowsserver2003/technologies/rightsmgmt/default.mspx

Enabling Information Protection in Microsoft Office 2003 with Rights Management Services and Information Rights Management

http://www.microsoft.com/technet/prodtechnol/office/office2003/maintain/rmsirm.mspx

Microsoft Windows Rights Management Services Client with Service Pack 1

http://go.microsoft.com/fwlink/?LinkID=18134

Lookout is a COM add-in to help users search their Outlook folders, including archives and other .pst files, much faster. It is available as a free download from Microsoft at http://www.microsoft.com/downloads/details.aspx?FamilyID=09b835ee-16e5-4961-91b8-2200ba31ea37.

Programming resources for managing folder permissions and simple server-side rules include:

ACL component documentation

http://msdn.microsoft.com/library/en-us/exchserv/html/comcpnts_8f04.asp

ACL COM component download

http://www.microsoft.com/downloads/details.aspx?FamilyID=D24EB917-9C06-4A4E-9BB4-5D2ABF45DB5D

Rule component documentation

http://msdn.microsoft.com/library/en-us/exchserv/html/comcpnts_93hw.asp

Rule COM component download

http://www.microsoft.com/downloads/details.aspx?FamilyID=CB3EF441-EEE3-4D05-940F-B3AF420A39F1

For resources for Microsoft Windows Management Instrumentation (WMI) scripting, see:

WMI Overview

http://www.microsoft.com/technet/scriptcenter/guide/sas_wmi_dieu.mspx

WMI Scripting Primer

http://msdn.microsoft.com/library/en-us/dnclinic/html/scripting06112002.asp

About the Authors

Sue Mosher is an independent consultant whose company, Turtleflock LLC (http://www.turtleflock.com), provides programming and other services to organizations that want to use Microsoft Office to become more productive. She has been recognized by Microsoft since 1994 as a Most Valuable Professional (MVP) for her efforts to help other users work with Microsoft products. Her Web site at http://www.outlookcode.com is a meeting place for Outlook programmers of all skill levels. This is her sixth book on Microsoft Outlook, her third for Digital Press.

Robert Sparnaaij, MCSE, Bachelor of Engineering, is an ICT consultant and Microsoft Outlook MVP and has been working professionally with Exchange and Outlook systems since 1999. Currently he works at an IT service desk with key tasks such as supporting internal clients, administering servers and business applications, setting up and guiding implementation and upgrade projects, setting up documentation and procedures for the department, company and end users, and advising and supporting the ICT Management department. He has a true ideal of creating the paperless office and maintaining information availability. With his web site at http://www.howto-outlook.com and his participation in the Microsoft Communities, he tries to help people to work efficiently with Outlook and related programs and systems on a daily basis. After the appearance of this book, Robert will go back to school and pursue a Master of Science for ICT in Business.

Robert writes: To Nienke, with whom I'd want to stay longer than Outlook can plan, thank you for your support during the writing of this book, giving me the time and pushing me to finish it. I'd like to thank my parents who have always backed me with every decision I made. I wouldn't be where I am today without them in every meaning of the sentence. The list of people to thank who had any influence on me while writing this is long and will always be incomplete—Microsoft, the Microsoft Communities, family, friends, fellow MVPs, my Web site visitors, and you as the reader of this book. Last but certainly not the least, I'd like to thank Sue Mosher for asking me to be a part of this.

Charlie Pulfer is the General Manager of Titus (http://www.titus.com) and has primary focus on the development of Titus' policy management software for Microsoft Outlook. Charlie also provides consulting services with expertise in PKI, e-mail policy and security, and Microsoft Rights Management Services.

David Hooker has written Exchange and Outlook code, including MAPI service providers and Outlook add-ins, since Outlook 98. He was an e-mail postmaster for an international organization for six years. He is a graduate of George Washington University, where he is currently pursuing further studies in computer science. In his spare time, he tries to paint like the 17th century Dutch masters.

David writes: I would like to thank the many people who encouraged me with my work in this book, including those who have given me interesting work over the years. I would also like to acknowledge Sue Mosher, from whom I received considerable guidance on the craft of writing really good computer books.

Index